Introduction to
STRUCTURAL EQUATION MODELING
USING IBM SPSS STATISTICS AND EQS

SAGE was founded in 1965 by Sara Miller McCune to support the dissemination of usable knowledge by publishing innovative and high-quality research and teaching content. Today, we publish more than 850 journals, including those of more than 300 learned societies, more than 800 new books per year, and a growing range of library products including archives, data, case studies, reports, and video. SAGE remains majority-owned by our founder, and after Sara's lifetime will become owned by a charitable trust that secures our continued independence.

Los Angeles | London | New Delhi | Singapore | Washington DC

NIELS J. BLUNCH

Introduction to STRUCTURAL EQUATION MODELING USING IBM SPSS STATISTICS AND EQS

Los Angeles | London | New Delhi
Singapore | Washington DC

Los Angeles | London | New Delhi
Singapore | Washington DC

SAGE Publications Ltd
1 Oliver's Yard
55 City Road
London EC1Y 1SP

SAGE Publications Inc.
2455 Teller Road
Thousand Oaks, California 91320

SAGE Publications India Pvt Ltd
B 1/I 1 Mohan Cooperative Industrial Area
Mathura Road
New Delhi 110 044

SAGE Publications Asia-Pacific Pte Ltd
3 Church Street
#10-04 Samsung Hub
Singapore 049483

Editor: Jai Seaman
Assistant editor: James Piper
Production editor: Victoria Nicholas
Copyeditor: Neville Hankins
Proofreader: Kate Campbell
Indexer: David Rudeforth
Marketing manager: Sally Ransom
Cover design: Shaun Mercier
Typeset by: C&M Digitals (P) Ltd, Chennai, India
Printed and bound by CPI Group (UK) Ltd,
Croydon, CR0 4YY

© Niels J. Blunch 2016

Apart from any fair dealing for the purposes of research or private study, or criticism or review, as permitted under the Copyright, Designs and Patents Act, 1988, this publication may be reproduced, stored or transmitted in any form, or by any means, only with the prior permission in writing of the publishers, or in the case of reprographic reproduction, in accordance with the terms of licences issued by the Copyright Licensing Agency. Enquiries concerning reproduction outside those terms should be sent to the publishers.

Library of Congress Control Number: 2015934011

British Library Cataloguing in Publication data

A catalogue record for this book is available from the British Library

ISBN 978-1-47391-621-0
ISBN 978-1-47391-622-7 (pbk)

At SAGE we take sustainability seriously. Most of our products are printed in the UK using FSC papers and boards. When we print overseas we ensure sustainable papers are used as measured by the Egmont grading system. We undertake an annual audit to monitor our sustainability.

Contents

How to use the companion website	vi
About the author	vii
Preface	viii

Part 1 Preparing Yourself and Your Data 1

  1 Introduction 3

  2 Measuring Your Variables: Reliability and Validity 27

  3 Factor Analysis 47

Part 2 The Three Basic Models 71

  4 Structural Equation Modeling with EQS 73

  5 Data Entering and Programming in EQS 107

  6 Models with Only Manifest Variables 123

  7 The Measurement Model in SEM: Confirmatory Factor Analysis 148

  8 The General Model 185

Part 3 Advanced Models and Techniques 217

  9 Mean Structures and Multi-group Analysis 219

  10 Incomplete and Non-normal Data 249

  11 Latent Curve Models 280

Appendices 307
Appendix A Statistical Prerequisites 309
Appendix B Glossary 326
Appendix C EQS Statements 336
Author Index 340
Subject Index 342

How to use the companion website

Introduction to Structural Equation Modeling Using IBM SPSS Statistics and EQS by Niels J. Blunch is supported by online resources for students, which are available at https://study.sagepub.com/bluncheqs and that includes, for students:

- Suggested readings using EQS to support your own research.
- PowerPoint slides featuring helpful diagrams and screenshots from the book to aid your revision.
- Exercises relating to each chapter to help test your understanding.
- Datasets allowing you to work through structural equation models at your own pace.
- Interactive Flashcards featuring glossary terms to help you get to grips with terminology.

About the author

Niels J. Blunch has an MSc in Business Administration from Copenhagen Business School. After a few years working in industry Niels went to the Department of Marketing at Aarhus School of Business in 1965, where he taught and carried out research in marketing and in research methodology in general. In parallel with his academic work he has worked as a consultant. He retired in 2007. *Introduction to Structural Equation Modeling Using IBM SPSS Statistics and EQS* is his eighth book, and his second in English.

Preface

This book contains what I consider to be the essentials for a non-mathematical introductory course in structural equation modeling (SEM) for the social and behavioral sciences.

It builds on material that I have used over the years in a compulsory course in behavioral science methods for first-year graduate students at Aarhus School of Business (Denmark).

In that course I used AMOS (another SEM program) and the present book parallels a book on AMOS that was published by Sage a few years ago.

The present book should be well suited for introductory courses in SEM for final-year undergraduate or first-year graduate students who have taken an introductory course in statistics up to and including multiple regression. The book contains an appendix on statistical prerequisites that could be used as a refresher. The appendix could be read as an introduction to the text or consulted when necessary during reading.

The examples in the book are real-life examples taken from a wide range of disciplines – including psychology, political science, marketing and health – and the same goes for the exercises that can be downloaded from the book's homepage; they build on real data.

A book on SEM could either illustrate the programming aspects by showing examples on how models are programmed in the various computer programs available (e.g. LISREL, EQS, AMOS, Mplus, Mx Graph), or concentrate on one and only one computer program and use it throughout.

I have chosen the latter method using SPSS and EQS as the workhorses. SPSS is a statistics program used at most universities and it should be well known to many students in the social and behavioral sciences. EQS is also widely used in the same disciplines and it is very easy to use. The programming language is very simple and you are offered two even simpler ways of programming: you can program by filling in a few empty tables; or you can just sketch your model in a user-friendly drawing environment. The program is also designed to work effectively together with SPSS.

I would like to thank the many people who have allowed me to use their data for examples and exercises – without them it would have been impossible to write the book. There are too many to mention personally here, but credit is given where the data are introduced.

Last – but not least – my thanks go to my wife Anne-Marie for her loving support during the long writing process.

PART 1

Preparing Yourself and Your Data

# 1

Introduction

After a presentation and an overview of the contents of the whole book, this chapter continues with an intuitive introduction to *structural equation modeling* (SEM) by presenting a few examples of such modeling.

These models are *very* simple, but are chosen to illustrate the broad spectrum of research problems that can be analyzed by the collection of tools in the bag called SEM. This will not only acquaint you with prototypes of problems and models discussed in more depth in later chapters, but also stress the way SEM solves the problem of measuring the vague concepts often met in the social and behavioral sciences (intelligence, preference, social status, attitude, literacy and the like), for which no generally accepted measuring instruments exist.

A short outline of the history of SEM follows subsequently.

Then you will learn how to cope with another problem. Unlike the natural sciences, the ideal way of doing causal research, namely experimentation, is more often than not impossible to implement in the social and behavioral sciences. This being the case, we face a series of difficulties of a practical as well as a philosophical nature.

You will also find a short introduction to the matrices appearing in the output from EQS, the computer program used in this book.

Rather than presenting a deep discussion of the mathematical and statistical calculations, which are the basis for SEM estimation, a brief, intuitive explanation of the principles is presented instead.

1 Purpose and Plan of the Book

As you can see from the title, this book is an *introduction* to structural equation modeling – or SEM for short. SEM is a very large subject indeed. It is not just one statistical method, such as regression analysis or analysis of variance, that you should know from your introductory course in statistics. In fact these two statistical techniques can be shown to be special cases of SEM, and the same goes for more advanced statistical models that you might have met, such as MANOVA, discriminant analysis and canonical correlation.

So you can see that general SEM is a rather large toolbox that can serve you in lots of different data analysis situations. This means that it is impossible to cover, in a rather slim volume like this one, the more advanced and complicated topics in this rapid developing area.

Furthermore, this is a *non-mathematical* treatment, which means that you will encounter very few formulas and, instead of mathematical deductions, you will find verbal explanations often of a more intuitive character.

The reader I have in mind is a student within the social and behavioral sciences who has completed an introductory course in statistics up to and including multiple regression analysis, and also has some experience of the IBM statistics program SPSS.

Plan of the book

The book consists of three parts.

Part 1 includes three chapters. This first chapter starts by presenting a few simple examples, each being a prototype of the kind of more complicated problems you will meet in later chapters. As you will learn from these examples, a central problem in SEM is the extent to which you can draw causal conclusions based on non-experimental data. A discussion of the problems involved takes up a good deal of space.

The variables you want to enter into your structural equation model must be measured. Chapter 2 considers problems connected with judging the quality of your measurements, by introducing the concepts of reliability and validity, and Chapter 3 presents principal components analysis and exploratory factor analysis as simple tools for examining the dimensionality in your data.

You should now be well equipped to embark on Part 2 of the book, where in Chapter 4 you are introduced to the steps in SEM and to the various problems that can arise as you go through these steps. In the process you will also be introduced to EQS programming by means of a very simple multiple regression example similar to those that you have probably met several times before.

In Chapter 5 you will learn how to enter data into an EQS data file, and you will be introduced to two interactive programming tools in EQS, namely '*Build EQS*' and '*Diagrammer*', the latter making it possible to program a model just by drawing it.

The next three chapters (6, 7 and 8) present the three 'main models' of SEM, the prototypes of which you met in Chapter 1 but now in more realistic (and complicated) forms. The examples are taken from a variety of disciplines: psychology, political science, health and marketing.

Part 3 of the book moves on to more advanced topics. In Chapter 9 the analysis is extended to deal with the *values* of the variables and not just the *relations* between them (as is most often the case in SEM). Chapter 9 also deals with models based on data from more than one population in order to compare populations and examine the extent to which the same model can be used to describe them all.

Chapter 10 will show you how to deal with problems caused by incomplete and non-normal data, while Chapter 11 introduces you to the so-called latent curve model used to model trends based on panel data.

2 Theory and Model

This is a book about drawing conclusions based on non-experimental data on the relationships between non-measurable concepts – and about using the computer program EQS to facilitate the analysis.

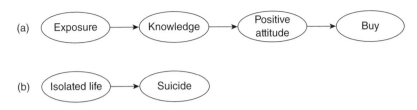

Figure 1 (a) The hierarchy-of-effects model; (b) Durkheim's suicide model

Scientific work is characterized by the fact that a scientist works with *models*, i.e. simplified descriptions of the phenomenon in 'the real world' that is the object of the research. An example of such a model is the hierarchy-of-effects model depicting the various stages through which a recipient of an advertising message is supposed to move from awareness to (hopefully) the final purchase (e.g. Lavidge & Steiner, 1961). See Figure 1a.

Another example comes from the theory of the pioneering French sociologist and philosopher Emile Durkheim: that living an isolated life increases the probability of suicide (Durkheim, 2002 [1897]). This theory can be depicted as in Figure 1b.

We can see that a scientific theory may be depicted as a graphic model in which the hypothesized connections among the concepts of the theory are shown as arrows.

What then is SEM?

SEM is a collection of tools for analyzing connections between various concepts in cases where these connections are relevant either for expanding our general knowledge or for solving some problem.

Examples of such problems are as follows:

1. Health officials might be interested in mapping a *possible* connection between smoking during pregnancy and infant health.
2. School authorities might be interested in examining the effects of various factors having a *possible* impact on students' academic achievement.
3. A psychologist might be interested in developing a questionnaire that could 'measure' the respondent's 'style of information processing', i.e. whether the respondent prefers a verbal and/or visual modality of processing information about his or her environment. In that connection the psychologist is interested in mapping the *possible* connection between a person's 'style of information processing' and the same person's answers to the various proposed questions.
4. A health researcher might be interested in mapping a *possible* connection between a person's psychical well-being and the same person's physical reactions.
5. An advertising manager or a health official might (for different reasons) be interested in mapping a *possible* connection between cigarette advertising and cigarette sales.

The key term is the word *possible*. We are not sure that a connection exists, but we want to find out whether it exists and, if so, to measure the strengths of the connection in numerical form.

So, SEM is a set of tools for verifying theories. In principle we start out with an a priori theory about the system we want to map, and then use SEM to test our model against empirical data. SEM is a *confirmatory* rather than an *exploratory* technique.

Our hope is that we can *confirm* our model and as a result be able to measure the *strength* of the various connections and in that way answer questions such as 'By how much can we expect each extra pack of cigarettes smoked during pregnancy to reduce birth weight?'

However, this does not exclude the possibility that our analysis might lead to modifications of the original model as we gain more insight while working with our model – so the distinction between confirmatory and exploratory is not a sharp one.

As the name 'structural equation *modeling*' suggests, the first step is to form a graphic depiction – *a model* – showing how the various concepts fit together.

Let us look at the examples above.

Example 1
Cigarette smoking during pregnancy and infant health (Mullahy, 1997)

If we measure cigarette smoking in 'total number of cigarettes smoked during pregnancy' and infant health by 'birth weight' we can suggest the model shown in Figure 2a. The concepts are shown in rectangles and the 'connection' between them is depicted as an arrow indicating the direction of a possible causal effect: we suspect the mother's cigarette smoking affects the child's birth weight and not the other way round.

In this example it is easy to decide on the direction of a (possible) effect, but at times this can be more problematic – for example, Example 5 in the list above, where an advertising manager hopes that advertising will promote sales but cannot rule out the possibility that a positive covariation between advertising and sales figures could be due to the way the advertising budget is compiled, e.g. using a fixed percentage of sales income for advertising. That is why I have avoided words like 'cause' and 'effect' in the list of examples above and used the more vague expression 'connection'. As you will learn in Section 4, it takes more than covariation to confirm a possible causal effect, and SEM is (in principle) only the analysis of covariations.

β is a measure of the strength of the connection and δ (*disturbance*) depicts the combined effect of all other factors influencing the child's birth weight.

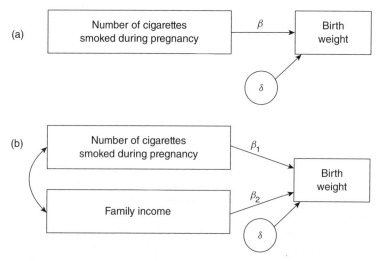

Figure 1.2 Example 1: a traditional regression model

There are many other such causes, most of which (in order to keep the model simple) could be summed up in economic terms as measured by total family income, so let us modify our model by including 'family income' as shown in panel (b). In this way we reduce the 'noise' summed up in δ. The two-headed arrow depicts a possible covariation between 'total number of cigarettes smoked during pregnancy and 'family income', a covariation not 'explained' by the model. You may know this phenomenon under the name of *multicollinearity* from when you learned multiple regression in your introductory statistics course. If you need a refresher, consult Appendix A.

So much for the word 'model' in *structural equation modeling*. But what about the words 'structural equation?

If we let the Greek letters β_1 and β_2 stand for the strength of the two effects while β_0 is a constant, we can just as well express our model in the *structural equation*

$$Y = \beta_0 + \beta_1 X_1 + \beta_2 X_2 + \delta \tag{1}$$

where Y is 'birth weight', X_1 is 'number of cigarettes smoked during pregnancy' and X_2 is 'family income'.

This is a traditional multiple regression model that most of us should know from our introductory course in statistics. So, you can see that multiple regression is a special case of SEM. As mentioned above, SEM is (mostly) about mapping 'relations', so the regressions coefficients β_1 and β_2 are the parameters of interest here (I have, however, added the intercept β_0 just to make the equation look familiar to you).

An obvious way to judge the correctness of the model in Figure 2b is to take a sample of mothers from the relevant population and question them about the three variables 'birth weight', 'number of cigarettes smoked during pregnancy' and 'family income'.

You can therefore test the model's agreement with empirical data by multiple regression and in that way verify the model.

In this case you do not need EQS to estimate the parameters (β_0, β_1, β_2 and the variance of δ) in the model, but if you do you will get exactly the same result as if you used traditional regression analysis.

(Note that covariances between independent variables are not considered parameters of the model in regression analysis – but they are in SEM, a point worth remembering!)

Usually, however, our models are a bit more complicated – and then regression analysis will not do the job. This can be illustrated using the second example above.

Example 2
Students' academic achievements

The model shown in Figure 3 was used by Joireman and Abbott (2004) to examine the impact of various factors that they suggested affected students' academic achievements.

This model is more representative of the complexity usually met in SEM – and here traditional regression analysis will (in general) not do the job.

In Example 1, 'number of cigarettes smoked' and 'family income' are traditionally called *independent variables* while 'birth weight' is the *dependent variable*; it depends on 'number of cigarettes smoked' and 'family income' – or at least that is what we think may be the case.

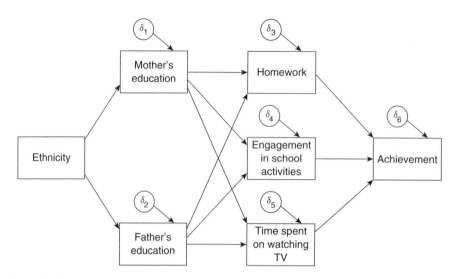

Figure 3 Example 2: model used to explain the impact of factors affecting students' academic achievements

A glance at the model in Figure 3 reveals that here things are a bit more complicated. Looking only at the connection between 'mother's education' and 'homework', you could say that 'mother's education' is the independent variable and 'homework' the dependent variable. However, 'mother's education' is dependent on 'ethnicity', so it is *also* a dependent variable.

This shows that we have to draw a very important distinction between *exogenous variables*, whose values are determined by variables not included in the model, and *endogenous variables*, the values of which are determined by other variables in the model.

In the model in Figure 3 (apart from δ-variables) the only exogenous variable is 'ethnicity' – all other variables are endogenous.

Example 3
Constructing a measuring instrument

A psychologist is constructing a questionnaire that can measure a person's 'style of processing', i.e. the person's preference to engage in a verbal and/or visual modality of processing information about his or her environment.

The psychologist decides to use a summated scale.

A summated scale is compiled by adding up scores obtained from answering a series of questions. One of the most popular scales is the *Likert scale*. Here the respondents are asked to indicate their agreement with a series of statements by checking a scale from, say, 1 (strongly disagree) to 5 (strongly agree) and the scores are then added to make up the scale. The scale values are in the opposite direction for statements that are favorably worded versus unfavorably worded in regard to the concept being measured.

Examples of such questions – or *items* as they are called in this connection – to measure 'style of processing' are as follows:

1. I enjoy work that requires the use of words.
2. There are some special times in my life that I like to relive by mentally 'picturing' just how everything looked.
3. When I'm trying to learn something new, I'd rather watch a demonstration than read how to do it.

The psychologist has formulated around 50 such items (statements) and is now wondering which of them should be chosen for inclusion in the questionnaire – the criteria of course being that the ones with the strongest 'connection' to the concept 'style of processing' should be the preferred ones.

The problem can be modeled as shown in Figure 4.

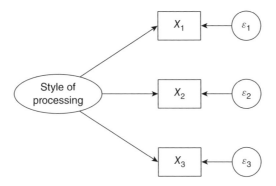

Figure 4 Example 3: model used in scale development

The X-variables in the figure are three items supposed to measure 'style of processing', and the three ε-variables indicate that factors other than the variable 'style of processing,' affect how people answer a question. ε is the combined effect of all such 'disturbing' effects. In other words, ε is the measurement error of the item in question.

You may wonder why the variable 'style of processing' in the model in Figure 4 is shown as an ellipse (just like the concepts in Figure 1), while the concepts in Figure 2 are depicted as rectangles. This is done because there is a fundamental difference between 'number of cigarettes', 'family income' and 'birth weight' on the one hand, and 'style of processing' on the other.

The first-mentioned concepts are *measurable,* i.e. there exist well-defined ways of measuring them. They are measured in number of cigarettes, in dollars (or whatever currency is relevant) and in pounds or kilograms. Such measurable variables are called *manifest variables*, and they are traditionally depicted as squares or rectangles.

A characteristic of the concept 'style of processing' in the model in Figure 4 is that it is not directly measurable by a generally accepted measuring instrument, a characteristic it shares with many concepts from the social and behavioral sciences – satisfaction, preference, intelligence, lifestyle, social class and literacy, just to mention a few. Such non-measurable variables are called *latent variables*. Latent variables are traditionally depicted as circles or ellipses

As such concepts cannot be measured directly, they are measured indirectly by *indicators* – in this case items in a Likert scale – and such indicators are *manifest variables*.

The arrows connecting a latent variable to its manifest variables should be interpreted as follows:

If a latent variable were measurable on a continuous scale – which of course is not the case as a latent variable is not (directly) measurable on *any* scale – variations in a person's (or whatever the analytical unit may be) position on this scale would be mirrored in variations in its manifest variables. This is the reason why the arrows point *from* the latent variable *towards* its manifest indicators and not the other way round.

The purpose is now to estimate the parameters in the model in Figure 4, these parameters being the three regression coefficients and the variances of the ε-variables, and then use the result to select the 'best' items (i.e. the ones with the strongest connection to 'style of processing') for use in the summated Likert scale.

In this case we cannot use traditional regression analysis, because one of the variables is latent, but EQS can do the job.

In fact, the three items in this example are taken from the 22-item SOP (Style of Processing) scale by Childers, Houston & Heckler (1985). We will return to this example in Chapter 7.

The selection of items for summated and non-summated scales is discussed in the next chapter.

Example 4
The effects of depression on the immune system

A health researcher is interested in evaluating the (possible) connection between depression and the state of the immune system, and tentatively suggests the model shown in Figure 5 (this figure is part of a more complicated model, to which we will return in Chapter 8).

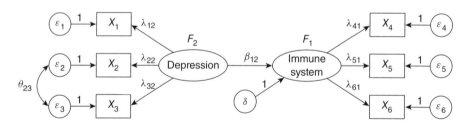

Figure 5 Example 4: a model with latent variables

As can be seen, the model contains the hypothesized effect of 'depression' on 'immune system' as well as the connections between the two latent (non-measurable) variables and their manifest (measurable) indicators.

The model thus consists of two parts:

1. The *structural model* describing the (causal?) connections between the latent variables. Mapping of this connection is the main purpose of the analysis.
2. The *measurement model* describing the connections between the latent variables and their manifest indicators.

We can translate the graphic model into a set of equations:

$$F_1 = \beta_{12}F_2 + \delta$$
$$X_1 = \lambda_{12}F_2 + \varepsilon_1 \qquad X_4 = \lambda_{41}F_1 + \varepsilon_4$$
$$X_2 = \lambda_{22}F_2 + \varepsilon_2 \qquad X_5 = \lambda_{51}F_1 + \varepsilon_5 \qquad (2)$$
$$X_3 = \lambda_{32}F_2 + \varepsilon_3 \qquad X_6 = \lambda_{61}F_1 + \varepsilon_6$$
$$COV(\varepsilon_2, \varepsilon_3) = \theta_{23}$$

where F_1 is the state of the immune system and F_2 depression. As in EQS, I use F as a designation for the latent variables, because such theoretical constructs are often referred to as *factors* (cf. Chapter 3 Factor Analysis). The first equation describes the structural model and the last seven the measurement model.

We note that a hypothesized causal structure can be depicted in two ways:

1. As a graph with variables shown as circles (or ellipses) and squares (or rectangles), (possible) 'causal' links shown as arrows and covariation not explained by the model shown as two-headed arrows.
2. As a system of equations.

Both ways of depicting models have their advantages. The graph has great communicative power, and the equations make it possible to use traditional algebraic manipulations. Usually during a study you sketch one or more models, and then translate the drawings into equations, which are used as input to calculations. Newer computer programs (such as EQS) also make it possible to draw a graph of the model, which the program then translates into program statements ('equations') and carries out the calculations necessary to estimate the parameters.

Throughout the book I will use the notation in Figure 5. Latent variables are depicted by circles or ellipses and manifest variables by squares or rectangles. A one-headed arrow depicts a hypothesized relationship between two variables, the arrow pointing from the independent to the dependent variable, while a two-headed arrow indicates covariance unexplained by other variables in the model. β denotes a coefficient in the structural model and λ a coefficient in the measurement model.

Coefficients usually have a subscript with two digits, the first indicating the head of the arrow and the second the foot. However, if no risk of misunderstanding exists, only one subscript is used.

Covariances between exogenous (predetermined) variables are denoted by ϕ and covariances between error terms are denoted by θ. Subscripts indicate the variables involved. If the two digits of the subscript are the same, it indicates a variance. Variances are not shown in the figure.

In this case we have several latent variables:

1. The two variables that are the center of our research: 'depression' and 'state of the immune system'.
2. δ (*disturbance*) is the combined effect of all factors having an effect on the dependent variable, but not explicitly included in the model.
3. The six ε-variables indicate that factors other than the latent variable ('depression' or 'state of the immune system') affect the result of a measurement – ε (*error*) is the combined effect of all such 'disturbing' effects.

Depression could be measured by Likert items such as:

X_1: I am sad all the time and I cannot snap out of it.

X_2: I am so restless and agitated that I have to keep moving or doing something.

X_3: I have as much energy as ever.

Most often you will have more than three items in a scale, but three will do as an illustration (in fact the three items mentioned above are taken from one of the most widespread scales for measuring the strength of depression: *'Beck's Depression Inventory'* (Beck, Ward, Mendelson, & Erbaugh, 1961)). Observe that the variables X_1 to X_3 are expected to correlate, because they are all functions of the same variable 'depression' – they are measuring the same concept. However, a glance at the wording of X_2 and X_3 shows that they are indeed very similar, and they could be expected to correlate *more* than by their mutual cause 'depression'. If that should be the case X_2 and X_3 measure not only the same latent variable 'depression', but also the same aspect of that concept, hence the two-headed arrow in Figure 5.

A characteristic of the summated scale is that in taking an unweighted sum of the various scores you implicitly assume that all the questions (or items) making up the scale measure the concept to the same precision. An advantage of SEM is that instead of summing the various items, you can use the items separately, and in that way weight them in accordance with their quality in measuring the concept in question.

Now, we cannot measure the state of the immune system by using a questionnaire. Instead we carry out a few tests to measure variables that could be used as indicators, such as number of leukocytes, number of lymphocytes and PHA-stimulated T-cell proliferation.

To sum up, a theory is a number of hypothesized connections among conceptually defined variables. These variables are often latent, i.e. they are not directly measurable and must be operationalized in a series of manifest variables.

These manifest variables and their interrelations are all we have at our disposal to uncover the connections among the latent variables.

The benefits of using latent variables

The variables with which the social science researcher works are usually more diffuse than concepts such as weight, length and the like, for which well-defined and generally accepted measuring methods exist. Rather, the social scientist works with concepts such as attitudes, literacy, alienation, social status, etc. Concepts that are not directly measurable and therefore must be measured indirectly via indicators, whether they are questions in a questionnaire or some sort of test.

If we compare SEM with a traditional regression model such as

$$Y_i = \beta_0 + \beta_1 X_i + \delta_i \qquad (3)$$

it is obvious that the latter is based on an assumption which is rarely mentioned but is nevertheless usually unrealistic: that all variables are measured without error. (The assumption of no measurement error always applies to the independent variable, whereas you can assume that δ_i includes measurement error in the dependent variable as well as the effect of excluded variables.)

An assumption of error-free measurements is of course always wrong in principle, but it will serve as a reasonable simplification when measuring, for example, weight, volume, temperature and other variables for which generally agreed measurement units and measuring instruments exist.

On the other hand, such an assumption is clearly unrealistic when the variables are lifestyle, intelligence, attitudes and the like. Any measurement will be an imperfect indicator of such a concept. Using more than one indicator per latent variable makes it possible to assess the connection between an indicator and the concept it is assumed to measure, and in this way evaluate the quality of the measuring instrument.

Introducing measurement models has the effect of freeing the estimated parameters in the structural model from the influence of measurement errors. Or – put another way – the errors in the structural model (*'errors in equations'* δ) are separated from the errors in the measurement model (*'errors in variables'* ε).

What then is SEM?

As should be clear from the examples, SEM is not a single statistical model, but rather a collection of models originated in different disciplines at different times and brought together, because they can be shown to be special cases of a general model.

In Example 1 you met the traditional regression model that you should already know from your introductory statistics course, and in Example 2 several such models were put together to form a system of regression functions. Such systems are known in psychology and related fields as *path models* and in economics as *simultaneous equation models* or *econometric models*.

The model in Example 3 is generally known as the *confirmatory factor model*, and in Example 4 the path model and the confirmatory factor model are brought together to form *the general structural equation model*, of which the models in the first three examples are special cases. In fact, the general model can be shown to include many of the linear models that are bases for statistical techniques you may already know: analysis of variance, canonical correlation and discriminant analysis, to mention a few. So the structural equation model is very general indeed and well suited for analyzing a broad spectrum of problems in many disciplines.

3 A Short History of SEM

SEM can trace its history back more than 100 years.

At the beginning of the twentieth century C. Spearman laid the foundation for factor analysis and thereby for the measurement model in SEM (Spearman, 1904). He tried to trace the different dimensions of intelligence back to a general intelligence factor. In the 1930s L.L. Thurstone invented multi-factor analysis and factor rotation (more or less in opposition to Spearman) and thereby founded modern factor analysis where intelligence, for instance, was thought of as being composed of several different intelligence dimensions (Thurstone, 1947; Thurstone & Thurstone, 1941).

About 20 years after Spearman, S. Wright developed so-called *path analysis* (Wright, 1918, 1921). Based on box and arrow diagrams like those in Figure 3, he formulated a series of rules that connected correlations among the variables to parameters in a model of the assumed data-generating process. Most of his work was on models with only manifest variables, but a few also included models with latent variables.

Wright was a biometrician and it is amazing that his work was more or less unknown to scientists outside this area, until it was taken up by social researchers in the 1960s (Blalock, 1961, 1971; Duncan, 1975).

In economics a parallel development took place in what came to be known as *econometrics*. However, this development was unaffected by Wright's ideas and was characterized by an absence of latent variables – at least in the sense of the word used in this book. However, in the 1950s econometricians became aware of Wright's work, and some of them found to their surprise that he had pioneered the estimation of supply and demand functions and in several respects was far ahead of econometricians of that time (Goldberger, 1972).

In the early 1970s path analysis and factor analysis were combined to form the general SEM of today. Foremost in its development was K.G. Jöreskog, who created the well-known LISREL (LInear Structural RELations) program for analyzing such models (Jöreskog, 1973).

However, LISREL is not alone in this. Among other similar computer programs, mention can be made of RAM (Reticular Action Model) (McArdle & McDonald, 1984), included in the SYSTAT package of statistics programs under the name RAMONA (Reticular Action Model Or Near Approximation), AMOS (Analysis of MOment Structures (Arbuckle, 1989) and of course EQS (EQuationS) (Bentler, 1985).

Jöreskog was a statistician but published much of his research in psychological journals. No wonder then that psychology was the area where this 'new' way of thinking first gained widespread use.

The first discipline to 'import' SEM – and the area where it has found most use outside of psychology – is marketing. One of the first articles on SEM in the *Journal of Marketing Research* was by Bagozzi (1977), and three years later this author published a book on the use of SEM in marketing (Bagozzi, 1980).

Since then there has hardly been an area within the social and life sciences where SEM has not gained more and more appreciation.

The reasons for this are very simple: we often have to struggle with measurement problems; and the possibilities to perform experiments are often limited.

Last but not least, SEM forces you to think in terms of hypotheses, models and verification, i.e. it *speaks* the language of science and forces you to think as a scientist.

There is an exception to the development sketched above, namely *economics*, where the use of latent variables (in the SEM sense) is not apparent, despite modern economists spending more and more time analyzing 'soft' variables like health, values, etc.

4 The Problem of Non-experimental Data

Basing causal conclusions on non-experimental data usually necessitates statistical models comprising several equations as opposed to traditional regression analysis and analysis of variance, which serve us so well in the simpler situations we meet when we analyze experimental data. Besides, the statistical assumptions underlying the models used are more difficult to fulfill in non-experimental research, and, last but not least, the concept of causality must be used with greater care in non-experimental research.

As is well known, we are not able to observe causation – considered as a 'force' from cause to effect. What we *can* observe is:

1. *Co-variation* – the fact that two factors A and B covary is an indication of the possible existence of a causal relationship, in one direction or the other.
2. *The time sequence* – the fact that the occurrence of A is generally followed by the occurrence of B is an indication of A being a cause of B (and not the other way round).

However (and this is a crucial requirement):

3. These observations must be made under conditions that rule out all other explanations of the observations than that of the hypothesized causation.

These three points could be used as building blocks in an operational definition of the concept of causation, even if this concept 'in the real world' is somewhat dim and perhaps meaningless except as a common experience facilitating communication between people (Hume, 2000 [1739]).

It is clear from the above that we can never *prove* a causal relationship; we can only render it probable. It is not possible to rule out all other explanations, but we can try to rule out the ones deemed most 'probable' to the extent that makes the claimed explanation 'A is the cause of B' the most probable.

The extent to which this can be done depends on the nature of the data from which the conclusions are drawn.

The data

The necessary data can be obtained in one of two different ways:

1. Data can be 'historical' in the sense that they mirror 'the real world', e.g. the actual consequences that a firm's pricing policy has had on sales.
2. Data can be experimental: you can make your own 'world' in which you can manipulate the variables whose effects you want to investigate.

Historical data are often called *observational* data in order to indicate that while in an experiment you deliberately manipulate the independent variables, you do not interfere with the variables in non-experimental research more than necessary in order to observe (i.e. measure) them.

The necessity of a closed system

To rule out all possible explanations except one is of course impossible, and since we can examine only a subset of (possible) explanations it is obvious that causal relationships can only be mapped in isolated systems. Clearly, experimental data are to be preferred to non-experimental data, because in an experiment we create our own world in accordance with an experimental plan designed to reduce outside influences.

It is much more difficult to cut out disturbing effects in a non-experimental study. In an experiment we create our own little world, but when we base our study on the real world we must accept the world as it is. We deal with historical data and cannot change the past.

While it seems obvious that causality can only be established – or according to Hume (2000 [1739]) only be meaningful – in a scientific model which constitutes a closed system, it is a little more complicated to define 'closed'.

Example 5
The determinants of cigarette sales

In Figure 6 – inspired by Bass (1969) – some of the factors determining cigarette sales are depicted. There are an enormous number of possible factors influencing cigarette sales – many more than shown in the figure. It would not be very difficult to expand the model to cover several pages of this book. In causal research it is necessary to keep down the number of variables – in this example (as Bass did) to the variables on the gray background.

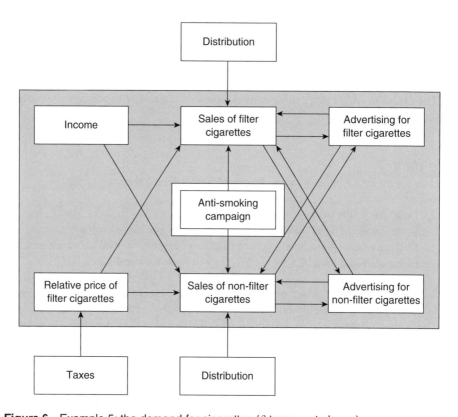

Figure 6   Example 5: the demand for cigarettes (δ-terms not shown)

As any limit on the number of variables must necessarily cut causal relations, we cannot demand that the system has no relation to the surrounding world. What we require is that all effects on a variable in the model, from outside the model, can be summarized in one variable which is of purely random (i.e. non-systematic) nature, and with a variance small enough not to 'drown' effects from variables in the model in 'noise'. If we use the Greek letter δ (disturbance) to designate the combined effects of excluded independent variables (noise), we can write

$$Y = f(X_1, X_2, X_3, ..., X_j, ..., X_p) + \delta \qquad (4a)$$

where Y is the dependent variable in the model, and X_j j ($j = 1, 2, ..., p$) are exogenous variables included in the model and supposed to influence Y. If the model is really 'closed', X_j (for $j = 1, 2, ...p$) and δ must be stochastically independent. This is the same as demanding that for each and every value of X_j the expected value of δ is the same and consequently the same as the unconditional expected value of δ. This can be written as

$$E(\delta \mid X_j) = E(\delta) = 0 \text{ for all values of } j \qquad (4b)$$

(for a definition of *expected value*, see Appendix A).

If condition (4b) is not met, a *ceteris paribus* interpretation of the parameters indicating the influence of the various independent variables is not possible, because the effects of variables included in the model are then mixed up with the effects of variables *not* included in the model.

Simon (1953, 1954) has given Hume's operational definition of causality a modern formulation.

Example 6
The disturbance must be independent of exogenous variables

As is well known (Appendix A), least squares estimation in traditional regression analysis forces δ to be independent of the exogenous variables $X_1, ..., X_j, ..., X_p$ *in the model* – and so do the estimation methods used in EQS. But the point is that this condition must hold in the population and not just in our model. So, be careful in specifying your model.

Consider the following model:

score obtained at exam = f (*number of classes attended*) + δ

Think about what variables are contained in δ: intelligence, motivation, age and earlier education, to name but a few. Do you think that it is likely that the 'number of classes attended' does not depend on any of these factors?

Three different causal models

Figure 7 shows three causal models from marketing, depicting three fundamentally different causal structures.

Dominick (1952) reported an in-store experiment concerning the effect on sales of four different packages for McIntosh apples. The experiment ran for four days in four retail stores. The causal model is shown in Figure 7a. In order to reduce the noise δ, the most influencing factors affecting sales (apart from the package) were included in the experiment, namely the effects on sales caused by differences among the shops in which the experiment was conducted, the effects caused by variations in sales over time, and the varying number of customers in the shops during the testing period.

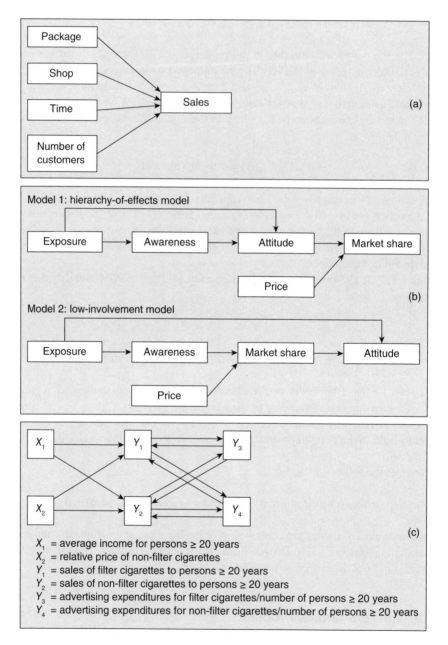

Figure 7 Three types of causal models (δ-terms not shown)

Aaker and Day (1971) tried to decide which of the two models in Figure 7b best describe buying behavior in regard to coffee. The question is whether buying coffee is considered a *high-involvement activity* (in which an attitude towards a brand is founded on assimilated information prior to the actual buying decision), or a *low-involvement activity* (where the attitude towards the brand is based on the actual use of the product). The non-experimental data came partly from a store panel (market shares and prices) and partly from telephone interviews (awareness and attitude). The models in the figure are somewhat simplified compared with Aaker and Day's original models, which additionally included a time dimension showing how the various independent variables extend their effects over subsequent periods of time.

Bass (1969) analyzed the effects of advertising on cigarette sales using the model in Figure 7c based on time series data.

The three examples illustrate three types of causal models of increasing complexity.

The model in Figure 7a has only one box with ingoing arrows. Such models are typical of studies based on experimental data, and the analysis is uncomplicated since:

1. There is no doubt about the orientation of the arrows – they depart from the variables being manipulated and from variables incorporated in the model in order to reduce the amount of noise.
2. The model can be expressed in only one equation.
3. The parameters in this equation can (subject to the usual assumptions) be estimated with regression analysis or analysis of variance (or in this case, analysis of covariance) – simple statistical techniques which can be found in any introductory statistics text.

In Figures 7b and c there are several boxes with both ingoing and outgoing arrows, so the model translates into more than one equation, because every box with an ingoing arrow is a dependent variable, and for every dependent variable there is an equation. For example, the hierarchy-of-effects model can be expressed by the following equations:

$$awareness = f_1(exposure) + \delta_1$$

$$attitude = f_2(exposure, awareness) + \delta_2$$

$$market\ share = f_3(attitude, price) + \delta_3$$

Such a system of equations, where some of the variables appear as both dependent and independent variables, is typical of causal models based on non-experimental data. This complicates the analysis, because it is not obvious a priori that the various equations are independent with regard to estimation, so can we then estimate the equations one by one using traditional regression analysis?

While the graphs in Figure 7b are *acyclic* (i.e. it is not possible to pass through the same box twice by following the arrows), the graph in 7c is *cyclic*: you can walk your way through the graph by following the arrows and pass through the same box several times. In a way you could say that such a variable has an effect on itself – a problem that I return to in Chapter 6. In the example the cyclic nature comes from reciprocal effects between advertising and sales: not only does advertising influence sales – which is the purpose – but sales could also influence advertising through budgeting routines.

We therefore have *two* (possible) causal relationships between advertising and sales, and the problem is to separate them analytically – to *identify* the two relationships.

This identification problem does not arise in acyclic models, at least not under certain reasonable assumptions. The causal chain is a 'one-way street', just as in an experiment. This means that not only is the statistical analysis simpler, but also the same thing applies to the substantive interpretation and the use of the results.

Causality in non-experimental research

Care must be taken in interpreting the coefficients in a regression equation when using non-experimental data.

To take a simple example from marketing research, suppose a market researcher wants to find the influence of price on sales of a certain product. The researcher decides to run an experiment in a retail store by varying the price and noting the amount sold. The data are then analyzed by regression analysis, and the result is

$$sales = a_0 + a_1(price) \tag{5a}$$

where a_0 and a_1 are the estimated coefficients.

Suppose the same researcher also wants to estimate the influence of income on sales of the same product. Now, the researcher cannot experiment with people's income, so he or she takes a representative sample from the relevant population and asks the respondents – among other things – how much of the product they have bought in the last week, and also asks them about their annual income. The researcher then runs a regression analysis, the result of which is

$$sales = b_0 + b_1(income) \tag{5b}$$

How do we interpret the regression coefficients a_1 and b_1 in the two cases?

The immediate answer we would get by asking anyone with a knowledge of regression analysis is that a_1 shows by how many units sales would change if the price were changed by one unit and b_1 by how many units sales would change if income were changed one unit.

However, this interpretation is only valid in the first case, where prices were actually changed.

In the second case, income is not actually changed, and b_1 depicts by how many units we can expect a household's purchase to change if it is *replaced* by another household with an income one unit different from the first.

Therefore the word 'causality' must be used with great care in non-experimental research, if we cannot rule out the possibility that, by replacing a household (or whatever the analytical unit may be) with another, the two units could differ on other variables than the one that is of immediate interest.

This is exactly the reason why an earlier name for SEM, – 'causal modeling' – went out of use.

It is only fair to mention that the use of SEM is in no way restricted to non-experimental research, although this is by far its most common use. Readers interested in exploring the possible advantages of using SEM in experimental research are referred to Bagozzi (1977) and Bagozzi and Yi (1994).

However, in this book you will find SEM used only on non-experimental data. The point to remember is that SEM is based on relations among the manifest variables measured as covariances, and (as you have probably heard several times before) 'correlation is *not* causation'. Therefore – as pointed out at the beginning of this section – it takes more than statistically significant relations to 'prove' causation.

If time series data are available you can also use the time sequence to support your theory, but – and this is the crucial condition – you cannot for pure statistical reasons rule out the possibility that other mechanisms could have given rise to your observations.

A claimed causal connection should be based on substantiated theoretical arguments.

5 The Data Matrix and Other Matrices

In the computer output from EQS, in the EQS manual and whenever you read an article where SEM is used, you will come across a wide variety of matrices. Therefore a few words on vectors and matrices are in order.

A *matrix* is a rectangular arrangement of numbers in rows and columns. In the data matrix in Table 1, X_{ij} is the value of variable j on observation i. In this book the observation is most often a person, and the variable is an answer to a question in a questionnaire.

The need to be able to describe manipulations, not of single numbers but of whole data matrices, has resulted in the development of *matrix algebra*. Matrix algebra can be considered a form of shorthand, where every single operator (e.g. + or –) describes a series of mathematical operations performed on the elements of the matrices involved. So, matrix algebra does not make it easier to do actual calculations, but does make it easier to describe the calculations.

Table 1 Data matrix

Variable → Observation ↓	1	2	...	j	...	p
1	X_{11}	X_{12}	...	X_{1j}	...	X_{1p}
2	X_{21}	X_{22}	...	X_{2j}	...	X_{2p}
⋮	⋮	⋮		⋮		⋮
i	X_{i1}	X_{i2}	...	X_{ij}	...	X_{ip}
⋮	⋮	⋮		⋮		⋮
n	X_{n1}	X_{n2}	...	X_{nj}	...	X_{np}

In matrix notation the data matrix is

$$\mathbf{X} = \begin{bmatrix} x_{11} & x_{12} & \cdots & x_{1j} & \cdots & x_{1p} \\ x_{21} & x_{22} & \cdots & x_{2j} & \cdots & x_{2p} \\ \vdots & \vdots & & \vdots & & \vdots \\ x_{i1} & x_{i2} & \cdots & x_{ij} & \cdots & x_{ip} \\ \vdots & \vdots & & \vdots & & \vdots \\ x_{n1} & x_{n2} & \cdots & x_{nj} & \cdots & x_{np} \end{bmatrix} \qquad (6)$$

Matrices are denoted by uppercase boldface letters and ordinary numbers (called *scalars*) by lowercase italicized letters. The matrix **X** is an $n \times p$ matrix, i.e. it has n rows and p columns.

A single row in the matrix could be considered as a $1 \times p$ matrix or a *row vector*, the elements of which indicate the coordinates of a point in a p-dimensional coordinate system in which the axes are the variables and the point indicates an observation. In this way we can map the data matrix as n points in a p-dimensional space – the *variable space*. Vectors are denoted by lowercase boldface letters:

$$\mathbf{x}_i = \begin{bmatrix} x_{i1} & x_{i2} & \ldots & x_{ij} & \ldots & x_{np} \end{bmatrix} \quad (7)$$

Alternatively, we could consider the data matrix as composed of p *column vectors* and map the data as p points each representing a variable in an n-dimensional coordinate system – the *observation space* – the axes of which refer to each of the n observations:

$$\mathbf{x}_j = \begin{bmatrix} x_{j1} \\ x_{j2} \\ \vdots \\ x_{ij} \\ \vdots \\ x_{nj} \end{bmatrix} \quad (8)$$

It is often an advantage to base arguments on such geometrical interpretations.

In addition to the data matrix you will meet a few other matrices. The *sum of cross-products* (*SCP*) for two variables X_j and X_k is defined as

$$\text{SCP} = \sum_{i=1}^{n}(X_{ij} - \bar{X}_j)(X_{ik} - \bar{X}_k) \quad (9)$$

If $j = k$ we obtain the *sum of squares* (*SS*). The $p \times p$ matrix

$$\mathbf{C} = \begin{bmatrix} SS_{11} & SCP_{12} & \ldots & SCP_{1j} & \ldots & SCP_{1p} \\ SCP_{21} & SS_{22} & \ldots & SCP_{2j} & \ldots & SCP_{2p} \\ \vdots & \vdots & & \vdots & & \vdots \\ SCP_{i1} & SCP_{i2} & \ldots & SCP_{ij} & \ldots & SCP_{ip} \\ \vdots & \vdots & & \vdots & & \vdots \\ SCP_{p1} & SCP_{p2} & \ldots & SCP_{pj} & \ldots & SS_{pp} \end{bmatrix} \quad (10)$$

containing the SCP and – on the main diagonal (the northwest–southeast diagonal) – the SS of p variables is usually called the *sum of squares and cross-products* (*SSCP*) *matrix*.

If all elements in **C** are divided by the *degrees of freedom* $n - 1$ (see Appendix A), we obtain the *covariance matrix* **S**, containing all covariances and, on the main diagonal, the variances of the p variables:

$$\mathbf{S} = \begin{bmatrix} s_{11} & s_{12} & \cdots & s_{1j} & \cdots & s_{1p} \\ s_{21} & s_{22} & \cdots & s_{2j} & \cdots & s_{2p} \\ \vdots & \vdots & & \vdots & & \vdots \\ s_{i1} & s_{i2} & \cdots & s_{ij} & \cdots & s_{ip} \\ \vdots & \vdots & & \vdots & & \vdots \\ s_{n1} & s_{n2} & \cdots & s_{nj} & \cdots & s_{np} \end{bmatrix} \qquad (11)$$

If all variables are standardized

$$X_{std} = \frac{X_{ij} - \bar{X}_j}{s_j} \qquad (12)$$

where $\bar{X}_j$ is the mean and s_j the standard deviation of X_j, to have mean 0 and variance 1.00 before these calculations, $\mathbf{S}$ becomes the *correlation matrix* $\mathbf{R}$:

$$\mathbf{R} = \begin{bmatrix} 1 & r_{12} & \cdots & r_{1j} & \cdots & r_{1p} \\ r_{21} & 1 & \cdots & r_{2j} & \cdots & r_{2p} \\ \vdots & \vdots & & \vdots & & \vdots \\ r_{i1} & r_{i2} & \cdots & r_{ij} & \cdots & r_{ip} \\ \vdots & \vdots & & \vdots & & \vdots \\ r_{n1} & r_{n2} & \cdots & r_{nj} & \cdots & 1 \end{bmatrix} \qquad (13)$$

6 How Do We Estimate the Parameters of a Structural Equation Model?

At first it seems impossible to estimate, for example, the regression coefficient β_{12} in Figure 5. After all, β_{12} connects two latent (i.e. non-measurable) variables. To give you an intuitive introduction to the principle on which estimation of parameters in models with latent variables is based, consider the simple regression model

$$Y = \beta X + \delta \qquad (14)$$

where both X and Y are measurable, and assume – without loss of generality – that both variables are measured as deviations from their mean. Under this assumption we have the following *expected values* E (see Appendix A):

$$E(Y) = E(X) = E(\delta) = 0 \qquad (15)$$

Further,

$$Var(Y) = E(Y^2) \qquad (16a)$$

$$Var(X) = E(X^2) \qquad (16b)$$

$$Cov(YX) = E(YX) \qquad (16c)$$

Now

$$Var(Y) = Var(\beta X + \delta) = \beta^2 \sigma_X^2 + \sigma_\delta^2 \quad (17a)$$

because $E(X\delta) = 0$ following the usual assumption of regression analysis, and from (16c) we get

$$Cov(YX) = E(YX) = E[(\beta X + \delta)X]$$
$$= \beta E(X^2) + E(X\delta) \quad (17b)$$
$$= \beta \sigma_X^2$$

We can then write the two covariance matrices

$$\begin{bmatrix} \sigma_X^2 & \\ \sigma_{YX} & \sigma_Y^2 \end{bmatrix} = \begin{bmatrix} \sigma_X^2 & \\ \beta \sigma_X^2 & \beta^2 \sigma_X^2 + \sigma_\delta^2 \end{bmatrix} \quad (18)$$

The model (14) implies a functional connection between the theoretical covariance matrix and the parameters of the model – here β and σ_δ^2.

If the empirical values are substituted for the theoretical ones, (18) becomes

$$\begin{bmatrix} s_X^2 & \\ s_{YX} & s_X^2 \end{bmatrix} \cong \begin{bmatrix} s_X^2 & \\ bs_X^2 & b^2 s_X^2 + s_\delta^2 \end{bmatrix} \quad (19)$$

The 'approximately equals' sign $\cong$ has been substituted for $=$ because we cannot in general expect the two matrices to be exactly equal, but the better the model describes the data, the more equal the matrices will be.

To generalize: if there is a one-to-one correspondence between the *sample covariance matrix* and the parameters of a model assumed to have generated the sample (i.e. if the model is *identified*) – which is not always the case – then the model can be estimated, its fit tested, and several measures of fit can be calculated based on the difference between the sample covariance matrix and the matrix implied by the model. This difference is called the *residual matrix*:

$$\begin{bmatrix} s_X^2 & \\ s_{YX} & s_Y^2 \end{bmatrix} - \begin{bmatrix} s_X^2 & \\ bs_X^2 & b^2 s_X^2 + s_\delta^2 \end{bmatrix} = \begin{bmatrix} 0 & \\ s_{YX} - bs_X^2 & s_Y^2 - b^2 s_X^2 + s_\delta^2 \end{bmatrix} \quad (20)$$

Therefore SEM is often called *analysis of covariance structures*.

In the regression case above, we can see that minimizing the elements of the residual matrix leads to the traditional estimates of β and σ_δ^2:

$$\beta \approx b = \frac{s_{YX}}{s_X^2} = \frac{\text{SCP}_{YX}}{\text{SS}_{XX}}$$
$$\sigma_\delta^2 \approx s_y^2 - s_{yx}^2 \quad (21)$$

which makes all entries in the residual matrix equal to zero.

You can therefore look at least squares not as a method to minimize the sum of squares for the residuals, but to minimize the difference between the two matrices in (19).

This is the basis on which estimation in SEM is built. Every model formulation implies a certain form for the covariance matrix of the manifest variables, and the parameters are estimated as the values that minimize the difference between the sample covariance matrix and the implied covariance matrix, i.e. the residual matrix – or to put it more precisely, a function of the residual matrix is minimized.

In this chapter you met the following concepts:

- theory and model
- exogenous and endogenous variable
- summated scale, Likert scale
- manifest and latent variables
- structural model and measurement model
- cyclic and acyclic models
- data matrix, SSCP matrix, covariance matrix and correlation matrix
- population and sample covariance matrix
- implied covariance matrix
- residual matrix

Questions

1. Why should a researcher prefer to work with latent variables? (List all the reasons you can.)
2. Explain the concepts 'measurement model' and 'structural model'.
3. To what extent is it possible to support a hypothesis of causal connections using SEM?
4. Explain the difference between cyclic and acyclic models.
5. Explain the various matrices **X**, **C**, **S** and **R**.
6. Look at Figure 3. Do you have any comments on the model? Do you have any suggestions for modifications of the model?

References

Aaker, D. A., & Day, D. A. (1971). A recursive model of communication processes. In D. A. Aaker (Ed.), *Multivariate analysis in marketing*. Belmont, CA: Wadsworth.

Arbuckle, J. L. (1989). AMOS: Analysis of moment structures. *The American Statistician, 43*, 66–67.

Bagozzi, R. P. (1977). Structural equation models in experimental research. *Journal of Marketing Research, 14*, 202–226.

Bagozzi, R. P. (1980). *Causal models in marketing*. New York: Wiley.

Bagozzi, R. P., & Yi, Y. (1994). Advanced topics in structural equation models. In R. P. Bagozzi (Ed.), *Advanced methods of marketing research* (pp. 1–51). Oxford: Blackwell.

Bass, F. M. (1969). A simultaneous study of advertising and sales – analysis of cigarette data. *Journal of Marketing Research, 6*(3), 291–300.

Beck, A. T., Ward, C. H., Mendelson, M., & Erbaugh, J. (1961). An inventory for measuring depression. *Archives of General Psychiatry, 4*, 561–571.

Bentler, P. M. (1985). *Theory and implementation of EQS: A structural equation program.* Los Angeles: BMDP Statistical Software.

Blalock, H. M. (1961). *Causal inferences in non-experimental research.* Chapel Hill, NC: University of North Carolina Press.

Blalock, H. M. (1971). *Causal models in the social sciences.* Chicago: Aldine-Atherton.

Childers, T. L., Houston, M. J., & Heckler, S. (1985). Measurement of individual differences in visual versus verbal information processing. *Journal of Consumer Research, 12*, 124–134.

Dominick, B. A. (1952). *An illustration of the use of the Latin square in measuring the effectiveness of retail merchandising practices.* Ithaca, NY: Department of Agricultural Economics, Cornell University Agricultural Experiment Station, New York State College of Agriculture, Cornell University.

Duncan, O. D. (1975). *Introduction to structural equation models.* New York: Academic Press.

Durkheim, E. (2002 [1897]). *Suicide.* London: Routledge.

Goldberger, A. S. (1972). Structural equation methods in the social sciences. *Econometrica, 40*, 979–1001.

Hume, D. (2000 [1739]). *A treatise of human nature.* Ed. D. Norton. Oxford: Oxford University Press.

Joireman, J., & Abbott, M. (2004). *Structural Equation Models Assessing Relationships Among Student Activities, Ethnicity, Poverty, Parents' Education, and Academic Achievement* (Technical Report #6). Seattle, OR: Washington School Research Center.

Jöreskog, K. G. (1973). A general method for estimating a linear structural equation system. In A. S. Goldberger & O. D. Duncan (Eds.), *Structural equation models in the social sciences* (pp. 85–112). New York: Seminar Press.

Lavidge, R. C., & Steiner, G. A. (1961). A model for predictive measurement of advertising effectiveness. *Journal of Marketing, 25*(Oct.), 59–62.

McArdle, J. J., & McDonald, R. P. (1984). Some algebraic properties of the Reticular Action Model for moment structures. *British Journal of Mathematical and Statistical Psychology, 37*, 234–251.

Mullahy, J. (1997). Instrumental-variable estimation of count data models: Applications to models of cigarette smoking behavior. *Review of Economics and Statistics, 79*, 586–593.

Simon, H. A. (1953). Causal ordering and identifiability. In W. C. Hood & T. C. Koopmans (Eds.), *Studies in Econometric Method.* New York: Wiley.

Simon, H. A. (1954). Spurious correlation: A causal interpretation. *Journal of the American Statistical Association, 49*(Sept.), 467–479.

Spearman, C. (1904). General intelligence, objectively determined and measured. *American Journal of Psychology, 15*, 201–293.

Thurstone, L. L. (1947). *Multiple factor analysis.* Chicago: University of Chicago Press.

Thurstone, L. L., & Thurstone, T. (1941). *Factorial studies of intelligence.* Chicago: University of Chicago Press.

Wright, S. (1918). On the nature of size factors. *Genetics, 3*, 367–374.

Wright, S. (1921). Correlation and causation. *Journal of Agricultural Research, 20*, 557–585.

2

Measuring Your Variables: Reliability and Validity

The concepts in your model will usually be rather diffuse (attitude, skill, preference, democracy), i.e. concepts for which no generally agreed measuring instruments exist. In such situations, therefore, you have to make your own measuring instruments – be they questions in a questionnaire or some sort of test.

The first requirement for such an instrument is that if you repeat the measurement under identical conditions, then you will end up with nearly the same result: your instrument must be *reliable*.

Another requirement – which seems just as obvious – is that the instrument should measure exactly what it is intended to measure and nothing else: the instrument must be *valid*.

Reliability and validity are the two main standards by which we evaluate a measuring instrument.

You will learn the classical versions of the two concepts, and you will learn how the use of SEM can illustrate the weaknesses of the classical ways of measuring reliability and validity and perhaps lead to more useful ways of judging these two central concepts.

In Example 3 in the previous chapter, mention was made of the SOP scale as an example of a summated scale. You will also learn how to construct such scales and how special computer programs can be used to that end.

From now on, you will need access to the companion website in order to carry out some of the activities used to demonstrate concepts and techniques and to take advantage of the exercises.

1 Reliability

We evaluate a measuring instrument by its reliability. The reliability of an instrument is its ability to give nearly identical results in repeated measurements under identical conditions. In other words, reliability is about reproducibility.

Let us consider the simple measurement model in Figure 1 as our point of departure.

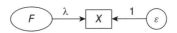

Figure 1 A simple measurement model

We can write

$$X = \lambda F + \varepsilon \tag{1a}$$

with the usual conditions

$$E(\varepsilon) = 0 \quad \text{and} \quad Cov(\varepsilon, F) = 0 \tag{1b}$$

The expectation of (1a) is

$$E(X) = E(\lambda F) = \lambda E(F) \tag{2a}$$

and the variance is

$$Var(X) = Var(\lambda F) + Var(\varepsilon) = \lambda^2 Var(F) + \sigma_\varepsilon^2 \tag{2b}$$

While we are able only to observe variation in X, it is of course the latent variable F and its variance – often referred to as the *true variance* – that are the center of our interest. Let us now define the *reliability coefficient* ρ_{XX} as the proportion of measured variance that can be traced back to F:

$$\rho_{XX} = \frac{\lambda^2 Var(F)}{\lambda^2 Var(F) + Var(\varepsilon)} = \frac{\lambda^2 Var(F)}{Var(X)} = 1 - \frac{Var(\varepsilon)}{Var(X)} \tag{3a}$$

It is obvious that (1) is an analogue of the simple regression model, and that ρ_{XX} is the squared correlation coefficient in this model. Unlike the traditional regression model, however, the independent variable F is unobservable.

When – as in this case – a latent variable has only one indicator, λ is only a scale factor, the value of which is arbitrary. Usually λ is then taken to have the value 1.00, in which case (3a) can be written as

$$\rho_{XX} = \frac{Var(F)}{Var(X)} = 1 - \frac{Var(\varepsilon)}{Var(X)} = \rho_{XF} \tag{3b}$$

Variances, covariances and reliability

Analysis of quantitative empirical data is basically analysis of variation and covariation. By how much do the attributes vary among observations, and to what extent do they covary?

Suppose you are interested in measuring the structural correlation $\rho_{F_1 F_2}$ between the two latent variables F_1 and F_2 in Figure 2.2. However, since you are able to observe only the empirical correlation r_{XY} between the manifest variables X and Y, you will underestimate the structural covariation.

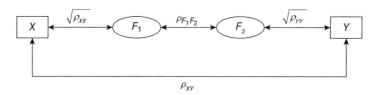

Figure 2 Correlation and reliability

2.1 Reliability

As you can see from the figure,

$$\rho_{XY} = \sqrt{\rho_{XX}}\, \rho_{F_1 F_2} \sqrt{\rho_{YY}} = \rho_{F_1 F_2} \sqrt{\rho_{XX} \rho_{YY}} \qquad (4)$$

from which you get

$$\rho_{F_1 F_2} = \frac{\rho_{XY}}{\sqrt{\rho_{XX} \rho_{YY}}} \qquad (5)$$

As the denominator is generally less than one you will underestimate the structural correlation, the size of underestimation depending on the reliability of the two measurements. It is therefore quite possible to overlook an existing correlation because of unreliable measurements.

In order to develop satisfactory measuring instruments we must find a way to estimate their reliability. This, however, means that we must have at least two measurements as shown in Figure 3.

From (3a) the reliability coefficients of the two measurements X_1 and X_2 are $\rho_{X_1 X_1} = \rho_{X_1 F}$ and $\rho_{X_2 X_2} = \rho_{X_2 F}$, respectively. However, because F is non-observable you cannot use (3a) for computation.

From Figure 3 it is evident that X_1 and X_2 – both being influenced by F – must correlate, and the more they correlate with F, the stronger their mutual correlation. It should therefore be possible to judge the reliabilities of the two measurements based on the empirical correlation between X_1 and X_2.

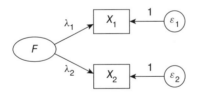

Figure 3 A measurement model with two indicators

We can now write

$$\begin{aligned} X_1 &= \lambda_1 F + \varepsilon_1 \\ X_2 &= \lambda_2 F + \varepsilon_2 \end{aligned} \qquad (6a)$$

with the usual regression assumptions

$$\begin{aligned} E(\varepsilon_1) &= E(\varepsilon_2) = 0 \\ Cov(\lambda_1, \varepsilon_1) &= Cov(\lambda_2, \varepsilon_2) = 0 \end{aligned} \qquad (6b)$$

to which we add one further assumption

$$Cov(\varepsilon_1, \varepsilon_2) = 0 \qquad (6c)$$

This leaves us with four possibilities:

$$\left.\begin{array}{l}\lambda_1 = \lambda_2 \\ \sigma^2_{\varepsilon_1} = \sigma^2_{\varepsilon_2}\end{array}\right\} \text{ the measurements are strictly parallel}$$

$$\left.\begin{array}{l}\lambda_1 \neq \lambda_2 \\ \sigma^2_{\varepsilon_1} = \sigma^2_{\varepsilon_2}\end{array}\right\} \text{ the measurements are weakly parallel}$$

$$\left.\begin{array}{l}\lambda_1 = \lambda_2 \\ \sigma^2_{\varepsilon_1} \neq \sigma^2_{\varepsilon_2}\end{array}\right\} \text{ the measurements are tau-equivalent} \tag{7}$$

$$\left.\begin{array}{l}\lambda_1 \neq \lambda_2 \\ \sigma^2_{\varepsilon_1} \neq \sigma^2_{\varepsilon_2}\end{array}\right\} \text{ the measurements are congeneric}$$

If the measurements are strictly parallel or tau-equivalent, the values of λ are arbitrary and are usually set to 1.00 – a tradition I will follow.

In classical test theory the latent variables F are not formally taken into account, which means that the coefficients λ are not known.

Consequently, classical theory builds on strictly parallel (and to a lesser extent tau-equivalent) measurements, where values of λ can be set to 1.00. Therefore, unless otherwise stated, parallel in the following means *strictly* parallel.

Parallel tests

Setting $\lambda = 1$, it follows from (6) and (7) that if X_1 and X_2 are parallel measurements, then

$$\begin{aligned} E(X_1) &= E(X_2) = E(F) \\ Var(X_1) &= Var(X_2) = Var(F) + Var(\varepsilon) \\ Cov(X_1, X_2) &= Var(F) \end{aligned} \tag{8}$$

It should be possible to use parallel measurements to evaluate the reliability. I will therefore calculate their correlation:

$$\rho_{X_1 X_2} = \frac{\sigma_{X_1 X_2}}{\sigma_{X_1} \sigma_{X_2}} = \frac{\sigma_{X_1 X_2}}{\sigma^2_X} = \frac{\sigma^2_F}{\sigma^2_F + \sigma^2_\varepsilon} = \frac{\sigma^2_F}{\sigma^2_F + \sigma^2_\varepsilon} \tag{9}$$

or, read from right to left,

$$\rho_{X_1 X_1} = \rho_{X_2 X_2} = \rho_{X_1 X_2} \tag{10}$$

In other words, parallel measurements have the same reliability, which is equal to their correlation.

If you are able to create parallel measurements, you can estimate their reliability. In the following subsections, I will show three different ways of doing so.

Test-retest

The obvious way to create parallel measurements is to repeat the measurement using the same instrument on the same respondents with a shorter or longer interval, and then estimate the reliability as the correlation coefficient between the two. The problem with this method is that it is difficult to say whether we are measuring reliability or changes in the latent variable. If the value of the latent variable has changed between the two points in time, the correlation could be small even if the measurements are reliable.

The correlation could also be large if a respondent remembered his or her answer to the first measurement, when the second is taken.

Alternative forms method

In order to rule out the possibility that the respondents at the second measurement remember their answer to the first – which will contradict assumption (6c) – it is necessary to construct another measuring instrument which is parallel to the first, and use that in the second round.

If for instance you intend to measure the skills of children in arithmetic by administering a test comprising various arithmetic problems, you can let the children do another test with different problems at a later time. Of course the two tests have to be of the same difficulty in order to obtain parallelism. One way to achieve this is to split the pool of problems between the two tests by randomization.

If you are interested in measuring attitudes or other more diffuse concepts it is difficult enough to construct one measuring instrument, so to construct two parallel ones can be a formidable task.

Split-half method

Both the above-mentioned methods require that two measurements are taken at shorter or longer intervals.

This is a drawback, but instead you can randomize the indicators of the latent variable in question into two equal-sized parts and calculate the correlation between these two measures. This can be considered as an approximation to the alternative forms method.

Let the two indicators X_1 and X_2 in Figure 3 be the results obtained by splitting the pool of arithmetic problems (after they have been administered) in the above example into two. If the two measurements can be considered parallel, the correlation between them is an estimate of the reliability of the two separate tests. However, we are interested in the reliability of the combined test. What then is the connection between the reliability of the two half-tests and the total, combined, test?

This, of course, depends upon how the two half-tests are combined, but if the combination is a simple addition $X = X_1 + X_2$, the reliability can be expressed as

$$\rho_{XX} = \frac{2\rho_{X_1 X_2}}{1 + \rho_{X_1 X_2}} \qquad (11)$$

This is the so-called *Spearman-Brown formula*.

Let the correlation coefficient between the number of correct answers to the two half-tests be 0.75. Since this is an estimate of the reliability of the half-tests, the reliability of the total test will, according to the Spearman-Brown formula, be

$$\rho_{XX} = \frac{2 \times 0.75}{1 + 0.75} = 0.86 \qquad (12)$$

A drawback with the split-half method is that the estimated reliability depends on how the test battery is split. I will return later with a possible solution to this problem.

2 Summated and Non-summated Scales

Adding together the number of correct answers to a test is an example of a *summated scale*. The answers are coded as '0' if the answer is wrong and as '1' if it is correct, and the total score is then taken to be the sum of the *item scores*.

We met another summated scale in Example 1.3, where a psychologist used SEM to develop a scale to measure 'style of processing' (SOP).

It is unrealistic to expect one question in a questionnaire to uncover all facets of complicated concepts such as 'style of processing'. A solution to the problem could be to use several questions – or *items* as they are called in this connection – per concept and to combine the scores obtained on each item into one measurement, usually by adding together the separate scores.

By adding several item scores we obtain a larger differentiation in the measurements. While a variable measured on a single five-point scale can have five different values (usually the values 1–5), a variable measured by summing over 10 five-point scales can take on 41 different values (usually the values 10–50), and thus give a more differentiated picture.

If you have several summated scales that differ in number of items, you could average the scores instead of summing them. In that way all your concepts would be measured on the same (e.g. 1–5) scale.

A further advantage is that while several objections could be raised against treating the separate items as interval scaled or even as normally distributed (a precondition for many statistical procedures including SEM), things look different when it comes to the sum or mean of several items.

The central limit theorem (Appendix A) states that under fairly general conditions the sum or mean of several stochastic variables will approach a normal distribution (and consequently be interval scaled) as the number of addends tends to infinity.

However, the following objections against the use of summated scales have been raised:

1. The simple summation of item scores presupposes that all items are equally good in measuring the underlying concept.
2. The respondents are scaled solely on their total score irrespective of how this score is obtained. Consequently, different respondents could have obtained the same score in very different ways. Are they then similar with regard to the attribute we intend to measure?

This last question can also be formulated as: 'Do the various items in the battery measure one and the same concept, or do they measure more concepts than one?' In the latter case it could, depending on the circumstances, be meaningless to add item scores that measure different concepts.

SEM offers a solution to both problems. By working with the individual items, the coefficients linking the latent variable to its manifest indicators (the λ_{ik} in Figure 1.5) are the 'optimal' ones, and *if* you choose to sum the items, you can use

SEM to calculate an optimally weighted sum of item scores instead of a simple sum. Also (as we will see in Chapter 7), SEM makes it possible to check whether a series of items are unidimensional, i.e. they all measure one and the same concept. However, a simpler method to deal with these two problems is to use factor analysis, the subject of the next chapter.

Nevertheless it has become quite common in recent years to use summated scales as indicators. Most often this is done by grouping items from a long scale (such as the 22-item SOP scale mentioned in Example 1.3) into bundles – or *parcels* as they are called – of 4–8 items and using a simple or weighted sum of the item scores as manifest indicators. The advantages of such a procedure are as follows:

1. The central limit theorem mentioned above could ensure that such indicators are 'more normal' than the separate items – especially if you group right-skew and left-skew distributed item scores into the same *parcel*.
2. You reduce the number of λ-parameters to be estimated, which could be an advantage, especially if the sample size is small.
3. It could be that *parceling* increases the stability of parameter estimates.

If your scale is very short – the extreme being binary variables of the yes/no type – parceling could also be an advantage.

Consider a test consisting of five yes/no questions. If you let 'No' count as '0' and 'Yes' as '1', summating the scores will give you a scale ranging from zero to five.

So, summated scales are not an obsolete technique as it was possibly the case when SEM was considered to be the answer to all problems.

Lastly, it should be mentioned that even if you have decided to use a summated scale in your research (e.g. for easier comparison with other research), it could still be advantageous to use SEM as a means of constructing the scale as mentioned in Example 1.3 and which will be demonstrated in Chapter 7.

However, parceling is not to be done carelessly: grouping the items could cover up problems that you should try to solve instead of hiding them. One such problem is *multidimensionality*. It should be obvious that if the concept you intend to measure is not unidimensional, there is a large risk that some or all of the parcels will also be multidimensional, i.e. cover more than one aspect of the concept. Then it could be difficult to find out what your latent concept really is, and there is a good chance that you will end up with a missspecified model.

So, discovering multidimensionality is an important issue in SEM, an issue that will be taken up in the next chapter.

My advice is: do not use parceling if you are working in a field that is new to you and/or you are developing a measurement model for a construct whose nature you are uncertain about. Only use parceling in situations where you are sure about the structure of the construct you are working with.

The many problems in parceling are summarized in the excellent article by Bandalos and Finney (2001).

Conceptual and operational definitions

It should be clear that it is very important for you to spend a good deal of time on defining your concepts and making their nature clear.

Traditionally you distinguish between a *conceptual definition* and an *operational definition*.

A *conceptual definition* is what you will find in a math book or in an encyclopedia. New concepts are defined with reference to concepts defined earlier or (in the case of an encyclopedia) to concepts that are assumed to be better known.

An *operational definition* defines a concept through the method used to measure it: 'temperature' is what you measure using *this* thermometer, 'intelligence' is what you measure using *this* test.

As it is impossible to trace a concept back to a few primitive concepts, the contents of which are interpreted by everyone in the same way, you could say that every conceptual definition is a circular definition – but then you will fail to see that during the process you are not moving in a plane but in a space. Therefore, when you have gone around the circle, you will be 'higher up' than when you started. The mental processes you have gone through will have given you a clearer understanding of the original concept as well as the auxiliary concepts you have had to introduce in order to clear your thoughts.

If you skip conceptual defining and go right to operationalization, it should be obvious that there is a great risk that you will end up with an inconsistent measuring instrument.

The conceptual definition tells you *what* to measure, and the operational definition tells you *how* to measure – but of course it is problematic to answer 'how' before 'what'.

Choosing items

Whether you choose to use the items separately or to summarize them in some way, you must be careful in their selection.

Good items require:

1. Large variances.
2. Expected values near the middle value.
3. All correlations between items to have about the same numerical magnitude, and if you choose to sum the items all the correlations should be positive.
4. All items to correlate with the sum of the rest.

The more these conditions are met, and the more the number of items, the larger the reliability.

As mentioned earlier, analysis of empirical data is basically analysis of variation and covariation. If a variable does not vary it is of no interest, because then it is part of the definition of the elements making up the population – and if a variable does not vary it cannot covary.

If the average of a variable is near one of the endpoints of a scale, we have denied respondents with more extreme attitudes the option to express their opinion. If a reformulation of the item brings the average nearer the midpoint of the scale, this will in most cases also increase the variance (and besides bring the distribution of scores nearer to normality – an advantage in many situations).

The correlations should be about the same (numerical) size. Two items having a numerically larger correlation between them than the rest indicate that they – apart from measuring the intended concept – also measure something else not measured by the other items, i.e. the scale is not unidimensional.

In a summated scale the inter-item correlations must necessarily all be positive. If an item shows negative correlations with the other items, the most obvious reason is that you have forgotten to reverse the scale of an item, which is worded in the opposite direction to the others. Another possibility is that the majority of respondents have failed to see a negation in the item. This risk is of course larger if only a few items have negations, so that the respondents do not get used to them. Good advice is to avoid negations altogether. An item having both positive and negative correlations to other items should be discarded.

Point 4 above is, of course, a logical consequence of point 3. Nevertheless, I mention it as a separate point because it expresses in a single number the value of adding an item to a scale.

The reliability of summated scales

In connection with the split-half method at the end of Section 1, mention was made of the Spearman-Brown formula

$$\rho_2 = \frac{2\rho}{1+\rho} \tag{13}$$

You can consider (13) to express the reliability of a scale that has twice the length (therefore ρ_2) of a scale with reliability ρ. If a summated scale has a reliability coefficient of 0.75, a scale of double the length will have a reliability of 0.86, provided the items are parallel.

Equation (13) is a special case of the general formula

$$\rho_k = \frac{k\rho}{1+(k-1)\rho} \tag{14}$$

expressing the reliability of a summated scale with k times the length of a scale with reliability ρ. If a summated scale has a reliability of 0.40, then the reliability of a scale five times as long is

$$\rho_5 = \frac{5 \times 0.40}{1+(5-1)0.40} = 0.77 \tag{15}$$

assuming parallel measurements. We see that – other things being equal – the longer the test battery, the larger the reliability.

Cronbach's α

Let the reliability of a single item X_j be ρ. The reliability of a scale made by the simple summation of k items is then

$$\rho_k = \frac{k\rho}{1+(k-1)\rho} \tag{16}$$

If we use the simple correlation coefficient r_{ij} between two arbitrary items as an estimate for ρ, we can estimate the reliability of the summated scale as

$$\hat{\rho}_k = \frac{kr_{ij}}{1+(k-1)r_{ij}} \tag{17}$$

In other words, in a test battery of k items we can calculate $k(k-1)/2$ different estimates of the reliability of the summated scale. But even if the tests are parallel these estimates will differ, so it is natural to insert the average correlation $\bar{r}$ in (17):

$$\hat{\alpha}_{std} = \frac{k\bar{r}}{1+(k-1)\bar{r}} \qquad (18)$$

This is *Cronbach's* α (Cronbach, 1951). The subscript *std* (for standardized) indicates that Cronbach's α also exists in an unstandardized version based not on correlations, but on covariances. It is possible to prove that $\hat{\alpha}_{std}$ equals the average of the $k(k-1)/2$ reliability coefficients that can be computed using (17).

If the measurements are not parallel the standardized version of α is of course not appropriate, and an unstandardized version based on the covariance matrix is to be preferred.

Then (18) becomes

$$\hat{\alpha} = \frac{k\bar{c}}{\bar{v}+(k-1)\bar{c}} \qquad (19)$$

where $\bar{v}$ is the average of the elements in the main diagonal and $\bar{c}$ is the average of the off-diagonal elements in the covariance matrix for X_j. If (19) is used on a correlation matrix, we get (18).

Equation (19) is a measure of the reliability of a summated scale whether the measurements are parallel or tau-equivalent. Moreover, (19) can be proved to indicate a lower limit of the reliability if the measurements are only congeneric (Bollen, 1989).

Usually (19) is written as

$$\hat{\alpha} = \frac{k}{k-1} \frac{s_L^2 - \sum s_i^2}{s_L^2} \qquad (20)$$

I leave it to you to demonstrate the equality of (19) and (20).

3 Computer-based Item Analysis

The process of choosing the 'best' items from a pool of items to be used in a research project is called *item analysis* or *reliability analysis*. Item analysis is usually done on a computer, and routines for this sort of analysis when using summated scales can be found in some of the most widespread statistics packages, e.g. SPSS, STATA and SYSTAT.

Example 1
Constructing a summated scale

Strangely enough, the consumption of fresh fish is much smaller in Denmark than in surrounding countries in spite of the fact that no Dane lives more than 60 miles (96 km) from the sea.

A research project was therefore launched in order to map the possible barriers for an increase in the consumption of fresh fish (Bredahl & Grunert, 1995; Grunert, Bisp, Bredahl, Sørensen, & Nielsen, 1995). Part of the project was a survey of the Danish population's attitudes towards fish and the use of fish in the household; one variable of interest was 'general experience/competence regarding preparation of fish'. Respondents were presented with the questionnaire in Table 1, and asked to check their agreement with the sentences on a scale from 1 (strongly agree) to 7 (strongly disagree). After reversal of item 36, the seven points were added, and the sum was proposed as a measure of a respondent's 'general experience/competence'.

Table 1 Example 1: extract from questionnaire

35.	I don't feel quite sure of how to clean fish:	☐
36.	It is quite natural for me to clean and fillet fish:	☐
37.	I think that fresh fish are unpleasant to touch:	☐
38.	I don't like the smell of fish:	☐
39.	I only rarely clean fresh fish:	☐
40.	If I want fresh fish, I usually get the fishmonger (or somebody else) to clean the fish, so that I don't have to handle it myself:	☐
41.	When I buy fish, I prefer ready-made dishes, so that I don't have to do anything myself:	☐
42.	I have never learned how to clean and fillet fish:	☐

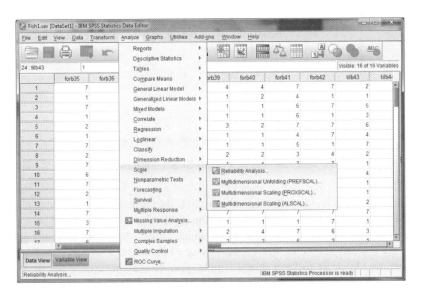

Figure 4 Example 1: reliability analysis using SPSS

Now open the SPSS file 'Fish' containing the data from the book's website. Choose 'Analyze/Scale/Reliability Analysis' as shown in Figure 4, and the dialog box shown in Figure 5a will appear.

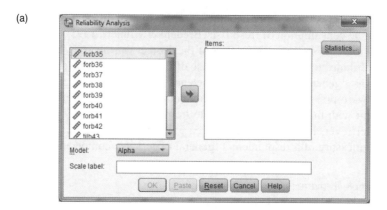

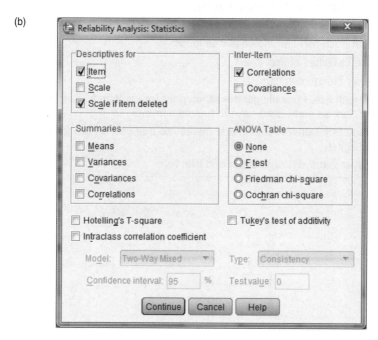

Figure 5 Example 1: reliability analysis using SPSS – the main window and dialog box

Select the items in the left column and click the little arrow (or double-click the selected items), whereby they are moved to the right column. In the model pane choose 'Alpha' (the default) and click 'Statistics', which makes the dialog box in Figure 5b appear. As you can see, SPSS offers a wide range of possibilities, which you can explore on your own. In order to keep things simple, you should check only the three boxes shown. That will result in the output given in Table 2, which I will briefly comment upon:

1. First in the output is Cronbach's α in unstandardized and standardized form. The two are of about equal size as a consequence of the items having nearly the same standard deviations.
2. Then average, standard deviation and number of answers to every single item are stated. We see that item 41 has a relatively small standard deviation and

therefore is a candidate for exclusion. The average is very extreme, so perhaps a reformulation of the item would be a good idea. Both items 37 and 38 also have extreme averages.
3. Next the correlation matrix is shown. All the correlations are positive after reversal of item 36 (hence 36r). However, item 41 correlates poorly with the other items, and a few of the correlations are a little too high compared with the rest, e.g. (forb35, forb42) and (forb39, forb40).
4. Towards the end of the output you will see the most interesting results of the analysis, where you can evaluate the consequences of deleting an item from the battery. Shown first for each item are the mean and variance for the summated scale if the item is deleted. 'Corrected Item-Total Correlation' is the simple correlation between the item and the sum of the rest, and 'Squared Multiple Correlation' is the coefficient of determination when the item is regressed on the others. Finally, the last column shows the size of (unstandardized) α, if the item is deleted.

Table 2 Example 1: reliability analysis using SPSS

Reliability Statistics (1)

Cronbach's Alpha	Cronbach's Alpha Based on Standardized Items	N of Items
.831	.823	8

Item Statistics (2)

	Mean	Std. Deviation	N
forb35	3.93	2.662	89
forb36r	3.00	2.454	89
forb37	5.56	2.164	89
forb38	5.22	2.152	89
forb39	2.31	2.156	89
forb40	2.57	2.235	89
forb41	6.15	1.736	89
forb42	4.21	2.643	89

Inter-Item Correlation Matrix (3)

	forb35	forb36r	forb37	forb38	forb39	forb40	forb41	forb42
forb35	1.000	.607	.326	.245	.538	.442	.179	.698
forb36r	.607	1.000	.439	.310	.689	.541	.240	.604
forb37	.326	.439	1.000	.524	.276	.280	.153	.249
forb38	.245	.310	.524	1.000	.264	.370	.171	.237
forb39	.538	.689	.276	.264	1.000	.691	.209	.484
forb40	.442	.541	.280	.370	.691	1.000	.119	.385
forb41	.179	.240	.153	.171	.209	.119	1.000	.043
forb42	.698	.604	.249	.237	.484	.385	.043	1.000

Item-Total Statistics (4)

	Scale Mean if Item Deleted	Scale Variance if Item Deleted	Corrected Item-Total Correlation	Squared Multiple Correlation	Cronbach's Alpha if Item Deleted
forb35	29.03	109.783	.671	.570	.795
forb36r	29.967	109.283	.760	.635	.782
forb37	27.40	127.016	.463	.375	.823
forb38	27.74	128.717	.429	.343	.827
forb39	30.65	117.389	.690	.632	.795
forb40	30.39	119.696	.605	.524	.805
forb41	26.82	142.263	.218	.111	.846
forb42	28.75	113.620	.598	.561	.806

If you remove item forb41, you can expect α to increase from 0.831 to 0.846. Also notice that the 'Corrected Item-Total Correlation' and 'Squared Multiple Correlation' are very small for this item. Often a minimum of 0.40 for the two is used as a rule of thumb.

If you remove item 41 and repeat the analysis, you get the output shown in Table 3.

Table 3 Example 1: reliability analysis using SPSS (second run)

	Scale Mean if Item Deleted	Scale Variance if Item Deleted	Corrected Item-Total Correlation	Squared Multiple Correlation	Cronbach's Alpha if Item Deleted
forb35	22.89	99.419	.674	.564	.814
forb36r	23.82	99.308	.755	.627	.801
forb37	21.26	116.148	.460	.375	.845
forb38	21.60	117.971	.421	.334	.850
forb39	24.51	106.935	.688	.630	.814
forb40	24.25	108.597	.615	.520	.824
forb42	22.61	101.991	.623	.545	.823

I will leave it to you to convince yourself that α can be further increased (to 0.866) by deleting both items 37 and 38.

It is also worth noting that these two items, together with item 41, are the only ones that mention reasons for (low) experience with the preparation of fish; that is, they are unpleasant to touch and do not smell good – and in the case of item 41 that ready-made dishes are preferred. These are not the reasons in the majority of cases (cf. the high means), hence the rather small 'Corrected Item-Total Correlation' and 'Squared Multiple Correlation' of these items.

Now, you could draw up a long list of reasons why a person would avoid preparing fish, *but there is no reason a priori to expect that the various reasons should correlate with each other or with any other item in the battery.*

The three items should never have been entered into the scale in the first place.

Item analysis is usually done on a small sample – a so-called *pilot sample* – prior to the main study. This was probably also done in this case, but the three items still made their way to the main study.

A final warning: remember that the last column in Table 3 shows the expected change in α *if a single item is removed*. Sometimes α cannot be increased by removing just one item, but can still be increased if more than one item is removed simultaneously. Therefore, also look at the 'Corrected Item-Total Correlation' and the 'Squared Multiple Correlation'.

As mentioned, 'Alpha' is the default in SPSS, but it is also possible (in the window in Figure 5a) to specify other measurement models:

1. *Split-half* calculates the split-half coefficient between the first and the second half of the items. In addition the Spearman-Brown coefficient (11) and the Guttman-Rulow coefficient, which only assumes tau-equivalence, are calculated.
2. *Guttman's lower bound on true reliability* calculates lower bounds for test-retest reliability under six different sets of assumptions, which are all weaker than the traditional assumption of parallel measurements. Besides, they are based on only one sample (Guttman, 1945).
3. *Parallel* estimates reliability under the assumption of weak parallel measurements and tests this hypothesis.
4. *Strictly parallel* estimates reliability under the assumption of strictly parallel measurements and tests this hypothesis.

It should be mentioned that the way SPSS calculates split-half is not the wisest one, as there could be a fatigue factor. It is preferable to calculate split-half between odd- and even-numbered items.

As should be evident, there is no such thing as 'the true reliability'. The various methods for calculating reliability measure different aspects of reliability: 'test-retest' is a measure of the *stability* of the measuring instrument, whereas 'alternative forms' measures the *equivalence* of two measuring instruments. In a way 'split-half' measures the equivalence of the two halves of the same measuring instrument and alpha the equivalence of the separate items. In that way 'split-half' and alpha are measures of the *internal consistency* of the measuring instrument.

4 Validity

It is of course not sufficient for a measuring instrument to be reliable, it must also be valid – it must measure what is intended. If your instrument is not reliable it measures only *uncertainty* or *noise* – and then it is of course meaningless to ask whether the instrument is valid. If on the contrary your measuring instrument is reliable, it measures something – but what? In other words, to be valid, a measurement must be reliable.

I have hitherto assumed that a measurement measures one and only one concept. However, this is not always the case. Often an indicator is connected to more than one latent variable, as is pictured in Figure 6.

This is not a problem if you can name the two factors, which usually can be done only if they both have several indicators. If, however, the measurement X_1 in addition to measuring the factor F is also influenced by the unknown factor F_*, for which it is the only indicator, then things become more complicated. A factor such as F_* is called measurement X_1's *specific factor*.

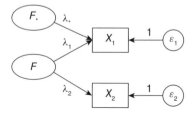

Figure 6 An indicator measures two different factors

The answer to the question 'How many times in the last five years have you been stopped by the police for drunk driving?' will be influenced not only by the true driving habits of the respondent (F), but also by his or her tendency to play down drunk driving (F_*). We can write

$$X_1 = \lambda_1 F + \lambda_* F_* + \varepsilon_1 \tag{21a}$$

with expected value

$$E(X_1) = \lambda_1 E(F) + \lambda_* E(F_*) \tag{21b}$$

and variance

$$Var(X_1) = \lambda_1^2 Var(F) + \lambda_*^2 Var(F_*) + Var(\varepsilon_1) \tag{21c}$$

$\lambda_1^2 Var(F)$ is called the *common variance* or *communality*. It is that part of the variable's variance that it shares with F and thus with the other variables, measuring the same factor (or factors). $\lambda_*^2 Var(F_*)$ is called the *specific variance*, as it relates to the specific factor, and $Var(\varepsilon_1)$ is the *error variance*.

In this notation

$$\rho_{X_1 X_1} = \frac{\lambda_1^2 Var(F) + \lambda_*^2 Var(F_*)}{Var(X_1)} \tag{22}$$

constitutes the reliable share of the variance, but only a share of

$$h^2 = \frac{\lambda_1^2 Var(F)}{Var(X_1)} \tag{23}$$

is valid.

As the validity of a measuring instrument expresses the agreement of the reading of the instrument with the true value, you could – at least in principle – judge the validity by comparing the imperfect measurement with that of a totally valid instrument. For example, the validity of the question 'How many times in the last five years have you been stopped by the police for drunk driving?' can be judged by comparing the answers with police reports.

However, this method presupposes that:

1. A totally valid measuring instrument exists.
2. It is possible to get access to it.

Usually at least one of these conditions will not be met. In such situations the concept of validity becomes ambiguous, and you talk about:

1. Content validity.
2. Criterion validity.
3. Construct validity.

A measurement has large *content validity* if it covers all (or many) aspects of the concept being measured. A trivial example is a test to measure children's ability in arithmetic. Such a test has content validity if it covers all of the examination requirements. On the other hand, if the test covers only a small part of the requirements, the content validity is low. Now, this example is special because the content of the concept 'examination requirements' is laid down in the curriculum. It is, however, very seldom that you are that lucky. In most cases content validity is evaluated in discussions with colleagues or other experts.

Criterion validity of a measuring instrument is evaluated by comparing the actual measurement with a criterion variable. We distinguish between *concurrent validity*, where the criterion is measured at the same time as the variable we wish to evaluate, and *predictive validity*, where the criterion is measured at a later time. A concurrent criterion is usually a measurement of the same concept with a different measuring instrument, while an example of a predictive criterion is the final exam result from a university as predicted by the entrance examination.

If a measurement is a valid measurement of construct F_1 it should correlate – positively or negatively – with measurements of other constructs ($F_2, F_3, F_4, \ldots$) with which concept F_1 is related in exactly the same way as the constructs $F_1, F_2, F_3, F_4, \ldots$ are expected to correlate, based on theory. A measuring instrument which stands such a test is said to have (a large) *construct validity*.

You could say that content validity is theoretically based and usually not measurable, while criterion validity is purely empirical, and construct validity is theoretically as well as empirically based.

Weaknesses of traditional validity measures

Criterion validity is fundamentally an empirical concept without much theoretical content. Concurrent validity is measured by the correlation coefficient between two or more simultaneous measurements assumed to measure the same theoretical construct. Let X_1 be the measurement whose validity you want to judge, and X_2 the criterion.

Then it is apparent that the correlation between the two, apart from the reliability of X_1, also depends on the reliability of X_2, and that the correlation could be inflated if the two measurement methods are not sufficiently different.

Construct validity suffers from many of the same weaknesses as criterion validity. Let F_1 with indicator X_1 and F_2 with indicator X_2 be two theoretical constructs, which – based on sound, substantiated theory – are expected to correlate. However, the correlation between X_1 and X_2 depends not only on the correlation between X_1 and F_1, but also on the correlation between X_2 and F_2, and on the correlation between F_1 and F_2.

Convergent and discriminant validity: the multitrait-multimethod technique

Campbell and Fiske (1959) proposed the so-called *multitrait-multimethod technique* for assessing validity: each of several concepts (traits) is measured by several methods.

Let three traits (latent variables) each be measured by two methods, and let the correlation matrix be as shown in Table 4.

Table 4 Multitrait–multimethod matrix

	X_1	X_2	X_3	X_4	X_5	X_6
method 1, trait 1 X_1	1.00					
method 1, trait 2 X_2	ρ_{21}	1.00				
method 1, trait 3 X_3	ρ_{31}	ρ_{32}	1.00			
method 2, trait 1 X_4	ρ_{41}	ρ_{42}	ρ_{43}	1.00		
method 2, trait 2 X_5	ρ_{51}	ρ_{52}	ρ_{53}	ρ_{54}	1.00	
method 2, trait 3 X_6	ρ_{61}	ρ_{62}	ρ_{63}	ρ_{64}	ρ_{64}	1.00

In order for the methods to be valid, Campbell and Fiske state the following requirements:

1. *Convergent validity*: The correlations of measurements of the same traits using different methods should be statistically significant and 'sufficiently large'. In this case these so-called convergent correlations are ρ_{41}, ρ_{52} and ρ_{63}.
2. *Discriminant validity*: Convergent correlations should be larger than correlations among measurements of different traits using the same method. In this case ρ_{41}, ρ_{52} and ρ_{63} should be larger than ρ_{21}, ρ_{31} and ρ_{32}.
3. *Discriminant validity*: Convergent correlations should be larger than correlations of measurements having neither trait nor method in common. i.e. ρ_{41}, ρ_{52} and ρ_{63} should be larger than ρ_{51}, ρ_{61}, ρ_{42}, ρ_{52}, ρ_{43} and ρ_{53}.
4. The pattern of correlations among traits should be the same across methods.

The multitrait-multimethod technique is an attempt to support the researcher in evaluating construct validity, but some of the fundamental problems still persist. This is easiest to see if we sketch the method in an SEM diagram as shown in Figure 7.

2.4 Validity

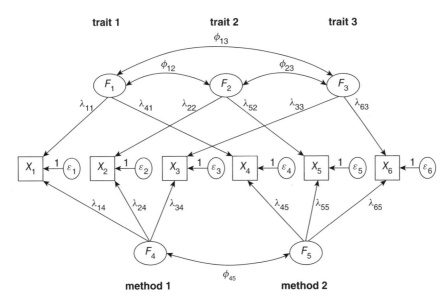

Figure 7 SEM model of multitrait-multimethod validation

Assuming all variables are standardized, we can write

$$\rho_{X_1 X_4} = \lambda_{11}\lambda_{41} + \lambda_{14}\lambda_{45}\phi_{45} \qquad (24)$$

and see that the convergent correlation $\rho_{X_1 X_4}$ does depend not only on F_1's influence on X_1 and X_4, which is implicit in the multitrait-multimethod philosophy, but also on the correlation ϕ_{45} between the two methods and their effects on X_1 and X_4.

The fundamental problem with the classical methods of reliability and validity assessment discussed so far is that they are all based exclusively on relations among manifest variables without explicitly taking the latent variables into account.

In Chapter 7 you will learn how SEM, by introducing latent variables, opens up for evaluations of reliability and validity that are based directly on the theoretical definition of these concepts.

In this chapter you met the following concepts:

- reliability and reliability coefficient
- parallel, tau-equivalent and congeneric measurements
- summated and non-summated scales
- parcel and parceling
- common variance
- specific variance
- error variance
- conceptual and operational definitions
- item analysis
- pilot sample
- validity
- content, criterion and concept validity
- convergent and discriminant validity

Questions

1. Define reliability and validity.
2. Discuss the various ways in which you can judge the reliability of a measuring instrument.
3. Discuss the demands that an item should meet in order to be included in a summated and/or a non-summated scale.
4. List the various steps you would take in constructing a summated scale.
5. Explain the concepts 'common variance', 'specific variance' and 'error variance'.
6. Explain the various forms of validity using examples from your own area of study or research.

References

Bandalos, D. L., & Finney, S. J. (2001). Item parceling issues in structural equation modeling. In G. A. Marcoulides & R. E. Schumacker (Eds.), *New developments and techniques in structural equation modeling*. Mahwah, NJ: Erlbaum.
Bollen, K. A. (1989). *Structural equations with latent variables*. New York: Wiley.
Bredahl, L., & Grunert, K. G. (1995). Determinants of the consumption of fish and shellfish in Denmark: An application of the theory of planned behavior. Paper presented at the International Seafood Conference: Seafood from producer to consumer, integrated approach to quality, Noordwijkerhout.
Campbell, D. T., & Fiske, D. W. (1959). Convergent and discriminant validation by the multitrait-multimethod matrix. *Psychological Bulletin, 56*, 81–105.
Cronbach, L. (1951). Coefficient alpha and the internal structure of tests. *Psychometrika, 16*, 297–334.
Grunert, K. G., Bisp, S., Bredahl, L., Sørensen, E., & Nielsen, N. A. (1995). *En undersøgelse af danskernes køb af fisk og skaldyr*. Aarhus: Aarhus School of Business. MAPP project paper.
Guttman, L. (1945). A basis for analyzing test-retest reliability. *Psychometrika, 10*(4), 255–282.

Further Reading

DeVellis, R. F. (2011). *Scale development* (3rd ed.). Thousand Oaks, CA: Sage.
de Gruijter, N. M., & van der Kamp, L. J. Th. (2008). *Statistical test theory for the behavioral sciences*. Boca Raton, FL: Chapman & Hall.

The first book is a rather elementary introduction, while the second is more advanced.

3
Factor Analysis

As mentioned in the previous chapter, we ideally require that a scale (summated or not, weighted or not) measures one and only one concept – that the scale is unidimensional. Another problem you faced was that of finding the optimal item weights when using parceling or other summated scales.

In this chapter you will therefore learn how to employ two classical and easy-to-use techniques for mapping the dimensionality of a data set and for calculating item weights.

The first technique is *principal components analysis* whereby a set of manifest variables (e.g. items) is transformed into new and fewer uncorrelated variables called *principal components*, each representing a dimension in the data.

The other is *exploratory factor* analysis where the roles, so to speak, are inverted. Instead of the 'new' variables being functions of the original manifest variables, the original variables are considered to be indicators (and thus functions) of underlying dimensions called *factors*.

This latter technique will, however, only be scantily treated as an introduction to *confirmatory factor analysis* in Chapter 7. The reason is that component analysis is less complicated and usually will give the same results as exploratory factor analysis. As the reason is purely pragmatic, you will no doubt find several examples on the use of component analysis, where factor analysis would have been more 'correct'.

Most often component analysis and exploratory factor analysis both go under the name of factor analysis, hence the title of this chapter.

1 Optimal Scales

In connection with Example 1.3, mention was made of summated scales as a means for measuring latent variables, and, in Chapter 2, you saw how item analysis based on a pilot sample could help you pick the best items for use in the main study.

It was mentioned that a large variance is an essential attribute of a good scale. As the aim is to study variations and covariations in variables across respondents or other objects, you could in fact consider the variance of a variable as an expression of the amount of information contained in that variable. The larger the variance, the larger the amount of information.

This, perhaps, might sound a bit strange to a reader who is used to looking at the variance as a measure of uncertainty or noise: the larger the variance, the larger the uncertainty, and thereby the less information. This, however, is only correct as long as we talk about the variance of a sampling distribution for an estimator (see Appendix A), but in scale construction we are interested in the variance in the population.

If all objects had the same value on a variable (in which case the variance is zero), measuring this variable would be of no interest, because the population would then partly be defined as the collection of objects having that value on the variable.

If we let X_j be the score on item j in a summated scale and L the total score, we can write

$$L = X_1 + X_2 + X_3 + \cdots + X_j + \cdots + X_p \tag{1}$$

and ask the question: 'Is it possible to obtain a larger variance (and thus a larger amount of information) by using a weighted sum such as the one shown in equation (2)?'

$$Y_1 = a_{11}X_1 + a_{12}X_2 + \cdots + a_{1j}X_j + \cdots + a_{1p}X_p \tag{2}$$

The answer is yes, and a simple example will illustrate the idea.

Example 1
Calculating the optimal weighting of a written and an oral exam

A class has obtained the marks shown in Figure 1 in an exam in French (measured on a 13-point scale as used in Denmark until 2007).

Most often the average of the two marks will appear on the certificate, i.e.

$$Y = 0.5X_1 + 0.5X_2 \tag{3}$$

A glance at the graph in Figure 1 will convince you that the points are more spread out along the X_1-axis than along the X_2-axis.

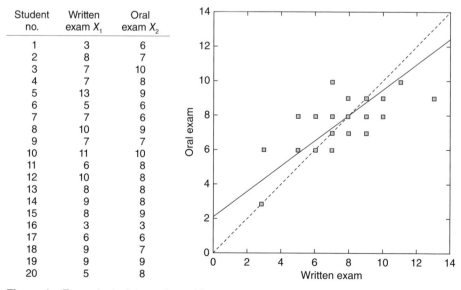

Figure 1 Example 1: data and graphics

X_1 has a variance of 6.37 and X_2 a variance of 2.79. The written exam does a better job in discriminating between the students, so should it then not also count more in the calculation of the combined mark for French?

In the figure a solid line is drawn through the cluster of points in such a way that the points are spread out more along this line than along any other line that could be drawn. If you project the points onto this line and provide a suitable scale, you might perhaps have a better expression of the students' abilities in French than if you use an unweighted average, which is tantamount to projecting the points onto the dashed 45° line.

The solid line has the equation

$$Y_1 = 0.64 X_1 + 0.36 X_2 \qquad (4)$$

and expresses the optimal weighting scheme for the two variables. Y_1 is called *the first principal component*.

Note that the Y_1-line is *not* the regression line. We can estimate two regression lines: the regression of X_1 on X_2 and the regression of X_2 on X_1. The first of these is placed so that the sum of squared *horizontal* distances from the points to the line is minimized, and the second so that the sum of the squared *vertical* distances is minimized. Both these lines pass through the point ($\bar{X}_1, \bar{X}_2$). The Y_1-line also passes through this point, minimizing the sum of squared *orthogonal* distances from the points to the line. See Figure 2.

So, a correlation (see Appendix A) between two or more variables could be considered a sign of a cause-effect relation – as in the structural part of an SEM model – in which case you can use regression analysis to map the relationship, or it could be interpreted as a sign that the variables measure the same underlying concept – as in the measurement part of the model – in which case the measurements could be combined to include as much information as possible from the original variables, using *principal components analysis*.

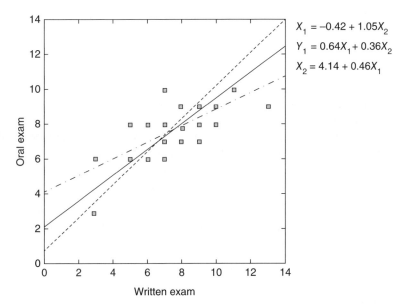

Figure 2 Example 1: the two regression lines and the (first) principal component

When the marks obtained in written and oral exams in French were combined into a single mark using the formula $Y = 0.64X_1 + 0.36X_2$, we treated the observations as if they were all placed on the Y_1-line, and thereby ignored the information contained in the distance from the various points to the Y_1-line.

This information can be utilized by introducing a Y_2-line perpendicular to the Y_1-line, thereby constructing a new coordinate system as shown in Figure 3. This Y_2-line is *the second principal component*.

It is obvious that Y_1 (by a suitable choice of scale) has a much larger variance than Y_2 (and any of the two original variables). Therefore Y_1 discriminates better among the students than any of the other three variables – it thus has the largest amount of information of the four variables, and Y_2 the least. Also observe that Y_1 and Y_2, contrary to X_1 and X_2, are uncorrelated (a regression line would coincide with the Y_1-axis).

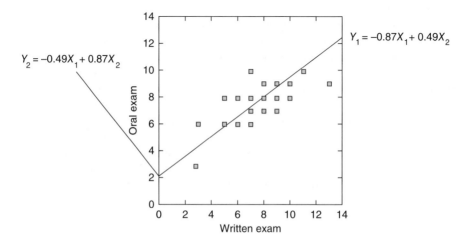

Figure 3   Example 1: the two principal components

The two components have the equations

$$Y_1 = 0.87X_1 + 0.49X_2 \quad \text{and} \quad Y_1 = -0.49X_1 + 0.87X_2 \qquad (5)$$

The first equation describes the same line as (4), because only the relative size of the coefficients matters.

If we measure the amount of information in the data by the variances of the variables, then the total amount of information in the X-variables is

$$VAR(X_1) + VAR(X_2) \qquad (6)$$

As the Y-coordinate system is just a rotation of the X-system, this transformation should not change the amount of information contained in the data, and consequently the coefficients in (5) are chosen so that

$$VAR(X_1) + VAR(X_2) = VAR(Y_1) + VAR(Y_2) \qquad (7)$$

In the present case

$$6.37 + 2.78 = 8.00 + 1.15$$

As our goal was to find the optimal weighting of the marks in the written and oral exam, we can disregard Y_2 and still keep

$$8.00 / (8.00 + 1.15) = 87\% \tag{8}$$

of the total amount of information in the X-variables. That is a lot more than the 41% kept in the simple average, which has a variance of 3.74.

2 Principal Components Analysis

The primary goal of component analysis is to reduce a number of correlating variables (i.e. variables sharing a certain amount of information) to a smaller number of – usually uncorrelated – variables. The p original variables X_j are transformed to p new variables Y_i called *principal components*:

$$\begin{aligned}
Y_1 &= a_{11}X_1 + a_{12}X_2 + \cdots + a_{1j}X_j + \cdots + a_{1p}X_p \\
Y_2 &= a_{21}X_1 + a_{22}X_2 + \cdots + a_{2j}X_j + \cdots + a_{2p}X_p \\
&\vdots \\
Y_i &= a_{i1}X_1 + a_{i2}X_2 + \cdots + a_{ij}X_j + \cdots + a_{ip}X_p \\
&\vdots \\
Y_p &= a_{p1}X_1 + a_{p2}X_2 + \cdots + a_{pj}X_j + \cdots + a_{pp}X_p
\end{aligned} \tag{9}$$

The total amount of information in the original variables (the X-variables) is then the sum of their variances, and the scales of the new variables (the Y-variables) are chosen to make

$$\sum_{i=1}^{p} Var(Y_i) = \sum_{i=1}^{p} Var(X_j) \tag{10}$$

in order to preserve the amount of information measured in this way. We have therefore not reduced the amount of data *unless we disregard some of the Y-variables*.

If we choose to keep only Y_1, then the coefficients a_{1j} are chosen so as to maximize the amount of information in Y_1 (i.e. to maximize $Var(Y_1)$ under the restriction (10)). If we also wish to keep the second principal component Y_2, then a_{2j} must be chosen so as to maximize $Var(Y_2)$ under the restriction that Y_2 is not correlated with Y_1 so that Y_2 only contains new information – and of course also under the restriction (10). This process is then continued with $Y_3, Y_4, \ldots$.

In other words, the coefficients are chosen so that the principal components, the Y-variables, are not correlated and are ordered by decreasing variance. The values of the Y-variables are called *component scores*, the coefficients a_{ij} are called *component score coefficients* and the covariances or correlations (depending on whether the analysis is based on a covariance or a correlation matrix) between the Y-variables and the X-variables are called *component loadings*.

The whole process groups the X-variables according to which component they correlate strongest with – *load most on*. By examining the variables loading on the same component it should be possible to interpret the component, i.e. to name it.

If the variables entering into a component analysis are very different in size (size of household, income, amount spent on a certain product or activity) it could be advantageous to standardize the variables to a variance of 1.00 before the analysis, because the variables with the largest variances would otherwise have the strongest influence on the outcome. This is tantamount to basing the analysis on the correlation matrix instead of the covariance matrix.

Although several good statistical reasons could be given in favor of basing component analysis on the covariance matrix (see e.g. Morrison, 2003), the use of correlations is almost universal – at least in the social and behavioral sciences.

Example 2
Interpreting dimensions in physical measurements

The correlations in Table 1 are based on the measurement of eight physical variables on 305 individuals (Harman, 1976).

Table 1 Example 2: correlations of eight physical measurements

	1	2	3	4	5	6	7	8
1. Height	1.000							
2. Arm span	0.846	1.000						
3. Forearm length	0.805	0.881	1.000					
4. Lower leg length	0.859	0.826	0.801	1.000				
5. Weight	0.473	0.376	0.380	0.436	1.000			
6. Bitrochanteric diameter	0.398	0.326	0.319	0.329	0.762	1.000		
7. Chest girth	0.301	0.277	0.237	0.327	0.730	0.583	1.000	
8. Chest width	0.382	0.415	0.345	0.365	0.629	0.577	0.539	1.000

From a correlation matrix of eight variables you can extract eight principal components, but the real question is: 'How many of these should you keep in order to retain most of the information in the data?' You can find some support for this decision in Figure 4.

Component	Variance	Variance in pct.
1	4.67	58
2	1.77	22
3	0.48	6
4	0.42	5
5	0.23	3
6	0.19	2
7	0.14	2
8	0.10	1
Total	8.00	100

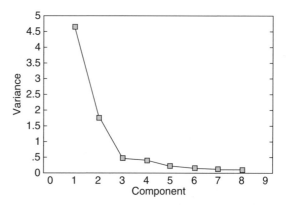

Figure 4 Example 2: component variances and elbow plot (scree plot)

The sum of the component variances is equal to the number of components. This comes as no surprise, because the original variables were standardized to have variance 1.00.

When deciding how many of the components to retain, the following rules of thumb are often used as starting points:

1. Extract components until a satisfactory share of the total information has been picked up. From the figure we see that by extracting one component we keep 58% of the information (variance), while extraction of two components brings this figure up to 80%:

$$\left(\frac{4.67+1.77}{8.00}\right)100\% = 58\% + 22\% = 80\%$$

2. From component 3 the variances are smaller than the average variance of the original variables (in this case 1.00). In other words, the last six components each contain less information than an average X-variable, and should therefore be discarded. According to this so-called *Kaiser criterion*, only the first two components should be retained.
3. If we look at the discarded components as uncertainty or noise, we should extract components until the next component is mainly made up of noise. But when is that? Usually you consider the remaining components to be noise, when the component variances begin to level off and have about the same size. This point is easier to find if the variances are depicted in an *elbow plot* (or *scree plot* as it is called in SPSS) as shown in Figure 4. The curve has a distinctive bend – an elbow – after the second component. According to this criterion a two-component solution should be chosen.

In this case the last two rules (and possibly also the first) lead to the same conclusion: extraction of two components. We measure two different attributes and not one or eight.

However, these are only rules of thumb – in the end the decision of how many components to retain depends on whether the components are substantively meaningful.

The transformation from the original variables to the first two principal components is

$$Y_1 = 0.4X_1 + 0.39X_2 + 0.38X_3 + 0.39X_4 + 0.35X_5 + 0.31X_6 + 0.29X_7 + 0.31X_8$$
$$Y_2 = 0.28X_1 + 0.33X_2 + 0.34X_3 + 0.30X_4 - 0.39X_5 - 0.40X_6 - 0.44X_7 - 0.31X_8 \quad (11)$$

Example 2 (continued)
Rotation of components

In order to interpret the components – to name them – we group the X-variables according to which component they correlate strongest with – *load most on*. The variables loading on the same component should have something in common, which could be used to name the component and thereby give it a substantive meaning. However, more often than not, the picture will be rather confusing.

The transformation (11) from X-variables to Y-variables is a mechanical process, and there is no reason to believe that the new variables should have any substantive meaning.

You might expect the variables to load most on the first component, and a look at the component loadings in Figure 5a shows that not a single variable loading is highest on component 2 – so are there really two *meaningful* components?

In Figure 5b the component loadings are depicted graphically, and you can see that they fall into two separate groups. There are in fact *two* components, the upper depicting the last four variables and the lower one the first four. However, our coordinate system is not able to disclose this unless we resort to a graph.

It is easily seen that a rotation of the coordinate system could bring the axes to pass nearer the two point clusters. By doing so, you obtain a simpler component structure, in that each variable has a large loading on one of the components and only a small loading on the other (or the others if there are more than two components). The result of this so-called *varimax rotation* is shown in Figure 6. You could name the first component 'bone structure' and the second 'flesh structure' (or 'height' and 'breadth').

It is possible, however, to let the axes go right through the point clusters of Figure 6, if we relax the restriction of orthogonal Y-axes. Such an *oblique rotation* is shown in Figure 7.

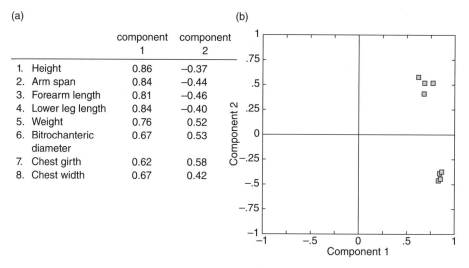

Figure 5 Example 2: original component structure

An oblique rotation means that the two components are no longer uncorrelated. In this case the correlation is 0.50. Whether to prefer an orthogonal or an oblique structure is not just a question of fit and figures, but a substantive question: 'Is it more reasonable to assume "bone structure" and "flesh structure" to be correlated, or is the opposite assumption more reasonable?'

In more complex cases there could be more than one among the infinite number of rotations that had meaningful but different substantive interpretations (Armstrong, 1967).

It is worth noting that SPSS (unfortunately!) does not allow you to use a covariance or correlation matrix as input when using roll-down menus. You have to write a command syntax. You can see how to do that on pages 421–422 of Norušis (2005).

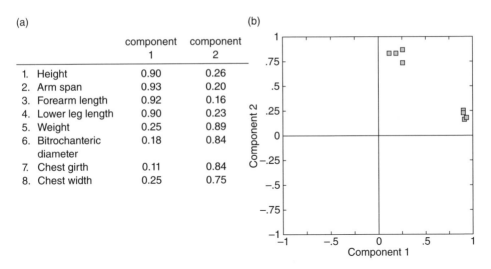

Figure 6 Example 2: varimax-rotated component structure

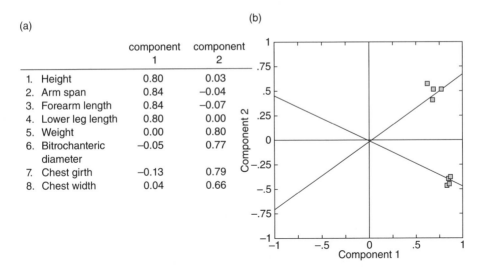

Figure 7 Example 2: oblique-rotated component structure

Checking whether a set of items is unidimensional

A set of items supposed to measure a certain construct ideally should measure only that construct and nothing else, i.e. the set of items should be unidimensional.

Consequently a component analysis should result in the following:

1. The first (unrotated) component should account for a large share of the total variance in the data.
2. Each of the following components should account for about the same variance.

Example 3 (continued from Example 2.1)
Using component analysis to do item analysis

You will recall from Example 2.1 how you could use traditional item analysis to locate three low-quality items in a scale that was used to measure respondents' 'general experience/competence regarding preparation of fish'. Let us see if a component analysis would point to the same problematic items.

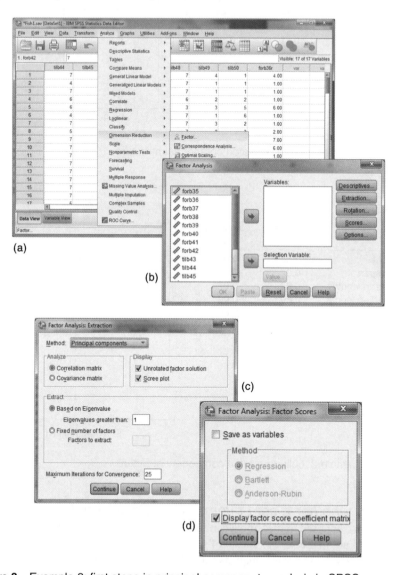

Figure 8 Example 3: first steps in principal components analysis in SPSS

After having opened the SPSS Data Editor, choose 'Analyze/Data Reduction/ Factor' (see Figure 8a). When you click 'OK', the dialog box in panel (b) appears. Select the variables in the left column and by clicking the upper little arrow move them to the right panel. Then click 'Extraction' and, in the dialog box in panel (c), choose 'Principal components' (the default). You are given the choice of whether you want your analysis to be based on the correlation matrix (the default) or the covariance matrix. Choose the covariance option, because all of your variables are measured on the same scale, check 'Unrotated factor solution' and 'Scree plot', and set the number of factors to be extracted to 1. Then click 'Continue', return to the dialog box in panel (b) and click 'Scores'. When the dialog box (d) appears, check 'Display factor score coefficient matrix', click 'Continue' and, when you return to the box in panel (b), click 'OK'.

Part of the output from the analysis is given in Table 2.

Table 2 Example 3: part of output from component analysis extracting one component (SPSS)

Communalities

	Raw		Rescaled	
	Initial	Extraction	Initial	Extraction
forb35	7.086	4.882	1.000	.689
forb36r	6.023	4.412	1.000	.733
forb37	4.681	1.283	1.000	.274
forb38	4.631	1.045	1.000	.226
forb39	4.650	2.864	1.000	.616
forb40	4.997	2.474	1.000	.495
forb41	3.013	.175	1.000	.058
forb42	6.988	4.382	1.000	.627

Extraction Method: Principal Component Analysis.

Total Variance Explained

	Component	Initial Eigenvalues(a)			Extraction Sums of Squared Loadings		
		Total	% of Variance	Cumulative %	Total	% of Variance	Cumulative %
Raw	1	21.517	51.148	51.148	21.517	51.148	51.148
	2	5.825	13.847	64.995			
	3	4.276	10.164	75.158			
	4	3.106	7.382	82.541			
	5	2.535	6.025	88.566			
	6	2.165	5.145	93.711			
	7	1.459	3.468	97.179			
	8	1.187	2.821	100.000			

Extraction Method: Principal Component Analysis.

Scree Plot

Component Matrix[a]

	Raw Component	Rescaled Component
	1	1
forb35	2.210	.830
forb36r	2.101	.856
forb37	1.133	.524
forb38	1.022	.475
forb39	1.692	.785
forb40	1.573	.704
forb41	.418	.241
forb42	2.093	.792

Extraction Method: Principal Component Analysis.
[a] 1 components extracted.

Component Score Coefficient Matrix[a]

	Component
	1
forb35	.273
forb36r	.240
forb37	.114
forb38	.102
forb39	.170
forb40	.163
forb41	.034
forb42	.257

Extraction Method: Principal Component Analysis.
[a] Coefficients are standardized.

1. First in the output are the communalities. Recall that the communality is that part of the variance of a measurement that it has in common with the latent variables – or in this case the one principal component – it is supposed to measure (and thus with all other variables supposed to measure that same latent variable). In principal components analysis, there is neither specific variance nor error variance as opposed the model in Chapter 2's equation (21). Consequently *all* variance is common variance if all components are extracted, and the raw initial communalities are just the variances of the various items, while the extracted communalities are the variances shared with the extracted component(s).

   The rescaled communalities are the same variances, after rescaling the initial communalities to have the value 1.00 (e.g. for the first item, $4.882/7.086 = 0.689$).

   The item forb41 catches the eye, because it shares only 6% of its variance with the extracted component. This item is therefore a candidate for exclusion and so are forb37 and forb38, the communalities of which are also much lower than the majority of items.

2. Then comes a listing of the principal components with their respective variances followed by an elbow plot that confirms the existence of only one component. You should compare this part of the output with Figure 4.

   Note that the variances of the principal components are called *eigenvalues*. Every symmetric $p \times p$ matrix (and that includes covariance matrices) has associated with it p eigenvalues. An eigenvalue is a function of the matrix. It is a mathematical concept, which in this case is interpreted as the variance of a principal component (more about eigenvalues will appear in Section 4.6).

   The first component extracts 51% of the variance, which is more than the 40% often recommended as a rule of thumb. Also the following components extract about the same amount of variance. So, the two conditions mentioned above are fulfilled.

3. Next come the so-called component loadings, the covariances and correlations between the original variables and the component scores – compare this part of the output with Figure 5. We see that the loading of forb41 is extremely small and therefore measures a different concept, and the loadings forb37 and forb38 are also smaller than the rest.

4. We could therefore expect forb41 to have a very small influence on the component score. Looking at the component score coefficients our expectation is confirmed. This item should be left out, as should forb37 and forb38. Running another component analysis after having left out these three items results in the output given in Table 3.

The first component now extracts 66% of the variance (not shown). All rescaled loadings are above the often recommended minimum value of 0.40, and the set of items would now be considered unidimensional according to that rule.

This is the same result we obtained in Example 2.1 based on traditional item analysis. From this, it is tempting to conclude that Cronbach's α is a measure of unidimensionality, but this is not the case: rather, *unidimensionality is a precondition for α*.

Unidimensionality means that correlations among items assumed to measure the same concept are only due to that concept; that is, controlling for the effect of the concept, there should be no excess correlation among the items: Equation (2.6c) is assumed to hold, whether the measurements are parallel, tau-equivalent or congeneric.

Table 3 Example 3: components analysis (second run)

Component Matrix[a]

	Raw Component 1	Rescaled Component 1
forb35	2.264	.850
forb36r	2.088	.851
forb39	1.723	.799
forb40	1.560	.698
forb42	2.182	.825

Extraction Method: Principal Component Analysis.
[a] 1 components extracted.

Component Score Coefficient Matrix[a]

	Component 1
forb35	.307
forb36r	.261
forb39	.189
forb40	.177
forb42	.294

Extraction Method: Principal Component Analysis.
[a] Coefficients are standardized.

Furthermore, we can see from Table 3 that the component score coefficients are roughly located in the interval 0.20–0.30, and consequently a simple summation of item scores could be used as an adequate approximation to the component scores.

While nowadays, since we hardly use hand calculation, it is just as easy to calculate a component score as a summated score, one strong point against using component scores could be put forward. If the scale is expected to be used repeatedly in several studies, or if you are comparing your research with that of others, you could argue that the simple summated scale is a more robust instrument than a weighted scale, because the weights (the component score coefficients) could vary across studies.

Mapping and interpreting multidimensional item sets

The more items you consider for the measurement of a concept, the larger the risk that more than one dimension will be revealed when you take a closer look at your data.

If that should happen, you also have to decide whether the various dimensions describe several aspects of the same concept, or whether in fact you are measuring several distinct concepts.

As will be demonstrated in Chapter 7, SEM can be used to that end, but the 'quick and dirty tool' is principal components analysis.

Example 4
Finding the dimensionality in a scale

In the same study (as the one in Example 3), measurement of the respondents' 'involvement in procuring and serving fish' was also required. The items used in a Likert scale are given in Table 4 and the data (Fish2) can be found on the book's website.

Table 4 Example 4: extract from the questionnaire

1. Fish is something I can talk about at length: ❏
2. I know so much about fish that I am able to evaluate the suitability of various types of fish for various dishes and various occasions: ❏
3. Fish is a product that interests me: ❏
4. I prefer some kinds of fish to others: ❏
5. Fish is a product or food product category which I don't believe that I have any use for: ❏
6. On the whole I don't know anything about fish: ❏
7. When I buy fish I usually buy the same kind every time: ❏
8. If I have decided to buy a certain type of fish, it is very possible that I change my mind if I have to go out of my way to get it: ❏
9. If somebody told me that the type of fish I have decided to buy was full of bones or maybe difficult to cook, I would stick to my decision no matter what: ❏
10. If I cannot get my favourite kind of fish where I usually shop, I don't mind buying another kind: ❏
11. Eating and serving fish add to the picture of me that I find ideal: ❏
12. Eating fish helps me live the life I strive for: ❏
13. There are many occasions and experiences in my life that I some way or another can connect to fish or eating fish: ❏
14. Fish is clearly something that I like: ❏
15. When I look at (fresh) fish or dishes made from (fresh) fish, there is a whole bunch of properties that I match them against: ❏
16. Eating fish is to a high degree something I do to express my 'ego': ❏
17. Personally it is of great importance to me to eat fish: ❏
18. On the basis of my personal values, I feel that I must eat fish: ❏
19. Eating and serving fish help me to express a way of life that I want: ❏
20. On the basis of what other people think, I feel that fish and eating fish is something I ought to be interested in: ❏
21. There is not much difference in the various types of fish that can be bought: ❏

Means and standard deviations are – after reversing items 5–7, 10 and 21 – given in Table 5. If we require the standard deviation to be at least 1.5 and the mean to be in the interval 2.5–5.5, the following items are candidates for exclusion: 4, 5r, 16, 20 and 21r.

Items having extreme means should be reformulated in order to bring the mean towards the middle of the scale; this will usually also increase the variance.

Table 5 Example 4: average and standard deviation for the 21 items

	Mean	Std. Deviation		Mean	Std. Deviation
involv1	4.45	2.06	involv12	4.67	2.25
involv2	4.18	2.26	involv13	4.25	2.39
involv3	3.85	2.13	involv14	2.22	1.86
involv4	1.45	.99	involv15	3.69	2.20
involv5r	1.44	1.22	involv16	6.02	1.46
involv6r	2.34	1.86	involv17	4.10	2.08
involv7r	4.75	2.22	involv18	3.61	2.17
involv8	3.70	2.49	involv19	4.89	2.31
involv9	4.03	2.50	involv20	5.68	1.82
involv10r	5.16	2.14	involv21r	1.66	1.36
involv11	5.40	1.97			

The inter-item correlations – after deletion of items 4, 5r, 16, 20 and 21r – are as given in Table 6.

The correlations vary in size from nearly 0.00 to nearly 0.80, which is a bad sign. Furthermore, it is possible to find clusters of items with satisfying intra-cluster correlations but with very small correlations to other clusters. For example, items 1, 2 and 3 seem to form a cluster, which is only very weakly linked to another cluster consisting of items 11, 12, 17 and 19. So, perhaps these two parts of the scale measure two different latent variables – and maybe there are more than two?

If so, the scale is not unidimensional and it might be a good idea to perform a principal components analysis in order to find out whether the items really make up a unidimensional scale, and, if not, how many dimensions it contains.

As in the previous example, choose 'Analyze/Data Reduction/Factor' and select the variables. In the 'Extraction' window choose to base your analysis on the covariance matrix, check the 'Scree plot' box and leave everything else at the default values, because at present you are only interested in finding out how many dimensions are present in your data. Then click 'Continue', return to the dialog box in Figure 8b, and click 'OK'.

In Figure 9 you can see the elbow plot, which indicates the existence of three dimensions. So, let us try a three-component solution.

You start all over again, and when the dialog box shown in Figure 8c appears you choose to extract 3 factors, click 'Continue' and when you return to the dialog box in Figure 8b, click 'Rotation'. In the dialog box in Figure 10a check 'Varimax' (the default method) and 'Display rotated solution', and click 'Continue'.

When you again return to the box in Figure 8b, open the dialog box in Figure 10b by clicking 'Options', and check 'Sorted by size'. Then click 'Continue', and, after returning to the 'Factor Analysis' dialog box, click 'OK'.

Taken together the first three principal components account for 56% of the variance in the data (output not shown).

Table 6 Example 4: inter-item correlations (decimal point not shown)

	1	2	3	6r	7r	8	9	10r	11	12	13	14	15	17	18
2	65														
3	77	69													
6r	47	56	56												
7r	24	42	32	23											
8	06	06	10	11	−18										
9	20	18	22	12	24	−04									
10r	17	20	23	22	14	47	01								
11	37	29	40	33	05	16	−05	16							
12	43	35	44	34	15	08	−01	15	61						
13	44	42	42	25	12	03	17	09	36	34					
14	49	45	59	43	30	03	38	23	37	46	26				
15	51	61	57	48	20	08	22	25	21	27	44	45			
17	35	40	44	34	10	16	18	10	31	49	26	56	26		
18	13	02	14	−04	03	−07	04	−08	12	36	13	24	−12	40	
19	26	21	23	26	05	−01	03	05	53	47	29	36	12	45	38

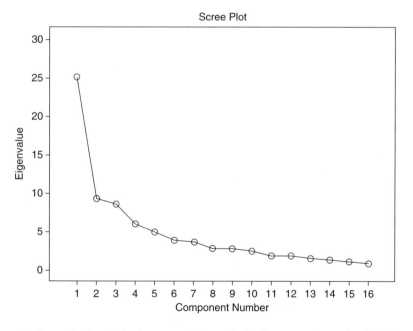

Figure 9 Example 4: principal components analysis, first run, elbow plot (SPSS)

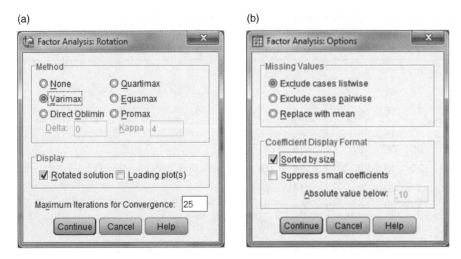

Figure 10 Example 4: principal components analysis, dialog boxes for second run

The rotated component matrix in Table 7 shows the relations between the various items and each of the three components in raw (covariances) and in rescaled (correlations) form.

Table 7 Example 4: principal components analysis (selected output from second run)

Rotated Component Matrix[a]

	Raw			Rescaled		
	Component			Component		
	1	2	3	1	2	3
involv2	1.806	.444	.337	.800	.197	.149
involv3	1.629	.694	.395	.766	.326	.186
involv15	1.635	.120	.522	.742	.054	.237
involv1	1.448	.675	.280	.703	.328	.136
involv14	1.124	.791	.039	.605	.425	.021
involv6r	1.092	.419	.444	.586	.225	.238
involv7r	1.261	-.116	-.534	.567	-.052	-.240
involv9	1.348	-.311	-.689	.539	-.124	-.275
involv13	1.164	.845	.154	.486	.353	.064
involv19	.190	1.834	-.107	.082	.795	-.046
involv12	.585	1.701	.290	.260	.757	.129
involv18	-.207	1.429	-.575	-.096	.659	-.265
involv11	.375	1.295	.510	.191	.658	.259
involv17	.672	1.312	.174	.322	.630	.084
involv8	-.140	.086	2.167	-.056	.034	.870
involv10	.478	-.021	1.461	.224	-.010	.683

Extraction Method: Principal Component Analysis.
Rotation Method: Varimax with Kaiser Normalization.
[a] Rotation converged in 4 iterations.

The first component is an expression of personal knowledge, interests and behavior while the second is some sort of lifestyle dimension incorporating psychological and social elements such as consumption of fish as a signal to other people. The third component includes only two nearly identical items expressing the respondents' determination or the strength of their preferences.

Now, you have a choice between considering the three factors as three aspects of the same concept 'involvement' or considering them as three distinct concepts.

That choice must of course be based on substantive thinking, taking into consideration all the information you have on the subject in the form of earlier research, discussions with colleagues, etc., and (not forgetting) common sense.

However, since it is obvious that if the dimensions are just three aspects of the same concept, the correlations across dimensions should be larger than if they were best considered as three fundamentally different concepts. You can get a first impression of the picture by looking at the correlation matrix after having sorted the items by dimension as shown in Table 8.

It seems to me that the first two dimensions are closer together and that the third dimension is separated from the first two. So, dimension 3 is definitely a separate concept, while the question of whether the first two dimensions should be considered two separate concepts or two aspects of the same concept depends on the actual use of the measuring instrument. In the latter case be careful not to mix items from the two dimensions in the same parcel if you use parceling.

Table 8   Example 4: inter-item correlations sorted by dimension (decimal point not shown)

	Dimension 1								Dimension 2					Dim. 3	
	2	3	1	15	14	6r	7r	13	9	12	11	19	18	17	8	10
3	69															
1	65	77														
15	61	57	51													
14	45	59	49	45												
6r	56	56	47	48	43											
7r	42	32	24	20	30	23										
13	41	42	44	44	26	25	12									
9	18	22	20	22	38	12	24	17								
12	35	44	42	27	46	34	15	34	–01							
11	29	40	37	21	37	33	05	36	–05	61						
19	21	23	26	13	36	26	05	29	03	47	53					
18	02	14	13	–12	24	–04	03	13	04	36	12	38				
17	40	44	35	26	56	34	10	26	18	49	31	45	40			
8	06	10	06	08	03	11	–18	03	–04	08	16	–01	–07	16		
10	20	23	17	25	23	22	14	09	01	15	16	05	–08	10	47	

If you use oblique rotation, the correlations between the three dimensions will be shown in the output, and that gives a clearer expression of the data structure. They are

$$\text{Corr(Dim 1, Dim 2)} = 0.26$$
$$\text{Corr(Dim 1, Dim 3)} = 0.13$$
$$\text{Corr(Dim 2, Dim 3)} = 0.15$$

However, be warned that exploratory techniques such as principal components analysis or exploratory factor analysis are not always the most efficient way to uncover the structure of a data set. Confirmatory techniques will (as shown in Chapter 7) often do a better job.

If you plan to use the items in a simple summated scale, and therefore do a traditional item analysis, it is possible to obtain a Cronbach's α of about 0.90. This does not seem that bad, but, as pointed out in Example 3, calculation of Cronbach's α across different dimensions is meaningless, and you should do an item analysis for each dimension. This is left to you as an exercise.

3 Exploratory Factor Analysis

The principal components Y_i are linear functions of the manifest variables X_i, as expressed in (9), which in a more compact form can be written as

$$Y_i = \sum_{j=1}^{p} a_{ij} X_j \quad \text{for} \quad i = 1, 2, \ldots, p \tag{12}$$

This is an exact mathematical transformation with a one-to-one correspondence between the *X*- and *Y*-variables. Principal components analysis is therefore *not* a statistical model, the parameters of which have to be estimated. Therefore it is possible to isolate the *X*-variables on the left side of the equality sign, and consider them as functions of the *Y*-variables:

$$X_j = \sum_{i=1}^{p} b_{ji} Y_i \quad \text{for} \quad j = 1, 2, \ldots, p \tag{13}$$

In this way the principal components are seen as latent variables, the values of which are mirrored in the manifest *X*-variables.

If there are theoretical reasons to assume that only $k < p$ *Y*-variables are 'significant', we can write

$$X_j = \sum_{i=1}^{k} \lambda_{ji} F_i + \lambda F_{j.\text{spec}} + \varepsilon_j \quad \text{for} \quad j = 1, 2, \ldots, p \tag{14}$$

This is the so-called *factor model*, where the 'significant' *Y*-variables are designated F_i. The 'non-significant' *Y*-variables are then considered either to express that an *X*-variable apart from measuring the *common factors* F_i also measures a *specific factor* F_{spec} (i.e. a factor which is measured only by the *X*-variable in question), or to express purely stochastic uncertainty or noise ε_j.

3.3 Exploratory Factor Analysis

It is not possible to isolate the specific factor in cross-sectional data and it will therefore be included in the error term. This means that the error term will not be purely stochastic, even if it is usually treated as such and attributed the assumptions

$$E(\varepsilon_j) = 0$$
$$Cov(\varepsilon_j, \varepsilon_i) = 0 \quad \text{for } j \neq i \quad (15)$$
$$Cov(\varepsilon_j, F_{ji}) = 0 \quad \text{for all } i \text{ and } j$$

Contrary to (13), (14) is a hypothetical model, often based on theoretically founded a priori assumptions, e.g. regarding the number of common factors. Contrary to (13) it is also a *statistical* model, as it includes a stochastic error ε_j, and its parameters therefore need to be estimated.

Note that while we can go from (12) to (13) and vice versa, the same simple operation is not possible on (14) because of the stochastic term ε_j. *Factor scores* can therefore not be calculated in a simple way, but have to be estimated. Several estimation methods exist, but none of them are very satisfying. The reason is that the factor model contains more parameters than there are data points – a rare situation in statistics! As a consequence we can estimate an unlimited number of factor models (and factor scores) all having the same mathematical properties. This is the so-called 'factor indeterminacy problem', see e.g. Thurstone (1947) or McDonald and Mulaik (1979).

The variance of X_j is

$$Var(X_j) = \underbrace{\sum_{i=1}^{k} \lambda_{ij}^2 Var(F_i)}_{\text{communality } h^2} + \lambda_{spec}^2 Var(F_{spec}) + Var(\varepsilon) \quad (16)$$

Leaving out the specific factor, the exploratory factor model can be depicted as shown in Figure 11, where the principal components model is also shown for comparison.

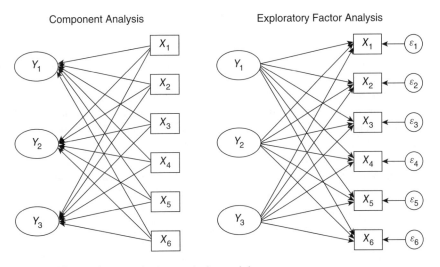

Figure 11 The exploratory factor analysis model

If you compare (14) and (16) with Chapter 2's equations (21a) and (21c) respectively, it is obvious that the factor model is an extension of the traditional measurement model from Chapter 2 to the case of several factors.

It is also obvious that the exploratory factor model is more in accordance with the measurement models of SEM than the principal components model is. Indeed, it only differs from the ideal measurement model in that the various indicators are related to *all* the latent variables (factors) in the model – analogous to principal components.

Therefore it would have been more 'correct' to use factor analysis instead of component analysis in the examples above. However, as mentioned in the introductory part of this chapter, the two techniques will usually give nearly the same results (even if there is a tendency for factor analysis to extract fewer factors than component analysis), and component analysis is in many ways less complicated – for example, there is no 'factor indeterminacy problem'.

The factor model resembles the traditional regression model but differs from this in that the independent variables (the F-variables) are not directly measurable. The name 'factor analysis' covers a rather large number of different estimation and rotation techniques (and usually component analysis is included under the same hat). Consult Kim and Mueller (1978a, 1978b) for a short introduction and Harman (1976) or Mulaik (2009) for a deeper treatment of the subject.

As the main purpose of factor analysis is to connect the X-variables to the common factors, it is clear that you cannot base the analysis on the variances of the variables, as stated in the main diagonal of the covariance matrix. These variances must be reduced by that part of the variance caused by the specific factor and the random error ε_j, so that only the common variances (the communalities) form the basis of the calculations.

Usually factor analysis is based on standardized variables, i.e. on the correlation matrix, and the treatment here will follow that tradition. Analogous reasoning can, however, be used if the analysis is based on the covariance matrix.

In most estimation methods the communalities are estimated first, so that they can be substituted for the ones in the main diagonal of the correlation matrix. The estimation is usually done by an iterative process using as starting values R^2 from a regression of the variable in question on all other variables.

Usually this process will initially result in a matrix in which the smallest eigenvalues are negative. This is not very fortunate, as the eigenvalues are the variances of the factors (cf. the comments to Table 2). Therefore the correlations outside the diagonal have to be 'regulated' so as to secure non-negative eigenvalues. This is done 'automatically' by the computer program.

As mentioned several times, the name 'factor analysis' covers a suite of different algorithms varying in the ways that communalities and factor structure are estimated.

The most popular technique today is, perhaps, *maximum likelihood estimation*.

Maximum likelihood estimation is based on the calculation of the *likelihood function*, which expresses the probability of obtaining the present data (covariance or correlation matrix) as a function of the parameters of the model. Then the parameters are estimated as the values of the parameters that maximize the likelihood function. In other words, parameters estimated by maximum likelihood are the values that have the largest probability of producing the covariance or correlation matrix on which the estimation is based. In maximum likelihood estimation, invented by D. N. Lawley (see e.g. Lawley and Maxwell, 1971) in the 1940s, communalities are not estimated at the beginning of the process, but are a product of the estimation of the number of factors.

The likelihood function can be deduced from the assumption that the common factors and error terms are multivariate normally distributed. As maximum likelihood estimates (in addition to other nice properties, to be mentioned in the next chapter) are asymptotically normally distributed, this enables statistical testing to be carried out.

It is, however, only fair to mention that, for example, Morrison (2003) and Johnson and Wichern (2007) presented several examples of statistical testing in principal components analysis too.

As you will see, exploratory factor analysis is one step from classical measurement theory towards the measurement model of SEM, both with regard to introducing several common factors and with regard to estimation, as maximum likelihood estimation is also the preferred estimation method in SEM.

Component analysis or factor analysis?

Which should then be the preferred technique: component analysis or factor analysis?

The two techniques have had their followers, and it is not unreasonable to say that at times the arguments between the two groups have developed into 'wars' (Velicer & Jackson, 1990). However, a simple answer to the question can be found in the structure of the covariance matrix on which the analysis is based. In principal components analysis, the main diagonal contains variances and the components are extracted in decreasing order of variance. In factor analysis, the diagonal elements are the communalities, i.e. that part of each variable's variance that is shared with the common factors (and in that way with all other variables), and the factors are extracted in decreasing order of covariation with the other variables.

Therefore the answer is as follows:

- If you are interested in summarizing a number of correlating variables in a few new variables with the smallest possible loss of information, then component analysis is the answer.
- If you are interested in explaining the correlations in a data set as a result of a few underlying factors, then factor analysis is the answer.

In most situations, component analysis and factor analysis will give nearly identical solutions, although factor analysis has a (very!) weak tendency to find a solution in fewer dimensions than component analysis. If you want to calculate scores, I would definitely recommend component analysis because of the unsatisfactory estimation methods offered by factor analysis.

In this chapter you met the following concepts:

- principal components analysis
- principal component
- component scores, component score coefficients
- component loading
- elbow plot and scree plot
- rotation
- pilot sample
- exploratory factor analysis
- maximum likelihood estimation
- Kaiser criterion

Questions

1. Explain the purpose and the principles of principal components analysis.
2. Define the following: principal component, component score, component score coefficient, component loading and communality.
3. What is the role of eigenvalues in component analysis?
4. Explain why and how you would employ rotation.
5. How do you use component analysis as item analysis?
   Compare component analysis and traditional item analysis. Discuss their vices and virtues.
6. What are the main differences between component analysis and (exploratory) factor analysis?
7. In many disciplines there are what we could call 'standard scales' (such as the SOP scale mentioned in Example 1.3). Select one from your own discipline and evaluate it using the techniques in this and the previous chapter. To get some inspiration take a look at Bearden, Netemeyer, and Haws (2011).

References

Armstrong, J. S. (1967). Deriviation of theory by means of factor analysis or Tom Swift and his electric analysis machine. *The American Statistician, 21*(5), 17–21.
Bearden, W. O., Netemeyer, R. G., & Haws, K. L. (Eds.). (2011). *Handbook of marketing scales*. Thousand Oaks, CA: Sage.
Harman, H. (1976). *Modern factor analysis* (3rd ed.). Chicago: University of Chicago Press.
Johnson, R. A., & Wichern, D. W. (2007). *Applied multivariate statistical analysis* (6th ed.). Upper Saddle River, NJ: Prentice Hall.
Kim, J.-O., & Mueller, C. W. (1978a). *Introduction to factor analysis: What it is and how to do it*. Beverly Hills, CA: Sage.
Kim, J.-O., & Mueller, C. W. (1978b). *Factor analysis: Statistical methods and practical issues*. Beverly Hills, CA: Sage.
Lawley, D. N., & Maxwell, A. E. (1971). *Factor analysis as a statistical method* (2nd ed.). Sevenoaks: Butterworths.
McDonald, R., & Mulaik, S. A. (1979). Determinacy of common factors: A nontechnical review. *Psychological Bulletin, 86*, 297–306.
Morrison, D. F. (2003). *Multivariate statistical methods* (4th ed.). New York: McGraw-Hill.
Mulaik, S. A. (2009). *The foundations of factor analysis* (3rd ed.). New York: McGraw-Hill.
Norušis, M. J. (2005). *SPSS 14.00 Statistical procedures companion*. Upper Saddle River, NJ: Prentice Hall.
Thurstone, L. L. (1947). *Multiple factor analysis*. Chicago: University of Chicago Press.
Velicer, W. F., & Jackson, D. N. (1990). Component analysis versus common factor analysis: Some issues in selecting an appropriate procedure. *Multivariate Behavioral Research, 25*, 1–28.

Further Reading

Child, D. (2006). *The essentials of factor analysis* (3rd ed.). London: Continuum.
Dunteman, G. H. (1989). *Principal components analysis*. Newbury Park, CA: Sage.
Mulaik, S. A. (2009). *The foundations of factor analysis* (3rd ed.). New York: McGraw-Hill.

The first two books are rather simple introductions to their subjects, while the third is more advanced.

PART 2

The Three Basic Models

4

Structural Equation Modeling with EQS

> In this chapter you are led through the various steps of structural equation modeling (SEM). On the way you will meet several problems that are connected with SEM.
>
> Among the questions you will have to answer are: 'Are there enough data to estimate the model?', 'Which estimation method should I use?', 'How do I get the computer to do what I want it to do?', 'How should I react to error messages?' and 'How do I interpret the computer output?'
>
> As a soft introduction to EQS, you will learn how to program a traditional multiple regression model and how to interpret the output from such an analysis.
>
> All through the chapter a number of concepts, which will be used in the remainder of the book, will be introduced and defined.

1 How Do You Proceed?

SEM is usually done by going through the following steps:

1. Statement of research questions.
2. Formulation of a structural equation model, which (hopefully!) will answer the research questions.
3. Examination of whether the model can be estimated – the so-called identification problem, which was briefly mentioned in connection with the model in Figure 1.7c.
4. If necessary, a reformulation of the model in order to make it estimable.
5. Data collection and estimation of the model.
6. Examination of computer output.
7. If necessary, modification of the model based on the interpretation of computer output.
8. Provisional acceptance of the model.
9. Testing the model on new data.
10. Acceptance or rejection of the model.

As should be clear from steps 4, 7 and 9, things are not always as simple as this list could lead you to believe. You must be prepared to run into problems at every step and therefore to go back and repeat earlier steps.

The first two steps above are problem-specific and are therefore treated through various examples later on. The rest are taken up in this chapter, roughly following the sequence stated above.

Even if it is difficult to say much on model specification without referring to a specific problem, a warning is in order: always remember that SEM is not all about statistics and technicalities. When starting a new project, learn as much as possible from published theory and earlier research on the subject. If you start modeling too early, there is a great risk that you will – at the very least – end up with a misspecified model.

Look at Example 1.6 once more – and think about it!

In the following I will use a very simple example to walk you through the process.

Example 1
Statement of research question and model formulation

Bredahl (2001) used SEM in a cross-national study of factors influencing consumers' attitudes and buying intentions towards genetically modified food products.

I will use part of Bredahl's German data to illustrate the programming and estimation of a multiple regression model. It must be emphasized, however, that this is not the way Bredahl analyzed her data.

The model is shown in Figure 1. The two-headed arrows indicate (possible) collinearity among the independent variables.

If you use EQS' drawing facilities (which you will be introduced to in the next chapter) to sketch the model, it will appear as shown in the figure.

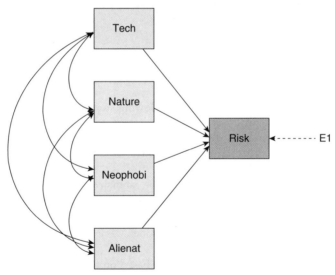

Variable name	Description	Measurement
Risk	Perceived risk by using genetically modified food	Six-item summated scale
Technology	Attitude to genetic modification in food production	Five-item summated scale
Nature	Attitude to nature	Six-item summated scale
Neophobia	Food neophobia	Five-item summated scale
Alienation	Alienation to the marketplace	Nine-item summated scale

Figure 1 Example 1: the model

Note: In the figure the variable names are abbreviated because EQS allows a maximum of 8 letters if the graphical interface is used for programming purposes. If you use more letters, EQS will automatically cut them off.

On the screen the endogenous variable box is yellow and the exogenous variable boxes are gray. Also the arrow connecting the error term E1 to the dependent variable is red, signaling that that regression coefficient is by default fixed at 1.00. As the figures in this book are in black and white, I have chosen to show red lines as dotted throughout the book.

As (in this case) we are only interested in relations between the variables and not in their values, the only input needed is the covariance matrix.

2 Identification

The identification problem was briefly touched upon in relation to Bass's model (Figure 1.7c) in Section 1.4. We can formulate the problem as follows: 'Are there enough data to estimate the parameters in the model?'

Intuitively, the data should contain at least as many data points as there are parameters to estimate. A simple analogy will illustrate the idea.

Let β_1 and β_2 in the equation

$$\beta_1 + \beta_2 = 10 \qquad (1)$$

be two parameters and let the number '10' be the collected data. It is clear that there are not enough data points for estimation. The equation has an unlimited number of solutions for β_1 and β_2, and the model is *under-identified*. If we add another equation to get

$$\beta_1 + \beta_2 = 10$$
$$\beta_1 - \beta_2 = 2 \qquad (2)$$

the two equations have one and only one solution

$$\beta_1 = 6$$
$$\beta_2 = 4 \qquad (3)$$

and the model is *just-identified*. However, this model will agree with more than one data set, implying that it cannot be tested. If we add the equation

$$\beta_1 \times \beta_2 = c \qquad (4)$$

we have 'one piece of information' left over for testing the model, which is now *over-identified*. If $c = 24$, the data are in agreement with the model, but if c is 'very' different from 24, the model is not supported by the data and should be rejected.

The number of surplus 'pieces of information' is called the *degrees of freedom* for the model. If the degrees of freedom are positive the model can be estimated and tested: the more degrees of freedom, the more precise the estimation and the more powerful the tests.

As – in most cases – the only data input needed is the sample covariance matrix, a model is identified if there are at least as many non-redundant elements in the covariance matrix as there are parameters to be estimated.

The so-called *t-rule*, that the number of 'pieces of information' should be at least as large as the number of parameters to be estimated for the estimation to be possible, is, however, a necessary but *not* a sufficient condition. As was demonstrated in Section 1.6, a postulated model implies a special form of the covariance matrix, as the elements of this matrix are functions of the parameters of the model. This should make it possible to estimate the parameters from the covariance matrix, but even if the number of equations is at least as large as the number of unknowns, a system of equations can still have more than one solution.

In principle, it is possible to determine whether or not a model is identified by examining the structure of the implied covariance matrix and finding out whether the resultant system of equations has more than one solution for each and every parameter. This can be a very complicated process, so a general necessary and sufficient condition for identification would be very useful.

Such a condition does not exist. What we have is a series of conditions for special model types, but these are all either necessary or sufficient – not both.

Two conditions must, however, always be satisfied for a model to be identified:

1. The *t*-rule must be met.
2. All latent variables must have a scale assigned. This is also true for the error terms (ε and δ). You cannot simultaneously estimate the coefficient and the variance of an error term. Usually (as in ordinary linear regression analysis) the coefficient is fixed at 1.00 and the variance is estimated. By fixing the coefficient at 1.00, the error term is measured in the same units as the dependent variable.

Remember: a model's parameters are regression coefficients and variances and covariances of the exogenous variables. An *exogenous variable* is a variable that does not appear as a dependent variable anywhere in the model. All other variables are called *endogenous variables*. Variances and covariances of endogenous variables are not parameters in the model, but consequences of the model.

In the model in Figure 1, we have four regression coefficients, five variances (the variances of the four exogenous variables plus the variance of E1) and six covariances, i.e. a total of 15 parameters to be estimated.

Our five variables have a covariance matrix containing five variances and ten covariances. So, we have 15 'pieces of information' at our disposal for the estimation of 15 parameters. In other words, our model is 'just-identified', and it can be estimated, but not tested.

Note that while covariances between endogenous variables are not considered parameters in a traditional regression model, they are in SEM!

What to do if a model is not identified

If a model is not identified, it must be made identifiable by increasing the number of manifest variables or by reducing the number of parameters to be estimated.

A reduction in the number of parameters to be estimated is done by *fixing* or *constraining* one or more parameters. Parameters are either *free*, *fixed* or *constrained*. A free parameter is a parameter that is 'free' to take on any value, and such a parameter is to be estimated from the data. A fixed parameter is a parameter whose value is

4.2 Identification

restricted a priori to take on a certain value and consequently such a parameter is not to be estimated. A parameter not in the model is considered fixed at zero. A constrained parameter is a parameter that is to be estimated from the data, but the possible estimated values are constrained to fulfill certain conditions.

In EQS a parameter can be constrained in three ways:

1. Two or more parameters can be restricted to have the same unspecified value.
2. Two or more parameters can be restricted to satisfy a linear equation.
3. A parameter can be restricted to have an upper and/or lower bound.

I strongly recommend examination of the model in order to find out whether it is identified prior to data collection. One reason for this is that you can often attain identification by introducing more manifest variables.

Consider the measurement model in Figure 2a.

After fixing the coefficients of the error terms to 1.00, the assignment of a scale to the latent variable F remains. We have two possibilities: (1) we can fix one of the coefficients (λ_1 or λ_2) to 1.00, in which case F will have the same scale as the X-variable in question; or (2) we can fix the variance of the latent variable to some arbitrary value – usually 1.00. Whatever we do, we have four parameters to estimate:

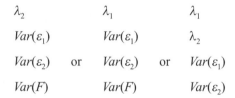

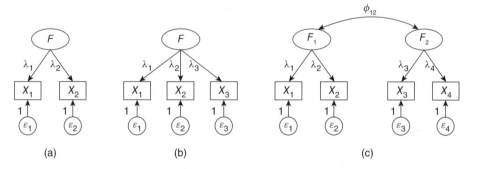

Figure 2 Identification

However, we have only three pieces of information: the variances of the two manifest variables and their covariance. Our model is under-identified.

Adding another indicator X_3 gives two further parameters to estimate, the coefficient λ_3 and the variance $Var(\varepsilon_3)$, but adds three new 'pieces of information': the variance of the new indicator and its covariances with the two other indicators – see panel (b). The model is just-identified.

In the model in panel (c), we have four indicators and consequently $(4 + 1)4/2 = 10$ pieces of information on which to base our estimation of the nine parameters:

$$\begin{array}{lll} \lambda_1 & Var(\varepsilon_1) & \phi_{12} \\ \lambda_2 & Var(\varepsilon_2) & \\ \lambda_3 & Var(\varepsilon_3) & \\ \lambda_4 & Var(\varepsilon_4) & \end{array}$$

assuming that the variances of the two latent variables are fixed. The model is over-identified with one degree of freedom.

However, suppose that ϕ_{12} is estimated to have a value near zero; then – because of rounding errors – you could end up in a situation similar to panel (a). This is an example of *empirical under-identification*. The problem is not with the model but with the data, and is therefore more difficult to foresee. The lesson is: always have at least five indicators per latent variable in order to obtain an over-identified measurement model and avoid estimation problems. Do not underestimate the problems with formulating good items. It is not unusual for half of them not to pass item analysis!

Due to the lack of a general necessary and sufficient condition for the identification of structural equation models, you will often have to fall back on empirical methods, i.e. try to estimate a proposed model and await the EQS error messages.

You could say that this is a little too late to find out that a model is under-identified, but it is not impossible to use this method prior to data collection. Just sketch your model, construct one or more covariance matrices that are comparable with your model, run the model in EQS and await the answer. If the model seems to be identified, run the analysis again with the implied covariance matrix as input. In your first run you order EQS output to include the implied covariance matrix by inserting the statement

/PRINT

COV = YES;

in the EQS program (more on programming in EQS appears in Section 4 below).

You could run the analyses several times with different *start values* (the values that the computer takes as initial 'guesstimates' of parameter values and steadily improves until the final solution – more about this below) and check that you obtain the same parameter estimates.

You will probably find it easier to construct a meaningful correlation matrix than a covariance matrix. Fortunately a correlation matrix will do, if you supplement it with standard deviations (see Example 1 below).

The identification problem is a consequence of the formulation of the model. However, sometimes the computer will tell you that the model is not identified even if all the sufficient conditions for identification are fulfilled. This could happen if computing problems arise. Because of rounding errors you could end up with calculations that are not defined, such as dividing by zero or taking the logarithm of zero. This is what I previously called *empirical under-identification*.

If a parameter seems to be under-identified, EQS will write an error message saying that the parameter in question is linearly dependent on other parameters.

A good introduction to the subject of identification in SEM is the one by Kenny & Milan (2012).

3 Estimation

In Section 1.6 I wrote that the model is estimated in such a way that the difference between the empirical covariance matrix and the covariance matrix implied by the model is minimized. It is more correct to say that a function, F, of that difference is minimized:

$$F = f\left(\mathbf{S} - \Sigma(\hat{\theta})\right) \qquad (5)$$

where $\mathbf{S}$ is the empirical covariance matrix and $\Sigma(\hat{\theta})$ is an estimate of the covariance matrix implied by a model with the estimated parameters $\hat{\theta}$.

As mentioned in Section 3.3, maximum likelihood estimation is the preferred estimation method in SEM. Parameters are estimated as the values that have the largest probability of producing the sample covariance matrix $\mathbf{S}$.

The likelihood function can be deduced from an assumption of multivariate normality of the manifest variables; it can, however, also be deduced under less demanding assumptions (Bollen, 1989; Browne, 1982).

Maximum likelihood (ML) estimation has a number of favorable qualities. First, it is consistent, i.e. the estimates $\hat{\theta}$ approach the parameter values θ asymptotically by increasing sample size, n. Furthermore, the ML estimator is asymptotically unbiased, asymptotically sufficient and asymptotically normally distributed. Also, $C = (n-1)F_{ML(min)}$, where n is the sample size and $F_{ML(min)}$ the minimum value of the fitting function, is asymptotically distributed as χ^2 with $p(p+1)/2 - t$ degrees of freedom, where p is the number of manifest variables and t the number of free parameters. This makes it possible to test the model against the data.

Note that all these are asymptotic qualities, and therefore cannot be guaranteed to hold in small samples.

Finding the parameter values that maximize the likelihood is too complicated to be done in an exact way. Instead the maximum is located by an iterative procedure, whereby the computer makes an initial 'guess' at the values of the parameters and then improves this initial guess step by step.

In a way you could compare this process with locating the top of a hill when you are blindfolded just by feeling with your feet.

From this picture it is obvious that the iterative process is not always successful in finding 'the top of the hill': an undulating landscape could have more than one hilltop, and perhaps the procedure does not find the highest one – or does not find any top at all.

The fitting function F can have many forms, as each estimation method has its own special F-function. EQS offers several estimation methods (to be mentioned in Section 5), but for this introductory example we will use ML estimation, which is also the default method in EQS, i.e. the method EQS will use if you do not demand otherwise.

The EQS model and notation

Before you can think of doing SEM using EQS, you must be familiar with the EQS representation and notation.

In EQS variables are classified either as *measurable* (manifest) or as *non-measurable* (latent) and either as *independent* or as *dependent*. A variable that performs as a dependent variable anywhere in the model is a dependent variable; *all other variables are independent*. Therefore in EQS terminology error terms and disturbances are also classified as (non-measurable) independent variables. That is why I have enclosed them in circles in the first part of the book.

So, in EQS terminology an independent variable is what I have hitherto called an exogenous variable and what EQS calls a dependent variable is the same as an endogenous variable. This special use of the words 'independent' and 'dependent' variable' can be a bit confusing when you want to talk about a single equation in a larger model (cf. the discussion in connection with Example 1.2).

All variables are given a name that consists of one of the letters below followed by a number:

V if they are manifest.

F if they are latent.

E if they represent 'noise' in a relation, where the dependent variable is a V-variable.

D if they represent 'noise' in a relation, where the dependent variable is an F-variable.

The V-variables are automatically numbered V1, V2, ... in accordance with the order in which they are appear in the data file. E- and D-variables are given the same number as the dependent V- or F-variable in the specific equation.

Until now I have – in accordance with traditional SEM literature – distinguished between 'noise' in structural models and in measurement models by using different symbols for the two, namely *d* and *e* respectively.

Note that in EQS, E is used as a symbol for 'noise' in a manifest variable regardless of whether it is part of a measurement model or a structural model, as illustrated in Figure 1.

Also, following SEM practice, a parameter was denoted by Greek letters: λ_{23}, β_{74} and θ_{13}, and so on.

EQS uses another naming system. Imagine a picture of your model. Then a parameter (a one- or two-headed arrow) is denoted by its endpoints:

A regression coefficient measuring the influence of V3 on V5 would be designed by 'V5,V3' (remember: arrow head first as in the subscripts in the first part of the book).

A covariance between V1 and V3 would be denoted 'V1,V3' or 'V3,V1' etc. Analogously the variance of E5 would be denoted 'E5, E5' etc.

4 Programming in EQS

It is now time to show you how actually to estimate the model in Figure 1.

EQS has one of the user-friendliest interfaces for this type of computer program. The programming can be done in three different ways:

1. You can write your program manually.
2. You can take advantage of an interactive user interface, where you fill out a few tables, and EQS then generates a program that you can save for documentation or later use.
3. You can sketch your model in a user-friendly drawing environment, where most of the drawing is done with a few mouse-clicks. EQS then translates the drawing into a program and performs the necessary calculations.

If you are a beginner, you will probably prefer one of the last two methods. However, as the end product in all three cases is the same written program, you will in this chapter familiarize yourself with the basic logic of the EQS programming language by using manual programming. In the next chapter you will then learn how to use the two other programming methods.

Example 1 (continued)
Multiple regression analysis in EQS

When you open EQS the screen looks as shown in Figure 3.a You click the 'new' icon ▯ (or choose File/New) and the window in panel (b) pops up. Then you click 'EQS Command file' and the screen changes to panel (c).

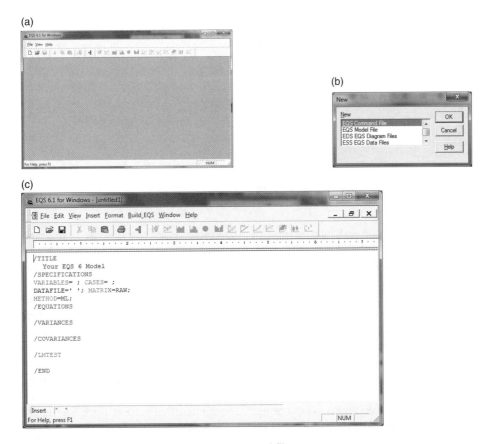

Figure 3 Example 1: opening a new command file

As you can see, the program is organized in paragraphs, some of which are required, while others are optional. Each paragraph starts with a slash, and within each paragraph you place your orders or statements, each statement ending with a semicolon.

Shown in Figure 4 is an EQS program that will do the necessary calculations.

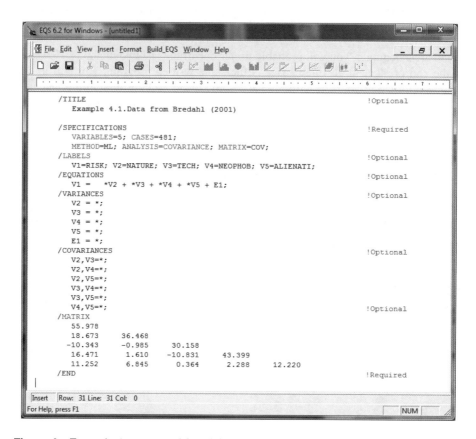

Figure 4 Example 1: command (.eqs) file

You can have several statements in the same line (as in the paragraph /SPECIFICATIONS) or you can choose to have only one statement on each line (as in the paragraph /VARIANCES).

Having several statements in a line could save a great deal of space in longer programs, but could perhaps make reading a bit difficult. Each paragraph can take up as much space as you want, and you are advised to take advantage of this and use the first paragraph to describe the actual EQS job as detailed as possible, so that you can keep track of the various steps in your project.

By the way, you may have noticed the text lines to the right in the program. You can always insert notes in your program. Just remember to start your note with an exclamation mark. This is another way to remember why you did a certain calculation, when some weeks later you return to your project. The exclamation mark tells EQS to ignore what comes next and not consider it as part of the program.

/SPECIFICATIONS contains the 'background information' EQS needs in order to carry out the calculations. We specify that there are seven variables and 481 cases. The statement

```
MATRIX = COV
```

tells EQS that the data input is a covariance matrix. Other possibilities are

```
MATRIX = CORR or MATRIX = RAW
```

specifying input as a correlation matrix or the raw data. In fact, when a covariance matrix is used as input, you do not need to specify it, as this will be assumed by default.

When doing structural modeling you will most often only be interested in the relations between the various variables, and not in their values. In such situations a data summary in the form of a covariance matrix is all that is needed. You do not need the raw data.

Irrespective of whether your input is a covariance matrix, a correlation matrix or the raw data, you can ask EQS to base the analysis on either a covariance matrix or a correlation matrix, thus

```
METHOD = ML; ANALYSIS = COVARIANCE
```

specifies ML estimation based on covariance matrix. In fact, these statements are not needed, as they are defalts.

You are allowed to abbreviate the statements as follows:

```
      DATA = DA
 VARIABLES = VA
     CASES = CAS
    MATRIX = MA
  ANALYSIS = AN
    METHOD = ME
```

As mentioned above, EQS by default names manifest variables V1, V2, ... However, it is a good idea to use labels that contain more information about the nature of a variable. This will be a great help when reading the output.

The paragraph /EQUATIONS contains the model to be analyzed. Here I use the default names for the variables for space considerations, but feel free to use the labels if you prefer.

You will also observe that every parameter to be estimated is marked with an asterisk, while a parameter that is fixed is not. In accordance with ordinary regression analysis, the coefficient of E is fixed at one by default (but feel free to fix it at any other number).

Also note that no intercept is specified. This does not mean that EQS cannot estimate models with explicit intercept terms – as we will see in Chapter 9 – but usually the intercept is of less interest and can be omitted. Therefore the only input needed is the covariance matrix.

Remember: the parameters of a structural equation model are regression coefficients and variances and covariances of *exogenous variables*.

In this case we cannot leave out the possibility of correlations among the exogenous variables – so-called collinearity – so we require the covariances between the exogenous variables to be freely estimated.

It is also worth mentioning that in this case the latter two paragraphs above could be specified as

```
/VARIANCES
V2 to V5 = *;

/COVARIANCES
V2 to V5 = *;
```

saving a great deal of time and space in larger models.

You may wonder why the paragraphs /EQUATIONS, /VARIANCES and /COVARIANCES are optional – after all, isn't the purpose to estimate parameters in these equations, and don't all exogenous variables have variances?

The answer is that it is possible to substitute one paragraph called /MODEL for the three paragraphs /EQUATIONS, /VARIANCES and /COVARIANCES. This will save you a lot of time and space in larger and more complicated models, as is demonstrated in Table 8.12. However, the role of /MODEL is to build the three paragraphs from a simpler input. Therefore the first two (and sometimes the third) of the three paragraphs will show up in the final program, which is echoed in the output – so you have to get acquainted with these paragraphs.

The paragraph /MATRIX contains the input data. Observe – no semicolons here!

If you want your analysis to be based on a covariance matrix (the default) and your input is a correlation matrix (which is often the case if your data come from a journal article or a research report), standard deviations must also be provided in order for EQS to calculate the covariance matrix.

In that case the /MATRIX paragraph in Figure 4 is replaced by

```
/MATRIX
    1.0000
    0.4133    1.0000
   -0.2517   -0.0297    1.0000
    0.3342    0.0405   -0.2994    1.0000
    0.4302    0.3242    0.0190    0.0993    1.0000

/STANDARD DEVIATIONS
    7.4818    6.0389    5.4917    6.5878    3.4957
```

If you choose not to include the data in the program, but to let EQS get them from an external file – which is always the case if your input is the raw data – you must of course tell EQS where to find the data, and you do that in the /SPECIFICATIONS as you will learn in the next chapter.

The paragraph /END indicates the end of the program.

When you save the program, it is given the suffix '.eqs'. Such eqs files are ordinary text files. You can therefore write and edit the program in ordinary word processors such as Word or WordPerfect. Just remember to save the file as a text file and give it the extension '.eqs'.

When you want to run the program, you choose 'Build EQS/Run EQS' (see Figure 5), and the output (which is also an ordinary text file) will appear immediately. When you save the output it is given the same name as the input file, but with the extension '.out'.

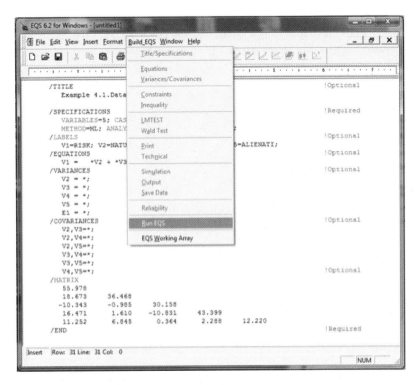

Figure 5 Example 1: starting the calculations

The output can be roughly divided into three sections. First comes a description of the input, then an evaluation of the model's fit to the input data, and – last but not least – the estimates of model parameters.

The first section of the output is shown in Table 1, on which I shall make the following comments:

1. First the program and the input matrix to be analyzed are echoed.
2. Then comes a summary of variables and parameters. We are told that there is one dependent variable (V1) and four independent variables (V2–V5 and E1).

    The number of free parameters is 15 (4 regression coefficients, 5 variances and 6 covariances). However, the number of data points (non-redundant elements in the covariance matrix) is also 15. Therefore we are left with zero degrees of freedom and a just-identified model.

As a consequence, the second section of the output with information on model fit is not very interesting: We know that the model fits the data perfectly.

3. Near the end of this section of the output we find the determinant of the input covariance matrix. Every quadratic matrix – and that includes covariance and correlation matrices – has a determinant associated with it. The determinant is a number that is a function of all elements in the matrix. You will, however, have to wait a few pages more to get an explanation of the use of this number, but for now just enjoy the feeling from reading the next two lines.

   First of all, look for these two lines – and if you do not find them, do not trust the output!

4. This part of the output ends with the residual covariance matrix. Since our model is just-identified, this is a zero matrix signaling a perfect fit.

Table 1 Example 1: output first part

```
1
    EQS, A STRUCTURAL EQUATION PROGRAM            MULTIVARIATE SOFTWARE, INC.
    COPYRIGHT BY P.M. BENTLER                     VERSION 6.2 (C) 1985 - 2012 (B101).


    PROGRAM CONTROL INFORMATION                                              (1)

         1        /TITLE
         2           Example 4.1.Data from Bredahl (2001)
         3        /SPECIFICATIONS
         4           VARIABLES=5; CASES=481;
         5           METHOD=ML; ANALYSIS=COVARIANCE; MATRIX=COV;
         6        /LABELS
         7           V1=RISK; V2=NATURE; V3=TECH; V4=NEOPHOB; V5=ALIENATI;
         8        /EQUATIONS
         9           V1 =    *V2 + *V3 + *V4 + *V5 + E1;
        10        /VARIANCES
                                                                      !Optional
        11           V2 = *;
        12           V3 = *;
        13           V4 = *;
        14           V5 = *;
        15           E1 = *;
        16        /COVARIANCES
        17           V2,V3=*;
        18           V2,V4=*;
        19           V2,V5=*;
        20           V3,V4=*;
        21           V3,V5=*;
        22           V4,V5=*;
        23        /MATRIX
        24           55.978
        25           18.673      36.468
        26          -10.343      -0.985      30.158
        27           16.471       1.610     -10.831      43.399
        28           11.252       6.845       0.364       2.288     12.220
        29        /END


    COVARIANCE  MATRIX TO BE ANALYZED:    5 VARIABLES (SELECTED FROM   5 VARIABLES)
    BASED ON    481 CASES.
```

```
                    RISK      NATURE     TECH     NEOPHOB    ALIENATI
                    V1        V2         V3       V4         V5
      RISK    V1    55.978
      NATURE  V2    18.673    36.468
      TECH    V3   -10.343    -0.985     30.158
      NEOPHOB V4    16.471     1.610    -10.831   43.399
      ALIENATI V5   11.252     6.845      0.364    2.288     12.220
```

BENTLER-WEEKS STRUCTURAL REPRESENTATION: (2)

```
      NUMBER OF DEPENDENT VARIABLES =   1
            DEPENDENT V'S :     1

      NUMBER OF INDEPENDENT VARIABLES =   5
            INDEPENDENT V'S :    2    3    4    5
            INDEPENDENT E'S :    1

      NUMBER OF FREE PARAMETERS =    15
      NUMBER OF FIXED NONZERO PARAMETERS =    1
```

*** WARNING MESSAGES ABOVE, IF ANY, REFER TO THE MODEL PROVIDED.
    CALCULATIONS FOR INDEPENDENCE MODEL NOW BEGIN.

*** WARNING MESSAGES ABOVE, IF ANY, REFER TO INDEPENDENCE MODEL.
    CALCULATIONS FOR USER'S MODEL NOW BEGIN.

3RD STAGE OF COMPUTATION REQUIRED   3543 WORDS OF MEMORY.
PROGRAM ALLOCATED   2000000 WORDS

DETERMINANT OF INPUT MATRIX IS   0.16215D+08   (3)

PARAMETER ESTIMATES APPEAR IN ORDER,
NO SPECIAL PROBLEMS WERE ENCOUNTERED DURING OPTIMIZATION.

RESIDUAL COVARIANCE MATRIX (S-SIGMA) :   (4)

```
                    RISK     NATURE    TECH     NEOPHOB    ALIENATI
                    V1       V2        V3       V4         V5
      RISK     V1   0.000
      NATURE   V2   0.000    0.000
      TECH     V3   0.000    0.000     0.000
      NEOPHOB  V4   0.000    0.000     0.000    0.000
      ALIENATI V5   0.000    0.000     0.000    0.000      0.000
```

As mentioned earlier, and as you can see from the residual matrix in Table 1, the model fits the data perfectly, so I will forgo the second section of the output and proceed directly to the third and last section given in Table 2:

1. We are first presented with estimates of the regression coefficients. This takes up three lines: the first line shows the regression function, and beneath each coefficient is shown the standard error of the estimate and the test statistic. This is the coefficient divided by its standard error and should be asymptotically normal distributed. The test statistic is followed by an '@' if it is significant at the 5% level. The null hypothesis is the usual one that the parameter in question is 0.00,

and the alternative hypothesis is that it is not. We see that all four coefficients are significant by traditional norms.

2. The estimated variances and covariances of the independent variables then follow. You could argue that we already know these, because they were part of the input. However, in overidentified models there could quite well be differences between an input parameter value and the estimated value, because the estimated values are freed from 'disturbing effects' from other variables in the model.

3. The standardized solution follows, i.e. a solution based on the assumption that the variables were standardized to have mean 0.00 and variance 1.00 before the estimation (see Appendix A).

   The standardized regression coefficients and the multiple coefficient of correlation squared (the coefficient of determination) are followed by the correlations (i.e. the standardized covariances) between the independent variables.

We observe that even if all the regression coefficients are highly significant, the four independent variables taken together explain less than 40% of the variation in 'Risk'.

As will be shown in Chapter 8, this is partly due to the fact that the measurements are not wholly reliable.

Table 2 Example 1: output, third part

```
MAXIMUM LIKELIHOOD SOLUTION (NORMAL DISTRIBUTION THEORY)


MEASUREMENT EQUATIONS WITH STANDARD ERRORS AND TEST STATISTICS           (1)
STATISTICS SIGNIFICANT AT THE 5% LEVEL ARE MARKED WITH @.



    RISK  =V1  =      .368*V2    -   .242*V3    +   .270*V4    +   .672*V5
                      .047           .051           .043           .082
                     7.814@         -4.714@         6.284@         8.221@

                +   1.000 E1



    VARIANCES OF INDEPENDENT VARIABLES                                   (2)
    ----------------------------------
    STATISTICS SIGNIFICANT AT THE 5% LEVEL ARE MARKED WITH @.

                              V                         F
                             ---                       ---
V2   -NATURE              36.468*I                                 I
                           2.354 I                                 I
                          15.492@I                                 I
                                I                                  I
V3   - TECH               30.158*I                                 I
                           1.947 I                                 I
                          15.492@I                                 I
                                I                                  I
V4   -NEOPHOB             43.399*I                                 I
                           2.801 I                                 I
                          15.492@I                                 I
                                I                                  I
V5   -ALIENATI            12.220*I                                 I
                            .789 I                                 I
                          15.492@I                                 I
                                I                                  I
```

VARIANCES OF INDEPENDENT VARIABLES   (2)

STATISTICS SIGNIFICANT AT THE 5% LEVEL ARE MARKED WITH @.

                         E   D
                        ---   ---
E1 - RISK   34.607*I   I
                       2.234 I   I
                      15.492@I   I
                             I   I

COVARIANCES AMONG INDEPENDENT VARIABLES   (2)

STATISTICS SIGNIFICANT AT THE 5% LEVEL ARE MARKED WITH @.

                         V   F
                        ---   ---
V3 - TECH   -.985*I   I
V2 -NATURE   1.514 I   I
                        -.650 I   I
                             I   I
V4 -NEOPHOB   1.610*I   I
V2 -NATURE   1.817 I   I
                        .886 I   I
                             I   I
V5 -ALIENATI   6.845*I   I
V2 -NATURE   1.013 I   I
                       6.758@I   I
                             I   I
V4 -NEOPHOB   -10.831*I   I
V3 - TECH   1.724 I   I
                      -6.284@I   I
                             I   I
V5 -ALIENATI   .364*I   I
V3 - TECH   .876 I   I
                        .415 I   I
                             I   I
V5 -ALIENATI   2.288*I   I
V4 -NEOPHOB   1.056 I   I
                       2.166@I   I
                             I   I

   STANDARDIZED SOLUTION: R-SQUARED (3)

RISK =V1 =   .297*V2   -   .178*V3   +   .238*V4
             + .314*V5   +   .786 E1   .382

CORRELATIONS AMONG INDEPENDENT VARIABLES

                         V   F
                        ---   ---
V3 - TECH   -.030*I   I
V2 -NATURE   I   I
                             I   I
V4 -NEOPHOB   .040*I   I
V2 -NATURE   I   I
                             I   I

```
V5   -ALIENATI              .324*I                    I
V2   -NATURE                    I                     I
                                I                     I
V4   -NEOPHOB              -.299*I                    I
V3   -  TECH                   I                     I
                               I                     I
V5   -ALIENATI              .019*I                    I
V3   -  TECH                   I                     I
                               I                     I
V5   -ALIENATI              .099*I                    I
V4   -NEOPHOB                   I                     I
                               I                     I
```

5 Estimation Methods Available in EQS

At present (version 6.2), EQS offers the following estimation methods:

1. Maximum likelihood (ML).
2. Least squares (LS).
3. Generalized least squares (GLS).
4. Elliptical LS (ELS).
5. Elliptical GLS (EGLS).
6. Elliptical reweighted LS (ERLS).
7. Heterogeneous kurtosis GLS (HKGLS).
8. Heterogeneous kurtosis RLS (HKRLS).
9. Arbitrary distribution GLS (AGLS).

These nine estimation methods vary in distributional assumptions, but they all require the variables to be interval scaled and the relations between them to be linear.

All nine estimation methods are so-called *full-information methods*, i.e. they estimate the parameters of the whole system in one go using all available data, while *limited-information methods* use only part of the available data. While full-information methods are generally more effective, they have two drawbacks:

1. There are sometimes difficulties in solving estimation problems, because specification problems in one part of the model can have their roots in another part of the model.
2. It is not possible to introduce non-identified relations into the model solely for the identification of other relations. The whole model must be identified for the estimation to work.

I will say a few words about the various estimation methods. A deeper treatment can be found in the program manual (Bentler, 2006) or in Bollen (1989).

You learned the principle behind ML estimation in Section 3 above, and in the following I have a few comments to make on the other estimation methods.

Least squares
LS is analogous to ordinary least squares (OLS) in traditional regression: OLS minimizes the sum of squared errors and LS minimizes the sum of squared values in the residual matrix. Like OLS, LS does not make any distributional assumptions, and it is consistent (so are all the estimation methods listed above), but it is not asymptotically the most efficient.

However, the statistics calculated in EQS presuppose that the variables are multivariate normal. If this is not the case, then you cannot be sure that $C = (n-1)F_{LS(min)}$ is asymptotically distributed as χ^2, and neither standard deviations nor test statistics for the various parameters can be trusted. Browne (1982) discusses some possibilities for making various tests if LS estimation has been used, but these are not at present implemented in EQS.

Like ML, LS also uses an iterative procedure (as do all estimation methods in EQS).

Generalized least squares

Just as LS is analogous to OLS, GLS is analogous to weighted least squares (WLS) in traditional regression.

OLS gives equal weight to all observations in calculating the regression coefficients. This will result in inefficient estimates if all observations do not have approximately the same error variance. The solution to this problem is WLS, where each observation is weighted in order to correct for unequal error variances. In much the same way GLS weights all elements in the residual matrix, taking variances and covariances of the elements into consideration.

GLS has the same asymptotic qualities as ML, and consequently the same tests can be performed. It is worth noting that GLS can be derived under less restrictive assumptions than ML (Bollen, 1989).

Elliptical LS (ELS), elliptical GLS (EGLS), elliptical reweighted LS (ERLS), heterogeneous kurtosis GLS (HKGLS) and heterogeneous kurtosis RLS (HKRLS)

We could call ML and GLS methods 'normal theory methods' because they require (to a larger or lesser degree) the variables to follow a multivariate normal distribution.

Now, among other things a normal distribution is characterized by:

1. Being symmetric.
2. Having a certain kurtosis (see Appendix A).

Normal theory methods are most sensitive to violation of the last condition, and the methods mentioned in the subsection heading are all methods that in different ways try to overcome problems with kurtosis – the elliptical models by assuming a multivariate population distribution that is similar to the multivariate normal, but has larger or smaller multivariate kurtosis. The last two open up the possibility of allowing the various variables to have distributions with different kurtosis.

These estimation methods will not be treated in this book, and interested readers are referred to the program manual (Bentler, 2006).

When non-normal estimation methods are used, they are preceded by their normal counterpart. You can overwrite this by specifying another first estimation method. In fact EQS is special in that it allows you to use several estimation methods in the same run.

Arbitrary distribution generalized least squares

This heading seems promising because such an estimation method should be able to avoid building analyses and conclusions on doubtful assumptions.

As the general rule in statistics is that the fewer restrictions in a model, the larger the required sample size, it comes as no surprise that arbitrary distribution GLS (AGLS) demands very large sample sizes indeed. A model need not be extremely complicated for AGLS estimation to require a sample size measured in thousands. Robust statistics (see below) or bootstrapping (treated in Chapter 10) could be a solution to the problem of ill-behaved distributions if the sample is too small to allow for AGLS estimation.

Robust statistics

It goes without saying that using a normal estimation method (or in fact using *any* method) where the distributional conditions are not fulfilled will involve the risk of drawing wrong conclusions from the output. Now, as the problem is often more with the test statistics than with the parameter estimates, a solution could be to use a normal theory method and then 'regulate' the test statistics using so-called *robust statistics*. EQS offers this possibility with any of the above-mentioned estimation methods except AGLS.

A few remarks on discrete (ordinal) variables

When AGLS estimation makes such large demands on the sample size, how do we then treat discrete (ordinal) data from the very popular five- or seven-point scales?

A special problem with ordinal scales is that the usual covariances cannot be used, and therefore special measures of covariation must be calculated. These methods all assume that the ordinal measurements cover underlying interval-scaled variables that fulfill the assumption of multivariate normality – a rather strong assumption that in most cases is difficult or impossible to verify.

In Chapter 10 I will illustrate the special methods that EQS uses to handle discrete variables; as you will have guessed, they are not without complications.

Alternatively you can treat the ordinal variables as if they are normally distributed interval-scaled variables. This will be most realistic if:

1. The variables can take on 'many' values.
2. The variables are 'nearly normal', i.e. symmetric with kurtosis (see Appendix A) near zero.
3. Any possible (limited) skewness falls on the same side for all variables.

If a scale has at least five possible values, the first condition can usually be taken as fulfilled. If your scale is shorter, you can use *parceling* (see Section 2.2).

If you treat categorical variables as continuous, you should of course request robust statistics.

6 Examining EQS Output

Examination of EQS output starts by looking for error messages – which are called *condition codes* in EQS – to see whether EQS has encountered any trouble during the estimation process. Examples of such problems are the following:

1. Parameters that (probably) are not identified.
2. The program fails to converge.
3. Negative variance estimates.
4. Covariance matrices that are not positive definite.

Point 1 was treated in Section 2 above; the other points in the list will be commented on below.

Convergence problems

If the program fails to converge, most often the cause is that the sample is too small, or the model is extremely misspecified, so that correlations among indicators for different latent variables are larger than correlations among indicators for the same concept.

In both cases the cure is simple: collect more data and/or reformulate the model.

Another cause of failing convergence could be that the variances of the manifest variables are very different in size, e.g. a family's yearly income in dollars and family size. In this case the solution is just as simple: change the measurement scale from dollars to thousands of dollars or tens of thousands of dollars or to whatever is necessary to obtain nearly comparable variances for the variables.

Extreme non-normal data can also give rise to convergence problems.

Computer programs such as EQS are generally good at finding start values for the iterations, but if bad start values are the problem, you can supply your own start values for some or all of the parameters yourself. Just put in your suggested start value for a parameter before the asterisk in the /EQUATIONS paragraph, e.g.

$$V1 = 0.5*V2 + *V3 + *V4 + V5 + E5;$$

If you are uncertain about specifying start values, you can use the RETEST statement. Inserting the statement

$$RETEST = RET.EQS$$

in the /PRINT paragraph creates a new program (.eqs) file named 'ret', where the final parameter estimates from the completed run are inserted as start values for a new run. Perhaps you will have to edit the new program by doing a few copy/paste operations between the new and the old program.

This feature will save you a lot of time – and is much preferred to increasing the number of maximum iterations. At first sight this possibility perhaps seems an obvious way to solve convergence problems, but it cannot be recommended. If EQS does not converge during the first 30 iterations (the default), then in most cases it will not find a meaningful solution however many iterations you allow.

Convergence problems could also arise as a consequence of the sample covariance matrix not being positive definite, a subject that is dealt with below.

As you will have guessed, the (optional) paragraph /PRINT is where you instruct EQS to print output you need to supplement the EQS default output. Compare the COV = YES statement in Section 2 above.

Negative variance estimates

Negative variances are of course meaningless. Most often it is the estimated variances of error terms (E and D) that are negative. The reason could be that a sample is too small. Often the reason is that existing correlations among some of the indicators for the same latent variables have not been taken care of. Such correlations will emerge in situations where there have been problems in formulating items that are sufficiently different, but nevertheless similar enough to measure the same concept.

Reformulating the model by introducing the relevant correlations can solve the problem. The perfectionist will consider such correlations as a blemish, because the ideal is that the only cause for correlation among the items is the latent variable itself. If two correlating indicators are very similar, you can omit one of them.

Correlating E-variables across latent variables in models based on cross-sectional data is difficult to defend, and should be avoided by reformulating the model (cf. Example 7.2).

If the calculations result in some variances being negative, most other SEM programs print the negative variance estimates in the output, but at the same time also print an error message. EQS uses another strategy: The variance estimate is given as zero, and you are given a warning in the form

```
E5,E5 constrained at lower bound
```

The way EQS treats this problem has a drawback: if the estimated negative variance is numerically very small, you could argue that in spite of the negative estimate, the population value could very well be positive, and perhaps fixing the variance to have a small positive value could have been a sensible solution to the problem.

Covariance matrices that are not positive definite

Every symmetric $p \times p$ matrix – and that includes covariance and correlation matrices – has associated with it p *eigenvalues* (some of which could be identical). If the *eigenvalues* are all positive, the matrix is said to be *positive definite* (if they are all negative, it is *negative definite*).

In component analysis (Chapter 3) we met a special interpretation of the eigenvalues of a covariance or correlation matrix – namely, as variances of the principal components. Since a variance cannot be negative, covariance and correlation matrices cannot be negative definite.

But can they have one or more zero eigenvalues (in which case the matrix is described as being *positive semi-definite*)? Yes, this is possible. It means that the data can be fully described in fewer than p dimensions. However, certain calculations, which could occur in the fitting function, are not defined for semi-definite matrices (because, for example, they lead to division by zero).

From (5) we can see that the fitting function F contains two covariance matrices **S** and $\Sigma(\hat{\theta})$ to which we can add a third matrix, i.e. a weight matrix **W** used for instance in GLS and AGLS estimation. As **W** shall also be positive definite, all three matrices could cause problems in the estimation process and lead to the error message.

If **S** is not positive definite, then either you have used pairwise deletion (see Chapter 10), or one or more of the variables is a linear function of one or more of the others.

If you cannot 'repair' the input and a positive semi-definite matrix **S** makes sense in the situation, I recommend using LS, as ML estimation then requires calculation of the logarithm of zero and GLS requires division by zero, both of which operations are of course undefined.

In this connection I must point out that, due to rounding errors, strong collinearity among manifest variables will lead to the same problems as if this matrix was semi-definite, i.e. it will result in empirical under-identification as mentioned in Section 2. So be prepared to face problems if you have correlations numerically larger than 0.80 among the manifest variables. However, there could also be more subtle collinearities involving more than two variables at a time. A simple way to get an indication of such multivariate collinearities is to calculate the multiple correlation coefficient for each variable when regressing it on the remaining variables. Large correlations signal collinearity problems, but say nothing about their nature. Detecting such collinearities can be a challenge. SPSS and other statistics packages have advanced output to assist you in such tasks. A simple explanation of the methods as implemented in SYSTAT (and SPSS!) can be found in Wilkinson, Grant, and Gruber (1996).

But what if the estimate $\Sigma(\hat{\theta})$ is not positive definite? It could be that the first guess for $\Sigma(\hat{\theta})$ is not positive definite. If this happens, EQS will in most instances iterate to a positive definite $\Sigma(\hat{\theta})$ in a few steps. If this does not happen, there is a risk that the process will not find the global minimum of the fitting function. As you can imagine, most often problems with $\Sigma(\hat{\theta})$ can be traced back to problems with **S** – after all, the whole idea is to minimize the discrepancy between the two matrices. Another reason could be that your model is 'very' wrong, and in that case you will have to respecify it.

If the problem arises with a matrix that emerges as a result of the calculations (i.e. covariance matrices of E and D), it can often be traced back to variances being estimated as negative (see above). Sometimes, however, a positive semi-definite covariance matrix is a natural (and meaningful!) consequence of the model. In such a case you can of course neglect the warning.

Last but not least, it should be pointed out that any of the three matrices could cause problems if the sample is too small.

Regardless, if there are problems of this sort, EQS will give you a warning such as

```
              MATRIX SMPLCOVA MAY NOT BE POSITIVE DEFINITE.
**********************************************************************
* *
* COVARIANCE MATRIX HAS A NON-POSITIVE DETERMINANT. ESTIMATION IS *
* ABORTED. *
* *
**********************************************************************
```

We have an example of the use of the determinant mentioned in the comments on the output in Table 4.1.

If a matrix is positive definite, its determinant is positive – but unfortunately you cannot argue that if the determinant is positive, then the matrix is positive definite.

Outliers and non-normality

Many of the problems discussed above can be traced back to the causes mentioned in the heading. Even if they do not result in error messages, estimates and the validity of the tests can, depending on the estimation method, be severely influenced by outliers and by data not being multivariate normal. Therefore it is advisable to examine the raw data very carefully before doing any calculations.

Outliers are observations which take on values that are very different from the main part of the data. As long as we consider each variable separately, it is not too difficult to locate outliers. A simple way to do so is to standardize all variables and then examine observations with one or more variables having values numerically larger than, say, 4.00. But when we look at two variables, we encounter problems. Consider Figure 6 where the first two variables from Example 3.4 are depicted. A small amount of error is added to the values so that all observations can be seen, even if they take on the same values. A contour ellipse including about 68% of the observations is also shown.

Three observations (A, B and C) are marked. Observation C is farther from the centroid than A and B, but which is farthest from the centroid, A or B?

By traditional standards A is farther from the centroid than B, but B has a *combination* of the variable values that is more unusual than those of A. You could therefore argue that B is farther away from the centroid if we use a measure where the units are smaller in directions where the Euclidean distance from the center to the limits of the cluster of observations is small. Such a measure is the *Mahalanobis squared distance D^2*.

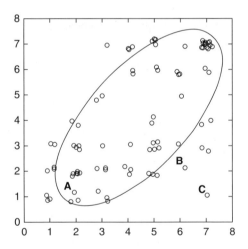

Figure 6 Example 3.4: identifying outliers

While most SEM programs calculate Mahalanobis distances, EQS does not – but SPSS does!

Originally I got the raw data from Bredahl in the form of an SPSS (.sav) file, and I could therefore take advantage of this.

The trick is that, when doing a regression analysis, SPSS gives you the possibility to save Mahalanobis distances from the center to every observation, taking only the independent variables into consideration.

Therefore (based on the raw data), you do a regression analysis (see Appendix A) using SPSS with all five variables as independent variables and an arbitrary variable as the dependent one.

When the window in Figure A.4b in Appendix A pops up, click the box marked 'Save' and choose Mahalanobis distances.

These are then added to your data set as shown in Figure 7. As you can see, I have sorted the observation by Mahalanobis distance in descending order. This makes it easier to detect the large distances. You simply choose 'Data/Sort' and then 'MAH_1'.

Now, what is an outlier? That is not an easy question to answer, but given the rather large drop in 'MAH_1' from respondent (resp) 238 to respondent 170, there is no doubt that observation 238 is an outlier. You can then (if you want) repeat the process after having deleted observation 238.

	risk	nature	tech	neophob	alienati	resp	MAH_1
1	33.00	42.00	12.00	28.00	4.00	238.00	27.66
2	28.00	20.00	11.00	7.00	20.00	170.00	22.39
3	30.00	41.00	32.00	20.00	5.00	239.00	22.05
4	12.00	40.00	19.00	20.00	20.00	184.00	20.74
5	27.00	12.00	29.00	17.00	21.00	324.00	18.24
6	13.00	24.00	12.00	29.00	14.00	410.00	17.85
7	27.00	42.00	30.00	16.00	7.00	69.00	15.67
8	42.00	33.00	35.00	35.00	18.00	356.00	15.45
9	38.00	37.00	10.00	23.00	9.00	371.00	15.42
10	19.00	24.00	35.00	32.00	12.00	43.00	14.84
11	28.00	41.00	10.00	16.00	20.00	445.00	14.73
12	36.00	34.00	9.00	24.00	9.00	317.00	14.68
13	41.00	20.00	31.00	21.00	16.00	82.00	14.35

Figure 7 Example 1: detection of outliers

Checking for normality is another important step in your data preparation. I will introduce you to the EQS tools for doing that by taking another look at Example 1.

Example 1 (Continued)
Checking for outliers and non-normality

In your data preparation you of course have to work with the raw data and not just a covariance summary.

As mentioned above, I originally got the raw data from Bredahl in the form of an SPSS (.sav) file, which was then read into EQS. I opened EQS and clicked the 'Open' icon (you can also choose 'File' (see Figure 3) and then chose 'Open' instead of 'New'). Then the window in Figure 8 popped up, where I could choose from a vide variety of file formats. I chose 'SPSS System Files' and selected the file 'Bredahl 2'. As a result the window in Figure 9 opened up.

Figure 8 Importing data to EQS

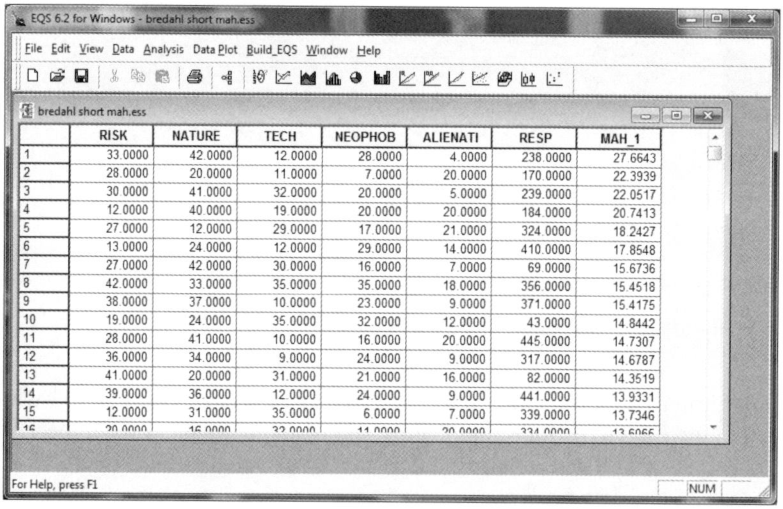

Figure 9 Example 1: EQS data file (.ess file)

As you can see, the file is automatically given the same name as the original SPSS file, but now with the extension .ess, which identifies it as an EQS system data file (remember to save it!).

The most popular estimation techniques in SEM assume multivariate normality, which means that:

1. All univariate distributions should be normal.
2. All bivariate regression functions should be linear.

As you can see from Figure 9. EQS offers you a variety of statistical tools, some of which you can also find in SPSS, while others are specific to EQS. One of the great things about EQS is that it is so easy to alternate between the two programs and thereby take full advantage of them both. In EQS you can:

1. Calculate statistics that characterize the variables in your data, such as mean, standard deviation, skewness and kurtosis (see Appendix A).
2. Plot your variables in histograms.
3. Plot your variables in normal probability plots.
4. Plot your variables in two-dimensional scatter plots.
5. Do linear regression analysis.

These are all techniques that can help you to detect (univariate and bivariate) outliers and check your data for (univariate and bivariate) normality.

I will not go into the details here, as they are very well described in the user's manual (Bentler & Wu, 2002).

Table 3 contains a program that will analyze the data in Figure 9. As the data reside in an external file (as is always the case when a raw data file is used), the paragraph /SPECIFICATIONS includes an instruction on where EQS will find the input data.

Table 3 Example 1 (continued): program using raw data as input

```
/TITLE
   Example 4.1. Data from Bredahl (2001)
regress
/SPECIFICATIONS
   DATA='C:\Users\Sony\Desktop\EQS bog\Example 4.1 NY\Bredahl regress.ESS';
   VARIABLES=5; CASES=481;
   METHOD=ML; ANALYSIS=COVARIANCE; MATRIX=RAW;
/LABELS
   V1=RISK; V2=NATURE; V3=TECH; V4=NEOPHOB; V5=ALIENATI;
/EQUATIONS
   V1 =    *V2 + *V3 + *V4 + *V5 + E1;
/VARIANCES
   V2 TO V5= *;
   E1 = *;
/COVARIANCES
   V2 TO V5=*;
/END
```

As far as the output is concerned, you will of course get exactly the same estimates, fit measures, etc., whether you use the program in Figure 4 or the one in Table 3, but when your input is raw data, then in addition you will get the output given in Table 4.

First, there is a summary description of the variables including their mean, standard deviation, skewness and kurtosis (see Appendix A).

Traditionally in SEM a skewness numerically larger than 3 is seen as 'large', whereas there is less agreement on how large the kurtosis should be in order to raise problems for estimation. As a compromise I suggest that you take a close look at variables with a kurtosis numerically larger than 10, as excessive kurtosis is more serious than skewness if you want to use normal theory estimation methods. All these of course are unidimensional characteristics.

Table 4 Example 1 (continued): checking for outliers and normality

```
SAMPLE STATISTICS BASED ON COMPLETE CASES


                            UNIVARIATE STATISTICS
                            ---------------------


     VARIABLE         RISK       NATURE        TECH       NEOPHOB     ALIENATI
                       V1          V2           V3          V4           V5
     MEAN           29.7983      32.3597     25.0042      18.9709     16.5759
     SKEWNESS (G1)  -0.5532      -0.3109     -0.3634       0.2111     -0.7200
     KURTOSIS (G2)  -0.2178      -0.4924      0.0224      -0.4213      0.2357
     STANDARD DEV.   7.4818       6.0389      5.4917       6.5878      3.4957


                            MULTIVARIATE KURTOSIS
                            ---------------------


     MARDIA'S COEFFICIENT (G2,P) =       3.8333
     NORMALIZED ESTIMATE         =       5.0242


                      ELLIPTICAL THEORY KURTOSIS ESTIMATES
                      ------------------------------------


     MARDIA-BASED KAPPA =    0.1095  MEAN SCALED UNIVARIATE KURTOSIS =    -0.0582

     MARDIA-BASED KAPPA IS USED IN COMPUTATION.  KAPPA=           0.1095


     CASE NUMBERS WITH LARGEST CONTRIBUTION TO NORMALIZED MULTIVARIATE KURTOSIS:
     ---------------------------------------------------------------------------

     CASE NUMBER       170          184         238         239         324

     ESTIMATE       614.1498     520.3319    961.3873    594.1370    392.1327
                    -----------------------------------

     MARDIA-BASED KAPPA =     .1119  MEAN SCALED UNIVARIATE KURTOSIS =    -.0558
     MARDIA-BASED KAPPA IS USED IN COMPUTATION.  KAPPA=            .1119

     CASE NUMBERS WITH LARGEST CONTRIBUTION TO NORMALIZED MULTIVARIATE KURTOSIS:
     ---------------------------------------------------------------------------

     CASE NUMBER       183          196         203         349         473
     ESTIMATE       958.4692     580.1100    387.7955    607.9674    520.2778
```

Next, there are estimates of Mardia's measure of multivariate kurtosis in standard and normalized form (Mardia, 1970, 1974) – but how big should it likely be to cause trouble as far as estimation is concerned?

The normalized measure is asymptotically distributed as standard normal, which suggests that a value larger than 4 to 5 could be a sign of problems.

The next few lines refer to the use of elliptical theory, which is beyond the scope of this book.

In the last line we have a list of the observations that contribute most to the multivariate kurtosis in descending order. You will see that this list contains exactly the same observations as the ones with greatest Mahalanobis distances in Figure 7. This is no surprise, as Mardia's multivariate kurtosis measure can be expressed as a function of the sum of Mahalanobis distances raised to the fourth power. In that way Mardia's kurtosis measure is both an expression of multivariate non-normality *and* a remedy for finding outliers.

As you can see from the discussion of kurtosis in Appendix A, kurtosis is influenced both by the tails (where you find the outliers) and by the peak of the distribution. Although the tails in most cases have the largest influence on kurtosis, the peak could also play a role: a large kurtosis does not *necessarily* signal an outlier.

My advice would therefore be as follows:

1. Judge the univariate normality of the variables based on histograms and probability plots.
2. If necessary, transform non-normal variables to (near) normality. Often this will also bring outliers nearer to the main body of the data.
3. After the transformations, use SPSS or EQS to detect outliers.

I am well aware that, in theory, the normality of marginal distributions does not guarantee multivariate normality. However, in my experience, you can in practice generally assume multivariate normality if all marginal distributions are normal.

In addition, if the data are multivariate normal, all bivariate regression functions are linear. This could also be used as a check for multivariate normality – but note that this is also a necessary and not a sufficient condition.

Samples that are too small

As pointed out several times, small samples can generate a lot of problems, but when is a sample too small?

I mentioned that AGLS estimation requires sample sizes measured in thousands, but apart from this it is difficult to give precise guidelines – seldom will you have so large a data set at your disposal.

The problem is twofold:

1. The sample size plays a multiple role in SEM. It determines the precision and stability with which the model is estimated and the power of statistical tests, and, further, it influences the size of the various fit measures that are discussed in the next chapter.
2. The required sample size depends on lots of factors: the complexity of the model, the estimation method and the distributional qualities of the data – and, what is more, these various factors interact in their demands.

The more complex the model, the larger the sample size required. As a rough rule of thumb it has been proposed that the sample size should be at least 10 times the number of free parameters, unless the model is *very* simple and the distribution of exogenous variables nearly multivariate normal.

Also, the more ill-behaved the distribution, the larger the sample size required. Remember: the arguments for using ML or GLS estimation are based on their asymptotic qualities.

As the decision on sample size is so complicated, many rules of thumb have emerged. Personally I think that a sample size of about 100 would suffice for regression models like the one in this chapter, or for the development of a simple measurement model like the SOP scale mentioned in Example 1.3 and discussed in more detail in Chapter 7. In more complicated models like the one you will meet in Chapter 8, I usually require 200–300 observations as a minimum.

The next steps

Having dealt with the problems that caused the error messages, you then move on to examine the output.

The first step is to look at the coefficients (and other parameters). Do they have the expected signs, and is their numerical magnitude in agreement with grounded theories, earlier empirical studies and common sense? Are any of the standard errors extremely large, causing uncertainties in the magnitude of the parameter estimates? Or are they perhaps extremely small, which could cause problems with the calculation of the test statistics?

Next, look at the global χ^2-test for the model as a whole and the long list of fit measures (to be discussed in Chapter 6). If the model fit is unsatisfactory you can try to improve it – usually by adding more parameters to the model – and if the fit is 'too good' the model can perhaps be simplified by fixing or deleting parameters. In both cases you can order output that can help with these modifications (you will find several examples on this in the following chapters).

In this step-by-step way you try to obtain a model which will give a satisfactory description of the data in as few parameters as possible, but at the same time is theoretically sound and substantively meaningful – a so-called *parsimonious* model.

I would like to emphasize the importance of simple models: the simpler the model, the more generalizable the model.

Exploratory use of SEM

This process is not without problems. The more revisions you go through, the larger the risk that you will profit from peculiarities in the sample at hand and that your model will not fit any other comparable data set.

In principle SEM is a confirmatory procedure, by which you test a model formulated a priori. However, the continual 'improvement' of the model is more exploratory and invalidates the 'testing': you test hypotheses on the same data that have given birth to them – a circular argument!

In this way the *P*-values lose their proper meaning and can only be used descriptively. This is the reason for including steps 9 and 10 in the list at the beginning of this chapter. Judging by published research, this cross-validation is very seldom done and, if you forgo it, it is extra important that:

1. Your original model is based on well-grounded substantive theory.
2. Stepwise alterations of the model are few in number and also based on substantive thinking.

The more you rely on computer output and 'automation', the greater the risk that you will neglect serious thinking based on substantive considerations. This is artificial intelligence in its worst form.

7 A Few Problems with SEM

I would like to end this chapter by pointing out three problems that you should always keep in mind when doing structural equation analysis: (1) the 'reverse' use of statistical tests; (2) the dependence of the χ^2-test on sample size; and (3) the existence of *equivalent models* that all have the same fit to the data.

The 'reverse' testing procedure

As is well known, the philosophy of traditional statistical testing goes as follows:

You formulate two hypotheses, a null hypothesis H_0 and an alternative hypothesis H_1. H_0 is the hypothesis that represents the status quo, while H_1 is the hypothesis you want to support. If the data do not support H_0, this hypothesis is rejected and H_1 is accepted – not as *true*, but as a *better* description of the data-generating process than H_0.

We accept H_1, not because we prove it is true but because we reject a competing hypothesis: statistical inference is 'the science of disproof'.

In SEM this logic is reversed: H_0 states that the model you actually want to support is true, and H_1 that it is not.

In a broader perspective this procedure conflicts with the basic philosophy of scientific discovery: that a new model proposed to explain an empirical phenomenon is only accepted if its explanation is better than the one taken to be 'true' hitherto. It is not 'true' in any absolute sense, only 'more true' than the old one, but it will in all probability give way to an even 'truer' model at some point in the future.

R. A. Fisher (1890–1962) – whom many believe was the greatest statistician of all time – often quoted Thomas Fuller (1654–1734): 'Nothing is good or bad but by comparison.' But this comparison very seldom takes place in SEM, except in implicit comparisons with the usually very unrealistic models that are the basis for fit measures.

There will in general be several processes that could be hypothesized to have generated the data at hand. It is therefore a good habit to start out with several models that are substantively meaningful (based on prior research, well-grounded theory or common sense), compare them and judge their relative ability to explain the data.

Based on published research this is very seldom done, in which case the researcher runs a risk of overlooking other plausible explanations of the data.

The example in Figure 1.7b is a positive exception to the usual way SEM is carried out.

The χ^2-test and the sample size

It is a well-known fact that the χ^2-test depends on sample size. In the case of SEM the test is based on $C = (n-1)F_{(min)}$ where $F_{(min)}$ is the minimum of the fitting function. If the sample size is sufficiently small, you will always accept H_0, and if it is sufficiently large you will always reject H_0.

The consequences of the combination of the 'reverse' test procedure and the dependence of χ^2 on sample size are therefore rather grotesque. Even if we know that our model is not literally 'true', we will accept it at small sample sizes and reject it at large sample sizes. This is the main reason for the invention of a long series of fit indices (some of them analogous to the well-known R^2), which you will meet in the next chapter.

Indeed, this is the problem with all two-sided tests, where a sharp null hypothesis is tested against a diffuse alternative. The null hypothesis is always false; it is only a matter of taking a sufficiently large sample to prove it is false!

This is one of several good reasons for using one-sided tests when testing estimated parameters – but remember to formulate your hypotheses before you look at the data! (Why?)

Equivalent models
If we estimate a simple regression model

$$y = \alpha_0 + \alpha_1 x + \delta_y \qquad (6a)$$

we will obtain exactly the same fit as in

$$x = \beta_0 + \beta_1 y + \delta_x \qquad (6b)$$

and in SEM where several equations and variables are involved, it will *always* be possible to find several different models with exactly the same fit but with different theoretical implications. While such *equivalent models* will include different parameters and different parameter values, they will show exactly the same values on all figures in the output used to measure the (global) 'goodness' of the model including the χ^2-test and fit measures.

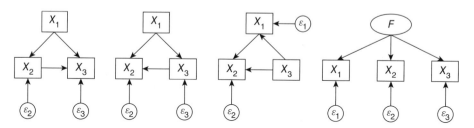

Figure 10 Equivalent models

Figure 10 shows a few of the models that will fit the data of a model with three manifest variables equally well: they are *equivalent*. In simple SEM models you might have only a limited number of equivalent models, but in larger models the number of equivalent models might be counted in hundreds or even thousands (in Figure 10 the models are just-identified, and all just-identified models are equivalent).

Even if most of the equivalent models are usually without any substantive meaning, in many cases there will exist a number of meaningful equivalent models. It is therefore the researcher's duty to explain why one meaningful equivalent model is preferred to others. Judging from published work this is very seldom done.

It can be cumbersome to specify all equivalent models (Herschberger, 1994; Lee, 1990), so the special computer program TETRAD was compiled to do this job (TETRAD Project homepage: www.phil.cmu.edu/projects/tetrad/).

The lesson learned is: an excellent fit guarantees that your model fits the data – but it does not prove that your model is a realistic picture of 'the real world'. Consequently, a bad fit is stronger evidence against the model than a good fit is evidence in support of it.

In this chapter you met the following concepts:

- identification
- *t*-rule
- fixed and free parameters
- maximum likelihood (ML)
- least squares (LS)
- generalized least squares (GLS)
- elliptical LS (ELS)
- elliptical GLS (EGLS)
- elliptical reweighted LS (ERLS)
- heterogeneous kurtosis GLS (HKGLS)
- heterogeneous kurtosis RLS (HKRLS)
- arbitrary distribution GLS (AGLS)
- EQS model and notation
- V, F, E and D variables
- parceling
- convergence
- positive definite and positive semi-definite covariance matrices
- equivalent models

You have also been introduced to the following EQS paragraphs:

```
/TITLE              /EQUATIONS
/SPECIFICATIONS     /COVARIANCES
/LABELS             /MATRIX
/VARIANCES
```

Questions

1. Using an example from your own area of study or research, sketch out the various steps in a typical SEM project.
2. Explain the identification problem and what can be done with an under-identified model.
3. Give a short description of the estimation methods currently available in EQS.
4. How would you go about examining EQS output?

References

Bentler, P.M. (2006). *EQS 6 Structural equations program manual*. Encino, CA: Multivariate Software, Inc.

Bentler, P. M., & Wu, J.C. (2002). *EQS 6.1 for Windows: User's guide*. Encino, CA: Multivariate Software, Inc.

Bollen, K. A. (1989). *Structural equation modeling with latent variables*. New York: Wiley.

Bredahl, L. (2001). Determinants of consumer attitudes and purchase intentions with regard to genetically modified foods – results of a cross-national survey. *Journal of Consumer Policy, 24*, 23–61.

Browne, M. W. (1982). Covariance structures. In D. M. Hawkins (Ed.), *Topics in multivariate analysis*. Cambridge: Cambridge University Press.

Herschberger, S. I. (1994). The specification of equivalent models before the collection of data. In A. E. von Eye & C. C. Clogg (Eds.), *Latent variables analysis*. Thousand Oaks, CA: Sage.

Kenny, D. A., & Milan, S. (2012). Identification: A nontechnical discussion of a technical issue. In R. H. Hoyle (Ed.), *Handbook of structural equation modeling*. New York: Guilford Press.

Lee, S. (1990). A simple rule for generating equivalent models in covariance structure modeling. *Multivariate Behavioral Research, 25*, 313–334.

Mardia, K. V. (1970). Measures of multivariate skewness and kurtosis with applications. *Biometrika, 57*(3), 519–530.

Mardia, K. V. (1974). Application of some measures of multivariate skewness and kurtosis in testing normality and robustness studies. *Sankhya, Series B, 36*, 115–128.

Wilkinson, L., Grant, B., & Gruber, C. (1996). *Desktop data analysis with SYSTAT*. Upper Saddle River, NJ: Prentice Hall.

Further Reading

In this chapter you have been introduced to a lot of problems and methods to cope with these problems. No doubt you are also curious and looking for answers to the many questions you may have asked yourself during reading – and to the many questions you will ask yourself when reading the following chapters.

I will therefore mention four books that should be of help to you in your further studies of structural equation models:

Bollen, K. A. (1989). *Structural equation modeling with latent variables*. New York: Wiley.

Hancock, G. R., & Mueller, R. O. (Eds.). (2013). *Structural equation modeling: A second course* (2nd ed.). Charlotte, NC: Information Age Publishing.

Hoyle, R. H. (Ed.). (2012). *Handbook of structural equation modeling*. New York: Guilford Press.

Marcoulides, G. A., & Schumacker, R. A. (Eds.). (2012). *New developments and techniques in structural equation modeling*. Mahwah, NJ: Psychology Press.

The book by Bollen is still a cornerstone of the SEM literature (and we are eagerly praying for a new edition).

Hancock & Mueller, and Marcoulides & Schumacker, are edited books which take up newer developments in a not-too-advanced form, and Hoyle is a veritable treasure trove, which in its more than 700 pages covers every aspect of SEM – from a historical treatment of its origin to the newest developments – and with lots of references.

5

Data Entering and Programming in EQS

In the previous chapter, among other things you learned how a program in EQS is organized in paragraphs, and you learned how to write a program manually.

In this chapter you will learn how to construct such a program using two interactive EQS programming tools: 'Build EQS' and 'Diagrammer'.

'Build EQS' leads you through a sequence of dialog boxes, each corresponding to a paragraph in the final program. By checking (at each step) a few boxes among the possibilities offered, that paragraph is added to the program, which is visible in the background.

Using 'Diagrammer' you draw the model in a friendly drawing environment, where you are helped on your way by a sequence of dialog boxes (as in 'Build EQS').

In the previous chapter you learned how to include the data in the program in the form of a covariance matrix or a correlation matrix supplemented with the variances.

It is often most convenient to let the data reside in an external file – and if you choose to work with the raw data they must be in an external file.

Therefore, you will first learn how to enter data into an EQS data file.

1 Entering Data

In the previous chapter I illustrated how to import an SPSS file and save it as an EQS (.ess) system data file. As a covariance matrix most often is the only data you need as input, I will show you how to create a covariance matrix such as the one in Table 1 as an .ess file. EQS can import several different file formats, and if you have your data in text format (.raw or .txt) or in SPSS format (.sav), the easiest way to get them into EQS would of course be to import them. But if your data come from a journal article or from your own research, you must type in your data.

Table 1 Lower triangular covariance matrix

```
0.722
0.214   0.360
0.184   0.260   0.384
0.217   0.204   0.211   2.890
0.087   0.054   0.045   0.571   0.360
```

After opening EQS, click the 'New' icon [] (or choose FILE/NEW) and the dialog box shown in Figure 1a will pop up. You are given the choice between several file formats; choose 'EQS Data File', and when you click 'OK', the 'Create a New Data File' dialog box shown in panel (b) will pop up. Select 'Create a Covariance Matrix', put in 5 for the number of variables and 247 for the number of cases, and click 'OK'.

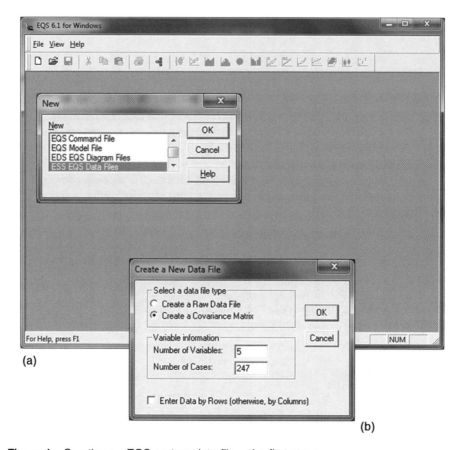

Figure 1 Creating an EQS system data file – the first steps

Now the Data Editor in Figure 2a pops up. As you can see, it contains two extra rows labeled 'STD_D' filled with 1.0000s and 'MEAN' filled with 0.0000s. For now you can ignore these two lines.

You can enter the figures by row or by column. Whichever you choose, EQS will fill in the corresponding column or row, so after you have filled in the first row or column, your Data Editor will look as in panel (b), while the finished Data Editor before saving is shown in panel (c).

Before you save the data, it is a good idea to label the variables. Assume that the model you have in mind is the one shown in Figure 3. This is the model you first met in Example 1.4, except that 'immune system' now has only two indicators.

5.1 Entering Data

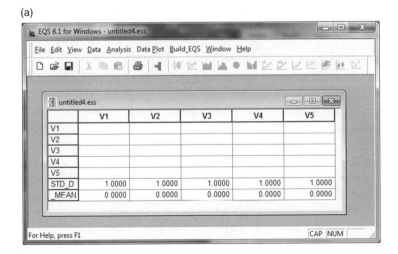

Figure 2 Creating a system data file – typing in the data

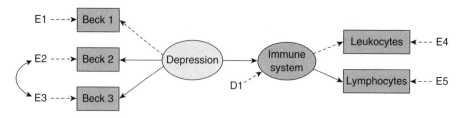

Figure 3 Model

Select 'Data/Information'. This brings up the dialog box shown in Figure 4a.

In 'List of Variables' double-click V1 and, when the box in panel (b) opens up, just select 'V1' and change the name from 'V1' to 'Beck 1'. When you click 'OK', you will return to the previous screen as shown in panel (c), and you can continue naming the next variable – but remember: the maximum number of letters is eight.

You may wonder why some of the variables in Figure 3 are longer than eight letters. The reason is that the original Figure 1.5 was used only for illustrating a model and not for programming purposes – no data were involved.

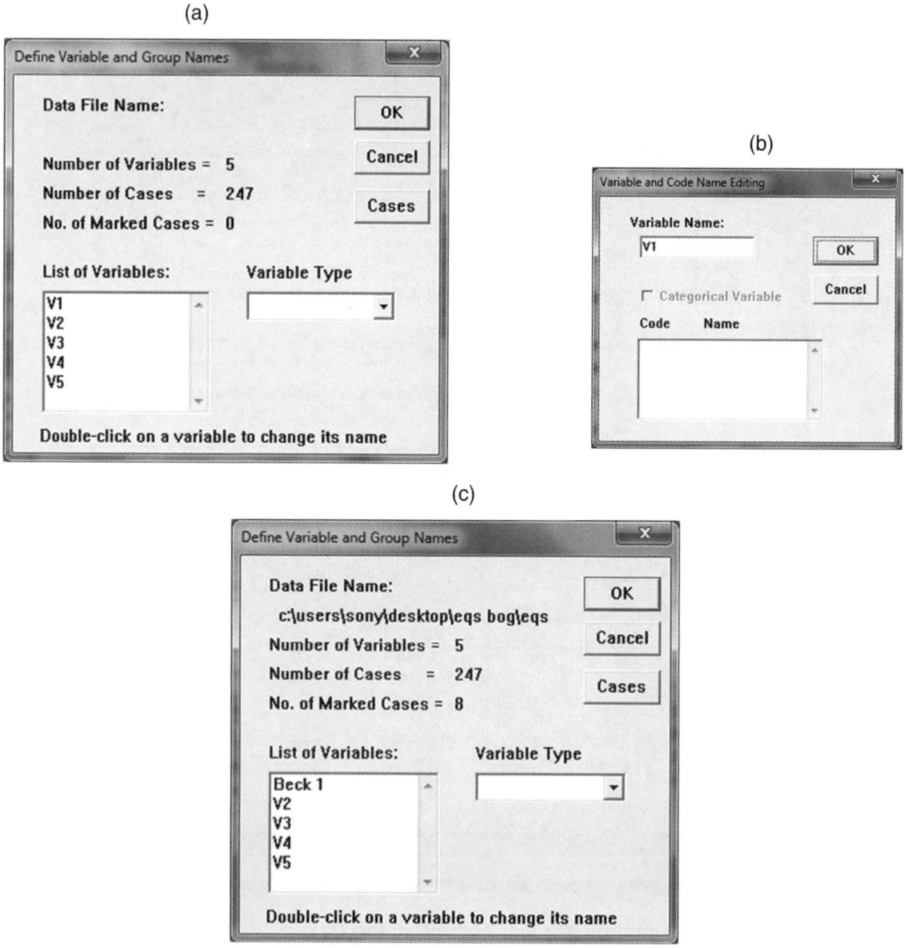

Figure 4 Labeling variables in an EQS System Data File

Now choose 'File/Save As' (you must save the file before you can use it), and when the window in Figure 5a pops up, just click OK and you will be shown the dialog box in panel (b). You can give the file any name you want (I use the name Chap 5). When you then click 'Save', *the covariance matrix is converted to a correlation matrix* as shown in Figure 6.

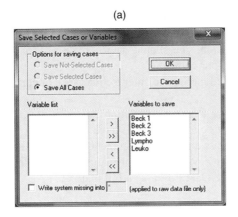

Figure 5 Saving your data

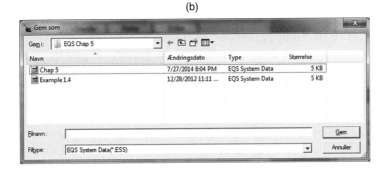

Figure 6 The saved data file in correlation form

This is done so that you can visually examine the covariation in the data. This is much easier to do when based on correlations than on covariances. Do not fear: before doing any calculations, EQS will automatically convert the correlation matrix back to a covariance matrix!

If you started by typing in a correlation matrix, you must type in the standard deviations yourself in order for EQS to create a covariance matrix as the basis for calculations. If you need the means (as you will in Chapter 9) you must also fill them in yourself.

After this demonstration, you should try to create a system data file of your own containing raw data of your choice.

I must admit that I find the way to enter a covariance or correlation matrix into EQS a bit confusing.

If you have your covariance (or correlation) matrix in lower triangular form from a journal article or similar source, or if you have calculated it in some other statistical package, you can save it as a pure text document and give it the extension '.cov'. EQS will then recognize it as a covariance or correlation matrix in lower triangular form and import it directly into the Data Editor as a full matrix.

2 Constructing an EQS Program Using 'Build EQS'

Build EQS is an interactive program that constructs the program as you go through a series of dialog boxes. For your convenience, Figure 7 shows the model we are working with.

Start by opening your data file in Figure 6 (if you have closed it!) and choose 'Build_EQS/Title/Specifications'. See Figure 8a. When the dialog box in panel (b) appears, fill in the model title and click 'OK'. You are of course welcome to examine the many possibilities, to which we will return later on. When you click 'OK', your screen will change to panel (c). This is the whole idea: every line in the roll-down menu in panel (a) corresponds to a paragraph in an EQS program, and as you walk your way through a series of dialog boxes, your clicking constructs an EQS model (.eqx) file with the same name as your data file, as shown in Figure 8c.

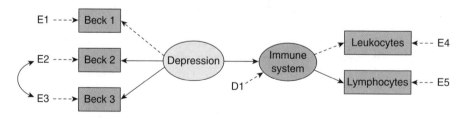

Figure 7 Model (same as Figure 3)

Next, choose 'Build_EQS/Equations' (Figure 9a), and the dialog box in Figure 9b will pop up. As you can see, the number of variables is already filled in, and what remains for you to do is to place a '2' in the 'Number of Factors' (i.e. latent variables) box and click 'OK'.

Figure 8 Using 'Build EQS': the first steps

Now the dialog box in Figure 10a,-b appears. What is shown here as panels (a) and (b) is in fact one window, and you go from (a) to (b) by using a horizontal scroll bar. Each of the seven lines corresponds to a possible equation, with the variable in the first column being a (possible) dependent variable, while the variables in the first row are the possible independent variables. When you click in a cell an asterisk will appear in that cell signaling that the corresponding regression coefficient should be estimated as a free parameter.

Click the relevant cells and the table will change to panel (c). As you can see from panel (b), the coefficients for the error terms are fixed at 1' – and if you want to fix other parameters, just enter a figure of your choice instead of an asterisk.

When you click 'OK', the table in panel (d) will pop up. The variances are already filled in, and you only have to enter an asterisk for the covariance between 'E2' and 'E3' as shown.

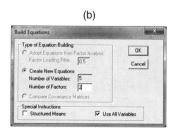

Figure 9 Using 'Build EQS': the next steps

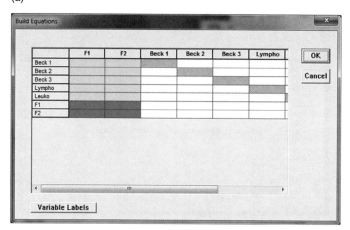
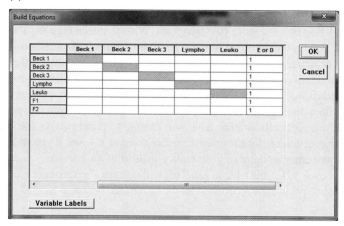

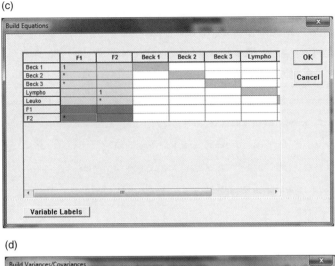

Figure 10 Using 'Build EQS': specifying the parameters to be estimated

When you click 'OK' you will see the program as shown in Figure 11. This is an EQS model (.eqx) file. Note that the .eqx file has only one statement per line. Therefore .eqx files can be very long for more complicated models.

It is very tempting to edit it to save space. But as a model file (an .eqx file) is an EQS system file, it cannot be edited. This, however, is not an inconvenience, because when you execute an .eqx file by choosing 'Build EQS/Run EQS', the output appears immediately and an editable .eqs file is constructed for modification, storage and possible later use. You could use that file to add labels for the two factors.

Note that Figure 11 has a new paragraph, /PRINT.

As you will have guessed, you use the paragraph to order special output. Now, you have not ordered special output in this case, but the thing to remember is that when you use the interactive tools 'Build EQS' or 'Diagrammer', a default/PRINT paragraph is automatically added to the program. This paragraph instruct EQS to print all fit measures and to print the third part of the output containing the parameter estimates in the (default) 'Equation' form used in Table 4.2.

I will return to the /PRINT paragraph in the next chapter.

3 Constructing an EQS Program Using 'Diagrammer'

Diagrammer is the name of the EQS graphic interface, which makes it possible to program EQS just by drawing the model. Like 'Build EQS' it is an interactive program that constructs the drawing as you go through a series of dialog boxes.

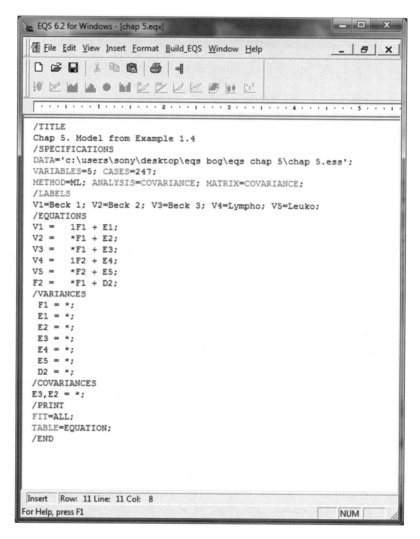

Figure 11 The final *.eqx program

As always, you must open a data file before you can write a program, so start by opening the data file in Figure 6. Then choose the 'Diagrammer' icon, which opens up the dialog box shown in Figure 12.

As you can see, there are four options of which the three first are a path model (as the one in Example 1.2), a simple factor model (as the one in Example 1.3) and a simple latent curve model (to be treated in Chapter 11). If your model is not too complicated, and it falls within one of these three categories, then clicking one of these icons would be a good choice. However, if your model is more complicated, choose the last option and click the Diagram Window, which opens up the drawing environment as in Figure 13. Here you can construct your model using the drawing tools on the left.

Irrespective of your choice, you are led through a series of dialog boxes, just as in 'Build EQS'.

5.3 Constructing an EQS Program Using 'Diagrammer'

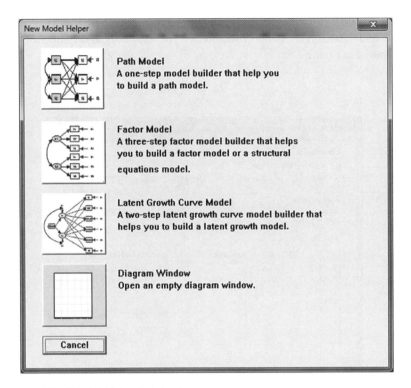

Figure 12 The 'Model Helper' dialog box

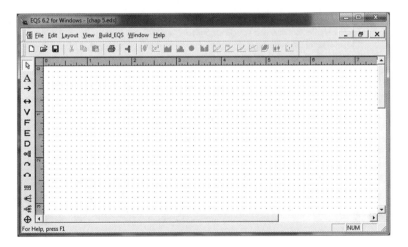

Figure 13 The drawing paper with tools

Choose the 'factor structure tool' from the tools on the left, and when you click on the position in your working space where you want the factor 'F1' to be placed, the window in Figure 14a will appear. Select 'Beck 1, Beck 2' and 'Beck 3', and by clicking the '>' move them to 'Indicator List' as shown in panel (b). Then click 'OK', and the factor structure for 'F1' will show up in the drawing area as in Figure 15a.

Repeat the process for the second factor (named 'F2' by default) using the indicators 'Lympho' and 'Leuko. Your window should now (perhaps after a bit of moving around) look as shown in Figure 15b.

(a)

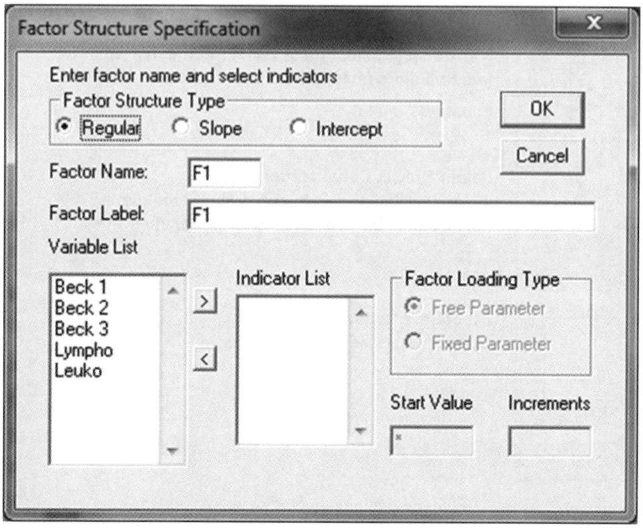

(b)

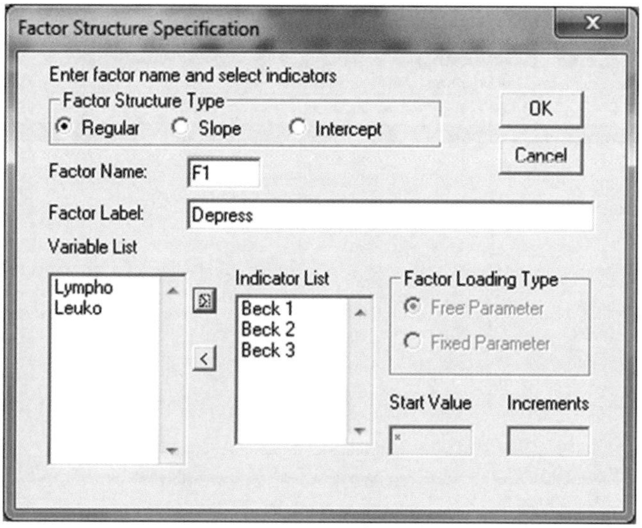

Figure 14 Building a factor structure

Click an element in the 'Depress' factor structure and when the six handles become visible, select 'Edit/Horizontal Flip'. The window now changes to the one in Figure 16a.

5.3 Constructing an EQS Program Using 'Diagrammer'

(a)

(b)

Figure 15 The 'Diagrammer' after placing (a) the first factor and (b) the second factor

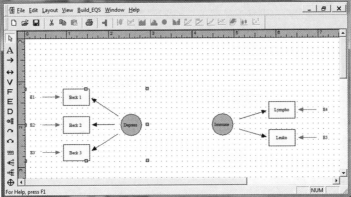

(a)

(Continued)

Figure 16 (Continued)

(b)

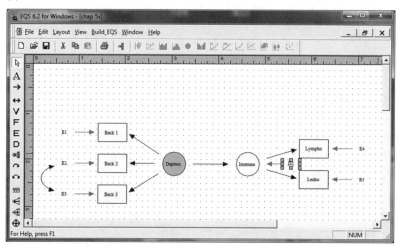

Figure 16 Your model after 'Horizontal Flip' of the 'Depress' factor (a) and after the addition of covariance between 'Beck 2' and 'Beck 3' and connection of the two factors (b)

What remains is to connect 'Beck 2' and 'Beck 3' by a two-headed arrow and to put in the arrow from 'Depress' to 'Immune'. First, select the 'curved arrow tool', move the mouse pointer to 'Beck 2' and with the left mouse button pressed, move the mouse to the 'Beck 3' factor, where you release the button. In much the same way, select the 'straight arrow tool' →, connect 'Depress' to 'Immune' and the window will change to the one in Figure 16b. Note that a disturbance variable is automatically added to the 'Immune' structure. However, its location is perhaps not the most pleasant one, so you can use the mouse to drag it to, for example, the position shown in Figure 17 – your final model.

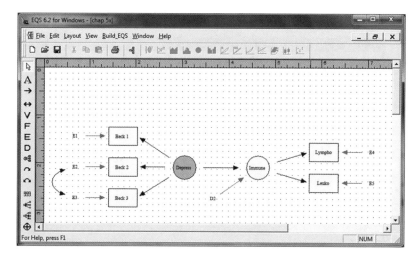

Figure 17 The final model

On the screen, dependent variables (the 'Immune' factor and the five indicators) are in yellow and the independent variable 'Depress' is grey. Freely estimated parameters are black and the six arrows connecting the E-terms and the D-term to their manifest or latent variables are red, indicating that they are fixed at 1.00 by default. Of course you are free to override the defaults.

As you will have noted, a tool is active until another tool is selected. So, when you have finished your drawing, select the 'reset tool' to reset the 'Diagrammer'.

Now you must think about providing the two factors with scales for the purpose of identification. One possibility is to fix one path aiming at each factor at 1.00. We were already offered this possibility in the window in Figure 14.

However, it is not too late. If you double-click a path of your own choice, the window in Figure 18 will appear. Check the 'Fixed Parameter' button, and the number '1.00' will appear in the 'Start Value' box. When you click 'OK' the arrow will change from black to red, indicating that the parameter is now fixed (by the way, does it matter which path you choose to fix?).

I will leave it to you to explore the possibilities by double-clicking the various parameters and variables in the model.

When you save the diagram (.eds) file, a model (.eqx) file similar to the one in Figure 11 appears. When you have run your program, a few fit measures are added to the diagram: chi square, with degrees of freedom and *P*-value, CFI and RMSEA.

Remember that when using 'Build EQS' a /PRINT paragraph was added to the program. When using 'Diagrammer' the following PRINT paragraph is added automatically:

```
/PRINT
EIS
FIT=ALL
TABLE=EQUATION
```

The EIS command will write all estimates to an external input (.eis) file. The 'Diagrammer' can read those estimates later, after the EQS job is done, and then embed them in the various parameters in the diagram. You just open the diagram and choose 'View/Estimates/parameter estimates' (I will give an example of this in the next chapter).

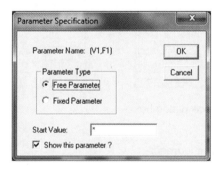

Figure 18 Fixing a parameter

A few concluding remarks on 'Diagrammer'

Sometimes it is necessary to construct a whole model or part of it using the separate elements as building blocks. In that case you can also use the various tools in the toolbox on the left of the drawing area.

You can use the 'Variable tool' V to draw a manifest variable (a rectangle), the 'Factor tool' F to draw a factor (a circle or an ellipsis), the 'Error tool' E to place an error, and the 'Disturbance tool' D to place a disturbance. In all cases, select the tool and click the place in the drawing area where you want the upper-left corner of the symbol to be. The 'Text tool' A works in the same way. You use it to place a textbox in your drawing, so that you can supplement your model with explanations of various kinds. In all cases you can of course move the elements around and resize them using the handles.

As you will have guessed, the 'One-way-arrows' → and ⤢, and the 'Two-way-arrows' ↔ and ⤡, are used to connect the various elements. Notice that whenever an element has a one-headed arrow pointing towards it, a D- or E-variable is added automatically, so it is very seldom that you need to use the D or E tools.

Sometimes you will want to label the factors or indicators in the diagrams with words that are too long to reside in the circle or rectangle of standard size.

You can of course 'ungroup' the factor structures, and then resize the circles or rectangles by dragging the handles. However, this is not the optimal way to solve the problem, because it could be a bit difficult to make sure that all symbols have the same size – which gives the nicest impression.

Choose 'Edit/Preferences' to open the window in Figure 19a and click the 'EQS Diagrammer' tab to open the window in panel (b). Remember: you need to have a data file open!

As you can see, EQS offers a rich palette of options for tailoring EQS to comply with your personal preferences. I have checked the 'Factor' radio button, and in the 'Object size' window you can resize the chosen object using the two scroll bars.

Feel free to explore the many other possibilities offered in Figure 19.

(a)

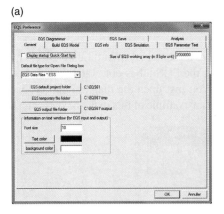

(b)

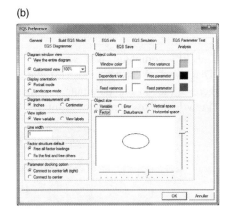

Figure 19 The 'Preference' dialog box

In this chapter you have learned:

- how to enter data into an EQS system data file
- how to label variables
- how to construct a program using 'Build EQS'
- how to construct a program using 'Diagrammer'

You have also been introduced to 'EQS preferences'.

6
Models with Only Manifest Variables

In this chapter you will be introduced to acyclic and cyclic models with only manifest variables.

As mentioned in Chapter 1, these models are commonly known as *path models*, and in economics as *simultaneous equation models* or *econometric models*.

You will first learn how to analyze acyclic models. You will meet two sufficient rules for identification and then be led through a simple example in which you will learn how to interpret the very extensive output from EQS, including the various fit measures you will find in the output.

Then we turn to cyclic models. The identification problem – which is much more of a problem in this kind of model – is illustrated using the cigarette advertising example from Chapter 1.

The very meaning of 'two-way causation' is discussed, and final advice is given: avoid cyclic models if at all possible!

1 Identifying and Estimating Acyclic Models

Of the few rules for identification in acyclic models with manifest variables, only two are mentioned here.

The zero B rule
A model with no variable that has both ingoing and outgoing arrows is always identified.

The recursive rule
If the regression coefficients can be arranged in a lower triangular matrix

$$\begin{aligned}X_1 &= \delta_1 \\ X_2 &= \beta_{21}X_1 + \delta_2 \\ X_3 &= \beta_{31}X_1 + \beta_{32}X_2 + \delta_3 \\ X_4 &= \beta_{41}X_1 + \beta_{42}X_2 + \beta_{43}X_3 + \delta_4 \\ X_5 &= \beta_{51}X_1 + \beta_{52}X_2 + \beta_{53}X_3 + \beta_{54}X_4 + \delta_5\end{aligned} \qquad (1a)$$

and

$$Cov(\delta_i, \delta_j) = 0 \text{ for all } i \text{ and } j \qquad (1b)$$

the model is said to be *recursive* and it is always identified. If some of the regression coefficients are zero, the model is over-identified.

The condition (1b) loosens any tie among the equations as far as estimation is concerned. Consequently, the equations can be estimated independently of each other, e.g. using OLS (Ordinary Least Squares), if the other conditions for that procedure are fulfilled.

It should be mentioned that traditionally all acyclic models are called recursive in SEM, unless they include correlations between errors for endogenous variables that also have a direct causal connection.

Example 1
Is the buying of coffee a high- or a low-involvement action?

If in Aaker and Day's hierarchy-of-effects model (Aaker & Day, 1971), first met in Figure 1.7b, we let

$$X_1 = \text{exposure}$$
$$X_2 = \text{price}$$
$$X_3 = \text{awareness}$$
$$X_4 = \text{attitude}$$
$$X_5 = \text{market share}$$

then the model can be written as in (1a), where

$$\beta_{21} = \beta_{32} = \beta_{42} = \beta_{51} = \beta_{53} = 0 \tag{2}$$

If the condition (1b) is met, the model is (over-identified according to the recursive rule. It is left to the reader to verify whether the low-involvement model is identified. The models are shown in Figure 1.

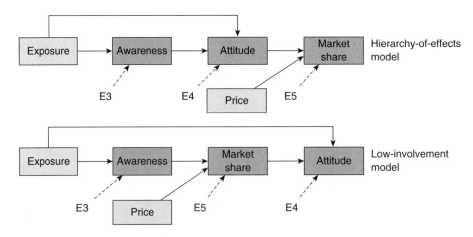

Figure 1 Example 1: acyclic causal models (from Figure 1.7b)

Example 2
Examining the stability of alienation

Wheaton, Muthén, Alwin, and Summers (1977) conducted a panel study covering the years 1966–1971 in order to study the stability of alienation as measured on two summated scales called 'anomia' and 'powerlessness'. Like several others – for example, Jöreskog and Sörbom (1984), Bentler (1995) and Browne (2009) – I will use the Wheaton et al. data to illustrate SEM analysis and to acquaint you with the extensive EQS output.

The study included several background variables, but here I will concentrate on the two variables 'anomia' and 'powerlessness' and the two years 1967 and 1971.

Figure 2 from Bentler (1995) shows a so-called cross-lagged panel design with 932 respondents.

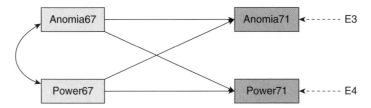

Figure 2 Example 2: the model (reproduced with kind permission from Peter Bentler)

With four variables there are $(4 \times 5)/2 = 10$ variances/covariances, on which to base the estimation, and the number of parameters to be estimated is $4 + 4 + 1 = 9$ (number of coefficients + number of variances + number of covariances). The model is therefore possibly identified with one degree of freedom. The identification is confirmed by the zero B rule.

Table 1 contains the data and a program for estimation of the model.

Table 1 Example 2: data and program (.eqs file)

	V2	V2	V3	V4
V1	11.834			
V2	6.947	9.364		
V3	6.819	5.091	12.532	
V4	4.783	5.028	7.495	9.986

```
/TITLE
   Example 6.2. Data from Wheaton et all. (1977)
/SPECIFICATIONS
   CAS=932; VAR=4; ME=ML;
/LABEL
   V1=ANOMIA67; V2=POWRLS67; V3=ANOMIA71; V4=POWRLS71;
```

(Continued)

(Continued)
```
/EQUATIONS
   V3 = *V1 + *V2 + E3;
   V4 = *V1 + *V2 + E4;
/VARIANCES
   V1 TO V2 = *;
   E3 TO E4 = *;
/COVARIANCES
   V2,V1= *;
/PRINT
   FIT=ALL
/MATRIX
   11.834
    6.947   9.364
    6.819   5.091  12.532
    4.783   5.028   7.495   9.986
/END
```

Before continuing, I suggest you read the data into an EQS data file and construct the program in Table 1 using 'Build EQS' – just to be sure you have mastered the two steps you learned in the previous chapter.

In the /PRINT paragraph I order a complete list of the measures that EQS can offer for judging the fit of my model. As a default EQS only prints fit measures down to IFI – see Table 2.

If you use 'Build EQS' you click 'Print' (see Figure 3a) and the window in panel (b) appears, offering you a wide selection of additional output from which to choose. Here you select 'Report full fit indices'.

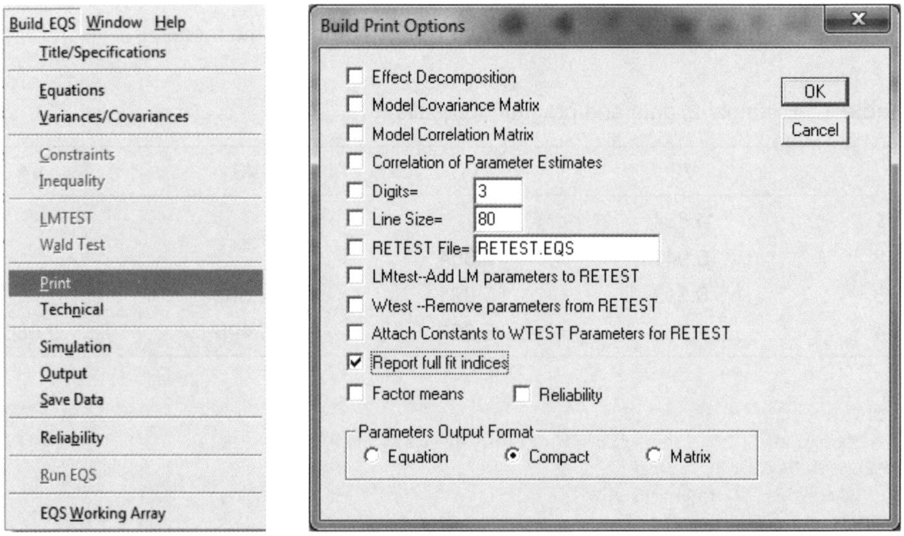

Figure 3 Example 2: choosing output

Now, let us take a look at the output. As usual the program output is in three sections:

1. A description of the input.
2. An evaluation of model fit.
3. Estimates of the models parameters.

For space considerations I will forgo the first part of the output that echoes the input program and be content to observe that:

PARAMETER ESTIMATES APPEAR IN ORDER,
NO SPECIAL PROBLEMS WERE ENCOUNTERED DURING OPTIMIZATION.

The second part covering model fit details is given in Table 2.

The most obvious way to judge the fit of a model is to look at the residual covariance matrix – as defined in Chapter 1's Equation (20). After all, the whole idea is to find a model that could reproduce the analyzed covariance matrix, and in this way 'explain' the covariations in the data at hand.

1. First in the output is the residual covariance matrix in raw and standardized (correlation) form.[1] As mentioned earlier, the residual covariance matrix is the difference between the sample covariance matrix and the covariance matrix implied by the model. The smaller the elements in the residual covariance matrix, the more the model is supported by the data.

    It may be easier to evaluate model fit by looking at the residual correlations. Small and not-too-different values are signs of a good fit, while large and very different values signal a bad fit and could point out where the problems are located.

    Generally large off-diagonal values are more serious than large diagonal values.

    The residual matrices in Table 2 are very far from the ideal, but at the same time they indicate where the problem is located.

    The model can reproduce the sample covariance matrix except for the covariance between the two 71-variables.

    As the residual covariance of Powerlessness71 and Anomia71 is positive, the model underestimates the covariance between the two variables. However, allowing the two variables (or rather their error terms) to correlate more than caused by the exogenous variables would eat up our only degree of freedom.
2. Next, there is a list of the ten largest standardized residuals and a graph of their distribution. The more 'normal' the distribution, the better.
3. A few lines below you find that the global χ^2-test of the model has a P-value of 0.000 with one degree of freedom. As mentioned in Section 4.7, *the null hypothesis is that the model is correct*. This means that there is practically zero chance of getting a sample like ours, or one that is less consistent with the model, if the model is true. Because of the 'reverse' testing, we are interested in getting *large* values of P. On the other hand very large P-values could be an indication of over-fitting, in which case the model should be simplified.

---

[1] LISREL and AMOS standardize by dividing the covariances by their standard errors.

4. Near the end of this section of the output is a wide assortment of fit indices. They will receive a deeper explanation in the next section.
5. Next is Cronbach's α. As you may have guessed, this is based on the assumption that all measured variables are indicators of one and the same latent variable. As this is obviously not the case, it is difficult to see how to use this information.
6. Last in the output is a summary of the iteration process. 'Parameter Abs Change' is a measure of the average change in the values of all estimated parameters at that iteration, and 'Function' is the value of the function (called F in Section 4.3) to be minimized. Both these measures should be gradually smaller through the process, and the changes from iteration to iteration should also be smaller and smaller. If this is not the general picture, it indicates iteration problems, and so do values other than 1.00 for 'Alpha'. See Bentler (2006).

Table 2 Example 5.2: output section 2 – model fit

```
RESIDUAL COVARIANCE MATRIX   (S-SIGMA) :                                          (1)


                      ANOMIA67    POWRLS67    ANOMIA71    POWRLS71
                        V1          V2          V3          V4
       ANOMIA67  V1     .000
       POWRLS67  V2     .000        .000
       ANOMIA71  V3     .000        .000        .000
       POWRLS71  V4     .000        .000       4.282        .000

                          AVERAGE ABSOLUTE RESIDUAL    =        .4282
                  AVERAGE OFF-DIAGONAL ABSOLUTE RESIDUAL =      .7137



STANDARDIZED RESIDUAL MATRIX:


                      ANOMIA67    POWRLS67    ANOMIA71    POWRLS71
                        V1          V2          V3          V4
       ANOMIA67  V1     .000
       POWRLS67  V2     .000        .000
       ANOMIA71  V3     .000        .000        .000
       POWRLS71  V4     .000        .000        .383        .000

                 AVERAGE ABSOLUTE STANDARDIZED RESIDUAL    =    .0383
         AVERAGE OFF-DIAGONAL ABSOLUTE STANDARDIZED RESIDUAL =  .0638


MAXIMUM LIKELIHOOD SOLUTION (NORMAL DISTRIBUTION THEORY)


LARGEST STANDARDIZED RESIDUALS:                                                   (2)

         NO.     PARAMETER    ESTIMATE
         ---     ---------    --------
          1      V4,   V3       .383
          2      V4,   V2       .000
          3      V3,   V2       .000
          4      V4,   V1       .000
          5      V3,   V3       .000
          6      V1,   V1       .000
          7      V3,   V1       .000
```

```
         8         V2,  V2           .000
         9         V2,  V1           .000
        10         V4,  V4           .000
```

DISTRIBUTION OF STANDARDIZED RESIDUALS

```
    ---------------------------------
    !                               !
 20-                                -
    !                               !
    !                               !
    !                               !
    !                               !                RANGE        FREQ PERCENT
 15-                                -
    !                               !        1   -0.5   -  --       0    .00%
    !                               !        2   -0.4   - -0.5      0    .00%
    !                               !        3   -0.3   - -0.4      0    .00%
    !                               !        4   -0.2   - -0.3      0    .00%
 10-                                -        5   -0.1   - -0.2      0    .00%
    !             *                 !        6    0.0   - -0.1      0    .00%
    !             *                 !        7    0.1   -  0.0      9  90.00%
    !             *                 !        8    0.2   -  0.1      0    .00%
    !             *                 !        9    0.3   -  0.2      0    .00%
  5-             *                  -        A    0.4   -  0.3      1  10.00%
    !             *                 !        B    0.5   -  0.4      0    .00%
    !             *                 !        C    ++    -  0.5      0    .00%
    !             *                 !       -------------------------------
    !             *       *         !               TOTAL           10 100.00%
    ---------------------------------
       1 2 3 4 5 6 7 8 9 A B C             EACH "*" REPRESENTS     1 RESIDUALS
```

MAXIMUM LIKELIHOOD SOLUTION (NORMAL DISTRIBUTION THEORY)

GOODNESS OF FIT SUMMARY FOR METHOD = ML

INDEPENDENCE MODEL CHI-SQUARE   =   1563.944 ON   6 DEGREES OF FREEDOM

INDEPENDENCE AIC =   1551.944   INDEPENDENCE CAIC =   1516.920
       MODEL AIC =   339.863   MODEL CAIC =   334.026

CHI-SQUARE =   341.863 BASED ON   1 DEGREES OF FREEDOM   (3)
PROBABILITY VALUE FOR THE CHI-SQUARE STATISTIC IS   .00000

THE NORMAL THEORY RLS CHI-SQUARE FOR THIS ML SOLUTION IS   286.123.

FIT INDICES   (4)

BENTLER-BONETT   NORMED   FIT INDEX =   .781
BENTLER-BONETT NON-NORMED   FIT INDEX =   -.313
COMPARATIVE FIT INDEX (CFI)   =   .781
BOLLEN'S   (IFI) FIT INDEX   =   .782
MCDONALD'S   (MFI) FIT INDEX   =   .833
JORESKOG-SORBOM'S GFI   FIT INDEX   =   .867
JORESKOG-SORBOM'S AGFI   FIT INDEX   =   -.332
ROOT MEAN-SQUARE RESIDUAL (RMR)   =   1.354
STANDARDIZED RMR   =   .121
ROOT MEAN-SQUARE ERROR OF APPROXIMATION (RMSEA)   =   .605
90% CONFIDENCE INTERVAL OF RMSEA   (.551,   .659)

(Continued)

Table 2 (Continued)

```
RELIABILITY COEFFICIENTS                                                      (5)
------------------------
CRONBACH'S ALPHA                        =       .831


                        ITERATIVE SUMMARY                                     (6)
                PARAMETER
ITERATION       ABS CHANGE          ALPHA               FUNCTION
    1           3.283068            1.00000             1.31707
    2           3.752208            1.00000              .36720
    3            .000041            1.00000              .36720
```

2 Fit Indices

As pointed out earlier, the χ^2-test has the weakness that if the sample is sufficiently small we will accept any model, and if it is sufficiently large any model will be rejected. To put it precisely, we test a hypothesis that we know a priori is false – and if the sample is large enough, the test will show what we expect it to show.

In order to overcome this problem a large number of fit indices have been constructed to help evaluate the extent to which the model is supported by the data (see Table 3). Some of these indices take on values in the interval 0.00–1.00 and, just like a determination coefficient, the closer to 1.00, the better the fit. However, a coefficient of determination has the advantage of a certain interpretation, i.e. as the share of the variance of a dependent variable that can be 'explained' by one or more independent variables. Unfortunately most fit indices lack such an interpretation, so only experience will tell us what is necessary for a specific fit index to show a good fit.

Fit indices are different ways of expressing the 'distance' between the sample covariance matrix $\mathbf{S}$ and the estimated implied covariance matrix $\Sigma(\hat{\theta})$, i.e. they are functions of the residual matrix $\mathbf{S} - \Sigma(\hat{\theta})$. But how do we measure this distance and express it in one number only?

As is evident from Table 2, this can be done in several ways. The many fit measures can be classified as in Table 3.

Table 3 Fit measures in EQS

Absolute Fit Measures	Relative Fit Measures	Fit Measures Based on the Non-Central Chi-Square Distribution	Information Theoretic Fit Measures
GFI	NFI	RMSEA	AIC
AGFI	NNFI	MFI	CAIC
RMR	CFI		
SRMR	IFI		

Absolute fit measures judge the fit of a model *per se* without reference to other models that could be relevant in the situation. This means that there is no standard or basis relative to which the actual model could be judged, for, again, as Fisher says: 'Nothing is good or bad but by comparison'. In a way you could say that a model is judged relative to no model at all.

Relative fit measures judge the fit of 'your' model relative to some standard. But which standard should we choose?

Usually the so-called 'independence model' is used. This model stipulates zero correlation among the manifest variables, and you could say that it is a rather unrealistic model, but it fulfills its purpose: to be a reference model in judging the fit of 'your' model.

Fit measures based on the non-central chi-square distribution have as their starting point the fact that no model is 'correct' – it can only be 'approximately correct'.

Information theoretic fit measures are not used for judging the fit of a single model, but are used in situations where you have to choose among several realistic but different models.

Information theoretic fit measures

First in the 'Goodness of fit summary' in Table 2 you meet the χ^2-values of the independence model and of 'your' model. These two chi-squares that are building blocks in several fit indices are designated χ^2_{indep} and χ^2_M in the following.

After the independence model chi-square, you then meet the two information-based fit measures AIC (Akaike Information Criterion (Akaike, 1973, 1987)) and CAIC (Consistent AIC, (Bozdogan, 1987)). These are also shown for both your model and the independence model.

These fit measures are both based on the idea of expressing the extent to which the present model will cross-validate with future samples of the same size from the same population. Also they both reward parsimony: you cannot get a better fit measure by just introducing more parameters and making the model more complex. Another common feature is that small *numerical* values are to be preferred, but that the measures have no upper (*numerical*) limit and therefore these fit measures are primarily used as a basis for choosing among several substantively meaningful models.

CAIC is a reformulation of AIC, carrying a greater penalty for model complexity.

It is worth mentioning that various SEM programs calculate these measures in different ways. For example, EQS calculates AIC as $\chi^2 - 2$(degrees of freedom) and LISREL and AMOS use the formula $\chi^2 + 2$(number of parameters). Whereas the first expression is always negative and the second always positive, the same rule applies: values nearer to zero are preferred.

Relative fit measures

As the saturated model (with zero degrees of freedom) has maximum fit and the independence model has the maximum number of constraints and consequently minimum fit, these two models indicate the limits between which 'your' model is placed.

You can therefore evaluate a model by looking at its 'location' between these two extremes.

You could, for example, calculate how far along the way from the independence model to the perfect fitting model 'your' model M has 'traveled':

$$\text{NFI} = \frac{\chi^2_{indp} - \chi^2_M}{\chi^2_{indp}} = \frac{1563.944 - 341.863}{1563.944} = 0.781 \qquad (3)$$

This is the so-called *Normed Fit Index* (Bentler & Bonnett, 1980), which is bounded within the interval 0–1.00.

Next is the *Non-Normed Fit Index* (NNFI), a variant of NFI that takes the degrees of freedom into account, and thereby 'punishes' over-fitting and also improves the behavior of the index near its upper limit.

In this case NNFI is negative, which should mean that not only is the model bad, but also it is worse than no model at all! This of course is nonsense. Negative values of NNFI are rare, but the fact that they can occur is a weakness of this index.

NFI has been used as a standard for many years, but because it has shown a tendency to underestimate the fit in small samples, it has been modified into CFI (*Comparative Fit Index* (Bentler, 1990)), which also takes the degrees of freedom into consideration:

$$\begin{aligned}\text{CFI} &= \frac{(\chi^2_{indp} - df_{indp}) - (\chi^2_M - df_M)}{(\chi^2_{indp} - df_{indp})} \\ &= \frac{(1563.944 - 6) - (341.863 - 1)}{1563.944 - 6} = 0.781\end{aligned} \qquad (4)$$

NFI- and CFI-values larger than 0.95 are usually taken as an indication of a good fit.

It is worth noting that if $\chi^2_M < f_M$ then CFI > 1.000, but CFI is reported as 1.000 in the output. Therefore CFI = 1.000 is not an indication of a perfect fit, but only indicates that $\chi^2_M < f_M$.

IFI (*Incremental Fit Index*) also include the degrees of freedom: IFI is derived from NFI by subtracting the degrees of freedom for the independence model in the denominator.

I will postpone discussion of the next fit index (MFI), and go on with the next four indices that all come under the same heading of absolute fit indices.

Absolute fit measures

The first is GFI, the classical *Goodness of Fit Index* introduced in LISREL many years ago. This index is calculated as

$$\text{GFI} = 1 - \frac{\text{minimum of the fit function after the model has been fitted}}{\text{the fit function before any model has been fitted}} \qquad (5)$$

It has been proposed that GFI is analogous to R^2 in multiple regression (see Appendix A) and, just like R^2, GFI takes on values between 0 and 1.00.

If GFI is adjusted for the number of degrees of freedom compared with the number of parameters, this gives AGFI (*Adjusted Goodness of Fit Index*), which rewards models with fewer parameters. In this case AGFI is negative just like NNFI.

The fit is expressed in the residual covariance matrix. Analogous to the standard deviation, we could compute the *root mean-square residual*:

$$\text{RMR} = \sqrt{\frac{(sum)^2}{p(p+1)/2}} = \sqrt{\frac{2(sum)^2}{p(p+1)}} \qquad (6)$$

where '*sum*' represents the sum of all non-redundant elements in the residual covariance matrix.

Now, the size of this expression depends on the units of measurement for the various variables, so that it is more relevant to carry out an analogous calculation based on the residual correlation matrix. This is shown next as 'Standardized RMR'. Usually an RMR (based on correlations) of less than 0.05 is taken as a sign of a good fit.

Fit Indices based on the non-central χ^2-distribution

As mentioned at the beginning of this section, the main reason for the introduction of many fit measures is that the global χ^2-test is a test of a null hypothesis that we a priori know is false: that our model is 100% correct.

As any model is only 'approximately true', $C=(n-1)F_{min}$ is actually distributed according to *the non-central χ^2-distribution with non-centrality parameter*

$$\delta = \chi^2 - df \qquad (7a)$$

As you will perhaps remember from your introductory statistics course, the expected value of the 'ordinary' χ^2-distribution is equal to the degrees of freedom, so δ measures how far the actual χ^2-distribution is from the one that would be a result of the test of a true model.

The ordinary χ^2-distribution (the central distribution) is thus a special variant of the non-central distribution with $\delta = 0$. The more 'wrong' our model, the larger the value of δ. Consequently, small values of δ are to be preferred, so δ is estimated as

$$\hat{\delta} = \max[C_{min} - df, 0] \qquad (7b)$$

Therefore $\hat{\delta} = 0$ does not indicate a perfect fit, only that $C_{min} < df$ (cf. the remarks in connection with (4)).

McDonald's Fit Index (MFI) (McDonald, 1989) is defined as

$$\text{MFI} = e^{-.5\hat{\delta}/n} \qquad (8)$$

Usually, MFI larger than 0.90 is taken as a sign of a good fit (but MFI could be larger than 1.00 due to sampling error).

The *root mean-square error of approximation* (Steiger & Lind, 1980) takes care of this problem by introducing the number of degrees of freedom:

$$\text{RMSEA} = \sqrt{\frac{\hat{\delta}}{n\,df}} \qquad (9)$$

Lower and upper 90% confidence limits are also shown in the output. Usually, RMSEA around 0.05 is considered a sign of a good fit, and models and values larger than 0.10 should not be accepted.

Remember that I demanded all the fit measures be printed. If I had not, only the following default measures would be shown: AIC, CAIC, NFI, NNFI, CFI.

Last in the output is a description of the iterations that have led to the estimated model. It should have few steps. If the process does not converge within the default number of steps (30), you should specify start values and not just increase the number of steps.

What indices should I report?

With so many fit indices to choose from, this question is not irrelevant.

As indices that are placed in the same group in Table 3 measure about the same aspect of model fit, the question boils down to choosing the best fit index from each group. My suggestion is that you should report the χ^2 with degrees of freedom and *P*-value and RMSEA with confidence interval. If you compare *non-nested models* (see Example 7.1 for a definition of *nested* models) these indices can be supplemented with one of the information theoretic fit measures – the most used is perhaps AIC.

If you want to report a relative fit measure I would suggest the use of CFI, but these measures have the common weakness that the baseline model is the very unrealistic independence model.

A common problem with most indices is that their sampling distribution is unknown. This means that decisions on whether the size of a fit index is satisfying is based on rules of thumb obtained through experience and by computer simulations.

Also, always remember that fit measures are measures of the *average* fit of the model to the data. Even if this general fit seems to be OK, the model could still have a bad fit in local places. Therefore be careful in checking the standard errors of the various parameters, and the coefficients of determination.

In this connection I should like to point out that in covariance-based SEM we are *not* predicting the dependent variables – we are predicting the covariance matrix. Therefore covariance-based SEM does not minimize the error variances. If you are more interested in making predictions than in explaining covariances, you should use another SEM methodology called *partial least squares*, invented by Wold (1975). For an introduction, see Fornell and Cha (1994). A deeper treatment with many examples can be found in Vinzi, Chin, Henseler, and Wang (2010). The newest textbook is by Hair, Hult, and Ringle (2014).

What can we conclude?

Now let us take a look at the third part of the output in Table 4, showing the estimates of the model's parameters.

As is evident from Figure 2, our model states that the covariance between Anomia71 and Powerlessness71 can be explained as a result of Anomia67 and Powerlessness67.

This hypothesis cannot be maintained, as a χ^2-value of about 342 is significant by any reasonable criterion – even if the sample is 'large'.

As mentioned earlier, the usual remedy in such a case, i.e. to introduce additional parameters, is not possible here. The only way to do so would be to allow E3 and E4 to correlate, and this would eat up our only degree of freedom, after which we would be left with a just-identified, i.e. a non-testable, model.

Nevertheless, let us take a look at the parameter estimates as given in Table 4.

All coefficients are statistically significant according to traditional criteria, and anomia seems to be slightly more stable than powerlessness. The two cross-effects are small and not very different in their standardized form. However, these conclusions must be taken with a pinch of salt, as they are based on an incorrect model.

As it is impossible to patch up the model, I will (in Chapter 8) construct a new one based on latent variables.

Table 4 Example 2: output section 3 – parameter estimates

```
MAXIMUM LIKELIHOOD SOLUTION (NORMAL DISTRIBUTION THEORY)


  MEASUREMENT EQUATIONS WITH STANDARD ERRORS AND TEST STATISTICS
  STATISTICS SIGNIFICANT AT THE 5% LEVEL ARE MARKED WITH @.

  ANOMIA71=V3   =      .455*V1     +    .206*V2    + 1.000 E3
                       .037             .041
                     12.407@           4.988@

  POWRLS71=V4   =      .158*V1     +    .420*V2    + 1.000 E4
                       .034             .038
                      4.658@           11.042@

MAXIMUM LIKELIHOOD SOLUTION (NORMAL DISTRIBUTION THEORY)

  VARIANCES OF INDEPENDENT VARIABLES
  ----------------------------------
  STATISTICS SIGNIFICANT AT THE 5% LEVEL ARE MARKED WITH @.

                       V                                F
                      ---                              ---
  V1  -ANOMIA67      11.834*I                           I
                       .548 I                           I
                     21.575@I                           I
                          I                             I
  V2  -POWRLS67       9.364*I                           I
                       .434 I                           I
                     21.575@I                           I
                          I                             I

MAXIMUM LIKELIHOOD SOLUTION (NORMAL DISTRIBUTION THEORY)

  VARIANCES OF INDEPENDENT VARIABLES
  ----------------------------------
  STATISTICS SIGNIFICANT AT THE 5% LEVEL ARE MARKED WITH @.

                       E                                D
                      ---                              ---
  E3  -ANOMIA71       8.379*I                           I
                       .388 I                           I
                     21.575@I                           I
                          I                             I
```

(Continued)

Table 4 (Continued)

```
E4   -POWRLS71                  7.120*I                              I
                                  .330 I                              I
                                21.575@I                              I
                                      I                              I

     MAXIMUM LIKELIHOOD SOLUTION (NORMAL DISTRIBUTION THEORY)

     COVARIANCES AMONG INDEPENDENT VARIABLES
     ---------------------------------------
     STATISTICS SIGNIFICANT AT THE 5% LEVEL ARE MARKED WITH @.

                         V                                    F
                        ---                                  ---
V2   -POWRLS67                  6.947*I                              I
V1   -ANOMIA67                   .413 I                              I
                                16.806@I                              I
                                      I                              I

     MAXIMUM LIKELIHOOD SOLUTION (NORMAL DISTRIBUTION THEORY)


     STANDARDIZED SOLUTION:                                    R-SQUARED


ANOMIA71=V3  =   .443*V1   +   .178*V2   +   .818 E3            .331
POWRLS71=V4  =   .172*V1   +   .407*V2   +   .844 E4            .287

     MAXIMUM LIKELIHOOD SOLUTION (NORMAL DISTRIBUTION THEORY)

     CORRELATIONS AMONG INDEPENDENT VARIABLES
     ----------------------------------------

                         V                                    F
                        ---                                  ---
V2   -POWRLS67                   .660*I                              I
V1   -ANOMIA67                        I                              I
                                      I                              I
```

Compact output

As is evident from Table 4, the last part of the output with parameter estimates takes up a lot of space even in this simple model. When reporting your findings in a journal article you can be sure that the editor will ask you to help by not wasting valuable paper just to present a lot of white space.

Luckily you only have to add the following statement in the /PRINT paragraph:

TA=COMPACT

Where TA is short for TABLE to get the parameter estimates and test statistics presented as in Table 5.

I will from now on present this part of the output in compact form – and for the same reason as the editor mentioned above!

Table 5 Example 2 (continued): output section 3 in compact form

```
PARAMETER ESTIMATES (B) WITH STANDARD ERRORS AND TEST STATISTICS (Z)
STATISTICS SIGNIFICANT AT THE 5% LEVEL ARE MARKED WITH @.

                                                              R-
DEP.VAR.       PREDICTOR        B        BETA    S.E.      Z        SQUARED
-----------------------------------------------------------------

   V3  (ANOMIA71)                                                    .331
           V1  (ANOMIA67)     .455*     .443    .037    12.407@
           V2  (POWRLS67)     .206*     .178    .041     4.988@
           E3  (ANOMIA71)    1.000      .818

   V4  (POWRLS71)                                                    .287
           V1  (ANOMIA67)     .158*     .172    .034     4.658@
           V2  (POWRLS67)     .420*     .407    .038    11.042@
           E4  (POWRLS71)    1.000      .844


VARIANCES OF INDEPENDENT VARIABLES
STATISTICS SIGNIFICANT AT THE 5% LEVEL ARE MARKED WITH @.


                              VARIANCE      S.E.      Z
------------------------------------------------------

VARIABLE
           V1  (ANOMIA67) 11.834*         .548    21.575@
           V2  (POWRLS67)  9.364*         .434    21.575@

ERROR
           E3  (ANOMIA71)  8.379*         .388    21.575@
           E4  (POWRLS71)  7.120*         .330    21.575@

COVARIANCES AMONG INDEPENDENT VARIABLES
STATISTICS SIGNIFICANT AT THE 5% LEVEL ARE MARKED WITH @.

                             COVA.       S.E.       Z               CORR.
-----------------------------------------------------------------

   V1,V2  (ANOMIA67,POWRLS67)  6.947*    .413    16.806@            .660
```

Programming using 'Diagrammer'/Path Model

In Figure 4 you will see the data, which you can find on the book's website under the name 'Wheaton.ess'.

Click the 'Diagrammer' icon and in the window in Figure 5.12b select 'Path Model' and the window in Figure 5a will appear.

Select 'anomia71' and, by clicking the upper little arrow, copy it to 'Dependent Variable' as shown in panel (b). Then, select 'anomia67' and 'power67', and by clicking the lower little arrow copy them to 'Its Predictors' as shown in panel (c). Then select 'Add', and the variables will be moved to the 'Path Model' as shown in panel (d).

Now, repeat the procedure selecting 'power71' as the dependent variable, and 'anomia67' and 'power67' as independent variables. Then when you click 'OK' the window in Figure 6 will appear – and you have finished your programming.

138   *Chapter 6* Models with Only Manifest Variables

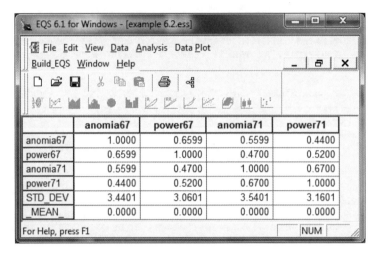

Figure 4   Example 2: input data (*.ess file)

As usual, run the program by selecting 'Build EQS/Run EQS'.

(a)

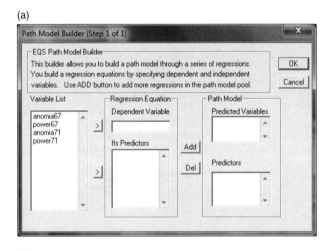

(b)

(c)

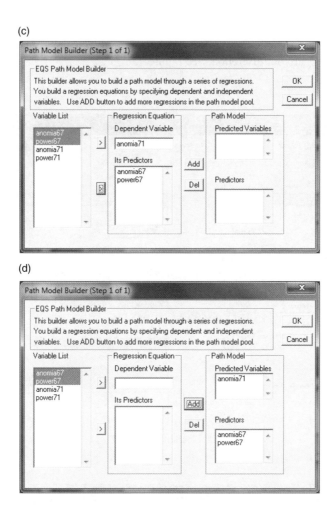

(d)

Figure 5 Example 2: programming in 'Diagrammer

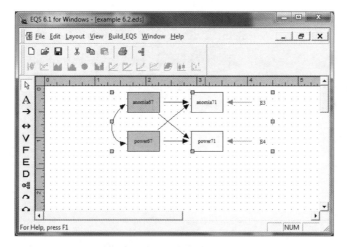

Figure 6 Example 2: the finished model

When you use 'Diagrammer' you can have the output printed in the model window. From the roll-down menus choose 'View/Estimates' and then choose 'un-standardized' or 'standardized' at your discretion. See Figure 7.

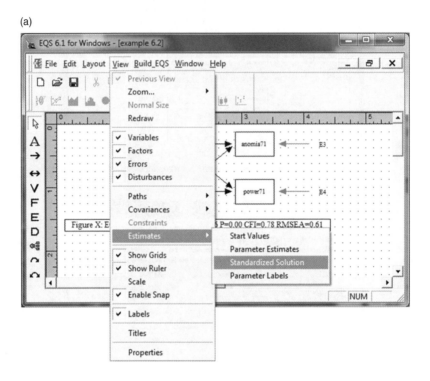

Figure 7 Example 2: placing output in the model window

3 The Identification Problem in Cyclic Models

In cyclic models identification problems arise more often than in acyclic models, and it is generally more difficult to judge whether a model is identified or not by inspection or the use of simple rules.

This is easily demonstrated using the Bass example we met in Figure 1.7c, which is repeated in Figure 8 with the missing disturbance terms added. From the figure we see that sales of filter cigarettes (Y_1) depend on advertising for filter cigarettes (Y_3) – which is of course the very purpose of advertising – but at the same time (Y_3) could also depend on (Y_1) through advertising budgeting routines. How is it possible to map such relationships? Can we analytically separate the two functions and identify them?

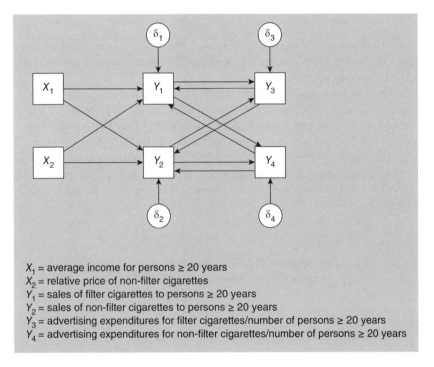

X_1 = average income for persons ≥ 20 years
X_2 = relative price of non-filter cigarettes
Y_1 = sales of filter cigarettes to persons ≥ 20 years
Y_2 = sales of non-filter cigarettes to persons ≥ 20 years
Y_3 = advertising expenditures for filter cigarettes/number of persons ≥ 20 years
Y_4 = advertising expenditures for non-filter cigarettes/number of persons ≥ 20 years

Figure 8 Cyclic causal model

Example 3
Mapping the effectiveness of advertising

Imagine you have collected data on sales and advertising over a long period of time.

The time series data can be graphed as shown in Figure 9. The observations form a nearly straight line and thus indicate a strong relationship between the two variables (for simplicity only four points are shown). The question, however, is: 'Is it the sales function $S = f_s(A)$ or the budget function $A = f_A(S)$ that is depicted in the figure?

Now, any observation in Figure 9 must lie on both the sales curve and the advertising curve, which means that, except for 'noise', the observations must be placed at the intersections of the two curves.

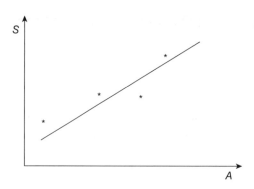

Figure 9 Example 3: scattergram of sales revenue S and advertising budget A

Figure 10 shows four possible situations with the 'true' functions marked. In reality, of course, we never know the exact position of the 'true' curves, because then there would be no need to estimate them.

In Figure 10a both functions were stable during the period covered by our data. Consequently, our observations are all clustered around the intersection of the curves, and they do not give us any information on the location of the two curves.

In panel (b) of the figure the budget function was stable in the period, while the sales function moved around, influenced by variables other than advertising. As a result of this the budget function can be identified. If instead the budget function had moved while the sales function had been stable, the sales function would have been identified.

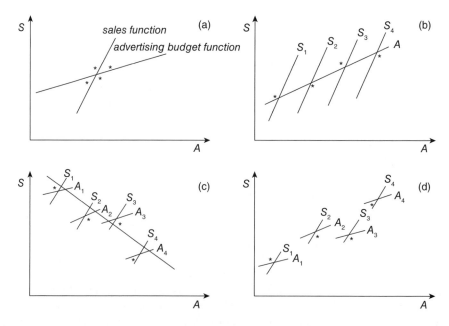

Figure 10 Example 3: the identification problem

In panel (c) both curves have moved, and consequently the points depict only the intersections of the two functions and say nothing about their location. However, the points run from northwest to southeast, so the analyst would hardly believe that the sales function has been located – if that was the purpose.

In panel (d), however, such a misinterpretation is more likely. But as you will know by now, if there is a two-way causation the points will mirror only the intersections of the curves and say nothing about their slopes.

To identify the functions in the model we must add to our model variables that can change the position of the functions, such as those shown in Figures 10b–d.

A necessary condition for identification: the order condition

Writing the sales function and the advertising budget function as

$$S = \beta_{S0} + \beta_{S1}A + \varepsilon_S \tag{10a}$$

$$A = \beta_{A0} + \beta_{A1}S + \delta_A \tag{10b}$$

it is easy to see that the problem is that we have two linear functions with exactly the same variables. Such functions are impossible to separate (identify) empirically (cf. Chapter 4's Equations 6(a) and 6(b)).

To identify a function we must add one or more variables to our model, the value of which is not determined within the model – that is, we must add exogenous variables.

If we add income, I, to Equation (10a), we get

$$S = \beta_{S0} + \beta_{S1}A + \beta_{S2}I + \delta_S \tag{11a}$$

$$A = \beta_{A0} + \beta_{A1}S + \delta_A \tag{11b}$$

As variations in I will cause the function (10a) to move, it is natural to assume that including I in (10a) will lead to identification of (10b). This is actually the case (cf. Figure 10b).

The model (11) comprises three variables: two endogenous variables (S and A) and one exogenous variable (I). If the number of exogenous variables not included in an equation is one less than the number of endogenous variables in that equation, the equation is *just-identified*. If there are fewer, the equation is *under-identified*, and if there are more, it is *over-identified*. This is the so-called *order condition*, which is necessary but not sufficient.

A sufficient condition for (11b) to be identified is that the coefficient β_{S2} is different from zero. This is the so-called *rank condition*, which for the two-equation model can be stated as follows: a necessary and sufficient condition for identification of an equation in a two-equation model is that the other equation contains at least one exogenous variable with a non-zero coefficient that is excluded from the equation in question. So identification depends not only on the structure of the model, but (unfortunately) also on parameter values.

Now, the sales function is probably of greater interest than the budget function, and to identify the former it is necessary to include in (11b) one or more exogenous variables that do not affect sales. This, however, is not as easy as it sounds, because most variables you could take into consideration when deciding how much to spend on advertising would also influence sales: namely, price of the product, degree of distribution, etc. A possible solution is to include the price of advertising.

The general order condition
If we have more than two equations in our model, the order condition is a little more complicated and can be stated as follows: a *necessary* condition for an equation to be identified is that the number of excluded *exogenous* variables is at least as large as the number of *endogenous* variables on the right hand side.

Let us use this rule on the model in Figure 8:

	Left-hand variable	Right-hand endogenous variables	Excluded exogenous variables	
Equation 1	Y_1	Y_3 Y_4	none	underidentified
Equation 2	Y_2	Y_3 Y_4	none	underidentified
Equation 3	Y_3	Y_1 Y_2	X_1 X_2	just-identified
Equation 4	Y_4	Y_1 Y_2	X_1 X_2	just-identified

We can see that only the budget functions are identified.

If these are the functions you are interested in, and equations 1 and 2 are only there to identify them, then of course that is OK and you can estimate functions 3 and 4 – but not using EQS. Unfortunately, EQS will not estimate part of a model. If just one parameter in a model is unidentified, EQS will give a warning and stop the calculation. Bass (partly) solved the identification problems by using two-stage least squares estimation – a limited information method not currently available in EQS.

If at all possible, you should examine the identification status of your model before you collect data, so that you can add the number of exogenous variables required to obtain identification.

A sufficient condition: the rank condition
As mentioned earlier, the order condition is only necessary but not sufficient. The reason is that the variables introduced in order to obtain identification must be independent of each other. If we introduce a variable which covaries with another already in the model, the new one will to a larger or smaller degree repeat information that we already have.

An exact formulation of the (general) rank condition is beyond the scope of this book (but for a simple explanation see e.g. Brown, 1991) because it is based on matrix algebra, but fortunately it is rare in practice to find a model that meets the order condition but does not also meet the rank condition.

4 What Does Two-Way Causation Really Mean?

In a model based on experimental data there is no doubt about the direction of the arrows: they point from the manipulated variables, and it is absurd to think about letting them point in the opposite direction. In models based on non-experimental data you may sometimes have your doubts as to the causal direction. Unfortunately, this subject

6.4 What Does Two-Way Causation Really Mean?

is rather poorly treated in the literature – but take a look at Davis (1985). However, some guidance can be found in the following two 'rules':

1. Cause is prior to effect.
2. Causes are often variables whose values are more stable than effects.

Nevertheless, you may often feel tempted to draw the arrows in both directions, and then end up with a cyclic model with all its complications.

What does a two-way causation really mean? Is it not absurd to think of letting A have an effect on B, and at the same time letting B have an effect on A? At the very least you should expect some delay, so that A 'now' affects B 'a little later' and then B affects A again 'a bit later', because, as Hume formulated it, cause precedes effect.

If we accept this premise, the model in Figure 11b should be substituted for the model in 11a. All cyclic causal models are absurd and all realistic models are – or should be – acyclic!

Formally this is correct, but if the time period in Figure 11b is measured in months and we only have quarterly data, then both cause and effect will take place within one (data) time period. In other words, the length of the data time period compared with the reaction time will determine whether we end up with a cyclic or an acyclic model.

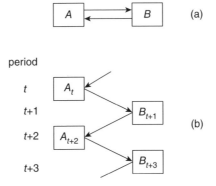

Figure 11 Cyclic and acyclic models

Example 3 (continued)
Mapping the effectiveness of advertising

If advertising affects sales in the same year while the budget is based on sales in the previous year, and we have yearly data, then Equations (10a) and (10b) can be written as

$$S_t = \beta_{S0} + \beta_{S1}A_t + \delta_S \tag{12a}$$

$$A_t = \beta_{A0} + \beta_{A1}S_{t-1} + \delta_A \tag{12b}$$

If you assume the error terms to be uncorrelated across the two equations, you will have a recursive system: S_{t-1} is pre-determined in Equation (12b), and A_t is predetermined in (12a), where S_t is the only post-determined variable.

If you have data only for two-year periods, you have to fall back on a cyclic model.

A final piece of advice

In the large majority of cases you will build your model on cross-sectional data, and then of course a cyclic model will be the only possible choice if you have reciprocal causation.

Now, it is clear from Figure 11b that two-way causation is a *dynamic* process, and we can think of each of the two effects in Figure 11a as the sum of an infinite series of loops. Only in cases where the two sums are defined, i.e. where the corresponding series converge, is it possible to estimate the two effects.

However, such estimates only make sense if the process in reality has gone through the whole process and brought it to an end. This is a rather hard assumption that is difficult (if not impossible) to judge.

As you can see, cyclic models are much more complicated than non-cyclic models. This is true both as far as identification and estimation are concerned and when it comes to the substantive interpretation and recommendations based on the model.

Therefore, a final piece of advice would be: if at all possible, avoid cyclic models.

I will, however, present a single example of a cyclic model with only manifest variables in Chapter 9.

In this chapter you met the following concepts:

- the zero B-rule and the recursive rule for identification in acyclic models
- the order condition and the rank condition for identification in cyclic models
- a wide range of fit indices:
- absolute fit measures
- relative fit measures
- fit measures based on the non-central χ^2-distribution
- information theoretic fit measures

You have also been introduced to the /PRINT paragraph and learned the following EQS statements:

```
FIT=ALL            TABLE=COMPACT
```

Questions

1. Explain the identification rules in your own words.

2. What characterizes each of the six groups of fit indices?

3. What are the numerical requirements usually used as rules of thumb in connection with the various indices?

4. Using examples from your own field of study or research, discuss the various problems raised by using cyclic models.

References

Aaker, D. A., & Day, D. A. (1971). A recursive model of communication processes. In D. A. Aaker (Ed.), *Multivariate analysis in marketing* (pp. 33–40). Belmont, CA: Wadsworth.

Akaike, H. (1973). Information theory and an extension of the maximum likelihood principle. Paper presented at the Proceedings of the 2nd International Symposium on Information Theory, Budapest.

Akaike, H. (1987). Factor analysis and AIC. *Psychometrika, 52*, 317–332.

Bentler, P. M. (1990). Comparative fit indexes in structural models. *Psychological Bulletin, 107*, 238–246.

Bentler, P. M. (1995). *EQS structural equations manual*. Encino, CA: Multivariate Software, Inc.

Bentler, P. M. (2006). *EQS 6 Structural equations program manual*. Encino, CA: Multivariate Software, Inc.

Bentler, P. M., & Bonnett, D. G. (1980). Significance tests and goodness of fit in the analysis of covariance structures. *Psychological Bulletin, 88*, 588–606.

Bozdogan, H. (1987). Model selection and Akaike's information criterion (AIC): The general theory and its analytical extensions. *Psychometrika, 52*, 345–370.

Brown, W. S. (1991). *Introducing econometrics*. St Paul, MN: West Publishing.

Browne, M. W. (2009). Path analysis (RAMONA). *SYSTAT 13 – Statistics III*. Chicago: SYSTAT Software Inc.

Davis, J. A. (1985). *The logic of causal order*. Beverly Hills, CA: Sage.

Fornell, C., & Cha, J. (1994). Partial least squares. In P. Bagozzi (Ed.), *Advanced methods of marketing research*. Oxford: Blackwell.

Hair, J. F., Hult, G. T. M., & Ringle, C. (2014). *A primer on least squares structural equation modeling*. Thousand Oaks, CA: Sage.

Jöreskog, K. G., & Sörbom, D. (1984). *LISREL 7: A guide to programs and applications* (3rd ed.). Chicago: SPSS Inc.

McDonald, R. P. (1989). An index of goodness-of-fit based on noncentrality. *Journal of Classification, 6*, 97–103.

Steiger, J. H., & Lind, J. C. (1980). *Statistically based tests for the number of common factors*. Paper presented at the Annual Meeting of the Psychometric Society, Iowa City, IA.

Vinzi, V. E., Chin, W. W., Henseler, J., & Wang, H. (2010). *Handbook of partial least squares: Concepts, methods and applications in marketing and related fields*. New York: Springer.

Wheaton, B., Muthén, B., Alwin, D. F., & Summers, G. F. (1977). Assessing reliability and stability in panel models. In D. R. Heise (Ed.), *Sociological methodology* (pp. 84–136). San Francisco: Jossey Bass.

Wold, H. (1975). Path models with latent variables: The NIPALS approach. In H. M. Blalock (Ed.), *Quantitative sociology: International perspectives on mathematical and statistical modeling*. New York: Academic Press.

7

The Measurement Model in SEM: Confirmatory Factor Analysis

> We start by examining the differences between the three models, which are usually put under the common designation of factor analysis: namely, principal components analysis, exploratory factor analysis and confirmatory factor analysis – the latter being in fact the measurement model of SEM.
>
> Next, you will learn two rules for identification in confirmatory factor models and you will explore estimation of confirmatory factor models through a classic example. You will also learn how EQS can help you to obtain parsimony, i.e. to find as simple and uncomplicated (but still well-fitting) model as possible.
>
> Then you will learn how confirmatory factor analysis can be used to select items for inclusion in a measurement model or for use in a summated scale. You will also learn how to use SEM to measure reliability and validity in ways that are more in accordance with the theoretical definition of these concepts than those presented in Chapter 2.
>
> The chapter ends with a short discussion of reflective and formative indicators, and points to a problem in item selection that has often led researchers astray.

1 The Three Factor Models

In component analysis the components are linear functions of the original variables, whereas in factor analysis – whether exploratory or confirmatory – the roles are reversed: the variables are considered functions of latent variables called factors.

However, there are a number of important differences between exploratory factor analysis and confirmatory factor analysis.

In exploratory factor analysis:

1. Every manifest variable is connected with every latent variable (as in component analysis).
2. Error terms are uncorrelated.
3. All parameters are estimated from the data.

In confirmatory factor analysis some or all of the above rules are violated:

1. Manifest variables are only connected with some pre-specified latent variables, the ideal being that every manifest variable is an indicator for one and only one factor.

2. Some error terms may be allowed to correlate.
3. Some of the parameters may be restricted to certain values or to have the same values as other parameters, or they may be restricted to fulfill other conditions.

The differences among the three factor models are depicted in Figure 1 (it deserves mentioning that the component model and the exploratory factor model are shown prior to a possible rotation that could introduce correlations among the components or factors).

Comparing Figure 1 with Figure 1.5, it is obvious that the measurement model in SEM is a confirmatory factor model, and that it is this model that was the basis for the arguments against the classical methods of measuring reliability and validity in Chapter 2.

Remember that an indicator X_i can be:

- a single item in a many-item scale;
- a simple sum of several items, i.e. a summated scale; or
- a weighted sum of several items, e.g. a principal component.

Component Analysis

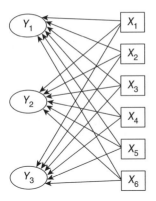

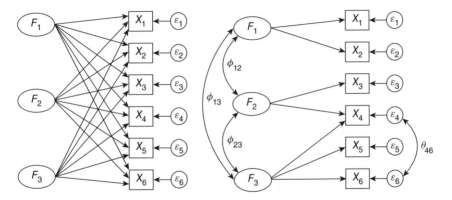

Figure 1 The three factor models

2 Identification and Estimation of Confirmatory Factor Models

In order to obtain identification every factor must be assigned a scale, either by fixing its variance or by fixing one of its regression coefficients; the same goes for the error terms. Further, the *t*-rule must be fulfilled but, as you have learned, this rule is only necessary, not sufficient.

Identification in confirmatory factor models

Two rules – both of which are sufficient, but not necessary – are worth mentioning (cf. Figure 4.2):

1. *The three-indicator rule*: A confirmatory factor model is identified if:

   (a) Every factor has at least three indicators.
   (b) No manifest variable is an indicator for more than one factor.
   (c) The error terms are not correlated.

2. *The two-indicator rule*: A confirmatory factor model with at least two factors is identified if:

   (a) Every factor has at least two indicators.
   (b) No manifest variable is an indicator for more than one factor.
   (c) The error terms are not correlated.
   (d) The covariance matrix for the latent variables does not contain zeros.

The main advantage of confirmatory models is that prior knowledge can be taken into account when formulating the model. Further, confirmatory models open up for various methods of testing the models.

Example 1
Democracy in developing countries

Bollen has published several studies on the determinants of democratic development (e.g. Bollen 1979, 1980). In this example I use data from Bollen (1989). The data given in Table 1 contain eight variables. The first four are indications of degree of democracy in 75 developing countries in 1960, the four variables being:

$V1$ = freedom of the press

$V2$ = freedom of group opposition

$V3$ = fairness of election

$V4$ = elective nature of the legislative body

The next four variables are the same variables measured the same way in 1965.

7.2 Identification and Estimation of Confirmatory Factor Models

Table 1 Example 1: covariance and means matrix

	V1	V2	V3	V4	V5	V6	V7	V8
V1	6.89							
V2	6.25	15.58						
V3	5.84	5.84	10.76					
V4	6.09	9.51	6.69	11.22				
V5	5.06	5.60	4.94	5.70	6.83			
V6	5.75	9.39	4.73	7.44	4.98	11.38		
V7	5.81	7.54	7.01	7.49	5.82	6.75	10.80	
V8	5.67	7.76	5.64	8.01	5.34	8.25	7.59	10.53
Means	5.46	4.26	6.56	4.45	5.14	2.98	6.20	4.04

A component analysis of the covariance matrix gives the first three eigenvalues as

$$57.17$$
$$8.47 \quad (1)$$
$$5.26$$

and presents a strong case for a one-component solution, although we know that in fact there are two sets of measurements, one for 1960 and one for 1965.

If we insist on a two-component solution, the component loadings (covariances) are (after a varimax rotation)

	F1	F2
V1	1.28	1.86
V2	3.53	0.96
V3	0.53	2.94
V4	2.23	1.94
V5	1.14	1.78
V6	2.79	1.09
V7	1.49	2.47
V8	2.12	1.80

(2)

where we see that the two components in no way represent the two time periods.

Of course you can try an oblique rotation (which will give a correlation of 0.63 between the two components), or use exploratory factor analysis instead of component analysis, but none of these techniques will separate the two time periods.

This shows the danger of letting the automatic use of exploratory methods lead you astray without theoretical considerations.

Now, let us see how such considerations can guide us:

1. We must maintain two factors, one expressing the degree of democracy in 1960 and the other the degree of democracy in 1965.
2. It is reasonable to assume that error terms in the same (manifest) measurement in the two years will correlate.
3. In the same way we will assume that the error terms for V2 and V4 (and V6 and V8) correlate, as these measurements are based on the same written source.

A model along these lines is shown in Figure 2.

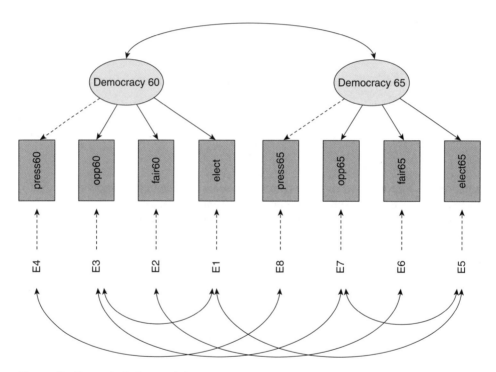

Figure 2 Example 1: the model

In order to estimate the model, two conditions must be satisfied:

1. We must create scales for the latent variables.
2. The model must be identified.

As mentioned earlier, the first condition can be met in two ways. The simpler way is to fix one of the regression coefficients for each factor to 1.00. This will transfer the scale of the indicator in question to its latent variable. Another possibility is to standardize the factors by fixing their variances to 1.00. On the screen the arrows connecting press60 and press65 to their respective factors are shown in red (as are the arrows connecting the E-variables to their manifest variables), signaling that I have chosen the first possibility.

Regarding point 2 above, we have 23 parameters to estimate:

$$6 \text{ coefficients}$$
$$7 \text{ covariances}$$
$$10 \text{ variances}$$

As input we have 8 variances and 28 covariances. We thus have 13 'pieces of information' or degrees of freedom left over for testing. The t-rule is satisfied. However, the three-indicator rule cannot be used because of the correlated error terms. So the model is *possibly* identified.

A program for estimation of the model is given in Table 2.

Table 2 Example 1: EQS program

```
/TITLE
   Example 7.1. First run. Data from Bollen 1989
/SPECIFICATIONS
   DATA='C:\Users\Sony\Desktop\EQS bog\EQS Chap 7\Bollen.ess';
   VARIABLES=8; CASES=75;
   METHOD=ML; ANALYSIS=COVARIANCE; MATRIX=COVARIANCE;
/LABELS
   V1=press60; V2=opp60; V3=fair60; V4=elect60; V5=press65;
   V6=opp65; V7=fair65; V8=elect65;
   F1=dem60; F2=dem65
/EQUATIONS
   V1 =    1F1 + E1;
   V2 =    *F1 + E2;
   V3 =    *F1 + E3;
   V4 =    *F1 + E4;
   V5 =    1F2 + E5;
   V6 =    *F2 + E6;
   V7 =    *F2 + E7;
   V8 =    *F2 + E8;
/VARIANCES
   F1 = *;
   F2 = *;
   E1 TO E8 = *;
/COVARIANCES
   F2,F1 = *;
   E4,E2 = *;
   E5,E1 = *;
   E6,E2 = *;
   E7,E3 = *;
   E8,E4 = *;
   E8,E6 = *;
/PRINT
   FIT=ALL;
   TABLE=COMPACT;
/END
```

The program format should be familiar to you by now. In the /SPECIFICATIONS paragraph I state that the data should be chosen from the EQS data file 'Bollen.ess' and ask for GLS estimation. No new commands are involved, so I do not expect you to have any trouble with the contents.

Table 3 shows selected output.

Table 3 Example 1: output from first run (extract)

STANDARDIZED RESIDUAL MATRIX: (1)

		PRESS60 V1	OPP60 V2	FAIR60 V3	ELECT60 V4	PRESS65 V5
PRESS60	V1	.001				
OPP60	V2	-.001	.014			
FAIR60	V3	.064	-.066	-.002		
ELECT60	V4	-.024	.018	-.004	.000	
PRESS65	V5	.002	.001	.026	.009	-.001
OPP65	V6	.038	.034	-.096	.048	-.025
FAIR65	V7	-.014	.002	-.014	-.006	.014
ELECT65	V8	-.012	.035	-.050	.017	-.025

		OPP65 V6	FAIR65 V7	ELECT65 V8
OPP65	V6	.010		
FAIR65	V7	-.022	-.003	
ELECT65	V8	.015	.013	.004

```
            AVERAGE ABSOLUTE STANDARDIZED RESIDUAL =              .0203
AVERAGE OFF-DIAGONAL ABSOLUTE STANDARDIZED RESIDUAL =              .0248

GOODNESS OF FIT SUMMARY FOR METHOD = ML

INDEPENDENCE MODEL CHI-SQUARE    =    454.661 ON  28 DEGREES OF FREEDOM

INDEPENDENCE AIC =     398.661    INDEPENDENCE CAIC =     305.771
       MODEL AIC =     -13.501           MODEL CAIC =     -56.628

CHI-SQUARE =       12.499 BASED ON    13 DEGREES OF FREEDOM          (2)
PROBABILITY VALUE FOR THE CHI-SQUARE STATISTIC IS          .48718

THE NORMAL THEORY RLS CHI-SQUARE FOR THIS ML SOLUTION IS       11.679.

FIT INDICES                                                          (3)
-----------
BENTLER-BONETT     NORMED   FIT INDEX =      .973
BENTLER-BONETT NON-NORMED   FIT INDEX =     1.003
COMPARATIVE FIT INDEX (CFI)           =     1.000
BOLLEN'S             (IFI) FIT INDEX  =     1.001
MCDONALD'S           (MFI) FIT INDEX  =     1.003
JORESKOG-SORBOM'S  GFI   FIT INDEX    =      .962
JORESKOG-SORBOM'S AGFI   FIT INDEX    =      .895
```

7.2 Identification and Estimation of Confirmatory Factor Models

```
ROOT MEAN-SQUARE RESIDUAL (RMR)        =      .324
STANDARDIZED RMR                       =      .030
ROOT MEAN-SQUARE ERROR OF APPROXIMATION (RMSEA)    =     .000
90% CONFIDENCE INTERVAL OF RMSEA  (         .000,         .111)


MAXIMUM LIKELIHOOD SOLUTION (NORMAL DISTRIBUTION THEORY)           (4)
PARAMETER ESTIMATES (B) WITH STANDARD ERRORS AND TEST STATISTICS (Z)
STATISTICS SIGNIFICANT AT THE 5% LEVEL ARE MARKED WITH @.

                                                                 R-
DEP.VAR.        PREDICTOR     B        BETA    S.E.    Z      SQUARED
-----------------------------------------------------------------
V1   (PRESS60 )                                                 .718
         F1   ( DEM60  ) 1.000    .848
         E1   (PRESS60 ) 1.000    .531
V2   (OPP60   )                                                 .516
         F1   ( DEM60  ) 1.267*   .719   .185   6.831@
         E2   (OPP60   ) 1.000    .695
V3   (FAIR60  )                                                 .524
         F1   ( DEM60  ) 1.069*   .724   .154   6.925@
         E3   (FAIR60  ) 1.000    .690
V4   (ELECT60 )                                                 .715
         F1   ( DEM60  ) 1.274*   .846   .148   8.626@
         E4   (ELECT60 ) 1.000    .534
V5   (PRESS65 )                                                 .620
         F2   ( DEM65  ) 1.000    .788
         E5   (PRESS65 ) 1.000    .616
V6   (OPP65   )                                                 .567
         F2   ( DEM65  ) 1.227*   .753   .182   6.755@
         E6   (OPP65   ) 1.000    .658
V7   (FAIR65  )                                                 .706
         F2   ( DEM65  ) 1.343*   .840   .174   7.736@
         E7   (FAIR65  ) 1.000    .542
V8   (ELECT65 )                                                 .692
         F2   ( DEM65  ) 1.309*   .832   .172   7.597@
         E8   (ELECT65 ) 1.000    .555


VARIANCES OF INDEPENDENT VARIABLES
STATISTICS SIGNIFICANT AT THE 5% LEVEL ARE MARKED WITH @.


                         VARIANCE     S.E.       Z
-------------------------------------------------
FACTOR
         F1   ( DEM60  )4.943*   1.132   4.368@
         F2   ( DEM65  )4.240*   1.086   3.905@
ERROR
         E1   (PRESS60 )1.937*    .454   4.269@
         E2   (OPP60   )7.427*   1.400   5.306@
         E3   (FAIR60  )5.130*    .975   5.264@
```

(Continued)

Table 3 (Continued)

```
        E4   (ELECT60 ) 3.195*   .754   4.240@
        E5   (PRESS65 ) 2.595*   .530   4.892@
        E6   (OPP65   ) 4.879*   .938   5.203@
        E7   (FAIR65  ) 3.183*   .723   4.405@
        E8   (ELECT65 ) 3.231*   .728   4.438@

COVARIANCES AMONG INDEPENDENT VARIABLES
STATISTICS SIGNIFICANT AT THE 5% LEVEL ARE MARKED WITH @.
                          COVA.     S.E.      Z       CORR.
-------------------------------------------------------------
F1,F2   (DEM60   ,DEM65   )  4.412*   .979   4.505@    .964
E1,E5   (PRESS60 ,PRESS65 )   .635*   .374   1.697     .283
E2,E4   (OPP60   ,ELECT60 )  1.292*   .714   1.810     .265
E2,E6   (OPP60   ,OPP65   )  2.073*   .744   2.786@    .344
E3,E7   (FAIR60  ,FAIR65  )   .828*   .619   1.336     .205
E4,E8   (ELECT60 ,ELECT65 )   .472*   .460   1.024     .147
E6,E8   (OPP65   ,ELECT65 )  1.274*   .588   2.165@    .321
```

A few comments should clarify the contents

1. The standardized residual covariances (i.e. the residual correlations) are all extremely small, so there is not much to gain by introducing more parameters. On the contrary, it is perhaps possible to simplify the model by placing restrictions on parameter values.
2. We see that a χ^2-test of the model has a P-value of 0.487. This means that there is a probability of 0.487 of getting this result or one that is more against our model, if the model is correct. Because of the reversed testing we are interested in the test *not* being significant. Therefore a P-value near 50% does not seem unsatisfying. We are, however, not interested in very large P-values, as this could be a sign of over-fitting, and therefore suggest that the model could be simplified.
3. All the fit measures point in the same direction: We should indeed look for simplifications of the model.
4. Next, there are the parameter estimates, their standard errors and test statistics. The only parameters that are not significant by traditional standards are (FAIR60,FAIR65) and (ELECT60,ELECT65) (one-sided tests, $\alpha = 0.05$. Remember that the '@' are for two-sided tests, but here one-sided tests seem more appropriate.

As the fit is so good, it should perhaps be possible to simplify the model. Generally, we want a parsimonious model with as few free parameters as possible. The danger with models that are 'too good' is that the good fit perhaps is obtained by profiting from peculiarities in the sample at hand, and that the results therefore would not show up in other samples from the same population. So, the simpler the model, the smaller the dangers of generalization – and also the simpler the model, the easier it is to interpret.

You could for instance argue that the connection between a latent variable and its indicator is the same in the two years, i.e. that the measuring instrument itself does not change between the two measurements. If so, you put in the following paragraph in the program in Table 2:

```
                /CONSTRAINTS
                (V2,F1)  =  (V6,F2);
                (V3,F1)  =  (V7,F2);                              (3)
                (V4,F1)  =  (V8,F2);
```

You will observe that these restrictions are not inconsistent with the data. The main results of this second run are shown in the model in Table 4, and the fit measures for the two models are:

First run	Second run
$\chi^2 = 12.232$	$\chi^2 = 15.074$
$df = 13 \quad P=0.487$	$df = 16 \quad P=0.519$

(4)

	χ^2	f
New model	15.074	16
Old model	12.232	13
Difference	2.842	3

(5)

We compare the two models as follows:

The difference in χ^2 is asymptotically distributed as χ^2 with three degrees of freedom. As a value of 2.842 with three degrees of freedom is not statistically significant according to traditional criteria, we prefer the new and simpler model.

This so-called χ^2-difference test is restricted to cases where one of the two models is nested under the other – that is, one model can be obtained by placing restrictions on the other.

Table 4 Example 1: selected output, second run

```
MAXIMUM LIKELIHOOD SOLUTION (NORMAL DISTRIBUTION THEORY)

PARAMETER ESTIMATES (B) WITH STANDARD ERRORS AND TEST STATISTICS (Z)
STATISTICS SIGNIFICANT AT THE 5% LEVEL ARE MARKED WITH @.

                                                              R-
DEP.VAR.        PREDICTOR    B         BETA   S.E.    Z       SQUARED
---------------------------------------------------------------------
V1   (PRESS60 )                                               .713
          F1   ( DEM60   ) 1.000       .845
          E1   (PRESS60  ) 1.000       .535
V2   (OPP60   )                                               .479
          F1   ( DEM60   ) 1.213*      .692   .144    8.423@
          E2   (OPP60    ) 1.000       .722
```

(Continued)

Table 4 (Continued)

```
V3   (FAIR60  )                                                    .582
          F1   ( DEM60  )  1.210*   .763   .126   9.619@
          E3   (FAIR60  )  1.000    .647
V4   (ELECT60 )                                                    .704
          F1   ( DEM60  )  1.273*   .839   .123  10.378@
          E4   (ELECT60 )  1.000    .544
V5   (PRESS65 )                                                    .644
          F2   ( DEM65  )  1.000    .802
          E5   (PRESS65 )  1.000    .597
V6   (OPP65   )                                                    .581
          F2   ( DEM65  )  1.213*   .762   .144   8.423@
          E6   (OPP65   )  1.000    .647
V7   (FAIR65  )                                                    .667
          F2   ( DEM65  )  1.210*   .817   .126   9.619@
          E7   (FAIR65  )  1.000    .577
V8   (ELECT65 )                                                    .695
          F2   ( DEM65  )  1.273*   .833   .123  10.378@
          E8   (ELECT65 )  1.000    .553
```

VARIANCES OF INDEPENDENT VARIABLES
  STATISTICS SIGNIFICANT AT THE 5% LEVEL ARE MARKED WITH @.

```
                          VARIANCE    S.E.     Z
-----------------------------------------------------
FACTOR
          F1   ( DEM60   ) 4.770*    1.050   4.545@
          F2   ( DEM65   ) 4.588*    1.043   4.398@
ERROR
          E1   (PRESS60  ) 1.916*     .442   4.334@
          E2   (OPP60    ) 7.633*    1.392   5.485@
          E3   (FAIR60   ) 5.027*     .985   5.104@
          E4   (ELECT60  ) 3.256*     .737   4.416@
          E5   (PRESS65  ) 2.538*     .529   4.793@
          E6   (OPP65    ) 4.874*     .943   5.166@
          E7   (FAIR65   ) 3.348*     .714   4.690@
          E8   (ELECT65  ) 3.267*     .735   4.448@
```

COVARIANCES AMONG INDEPENDENT VARIABLES
  STATISTICS SIGNIFICANT AT THE 5% LEVEL ARE MARKED WITH @.

```
                                 COVA.    S.E.     Z      CORR.
-------------------------------------------------------------------
   F1,F2   (DEM60   ,DEM65   )   4.520*   .987   4.578@   .966
   E1,E5   (PRESS60 ,PRESS65 )    .582*   .372   1.564    .264
   E2,E4   (OPP60   ,ELECT60 )   1.411*   .699   2.017@   .283
   E2,E6   (OPP60   ,OPP65   )   2.098*   .748   2.806@   .344
   E3,E7   (FAIR60  ,FAIR65  )    .741*   .624   1.188    .181
   E4,E8   (ELECT60 ,ELECT65 )    .480*   .462   1.039    .147
   E6,E8   (OPP65   ,ELECT65 )   1.275*   .595   2.143@   .319
```

In introducing these restrictions I had an eye on the output in Table 3, but my choice of restrictions was based on substantive reasoning. I was not just fishing in the output.

The revision of the original model was theory driven, but if model revision is more or less driven by empirical evidence the 'testing' is not meaningful, because you test on the same data that have formed the hypotheses. For example, if you drop non-significant parameters from a model you can be almost sure that the χ^2-difference test will also be non-significant.

A digression: if you cannot substantiate that the measuring instrument functions in the same way on the two occasions, you cannot compare the degree of democracy at the two points in time, if you should want to do so (more about this in Chapter 9).

Sample or population?

There is a problem with the analysis in Example 1: should we consider the 75 developing countries as a random sample drawn from a larger population (and, if so, how is that population defined?), or do they constitute the complete population? This is a fundamental question.

The basic idea in statistical estimation and testing is that you use a sample to draw conclusions about the unknown parameters of the population, taking the sampling error into consideration. But if your 'sample' is in reality the population, your 'parameter estimates' *are* the population parameters, and consequently there is no need for testing!

Even if the sample could be considered as drawn at random from some population, it is in all probability so large a fraction of that population that special formulas should be used to calculate the standard errors. Remember this if your analysis in based on macro data.

Programming using the 'Diagrammer'/'Factor Model'

After opening the data file (Bollen.ess), click the 'Diagrammer' icon ⚙ and in the window in Figure 5.12 select 'Factor Model'. The window in Figure 3a will appear.

(a)

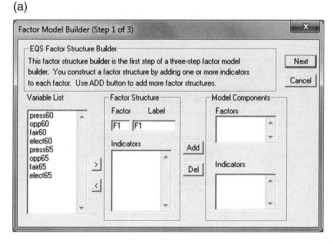

(Continued)

Figure 3 (Continued)

(b)

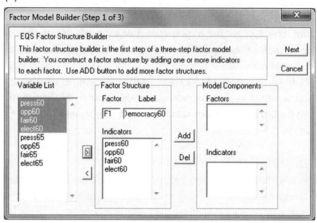

(c)

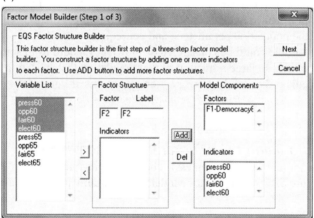

(d)

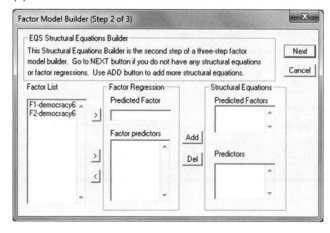

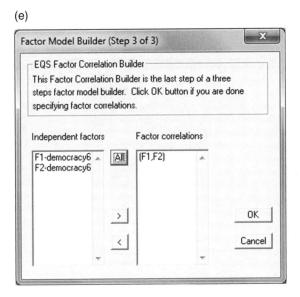

Figure 3 Example 1: the three steps in the 'Diagrammer/Factor Model

Label Factor 1 'democracy60'. Then select 'press60', 'opp60', 'fair60' and 'elect60' and by clicking the little arrow copy them to 'Indicators' as shown in panel (b). Then select 'Add', and the variables are moved to the 'Model Components' as shown in panel (c).

At the same time 'F2' appears in the 'Factor Structure' section of the window and you repeat the procedure, labeling F2 'democracy65' and using the last four indicators.

Pressing 'OK' moves you to the next step in the process – see panel (d). This gives you the possibility to include causal paths between factors, i.e. to build a general structural equation model like the ones treated in the next chapter. As such a connection is irrelevant in this case, just press 'OK' to go the third and last step.

The window in panel (e) appears. Select 'All' and when you click 'OK' the window in Figure 4 will appear – and you have finished your programming.
As you can see, the drawing in Figure 4 differs from the one in Figure 2, but feel free to experiment on your own with modifications to the drawing.

On the screen the arrows connecting the first indicator to its factor are red, signaling that the regression coefficient is fixed at 1.00 by default.

There is, however, a hidden problem here. You will remember that EQS allows only eight characters in labels, whereas 'Diagrammer' does not have such a restriction. This means that when you try to run the program shown in Figure 4, EQS will cut off all letters but the first eight, and you will receive an error message that F1 and F2 have the same label, so you have to rename the two factors before you run the program (e.g. call them dem60 and dem65 as in Table 2).

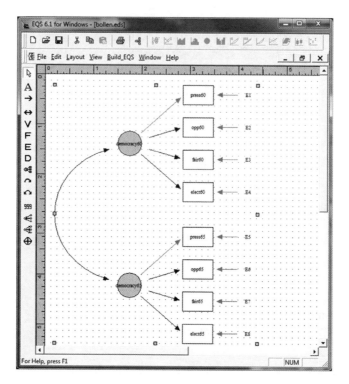

Figure 4 Example 1: the final model

3 Item Selection and Scale Construction

Very often confirmatory factor analysis will give a more differentiated picture of a scale's characteristics than traditional item analysis or exploratory factor analysis.

In Example 2.1 an item analysis in SPSS reduced the scale by three items and increased Cronbach's α from 0.831 to 0.866. In Example 3.3 we reached the same conclusion using principal components analysis.

These are the two classical techniques for item analysis, but they are not without drawbacks:

1. A large Cronbach's α and/or large item–rest correlations are no guarantee of unidimensionality.
2. In component analysis (and exploratory factor analysis) every manifest variable is connected to every latent variable, whereas in the ideal scale, every manifest variable is connected to only one factor. This blurs the picture (cf. Figure 1).
3. In both cases the possibilities for statistical testing are limited.

Example 2
Constructing a scale to measure 'style of processing

Childers, Houston, and Heckler (1985) constructed a summated scale for measuring 'style of processing' (SOP), i.e. a person's preference to engage in a verbal and/or visual modality of processing information about his or her environment.

7.3 Item Selection and Scale Construction

You met this scale in Example 1.3.

The SOP scale is a 22-item, four-point scale, of which 11 items are assumed to reflect a verbal processing style and 11 a visual processing style. Childers et al. proposed the two sub-scales to be used either separately or in combination as one scale – although they preferred using the combined scale.

The items are shown in Table 5.

The scale was used by Sørensen (2001) in a project on consumer behavior, the respondents being 88 randomly selected Danish housewives. The scale used was a seven-point scale and not a four-point scale like the original one. You can find Sørensen's data on the companion website.

Table 5 Example 2: SOP scale

1. I enjoy work that requires the use of words.
2. There are some special times in my life that I like to relive by mentally 'picturing just how everything looked.*
3. I can never seem to find the right word when I need it.*
4. I do a lot of reading.
5. When I'm trying to learn something new, I'd rather watch a demonstration than read how to do it.*
6. I think I often use words in the wrong way.*
7. I enjoy learning new words.
8. I like to picture how I could fix up my apartment or a room if I could buy anything I wanted.*
9. I often make written notes to myself.
10. I like to daydream.*
11. I generally prefer to use a diagram rather than a written set of instructions.*
12. I like to 'doodle'.*
13. I find it helps to think in terms of mental pictures when doing many things.*
14. After I meet someone for the first time, I can usually remember what they look like, but not much about them.*
15. I like to think in synonyms of words.
16. When I have forgotten something I frequently try to form a mental 'picture' to remember it.*
17. I like learning new words.
18. I prefer to read instructions about how to do something rather than have someone show me.
19. I prefer activities that don't require a lot of reading.*
20. I seldom daydream.
21. I spend very little time trying to increase my vocabulary.*
22. My thinking often consists of mental 'pictures' or images.*

Notes: *Denotes items that are reverse scored. Items 1, 3, 4, 6, 7, 9, 15, 17, 18, 19, and 21 compose the verbal component. Items 2, 5, 8, 10 through 14, 16, 20, and 22 compose the visual component.

Cronbach's α was 0.76 for the verbal sub-scale and 0.71 for the visual sub-scale, while for the combined scale it was 0.74. In their original paper Childers et al. stated the same α to be 0.81, 0.86 and 0.88 respectively. In most circumstances, values of α of this size will lead to acceptance of the scales as reliable *and unidimensional*.

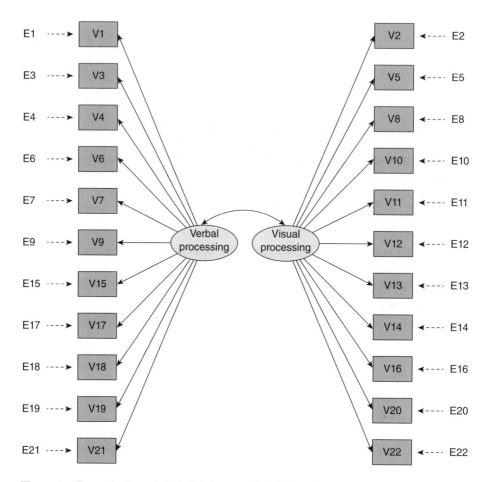

Figure 5 Example 2: model of Childers et al.'s SOP scale

Here I will use Sørensen's data in order to evaluate the scale; the measurement model is shown in Figure 5.

In the program shown in Table 6, you will meet one new paragraph:

/LMTEST

PROCESS=SIMULTANEOUS;

SET=PEE,GVF;

This deserves a few remarks, but you will have to wait till I comment on the output in Table 8.

But, first, let us first take a look at the fit measures in Table 7.

Table 6 Example 2: program for first run

```
/TITLE
  Example 7.2. First run. Data from Sørensen (2001)
/SPECIFICATIONS
  DATA='C:\Users\Sony\Desktop\EQS bog\EQS Chap 7\SOPX.ESS';
  VARIABLES=22; CASES=88;
  METHOD=GLS; ANALYSIS=COVARIANCE; MATRIX=COVARIANCE;
/LABELS
  F1=VERBAL PROCESSING; F2=VISUAL PROCESSING;
/EQUATIONS
  V1  = *F1 + E1;   V3  = *F1 + E3;   V4  = *F1 + E4;   V6  = *F1 + E6;
  V7  = *F1 + E7;   V9  = *F1 + E9;   V15 = *F1 + E15;  V17 = *F1 + E17;
  V18 = *F1 + E18;  V19 = *F1 + E19;  V21 = *F1 + E21;

  V2  = *F2 + E2;   V5  = *F2 + E5;   V8  = *F2 + E8;   V10 = *F2 + E10;
  V11 = *F2 + E11;  V12 = *F2 + E12;  V13 = *F2 + E13;  V14 = *F2 + E14;
  V16 = *F2 + E16;  V20 = *F2 + E20;
  V22 = *F2 + E22;
/VARIANCES
  F1 = 1;
  F2 = 1;
  E1 TO E22 = *;
/COVARIANCES
  F2,F1   = *;
/LM TEST
  PROCESS=SIMULTANEOUS;
  SET=PEE, GVF;
/PRINT
  FIT=ALL;
  TABLE=COMPACT;
/END
```

Table 7 Example 2: fit indices for first run

```
CHI-SQUARE =        242.239 BASED ON       208 DEGREES OF FREEDOM
   PROBABILITY VALUE FOR THE CHI-SQUARE STATISTIC IS        0.05189


   FIT INDICES
   -----------
   BENTLER-BONETT     NORMED  FIT INDEX    =    0.203
   BENTLER-BONETT NON-NORMED  FIT INDEX    =    0.479
   COMPARATIVE  FIT  INDEX  (CFI)          =    0.531
   BOLLEN'S           (IFI) FIT INDEX      =    0.643
   MCDONALD'S         (MFI) FIT INDEX      =    0.823
   JORESKOG-SORBOM'S   GFI  FIT INDEX      =    0.747
   JORESKOG-SORBOM'S AGFI   FIT INDEX      =    0.692
   ROOT MEAN-SQUARE RESIDUAL (RMR)         =    0.899
   STANDARDIZED RMR                        =    0.230
   ROOT MEAN-SQUARE ERROR OF APPROXIMATION (RMSEA)    =    0.043
   90% CONFIDENCE INTERVAL OF RMSEA  (         0.000,          0.065)
```

A chi-square of 242.239 with 208 degrees of freedom giving a P-value of 0.052 is a little on the low side. What is more serious is that the fit indices are not quite satisfactory: the IFI and CFI indices below 0.80 should be taken seriously, so it is time to look at freeing parameters.

In the previous example you met the χ^2-difference test which was used to test if two models, one of which was nested under the other, were statistically different as far as fit was concerned.

You could of course use that same test here. For every fixed parameter (in this case parameters fixed at zero) – or groups of parameters – you would consider for 'unfixing', you could add them to the model and test whether the new model was significantly better than the old one.

That, however, would be a very tedious job, with a lot of model building and a lot of testing.

Fortunately EQS offers a way to do all the tests in one go without having to construct the various models you want to consider.

If you consider adding free parameters, use the Lagrange multiplier (LM) test, and if you think of fixing free parameters (not relevant in this case) use the Wald (W) test. The χ^2-difference, LM and W tests are asymptotically equivalent, i.e. in large samples they will give the same results.

The command

```
/LMTEST

PROCESS=SIMULTANEOUS;
```

orders EQS to do an LM test roughly equivalent to a series of χ^2-difference tests, one for each fixed parameter, starting with the one that is expected to contribute most to a better fit, and then proceeding with the second most significant etc.

If I had not inserted the command

```
SET=PEE,GVF;
```

the output would have printed out a list of every fixed parameter in the model – and that would have been a very long list indeed. Remember that all parameters that are not in the model are considered fixed (at zero) and, for most of them, including them in the model would make no sense, e.g. introducing causal paths between manifest variables. The SET command restricts the number of parameters that are considered for inclusion in the model.

To understand the meaning of this command, you must understand that EQS groups parameters in three groups (or matrices):

1. A group (matrix) called PHI and abbreviated P consists of covariances between independent variables.
2. A group called GAMMA and abbreviated G consists of regression coefficients involving both dependent and independent variables.
3. A group called BETA and abbreviated B that contains regression coefficients involving only dependent variables.

Dependent and independent are used here in the EQS sense. In the present case, only the modifications in the connections between V and F variables (i.e. VF parameters) and correlations between the Es (i.e. EE parameters) are worth considering.

The command SET = PEE, GVF tells EQS that the parameters to be considered are EE variables (found in the P matrix) and VF parameters (found in the G matrix).

If you use interactive programming, you will at one point choose 'Build EQS/LMTEST' (see Figure 6a) to activate the window in panel (b), where you can see the three parameter matrices and their sub-matrices. When this window opens, several of the check boxes are checked by default, but just uncheck them and instead place your check marks as shown in the panel (c).

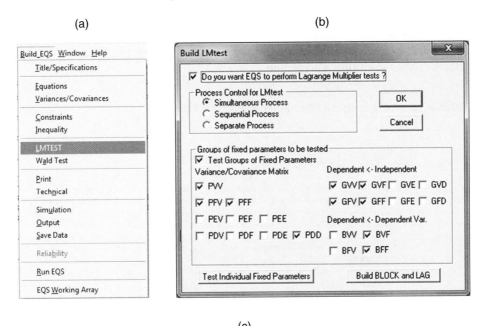

Figure 6 Programming 'LMTEST'

From panel (b), you will guess that

PROCESS=SIMULTANEOUS;

is the default, so I could just as well have omitted it. The two alternatives

PROCESS=SEQUENTIAL;

and

PROCESS=SEPARATE;

give you the possibility to specify the sequence of the tests – for example, to specify a sequence in accordance with an a priori theory. You will have to consult the manual (Bentler, 2006) for further information.

Table 8 Example 2: output first run – Lagrange multiplier test

```
LAGRANGE MULTIPLIER TEST (FOR ADDING PARAMETERS)

ORDERED UNIVARIATE TEST STATISTICS:
                                            HANCOCK              STANDAR-
                              CHI-          208 DF      PARAM.   DIZED       PREDICTED
  NO   CODE   PARAMETER     SQUARE   PROB.  PROB.       CHANGE   CHANGE    RMSEA    CFI
  --   ----   ---------    -------  ------  ------     -------  -------   ------  ------
   1    2  6   E13,E11       9.146   0.002   1.000       0.820    0.580    0.038  0.642
   2    2  6    E8,E6        7.163   0.007   1.000      -0.371   -0.521    0.039  0.615
   3    2  6    E8,E3        6.908   0.009   1.000       0.487    0.584    0.040  0.612
   4    2  6    E8,E7        6.884   0.009   1.000      -0.255   -0.572    0.040  0.611
   5    2  6    E3,E2        6.884   0.009   1.000      -0.658   -0.578    0.040  0.611
   6    2  6   E15,E5        5.972   0.015   1.000      -0.688   -0.393    0.040  0.599
   7    2  6   E21,E6        5.673   0.017   1.000       0.454    0.434    0.041  0.595
   8    2  6    E6,E3        5.554   0.018   1.000       0.517    0.635    0.041  0.593
   9    2  6    E9,E4        5.530   0.019   1.000      -0.885   -0.370    0.041  0.593
  10    2  6   E18,E5        5.382   0.020   1.000       0.670    0.565    0.041  0.591
   -    -  -      -             -       -       -           -        -        -      -
   -    -  -      -             -       -       -           -        -        -      -
   -    -  -      -             -       -       -           -        -        -      -
   -    -  -      -             -       -       -           -        -        -      -
 253    2  6   E16,E2        0.000   0.993   1.000      -0.002   -0.001    0.044  0.517
 254    2  0    F2,F2        0.000   1.000   1.000       0.000    0.000    0.044  0.517
 255    2  0    F1,F1        0.000   1.000   1.000       0.000    0.000    0.044  0.517


MULTIVARIATE LAGRANGE MULTIPLIER TEST BY SIMULTANEOUS PROCESS IN STAGE 1

  PARAMETER SETS (SUBMATRICES) ACTIVE AT THIS STAGE ARE:
  PEE GVF

          CUMULATIVE MULTIVARIATE STATISTICS        UNIVARIATE INCREMENT
          ----------------------------------     -----------------------------
                                                                 HANCOCK'S
                       CHI-                       CHI-           SEQUENTIAL     PREDICTED
  STEP   PARAMETER   SQUARE   D.F. PROB.        SQUARE PROB.     D.F. PROB.    RMSEA   CFI
  ----   ---------   ------   ---- -----        ------ -----     ---- -----    -----  -----
    1     E13,E11     9.146     1  0.002         9.146 0.002      208 1.000    0.038  0.642
    2      E8,E6     16.389     2  0.000         7.242 0.007      207 1.000    0.033  0.728
```

3	E8,E7	23.177	3	0.000	6.788	0.009	206 1.000	0.028	0.807
4	E12,E8	28.917	4	0.000	5.740	0.017	205 1.000	0.023	0.872
5	E19,E10	34.706	5	0.000	5.789	0.016	204 1.000	0.016	0.938
6	E9,E4	40.215	6	0.000	5.509	0.019	203 1.000	0.001	1.000
7	E3,E2	45.211	7	0.000	4.996	0.025	202 1.000	99.999	1.000
8	E21,E6	50.094	8	0.000	4.883	0.027	201 1.000	99.999	1.000
9	E15,E5	55.044	9	0.000	4.950	0.026	200 1.000	99.999	1.000
10	E2,E1	59.898	10	0.000	4.854	0.028	199 1.000	99.999	1.000
11	E6,E3	64.340	11	0.000	4.443	0.035	198 1.000	99.999	1.000
12	E19,E6	68.959	12	0.000	4.619	0.032	197 1.000	99.999	1.000

```
*** NOTE *** IF PREDICTED RMSEA COULD NOT BE CALCULATED, 99.999 IS PRINTED.
             IF PREDICTED  CFI  COULD NOT BE CALCULATED,  9.999 IS PRINTED.
```

You do not need to bother with the first two columns in Table 8 as they are only technical codes. In the third column you will find a list of fixed parameters (in this case they are all fixed at zero) sorted according to the size of increase in the model fit they would cause if the were freely estimated. The fourth and fifth columns show the chi-square and *P*-value of a test of the null hypothesis that the model fit would *not* increase if the parameter in question were freely estimated.

As all the *P*-values in the first ten cases are less than 0.05 you would reject this null hypothesis in (at least) the first ten cases based on traditional criteria, but the problem with such a decision is that the various tests are not independent. They do not tell you what would happen if more than one parameter were set free simultaneously.

The next column shows the Hancock *P*-values, which are some sort of Bonferroni probabilities analogous to what you have probably met in your introductory statistics course. As you will guess from the *P*-values of 1.000, this criterion is much too conservative, and I will not recommend basing any conclusions on it.

The next two columns show the expected change in parameter values if the parameter in case were set free. At present these parameters are not in the model, i.e. they are fixed at zero. Consequently the expected parameter changes are the expected parameter values.

Because of the interdependencies among the marginal LM tests, it is safer to base decisions on the multivariate tests in the second panel in the table.

The first line shows the consequences of freeing the parameter (E13,E11), the next the consequences of simultaneously freeing (E13,E11) and (E8,E6), the third the consequences of freeing (E13,E11), (E8,E6) and (E8,E7), etc.

In the third, fourth and fifth columns you will see the chi-square, df and *P* for simultaneously freeing the parameters, mentioned in the line and the lines above. The next two columns show marginal tests of freeing a parameter if all parameters in the lines above have also been freed.

It is tempting to free parameters, starting from the top until the marginal test becomes insignificant, but do not yield to the temptation.

As I advocated earlier, it is usually a good idea to base suggestions for modifications to a model on substantive rather than purely empirical evidence, so let us take a look at the items in Table 5.

A few of them catch the eye:

1. Items 10 and 20 say nearly the same thing and serve as mutual controls on the consistency of the answers, so they should correlate more than by their common cause: 'visual'.

2. The same can be said of items 7 and 17.
3. Items 3 and 6 are also very close. If you cannot find a special word when you need it and therefore use another word, I think you will find that other word less suitable in the situation.

At least you should consider introducing these correlations in the model.

4. You should also expect correlations among items 5, 11 and 18. Whereas most of the other items only mention one of the processing styles, these three explicitly mention both, and compare them.
   According to their wording these three items could be placed in both subscales. You should therefore consider letting them load on both factors.

A program along these lines is given in Table 9 and the output in Table 10.
If you compare Table 10 with Table 7, you will observe that I have omitted the lines with E variables to save space. This will be done in all output tables from now on.

Table 9 Example 2: program for the second run

```
/TITLE
  Example 7.2. Second run. Data from Sørensen (2001)
/SPECIFICATIONS
  DATA='C:\Users\Sony\Desktop\EQS bog\EQS Chap 7\SOPX.ESS';
  VARIABLES=22; CASES=88;
  METHOD=GLS; ANALYSIS=COVARIANCE; MATRIX=COVARIANCE;
/LABELS
  F1=VERBAL PROCESSING; F2=VISUAL PROCESSING;
/EQUATIONS
  V1  =   *F1 + E1;   V3  = *F1 + E3;   V4  = *F1 + E4;   V6  = *F1 + E6;
  V7  =   *F1 + E7;   V9  = *F1 + E9;   V15 = *F1 + E15;  V17 = *F1 + E17;
  V18 =   *F1 + *F2 + E18;                V19 = *F1 + E19;  V21 = *F1 + E21;

  V2  =   *F2 + E2;   V5  = *F1 + *F2 + E5;                V8  = *F2 + E8;
  V10 =   *F2 + E10;  V11 =   *F1 + *F2 + E11;             V12 = *F2 + E12;
  V13 =   *F2 + E13;  V14 = *F2 + E14;  V16 = *F2 + E16;   V20 = *F2 + E20;
  V22 =   *F2 + E22;
/VARIANCES
  F1 = 1;
  F2 = 1;
  E1 TO E22 = *;
/COVARIANCES
  F2,F1   = *;
  E10,E20 = *;
  E7,E17  = *;
  E3,E6   = *;
/LM TEST;
  PROCESS=SIMULTANEOUS;
  SET=PEE, GVF;
/PRINT
  FIT=ALL;
  TABLE=COMPACT;
/END
```

Table 10 Example 2: selected output (second run) (E lines removed to save space)

```
CHI-SQUARE =       216.290 BASED ON      202 DEGREES OF FREEDOM
   PROBABILITY VALUE FOR THE CHI-SQUARE STATISTIC IS          .23235

   PARAMETER ESTIMATES (B) WITH STANDARD ERRORS AND TEST STATISTICS (Z)
   STATISTICS SIGNIFICANT AT THE 5% LEVEL ARE MARKED WITH @.

                                                            R-
DEP.VAR.         PREDICTOR    B       BETA    S.E.    Z     SQUARED
----------------------------------------------------------------
V1  ( V1    )                                               .276
          F1 (VERBALPR) .543*   .526    .177  3.075@
V2  ( V2    )                                               .367
          F2 (VISUALPR) .807*   .606    .198  4.067@
V3  ( V3    )                                               .286
          F1 (VERBALPR) .760*   .535    .204  3.735@
V4  ( V4    )                                               .045
          F1 (VERBALPR) .294*   .212    .219  1.345
V5  ( V5    )                                               .598      (1)
          F1 (VERBALPR) 1.731*  .901    .349  4.956@
          F2 (VISUALPR) -.417*  -.217   .373  -1.117
V6  ( V6    )                                               .245
          F1 (VERBALPR) .559*   .495    .169  3.299@
V7  ( V7    )                                               .097
          F1 (VERBALPR) .256*   .311    .137  1.863
V8  ( V8    )                                               .551
          F2 (VISUALPR) .874*   .742    .161  5.436@
V9  ( V9    )                                               .173
          F1 (VERBALPR) .779*   .416    .267  2.920@
V10 ( V10   )                                               .135
          F2 (VISUALPR) .561*   .367    .211  2.656@
V11 ( V11   )                                               .386      (1)
          F1 (VERBALPR) 1.243*  .691    .317  3.915@
          F2 (VISUALPR) -.204*  -.113   .338  -.602
V12 ( V12   )                                               .036
          F2 (VISUALPR) .323*   .189    .244  1.324
V13 ( V13   )                                               .630
          F2 (VISUALPR) 1.280*  .794    .218  5.884@
V14 ( V14   )                                               .137
          F2 (VISUALPR) .698*   .370    .233  3.000@
V15 ( V15   )                                               .055      (2)
          F1 (VERBALPR) .341*   .235    .236  1.442
V16 ( V16   )                                               .204
          F2 (VISUALPR) .680*   .452    .213  3.185@
V17 ( V17   )                                               .079      (2)
          F1 (VERBALPR) .227*   .282    .136  1.665
V18 ( V18   )                                               .722      (1)
          F1 (VERBALPR) 1.833*  1.124   .377  4.861@
          F2 (VISUALPR) -.977*  -.599   .413  -2.363@
V19 ( V19   )                                               .536
          F1 (VERBALPR) 1.264*  .732    .203  6.218@
V20 ( V20   )                                               .173
          F2 (VISUALPR) .647*   .416    .229  2.827@
```

(Continued)

Table 10 (Continued)

```
V21 ( V21    )                                              .010       (2)
       F1 (VERBALPR)  .125*  .099  .210  .596
V22 ( V22    )                                              .591
       F2 (VISUALPR) 1.284*  .769  .198  6.486@
```

COVARIANCES AMONG INDEPENDENT VARIABLES
STATISTICS SIGNIFICANT AT THE 5% LEVEL ARE MARKED WITH @.

```
                                      COVA.   S.E.     Z       CORR.
-----------------------------------------------------------------------
F1,F2    (VERBALPR,VISUALPR)          .669*   .126   5.308@    .669     (3)
E3,E6    ( V3   ,  V6  )              .460*   .213   2.158@    .391
E7,E17   ( V7   ,  V17 )              .353*   .106   3.330@    .585
E10,E20  ( V10  ,  V20 )             1.425*   .359   3.965@    .708
```

With a chi-square of 216.290 with 202 degrees of freedom giving a P-value of 0.233, the model seems satisfactory, and a look at the fit indices confirms this:

CFI	SRMR	RMSEA	LO 90	HI 90
0.804	0.197	0.029	0.000	0.055

Although CFI is not quite up to standard (> 0.90–0.95), it is considerably larger than in the first run, and the other indices are all fine.

By studying the parameters of the model, you can observe the following:

1. Item 18 has significant loadings on both factors whereas items 5 and 11, which were supposed to measure visual processing style, actually both have significant loadings on 'verbal' and non-significant loadings on 'visual'. However, all coefficients have the expected signs.
2. The following regression coefficients are non-significant (one-sided test, $\alpha = 0.05$): 15, 17, 21, 5, 11 and 12.
3. All the covariances are significant, and the correlation between the two factors is 0.669 (as the two factors are standardized, the correlation equals the covariance).

What, then, can we conclude?

1. The SOP scale has two dimensions as suggested by Childers et al. – in fact it has *more* than two dimensions showing up as highly significant correlations between items in the same main dimension.
2. Some of the items have very little loading on the factor they are supposed to measure. A reformulation or exclusion should be considered.
3. Although the two sub-scales correlate, there are in fact *two* dimensions, and treating them as one scale could – depending on the research question – cause problems, because it assumes that the two ways of processing are alternatives.
4. In fact it has long been known that verbal and visual processes take place in functionally separate cognitive systems and thus are not alternatives (Paivio, 1971).

From this last point you will learn that it is of the utmost importance to spend a good deal of time making clear the nature of the concepts you intend to measure. This preliminary step is all too often not given the necessary care.

Now, in light of point 4 above, you may wonder: 'Why do the two factors correlate at all?'

A possible explanation is that the correlation is caused by item 18 loading on both factors, and that the correlation would disappear if this item (together with items 5 and 11) were removed.

This line of reasoning immediately gives birth to another question: the SOP scale is intended to measure preference, but do all items really measure preference? It seems to me that items 3, 6 and 14 measure ability rather than preference. Of course preference and ability must be expected to correlate, because we generally prefer activities where we feel we have the largest potential – but is ability not exogenous, and should the arrows connecting items 3, 6 and 14 to their latent variables not point in the opposite direction?

These two last points have taught us an important lesson: that serious thinking about the subject area is much preferred to thoughtless dependence on computer output.

If we delete items 5, 11 and 18 together with the three 'ability questions' we get the output in Table 11.

Table 11 Example 2: output from third run

```
CHI-SQUARE =        108.183 BASED ON       101 DEGREES OF FREEDOM
   PROBABILITY VALUE FOR THE CHI-SQUARE STATISTIC IS        0.29440

PARAMETER ESTIMATES (B) WITH STANDARD ERRORS AND TEST STATISTICS (Z)
   STATISTICS SIGNIFICANT AT THE 5% LEVEL ARE MARKED WITH @.

                                                                    R-
   DEP.VAR.          PREDICTOR  B       BETA   S.E.    Z      SQUARED
   -----------------------------------------------------------------
   V1  ( V1   )                                                 .552
              F1   (VERBALPR) 1.030*   .743   .177   5.812@
   V2  ( V2   )                                                 .171
              F2   (VISUALPR)  .610*   .413   .209   2.923@
   V4  ( V4   )                                                 .219
              F1   (VERBALPR)  .787*   .468   .232   3.397@
   V7  ( V7   )                                                 .595
              F1   (VERBALPR)  .851*   .771   .141   6.027@
   V8  ( V8   )                                                 .219
              F2   (VISUALPR)  .497*   .468   .164   3.028@
   V9  ( V9   )                                                 .039   (3)
              F1   (VERBALPR)  .392*   .198   .293   1.337
   V10 ( V10  )                                                 .079
              F2   (VISUALPR)  .441*   .281   .229   1.922
   V12 ( V12  )                                                 .019   (3)
              F2   (VISUALPR)  .244*   .137   .255    .958
   V13 ( V13  )                                                 .655
              F2   (VISUALPR) 1.501*   .809   .221   6.788@
   V15 ( V15  )                                                 .123
              F1   (VERBALPR)  .577*   .350   .242   2.383@
```

(Continued)

Table 11 (Continued)

```
V16 ( V16   )                                        .225
         F2  (VISUALPR)  .800*   .474  .219  3.660@
V17 ( V17   )                                        .493
         F1  (VERBALPR)  .770*   .702  .142  5.422@
V19 ( V19   )                                        .132
         F1  (VERBALPR)  .564*   .364  .231  2.443@
V20 ( V20   )                                        .224
         F2  (VISUALPR)  .926*   .473  .252  3.674@
V21 ( V21   )                                        .223
         F1  (VERBALPR)  .744*   .473  .215  3.464@
V22 ( V22   )                                        .559
         F2  (VISUALPR) 1.259*   .748  .198  6.367@

COVARIANCES AMONG INDEPENDENT VARIABLES
STATISTICS SIGNIFICANT AT THE 5% LEVEL ARE MARKED WITH @.

                                  COVA.   S.E.    Z         CORR.
----------------------------------------------------------------
  F1,F2    (VERBALPR,VISUALPR)  -.064*   .163   -.394    -.064   (1)
  E7,E17   ( V7    ,  V17  )    .278*   .143   1.939     .506   (2)
  E10,E20  ( V10   ,  V20  )   1.997*   .423   4.722@    .767   (2)
```

The fit of this model is not too bad:

CFI	SRMS	RMSEA	LO 90	HI 90
0.893	0.171	0.029	0.000	0.064

Of the three models, the third one is the best fitting. However, the most striking support for this model is found using the decision theoretic measures:

	Model 1	Model 2	Model 3
AIC	−174	−188	−94
CAIC	−897	−890	−445

Looking at the parameter estimates, we can see the following:

1. The correlation between the two factors disappeared, as it should according to theory.
2. The other two correlations are significant (remember: one-sided tests!).
3. Items 9 and 12 are not significant.

The purist would remove items 7 and 20 in order to get rid of the remaining correlations. However, as these correlations would probably be (nearly) constant and repeat themselves in future uses of the scale, they would not reduce its reliability. You could also consider removing or rephrasing the non-significant items.

If your research demands that you compare your study with others that used the SOP scale, it will perhaps be necessary for you to use the items as a summated scale (or scales). If that is not a demand, I would prefer to use the items un-summated. You could consider parceling if you need to keep down the number of parameters.

Example 1 (continued)
Democracy in developing countries

In the previous example you were introduced to the LM test. Now, I revert to Example 1 to show you how this test works in connection with constrained parameters.

If you add the paragraph

/LM TEST;

PROCESS=SIMULTANEOUS;

to the program for the second run, the output will include the lines in Table 12, which clearly shows that none of the restrictions are unwarranted. You should compare the content of this table with the result of the χ^2-difference test used earlier.

The last part of the section, testing the addition of parameters, is of course irrelevant in this case.

Table 12 Example 1: using the LM test to test constraints

```
LAGRANGE MULTIPLIER TEST (FOR RELEASING CONSTRAINTS)

    CONSTRAINTS TO BE RELEASED ARE:
         CONSTR:    1    (V2,F1)-(V6,F2)=0;
         CONSTR:    2    (V3,F1)-(V7,F2)=0;
         CONSTR:    3    (V4,F1)-(V8,F2)=0;

              UNIVARIATE TEST STATISTICS:
                                                    PARAM.
    NO    CONSTRAINT      CHI-SQUARE   PROBABILITY  CHANGE
    --    ----------      ----------   -----------  ------
    1     CONSTR:   1        0.361        0.548      0.095
    2     CONSTR:   2        2.402        0.121     -0.272
    3     CONSTR:   3        0.004        0.950      0.009


           CUMULATIVE MULTIVARIATE STATISTICS          UNIVARIATE INCREMENT
           ---------------------------------          --------------------

    STEP  PARAMETER    CHI-SQUARE  D.F.  PROBABILITY    CHI-SQUARE  PROBABILITY
    ----  ---------    ----------  ----  -----------    ----------  -----------
    1     CONSTR:  2      2.402     1       0.121         2.402        0.121
    2     CONSTR:  1      2.550     2       0.279         0.148        0.701
    3     CONSTR:  3      2.577     3       0.462         0.027        0.869


    LAGRANGE MULTIPLIER TEST (FOR ADDING PARAMETERS)

    ORDERED UNIVARIATE TEST STATISTICS:
```

(Continued)

Table 12 (Continued)

```
                                          HANCOCK              STANDAR-
                              CHI-        16 DF    PARAM.      DIZED
PREDICTED
   NO  CODE   PARAMETER   SQUARE   PROB.   PROB.   CHANGE   CHANGE   RMSEA    CFI
   --  ----   ---------   ------   -----   -----   ------   ------   ------   -----
    1  2 12     V3,F2      2.982   0.084   1.000   -0.305   -0.041   99.999   1.000
    2  2 12     V7,F1      1.943   0.163   1.000    0.235    0.034   99.999   1.000
    3  2  0     V1,F1      0.523   0.469   1.000    0.095    0.017   99.999   1.000
    4  2  0     V5,F2      0.523   0.469   1.000   -0.095   -0.017   99.999   1.000
    5  2 12     V2,F2      0.508   0.476   1.000    0.113    0.014   99.999   1.000
    6  2 12     V1,F2      0.451   0.502   1.000    0.088    0.016   99.999   1.000
    7  2 12     V5,F1      0.420   0.517   1.000   -0.083   -0.014   99.999   1.000
    8  2 12     V6,F1      0.188   0.664   1.000   -0.066   -0.009   99.999   1.000
    9  2 12     V8,F1      0.024   0.877   1.000   -0.021   -0.003    0.007   1.000
   10  2 12     V4,F2      0.020   0.887   1.000    0.020    0.003    0.007   1.000

*** NOTE *** IF PREDICTED RMSEA COULD NOT BE CALCULATED, 99.999 IS PRINTED.
             IF PREDICTED  CFI  COULD NOT BE CALCULATED,  9.999 IS PRINTED.


***** NONE OF THE UNIVARIATE LAGRANGE MULTIPLIERS IS SIGNIFICANT,
***** THE MULTIVARIATE TEST PROCEDURE WILL NOT BE EXECUTED.
```

4 Reliability and Validity

The classical methods of judging the reliability and validity of a measuring instrument all have their shortcomings since none of them actually take the latent variables explicitly into account as part of the measurement model.

Therefore the theoretical definitions of reliability and validity as coefficients of determination when regressing the measurement on the theoretical constructs cannot be used as a basis for calculations. However, using SEM as the basis for judging reliability and validity should open up this possibility.

Reliability

In Equation (2.3a) the reliability coefficient was defined as the coefficient of determination when a measurement (an indicator, a manifest variable) is regressed on its latent variable(s). Using SEM, you can use this definition to calculate reliability coefficients.

In the various outputs in this chapter you will find these squared multiple correlations in the last column of the estimated regression coefficients.

It comes as no surprise that the two items with the smallest reliabilities are the ones that have non-significant regression coefficients. However, a few of the highly significant items have rather small reliabilities and should be discarded or reformulated.

Anyway, if apart from measuring SOP you also want to measure several other concepts in order to construct a 'causal' model, 16 (not to mention 22!) items are quite a lot. If the other latent variables in your model require a similar number of items your questionnaire will easily grow to a length that could cause messy data, because respondents might refuse to participate, not answer all the questions, or fill out the questionnaire more or less at random in order to get the job done as quickly as possible.

In their efforts to obtain perfection scale, constructors very often end up with scales that are too long for practical use. The SOP scale is perhaps an example of this.

7.4 Reliability and Validity

This way of calculating a reliability coefficient has at least five advantages:

1. It is based on the very definition of reliability.
2. It is possible to calculate the reliability of every single item and not just a sum of them.
3. It can be used whether the measurements are parallel, tau-equivalent or congeneric.
4. It does not assume errors to be uncorrelated across items.
5. It can be used when an item is an indicator for more than just one latent variable.

If you have only cross-sectional data it is in general not possible to estimate the specific variance, which is then absorbed into the error variance. In this case you must either assume that the specific variance is zero or consider the estimated reliabilities to be lower bounds.

Reliability in EQS

You can order EQS to print a wide assortment of reliability coefficients, all building on different assumptions, but you must be careful to use only coefficients that make sense in the actual case – remember from Example 6.2 that EQS printed Cronbach's α although it had absolutely no meaning in the context.

Before we look at the complications involved in measuring reliability in a multi-factor model such as the SOP scale, let us revert to a simpler one-factor example.

Example 3
Reliability of a one-factor scale

As mentioned several times in Chapter 2, calculation of Cronbach's α presupposes that the scale in question is unidimensional. So let us open the data set 'Fish1' (used in Example 2.1) as an EQS data file and construct the program in Table 13.

The output is given in Table 14, on which I will give the following comments:

Table 13 Example 3: program for EQS calculation of reliability for a one-factor model

```
/TITLE
   Reliability Analysis using the dataset 'Fish1'
/SPECIFICATIONS
   DATA='c:\users\sony\documents\fish1.ess';
VARIABLES=17; CASES=89;
   METHOD=ML; ANALYSIS=COVARIANCE; MATRIX=RAW;
/LABELS
   V1=FORB35;   V2=FORB36;   V3=FORB37;   V4=FORB38;   V5=FORB39;
   V6=FORB40;   V7=FORB41;   V8=FORB42;   V9=TILB43;   V10=TILB44;
   V11=TILB45;  V12=TILB46;  V13=TILB47;  V14=TILB48;  V15=TILB49;
   V16=TILB50;  V17=FORB36R;
/RELIABILITY
   SCALE=V1,V3,V4,V5,V6,V7,V8,V17;
/PRINT
   TABLE=EQUATION;
/END
```

Table 14 Example 3: EQS calculation of reliability for a one-factor model: output

```
RELIABILITY COEFFICIENTS
------------------------
CRONBACH'S ALPHA                                  =      0.831             (1)
RELIABILITY COEFFICIENT RHO                       =      0.847             (2)
MAXIMAL WEIGHTED INTERNAL CONSISTENCY RELIABILITY =          0.886         (3)

MAXIMAL RELIABILITY CAN BE OBTAINED BY WEIGHTING THE VARIABLES AS FOLLOWS:
FORB35     FORB37     FORB38     FORB39     FORB40     FORB41     FORB42
0.2146     0.0954     0.0793     0.3590     0.2055     0.0523     0.1812
FORB36R
0.4440

STANDARDIZED FACTOR LOADINGS FOR THE FACTOR THAT GENERATES              (4)
MAXIMAL RELIABILITY FOR THE UNIT-WEIGHT COMPOSITE

BASED ON THE MODEL (RHO):
FORB35     FORB37     FORB38     FORB39     FORB40     FORB41     FORB42
0.7344     0.4561     0.4001     0.7950     0.6833     0.2390     0.6936
FORB36R
0.8490
```

1. First in the output is Cronbach's α (which of course has exactly the same value as in Table 2.2). As you will remember, classical test theory does not include latent variables, and as calculation of α uses only manifest variables, it does not build the theoretical definition of reliability as formulated in Equation (2.3a).

    Also remember that α builds on the restrictive assumption that the items are at least equivalent.

2. Next comes Raykov's ρ, which builds on the theoretical definition of reliability and is more general than α as it only demands the measurements to be congeneric; ρ is in most cases larger than α. Furthermore, ρ builds on the actual measurement model, which could have more than one factor. However, when you use the /RELIABILITY paragraph a one-factor model is assumed. ρ maintains the equal weighting of items.

    Raykov (1997) presents a fine discussion and a comparison of the two reliability coefficients and even shows an EQS program for calculating ρ in the one-factor case.

3. The next few lines show the reliability (ρ) that could be obtained if the items were optimally weighted and the optimal weights. As you will observe, the three items with the lowest weights are exactly the same as those that were discarded in our traditional item analyses in Examples 2.1 and 3.3.

4. Last in the output are the standardized factor loadings (regression coefficients) for a model with equal-weighted items.

Example 4 (continued from Example 2)
Reliability of a multi-factor scale

If you include the statement

$$\text{RELIABILITY = YES}$$

7.4 Reliability and Validity

In the /PRINT paragraph in the program in Table 6, the output will include the reliability coefficients shown in Table 15.

Table 15 Example 2: Reliability coefficients in a many-factor model

```
RELIABILITY COEFFICIENTS
------------------------
CRONBACH'S ALPHA                                              =  0.745   (1)
COEFFICIENT ALPHA FOR AN OPTIMAL SHORT SCALE                  =  0.862   (2)
BASED ON THE FOLLOWING   2 VARIABLES
  V7        V17
RELIABILITY COEFFICIENT RHO                                   =  0.540   (3)
GREATEST LOWER BOUND RELIABILITY                              =  0.921   (4)
LI-BENTLER CORRECTED GREATEST LOWER BOUND RELIABILITY         =  0.901
GLB RELIABILITY FOR AN OPTIMAL SHORT SCALE                    =  0.928   (5)
BASED ON 19 VARIABLES, ALL EXCEPT:
  V9        V12       V14
BENTLER'S DIMENSION-FREE LOWER BOUND RELIABILITY              =  0.921   (6)
LI-BENTLER CORRECTED DIMENSION-FREE LOWER BOUND RELIABILITY   =  0.901
SHAPIRO'S LOWER BOUND RELIABILITY FOR A WEIGHTED COMPOSITE    =  0.947   (7)

WEIGHTS THAT ACHIEVE SHAPIRO'S LOWER BOUND:
  V1        V2        V3        V4        V5        V6        V7
  0.2679    0.0401    0.3213    0.1406    0.3282    0.2637    0.2418
  V8        V9        V10       V11       V12       V13       V14
  0.2400    0.1928    0.0268    0.2368    0.1308    0.1459    0.1575
  V15       V16       V17       V18       V19       V20       V21
  0.2102    0.1348    0.2427    0.2744    0.3218    0.0553    0.1430
  V22
  0.1720

STANDARDIZED FACTOR LOADINGS FOR THE FACTOR THAT GENERATES
MAXIMAL RELIABILITY FOR THE UNIT-WEIGHT COMPOSITE

BASED ON THE MODEL (RHO):
  V1        V2        V3        V4        V5        V6        V7
  0.2651    0.4266   -0.1454    0.1065    0.0909    0.0762    0.3562
  V8        V9        V10       V11       V12       V13       V14
  0.3425    0.0308    0.6107   -0.0265   -0.0897    0.2935    0.0940
  V15       V16       V17       V18       V19       V20       V21
  0.1512    0.1041    0.3651    0.0234    0.0969    0.6580    0.1724
  V22
  0.2782

BASED ON THE GREATEST LOWER BOUND (GLB):
  V1        V2        V3        V4        V5        V6        V7
  0.4536    0.2801    0.5299    0.3045    0.5899    0.5632    0.4042
  V8        V9        V10       V11       V12       V13       V14
  0.4487    0.3019    0.2605    0.4932    0.2171    0.3797    0.2985
  V15       V16       V17       V18       V19       V20       V21
  0.2630    0.3624    0.3503    0.5012    0.6250    0.2677    0.2231
  V22
  0.4393
```

1. First in the list is *Cronbach's α*. In this case it is irrelevant, because it builds on a one-factor model and in addition demands that all regression coefficients and all error variances are equal and that all errors are uncorrelated. This is indeed a very unrealistic model in most cases. The two-factor structure in this case is reason enough to invalidate α.

2. The next two lines, which tell us that we could obtain a maximal α using only the two items V7 and V17, are of course irrelevant for the same reason.
3. Next is ρ, which takes into account the two-factor structure of the model. ρ also assumes unit weighting of the items and, in case of correlated error terms, these correlations are considered to be 'noise'.

    Perhaps this last remark deserves a few more words for clarification.
    Recall Equation (2.2b), which in a 'rougher' form could be formulated as follows:

    variance of X = variance explained by model + unexplained variance (6)

    where X is a manifest variable, and we defined the reliability as

    $$\rho_{xx} = \frac{\text{variance explained by model}}{\text{variance of } X} \quad (7)$$

    In the general factor model (whether it has one or more factors), we have several Xs, i.e. we have a *vector* of Xs, and consequently a covariance *matrix* (the input covariance matrix), which is divided into an implied (or model) matrix and a residual (or error) matrix (cf. Chapter 1's Equation (20)):

    $$\hat{\Sigma} = \hat{\Sigma}_m + \hat{\Sigma}_\varepsilon \quad (8)$$

    The reliability is calculated using a formula analogous to (7), but with covariance matrices substituted for variances. By considering error covariances as 'noise', error variances *and* error covariances are put into $\hat{\Sigma}_\varepsilon$, and $\hat{\Sigma}_m$ takes everything else.

    Whereas α assumes a one-factor structure and ρ builds on the actual model (in this case a two-factor structure), the following reliability measure builds on a many-factor structure with an unspecified number of factors and they consider all covariances to be 'true' – that is, all covariances are put into $\hat{\Sigma}_m$.

4. *Greatest lower bound reliability* demands that all variances are non-negative, whereas *Bentler's dimension-free lower bound reliability* does not. However, they both have an upward bias that could be serious in small samples. The two Li-Bentler corrections allow for this.
5. Also shown in the output is the reliability of an optimal short GLB scale together with a description of which items are included in this scale.
6. *Shapiro's lower bound reliability for a weighted composite* (Shapiro, 1982) is based on weighting the items using the weights that maximize reliability, the weights also being shown in the output.
7. Last in the output are standardized factor loadings that maximize the reliability measures ρ and GLB (both of which presuppose unit weighted scores).

Validity

Calculation of a suitable measure for the validity is more complicated.

Let us assume that we have a manifest variable V, which is an indicator of more than one latent variable in our model. If as our starting point we take the validity of V to be the extent to which V is connected to each concept, F1, F2, ... it is assumed to measure, then the most straightforward measures of validity are the regression coefficients (V1,F1), (V1,F2), … in raw or standardized form. Each of these measures has the same advantages and drawbacks that we know from traditional regression analysis. One advantage of the standardized coefficients is that they are independent of the measurement units. This is very important in the case of SEM, where the measurement scales of the variables and especially those of the latent variables are often more or less arbitrary. On the other hand, standardized coefficients depend on the variances in the populations, and if we wish to compare several groups from different populations this could be a problem.

Another way is to start with the reliability coefficient as the coefficient of determination when regressing the variable V on all variables that have a direct effect on it. This is of course the squared correlation coefficient as defined in the section above on reliability.

If we want the validity coefficient to measure that part of the variance in V attributable to, for example, F1, we must deduce from the squared multiple correlation coefficient the variation caused by all other factors influencing V.

We can then define the validity coefficient of V with regard to F1 as

$$U_{V.F1} = R_V^2 - R_{V(F1)}^2 \tag{9}$$

where R_V^2 is the coefficient of determination obtained by regressing V on all variables that have a direct influence on V, while $R_{V(F1)}^2$ is the coefficient of determination obtained by regressing V on the same variables except F1. The symbols in (9) are taken from Bollen (1989), who proposed the measure, to designate *unique validity variance*.

Example 2 (continued)
Constructing a scale to measure 'style of processing'

Let us estimate the unique validity variance of *process18* with regard to *verbal* in the model for the second run.

We have

$$U_{V18.verbal} = R_{V18}^2 - R_{V18(verbal)}^2 \tag{10}$$

R_{V18}^2 can be read from Table 10, and $R_{V18(verbal)}^2$ is obtained by regressing process18 only on 'visual':

$$U_{V18, verbal} = 0.722 - 0.064 = 0.658 \tag{11}$$

As pointed out several times, the concept of validity is much more problematic both to define and to measure than reliability. The reader is referred to Bollen (1989) and Raykov (2012) for further reading.

5 Reflexive and Formative Indicators

In a confirmatory factor model (and also in an exploratory factor model), the arrows point *from* the latent variable to its manifest indicators. As a consequence, indicators of the same latent variable must correlate (cf. Figure 9a).

It is a very common mistake among newcomers to SEM to overlook this simple fact, and to use indicators that are not *necessarily* correlated.

The classic example is that you want to measure a person's consumption of alcoholic beverages, and to that end you use a series of questions each measuring the consumption of one single beverage. That is, indicators such as:

Consumption of beer

Consumption of wine

Consumption of whisky

Consumption of cognac

etc.

While a (weighted) sum of these variables is a measure of total consumption of alcohol, there is no reason to believe that all these indicators should be correlated.

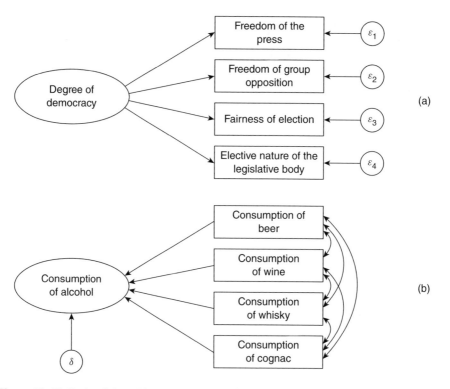

Figure 7 Reflexive (a) and formative (b) indicators

In a graphic illustration of this situation, the arrows should point *from* the indicators and *to* the latent variable (cf. Figure 9b).

The indicators in panel (a) of the figure are called *reflexive*: they *reflect* the underlying latent variable. In contrast the indicators in panel (b) are called *formative*: they *form* or define the latent variable, which in this case is not latent at all, as it is a function of manifest variables.

While a certain amount of correlation should exist among reflexive indicators for the same latent variable, correlations among formative indicators are not a necessity.

It is important to be aware that classical test theory and concepts like reliability and validity assume indicators to be reflexive. Using formative indicators in SEM programs like EQS is rather complicated. Apart from identification problems (that can be very tricky to solve) you can see from the figure that making the indicators exogenous means that they lose their error terms, and that measurement errors will instead be absorbed in the disturbance of the latent variable together with other sources of unexplained variance if the latent variable is affected by other variables in a larger model.

In fact, you have already met examples of indicators that could perhaps be considered formative, namely the three problematic items forb38, forb39 and forb41 in the first fish example (Example 2.1).

In many applications of SEM, socio-economic variables are used to characterize a person. The various indicators used are most realistically seen as formative, but it is not uncommon to see them treated as reflexive.

The many problems with using formative indicators in traditional SEM are given an excellent treatment by Kline (2006).

If your model includes several latent variables with formative indicators, you could try using another SEM technique, namely *partial least squares* (PLS) invented by Herman Wold (Wold, 1975). An introduction to this technique can be found in Fornell and Cha (1994). A deeper treatment with many examples is given by Vinzi, Chin, Henseler, and Wang (2010). The newest textbook is by Hair, Hult, and Ringle (2014).

You could say that PLS relates to covariance-based SEM like component analysis relates to factor analysis (Compare Figure 7 with Figure 1).

In this chapter you met the following concepts:

- confirmatory factor analysis
- three-indicator rule
- two-indicator rule
- R^2 as a measure of reliability
- unique variance as a measure of validity
- χ^2-difference test
- Lagrange multiplier test

You have also been introduced to the EQS paragraphs:

/CONSTRAINTS

and

/RELIABILITY

and to the various reliability measures in EQS.

Questions

1. State the differences among the three (main) factor models, and discuss their virtues and vices.

2. Can you suggest further modifications to the model in Figure 3?

3. Reflecting on your own studies or research, comment on the various instruments EQS offers for helping you with model modifications. Discuss their virtues and vices.

4. Comment on the differences between reflective and formative indicators. Why is this distinction important?

References

Bentler, P. M. (2006). *EQS 6 Structural equations program manual*. Encino, CA: Multivariate Software, Inc.

Bollen, K. A. (1989). *Structural equation modeling with latent variables*. New York: Wiley.

Bollen, K. A. (1979). Political democracy and the timing of development. *American Sociological Review, 44*, 572–587.

Bollen, K. A. (1980). Issues in the comparative measurement of political democracy. *American Sociological Review, 45*, 370–390.

Bollen, K. A. (1989). *Structural equation modeling with latent variables*. New York: Wiley.

Childers, T. L., Houston, M. J., & Heckler, S. (1985). Measurement of individual differences in visual versus verbal information processing. *Journal of Consumer Research, 12*, 124–134.

Fornell, C., & Cha, J. (1994). Partial least squares. In P. Bagozzi (Ed.), *Advanced methods of marketing research*. Oxford: Blackwell.

Hair, J. F., Hult, G. T. M., & Ringle, C. (2014). *A primer on least squares structural equation modeling*. Thousand Oaks, CA: Sage.

Kline, R. B. (2006). Reverse arrow dynamics: Formative measurement and feedback loops. In G. R. Hancock & R. O. Mueller (Eds.), *Structural equation modeling: A second course* (pp. 43–68). Charlotte, NC: Information Age Publishing.

Paivio, A. (1971). *Imagery and verbal processes*. New York: Holt, Rinehart & Winston.

Raykov, T. (1997). Estimation of composite reliability for congeneric measures. *Applied Psychological Measurement, 21*, 173.

Raykov, T. (2012). Scale construction and development using structural equation modeling. In R. H. Hoyle (Ed.), *Handbook of structural equation modeling* (pp. 472–492). New York: Guilford Press.

Shapiro, A. (1982). Weighted minimum trace factor analysis. *Psychometrika, 47*, 243–264.

Sørensen, E. (2001). *Means-end chains og laddering i et kognitivt perspektiv*. PhD thesis, Aarhus School of Business, Aarhus, Denmark.

Vinzi, V. E., Chin, W. W., Henseler, J., & Wang, H. (2010). *Handbook of partial least squares: Concepts, methods and applications in marketing and related fields*. New York: Springer.

Wold, H. (1975). Path models with latent variables: The NIPALS approach. In H. M. Blalock (Ed.), *Quantitative sociology: International perspectives on mathematical and statistical modeling*. New York: Academic Press.

8

The General Model

In this chapter the structural model (Chapter 6) and the measurement model (Chapter 7) are brought together to form the general structural equation model.

This model is introduced by way of Example 4.1, which is modified by letting the structural variables be latent instead of manifest. After this simple example has demonstrated the advantages of basing your analyses on latent variable models, we move on to a larger example.

In this example you will learn the two-step strategy: separate analyses of the measurement and structural models. Among other things, you will also learn how to analyze indirect effects, i.e. effects that are mediated by other variables.

Next you will look at a time series model, which has one real advantage compared with cross-section models: there is no doubt about the causal directions.

1 Combining the Structural and Measurement Model

As you will probably have guessed, combining the structural and the measurement model into one model complicates the analysis. Among the questions to be answered are the following:

1. If I have problems with model fit, is the problem then with the measurement model or the structural model?
2. Combining the two models into one makes them dependent on each other. Therefore the parameter estimates in one sub-model could depend on the parameter estimates in the other. What are the consequences for the substantive interpretation if that happens?

Before answering these questions, let us examine what happens when we transform a model with only manifest variables into one with latent variables.

Example 1 (continued from Example 4.1)
Mapping European consumers' willingness to buy genetically modified food: from manifest to latent variables

In Example 4.1 you were introduced to EQS programming by way of a simple multiple regression example (you may wish to look back at this before moving on) using only manifest variables – in this case summated scales. This presupposes that measurement error is absent – that the measurements are totally reliable. This is of course a very unrealistic assumption, but we can loosen it by introducing latent variables. In Figure 1 you can compare the original regression model in panel (a) with the model in panel (b), obtained by splitting the various summated scales into their separate items.

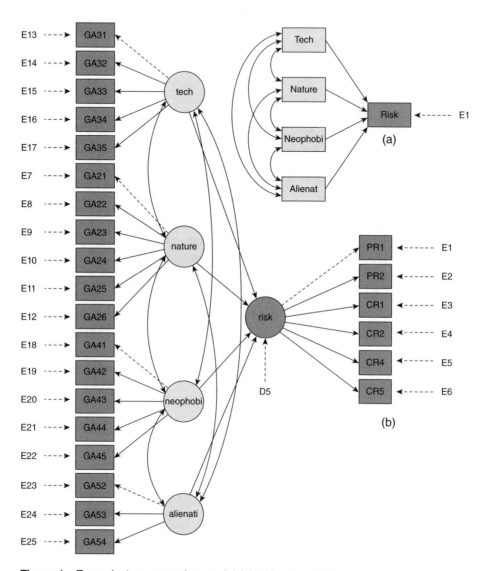

Figure 1 Example 1: a regression model (a) without and (b) with latent variables

Identification: the two-step rule

As already mentioned, there is no general necessary and sufficient condition for identification, so often you have to rely on the computer's messages about 'probably non-identified' parameters.

As the general model consists of two sub-models – a measurement model and a structural model – intuitively the total model must be identified if its two parts are identified when considered separately. This can in fact be proved to be the case, and can be formulated in the so-called *two-step rule*.

First you look at the model in Figure 1b as a confirmatory factor analysis model (i.e. you let the one-headed arrows in the structural model be substituted by two-headed arrows depicting covariances) and make sure that it is identified. Then you regard the structural part of the model as consisting of only manifest variables, and you make sure that this model is identified too. If both conditions are fulfilled this is *sufficient* (but not necessary) to secure identification of the original model.

The first condition is met according to the three-indicator rule (mentioned in Section 7.2), and the second follows from the zero B-rule (mentioned in Section 6.1).

Estimation

A program for estimating the model is given in Table 1 and the data can be found on the book's website.

As you can see, I have not written out the individual variances and covariances, but used the 'short form' you first met in Section 4.4. A similar method can be used in the /EQUATIONS paragraph, which can be written

```
                    /EQUATIONS
                  V1 TO V6 ON F5;
                  V7 TO V12 ON F2;
                  V8 TO V17 ON F1;
                  V18 TO V22 ON F3;
                  V23 TO V25 ON F4;
```

Part of the output is given in Table 2.

Table 1 Example 1: the program

```
/TITLE
  Example 8.1. Data from Bredahl (2001)
/SPECIFICATIONS
  DATA='c:\users\sony\desktop\eqs bog\eqs chap 8\bredahla.ess';
  VARIABLES=30; CASES=481;
  METHOD=ML; ANALYSIS=COVARIANCE; MATRIX=RAW;
/LABELS
  V1=PR1; V2=PR2; V3=CR1; V4=CR2; V5=CR4;
  V6=CR5; V7=GA21; V8=GA22; V9=GA23; V10=GA24;
  V11=GA25; V12=GA26; V13=GA31; V14=GA32; V15=GA33;
  V16=GA34; V17=GA35; V18=GA41; V19=GA42; V20=GA43;
  V21=GA44; V22=GA45; V23=GA52; V24=GA53; V25=GA54;
/EQUATIONS
```

(Continued)

Table 1 (Continued)

```
    V1  =  1F5 + E1;   V2  =  *F5 + E2;   V3  =  *F5 + E3;    V4  =  *F5 + E4;
    V5  =  *F5 + E5;   V6  =  *F5 + E6;   V7  =  1F2 + E7;    V8  =  *F2 + E8;
    V9  =  *F2 + E9;   V10 =  *F2 + E10;  V11 =  *F2 + E11;   V12 =  *F2 + E12;
    V13 =  1F1 + E13;  V14 =  *F1 + E14;  V15 =  *F1 + E15;   V16 =  *F1 + E16;
    V17 =  *F1 + E17;  V18 =  1F3 + E18;  V19 =  *F3 + E19;   V20 =  *F3 + E20;
    V21 =  *F3 + E21;  V22 =  *F3 + E22;  V23 =  1F4 + E23;   V24 =  *F4 + E24;
    V25 =  *F4 + E25;
      F5 = *F1 + *F2 + *F3 + *F4 + D5;
/VARIANCES
 F1 TO F4= *;
 E1 TO E25= *;
 D5 = *;
/COVARIANCES
 F1 TO F4 = *;
/PRINT
 FIT=ALL;
 TABLE=COMPACT;
/END
/PRINT
 FIT=ALL;
 TABLE=COMPACT;
/END
```

Table 2 Example 1: output

```
MAXIMUM LIKELIHOOD SOLUTION (NORMAL DISTRIBUTION THEORY)

    PARAMETER ESTIMATES (B) WITH STANDARD ERRORS AND TEST STATISTICS (Z)
    STATISTICS SIGNIFICANT AT THE 5% LEVEL ARE MARKED WITH @.

                                                                            R-
   DEP.VAR.         PREDICTOR              B      BETA    S.E.     Z      SQUARED
   ---------------------------------------------------------------------------
   V1  ( PR1  )    F5  (  RISK   )      .815*    .619    .063   12.988@   .383
   V2  ( PR2  )    F5  (  RISK   )     1.073*    .762    .066   16.208@   .581
   V3  ( CR1  )    F5  (  RISK   )     1.000     .771                     .595
   V4  ( CR2  )    F5  (  RISK   )      .696*    .569    .059   11.880@   .324
   V5  ( CR4  )    F5  (  RISK   )      .662*    .622    .051   13.058@   .386
   V6  ( CR5  )    F5  (  RISK   )      .851*    .684    .059   14.471@   .468
   V7  ( GA21 )    F2  (NATURE   )     1.000     .755                     .570
   V8  ( GA22 )    F2  (NATURE   )      .830*    .534    .089    9.316@   .285
   V9  ( GA23 )    F2  (NATURE   )      .660*    .405    .090    7.341@   .164
   V10 ( GA24 )    F2  (NATURE   )      .738*    .399    .102    7.233@   .159
   V11 ( GA25 )    F2  (NATURE   )      .555*    .309    .097    5.705@   .096
   V12 ( GA26 )    F2  (NATURE   )      .692*    .410    .093    7.424@   .168
   V13 ( GA31 )    F1  (  TECH   )     1.000     .657                     .431
   V14 ( GA32 )    F1  (  TECH   )      .979*    .712    .080   12.208@   .507
   V15 ( GA33 )    F1  (  TECH   )      .934*    .700    .077   12.063@   .489
   V16 ( GA34 )    F1  (  TECH   )      .880*    .632    .079   11.190@   .400
   V17 ( GA35 )    F1  (  TECH   )      .888*    .646    .078   11.374@   .417
   V18 ( GA41 )    F3  (NEOPHOBI )     1.000     .529                     .280
   V19 ( GA42 )    F3  (NEOPHOBI )     1.306*    .682    .132    9.903@   .465
   V20 ( GA43 )    F3  (NEOPHOBI )     1.319*    .639    .138    9.566@   .409
```

8.1 Combining the Structural and Measurement Model

```
V21  ( GA44 )   F3   (NEOPHOBI )    1.505*   .785    .143    10.510@    .617
V22  ( GA45 )   F3   (NEOPHOBI )    1.308*   .640    .137     9.570@    .409
V23  ( GA52 )   F4   (ALIENAT  )    1.000    .756                       .572
V24  ( GA53 )   F4   (ALIENAT  )    1.097*   .792    .085    12.976@    .627
V25  ( GA54 )   F4   (ALIENAT  )     .899*   .583    .082    10.992@    .340
F5   ( RISK )   F1   (  TECH   )    -.326*  -.254    .067    -4.867@    .584
                F2   (NATURE   )     .617*   .464    .090     6.820@
                F3   (NEOPHOBI )     .378*   .256    .080     4.717@
                F4   (ALIENAT  )     .341*   .256    .079     4.334@

COVARIANCES AMONG INDEPENDENT VARIABLES
STATISTICS SIGNIFICANT AT THE 5% LEVEL ARE MARKED WITH @.

                                   COVA.    S.E.      Z        CORR.
----------------------------------------------------------------------
F1,F2    ( TECH    ,NATURE   )     .065*    .065    1.000       .061
F1,F3    ( TECH    ,NEOPHOBI)     -.360*    .067   -5.370@     -.374
F1,F4    ( TECH    ,ALIENAT  )     .014*    .062     .231       .013
F2,F3    (NATURE   ,NEOPHOBI)      .029*    .057     .514       .031
F2,F4    (NATURE   ,ALIENAT  )     .511*    .074    6.913@      .497
F3,F4    (NEOPHOBI ,ALIENAT  )     .107*    .055    1.948       .115
```

The main results from the analysis in Example 4.1 and the present analysis are most easily compared as in Table 3.

Table 3 Example 1: comparing the results of the two analyses. Estimated regression coefficients (standard errors in parentheses) and coefficients of determination

	Manifest variables	Latent variables
Technology	−0.242	−0.326
	(0.051)	(0.067)
Nature	0.368	0.617
	(0.047)	(0.090)
Neophobia	0.270	0.378
	(0.043)	(0.080)
Alienation	0.672	0.341
	(0.082)	(0.079)
R^2	0.382	0.584

What first catches the eye is the increase in the coefficient of determination caused by introducing latent variables: from 0.382 to 0.584, an increase of no less than 53%. So part of the reason for the apparently low overall explanatory power in the original regression model is the low reliability of the measurements.

Also observe that rather dramatic changes in regression coefficients have taken place, and that neglecting the measurement errors underestimates most of the standard errors.

The effects of introducing latent variables

From the above example, you will see that neglecting the inevitable measurement error ε has the following consequences:

1. Unreliable measurement of the dependent variable deflates the coefficient of determination and increases the standard error of the estimated regression coefficients.
2. Unreliable measurements of independent variables bias the estimated regression coefficients and the coefficient of determination.

Both problems can be solved by regarding the variables in question as latent.

2 Analysis of the General Model

In Example 1 the measurement model is over-identified and the structural model is just-identified. This means that the χ^2-test is a test of the measurement model only and that all the fit indices only measure the fit of the measurement part of the model. If you substitute unexplained covariances for the one-headed arrows in the structural part of the model, you end up with exactly the same fit measures. The two models are equivalent.

Therefore the only measure of 'fit' for the structural part of the model is R^2.

Often the measurement model and the structural model are estimated in one go – the so-called *one-step strategy*. However, this could raise problems, one of which is that if the (complete) model does not fit the data, it can sometimes be complicated to find out whether the structural model depicting your theory is wrong, or the bad fit is due to unreliable measurements.

Therefore, a two-step rule should also be applied to the analysis of the model. First analyze the model as a confirmatory factor model and then put in the one-headed arrows and analyze the full model. This is the so-called *two-step strategy*. Anyway, it is meaningless to analyze the structural part of the model if the measurement model does not show satisfactory reliabilities.

Another problem is this: if the model fits the data, and a measurement model shows a satisfactory reliability, can we then be sure that it will show the same excellent qualities if used in connection with another structural model? In other words, a measuring instrument should ideally work in the same way whenever it is used, irrespective of the structural model. Therefore the regression coefficients in the measurement model should not change significantly when making modifications to the structural part of the model.

The two-step strategy could therefore easily be expanded to a many-step procedure. One example is given by Mulaik and Millsap (2000) who proposed a four-step strategy starting with an exploratory factor analysis. However, using an exploratory technique as the first step could be a bit dangerous if no more than two samples are used for cross-validation – and if you forgo substantive thinking.

Another point to consider is whether the measuring instruments also generalize to other populations, other points in time, etc. – a subject I will take up in the next chapter.

Example 2
Does mental condition influence the immune system?

Using Danish data, Thomsen et al. (2004) mapped the relationships between rumination (negative recurrent thoughts), immune parameters and health care utilization for two samples, one of young and one of elderly people. I will use only the elderly sample. The data (ThomsenElder) can be found on the book's website.

The model that seems to be the basis for their analysis is shown in Figure 2.

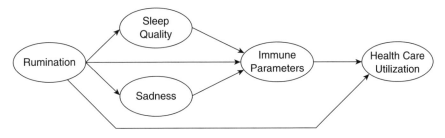

Figure 2 Example 2: the structural model

Rumination was measured using the rehearsal sub-scale from the *Emotional Control Questionnaire version 2* (Roger & Narajian, 1989), sadness by the depression–dejection sub-scale from the short version of the *Profile of Moods Scale* (McNair, Lorr, & Dopplemann, 1981; Shacham, 1983) and sleep quality by the one item on subjective sleep quality from the *Pittsburgh Sleep Quality Index* (Buysse, Reynolds, Monk, Berman, & Kupfer, 1989). The items used are shown in Table 4.

Table 4 Example 2: scales used for measuring the psychological constructs

Rumination	
ecq 1	I remember things that upset me or make me angry for a long time afterwards
ecq 2	I generally don't bear a grudge – when something is over, it's over, and I don't think about it again
ecq 3	I get 'worked up' just thinking about things that have upset me in the past
ecq 4	I often find myself thinking over and over about things that have made me angry
ecq 5	I can usually settle things quickly and be friendly again after an argument
ecq 6	If I see or hear about an accident, I find myself thinking about something similar happening to me or to people close to me
ecq 7	I think about ways of getting back on people who have made me angry a long time after the event has happened

(Continued)

Table 4 (Continued)

Rumination	
ecq 8	I never forget people making me angry or upset, even about small things
ecq 9	I find it hard to get thoughts about things that have upset me out of my mind
ecq 10	I often daydream about situations where I'm getting my own back on people
ecq 11	If I see something that frightens or upsets me, the image of it stays in my mind for a long time afterwards
ecq 12	Thinking about upsetting things just seems to keep them going, so I try to put them out of my mind
ecq 13	If I lose out on something, I get over it quickly
ecq 14	If I have to confront someone, I try not to think too much about it beforehand
Sadness	(5-point scale, scaled 'not at all' to 'extremely')
poms4d	Unhappy
poms8d	Sad
poms12d	Blue
poms14d	Hopeless
poms20d	Discouraged
poms23d	Miserable
poms28d	Helpless
poms33d	Worthless
Subjective sleep quality: psqik1	During the past month, how would you rate your sleep quality overall (scaled 0–4, the smaller, the better)?

Looking at the items in Table 4, it is noticeable that ecq 7, ecq 8, ecq 9 and ecq 10 are very similar, so I would expect them to correlate more than due to their common factor rumination. Furthermore, they are placed together, which could strengthen the correlations. This is not the only example of similar items being placed together. I sincerely hope that the researchers randomized the order of items in the questionnaire they used!

I will tentatively include these correlations in the measurement model.

The following immune parameters were measured: number of leukocytes, number of lymphocytes, number of $CD19^+$ lymphocytes and PHA-stimulated T-cell proliferation. Data on health care utilization were extracted from the country's central register where the following two variables were used: number of personal consultations with GP during follow-up period and number of telephone consultations during the same period. In the following analysis both these variables are divided by five in order to put their variances on a level with the other manifest variables (cf. the comments in Section 4.6).

Thomsen et al. analyzed the various effects on immune parameters and on health care utilization in two separate sets of stepwise regressions, one with immune parameters as dependent variables and one with health care utilization as a dependent variable.

I will reanalyze their data using SEM, taking as my point of departure the model sketched in Figure 2.

There are a rather large number of missing values in the data, which means that only two of the four immune indicators will be used. Furthermore, I will use only respondents who have no missing values on any measurement.

This limits the sample to 247 respondents and is of course not the most efficient use of the data. However, this choice is taken for pedagogical reasons. In Chapter 10 you will learn how to analyze incomplete datasets in ways that makes full use of all available data.

It is always a good idea to look at the covariations between the manifest variables before doing any calculations. This will often give you a first check on the realism of a proposed model. This is the reason why EQS transforms an inputted covariance matrix to a correlation matrix when it is saved: correlations are easier to interpret than covariances.

	ecq1	ecq2	ecq3	ecq4	ecq5	ecq6	ecq7	ecq8	ecq9	ecq10	ecq11	ecq12
ecq7	0.3354	0.0699	0.3578	0.4528	0.0693	0.2051	1.0000	0.3103	0.1620	0.5303	0.2044	0.006
ecq8	0.4568	0.1599	0.3497	0.3976	0.1389	0.2136	0.3103	1.0000	0.5343	0.3261	0.2440	0.038
ecq9	0.5806	0.1527	0.4820	0.5281	0.1881	0.3006	0.1620	0.5343	1.0000	0.2442	0.4547	0.040
ecq10	0.2572	0.1594	0.2376	0.2590	0.2166	0.1324	0.5303	0.3261	0.2442	1.0000	0.2787	0.004
ecq11	0.3471	0.1673	0.4185	0.3060	0.2779	0.3012	0.2044	0.2440	0.4547	0.2787	1.0000	0.097
ecq12	0.0362	0.2868	0.0415	-0.0027	0.3848	-0.0346	0.0064	0.0382	0.0403	0.0045	0.0971	1.000
ecq13	0.1610	0.3458	0.1010	0.1310	0.5130	0.0434	0.1274	0.1130	0.1716	0.1233	0.2227	0.553
ecq14	-0.0181	0.2450	-0.0631	-0.0382	0.1955	-0.1872	-0.0247	0.0437	-0.0027	0.0094	-0.0437	0.322
poms4d	0.2687	0.1592	0.2806	0.2247	0.1127	0.0249	0.1121	0.1461	0.3030	0.0825	0.2051	0.051
poms8d	0.2570	0.1573	0.2154	0.1852	0.0893	0.0539	0.0965	0.1821	0.2865	0.1450	0.1705	-0.012
poms12	0.2685	0.1438	0.2478	0.2222	0.1428	0.1435	0.1650	0.1929	0.3208	0.1992	0.3053	0.025
poms14	0.1979	0.1755	0.2416	0.1912	0.1950	-0.0170	0.0389	0.1281	0.2449	0.1159	0.1586	0.011
poms20	0.2437	0.1503	0.2518	0.2077	0.0848	0.0956	0.0568	0.1562	0.3624	0.1236	0.1750	-0.085
poms23	0.1668	0.0370	0.2348	0.1694	0.0136	0.0358	0.0592	0.1164	0.1176	0.0392	0.1075	0.065
poms28	0.1816	0.1276	0.2206	0.1765	0.1467	0.0913	0.1199	0.1872	0.1945	0.2034	0.1308	-0.022
poms33	0.1153	0.0458	0.1590	0.0837	0.0717	0.0487	0.1212	0.0792	0.1507	0.1456	0.1929	0.029
psqik	0.2665	0.1444	0.1744	0.0782	0.2080	0.0352	0.0758	0.0324	0.2380	0.1563	0.1593	0.116
leukocy	0.1396	0.1239	0.1209	0.1002	0.0621	0.1265	0.1085	0.0642	0.1275	0.1308	0.1375	0.032
lympho	0.1620	0.0674	0.1540	0.0774	0.0960	0.0318	0.1460	0.0653	0.0756	0.1710	0.1659	0.040
consult	0.0098	0.0307	0.0502	0.0159	0.0137	0.0078	-0.0133	-0.0934	0.0334	-0.0192	-0.0426	0.028
telepho	0.1769	-0.0067	0.2179	0.1188	0.0333	0.0748	0.0526	-0.0059	0.2043	0.0046	0.1738	0.020
STD_D	1.1094	1.2275	0.9611	0.9090	1.0933	1.0657	0.6280	0.8419	0.9975	0.4299	0.9500	1.145
MEAN	0.0000	0.0000	0.0000	0.0000	0.0000	0.0000	0.0000	0.0000	0.0000	0.0000	0.0000	0.000

Figure 3 Example 2: input correlation matrix (detail)

One thing that you will immediately observe when you examine the input correlations is that variable V26 (CONSULT) has no connection to any other variable than V27 (TELEPHON): its average correlation to other variables is 0.05, the median correlation is 0.04 and the maximum 0.15. The preceding factors seem to have a larger effect on telephone consultations than on face-to-face consultations (for space reasons only a small part of the input matrix is shown in Figure 3).

Telephone consultations are typically used for less severe health problems such as colds, influenza and milder pains, and for the renewal of prescriptions for sleeping pills and nerve medicine. If the model should end up connecting telephone calls with rumination, sleeping problems and depression, the simple explanation could also be that people ruminate about health problems!

In contrast face-to-face consultations are used for more serious health problems. Such problems could of course also have their roots in rumination, but they are less likely to show up during the rather short follow-up period, where the data were collected.

I therefore decided to measure health care utilization only by TELEPHON, and to fix its coefficient at 1.00 and its variance at 0.00.

This seems not to be too unrealistic: data about telephone (as well as face-to-face) consultations are taken from a national register – and it is not too unrealistic to assume the errors in the register to be negligible. At this early stage, using the same procedure with the factor 'Sleep Quality' is more unrealistic, but will do at this stage. I will return to the problem later.

As a first step, I will analyze the model as a confirmatory factor model, as shown in Figure 4.

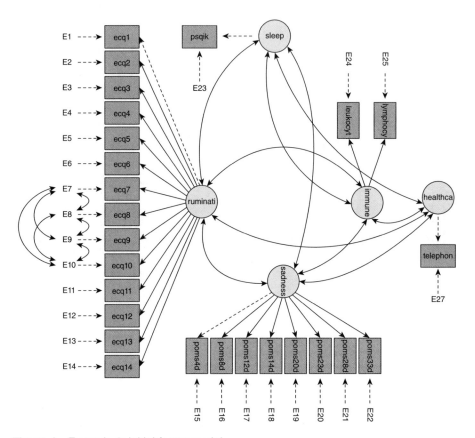

Figure 4 Example 2: initial factor model

The program is given in Table 5 and the output in Table 6.

Table 5 Example 2: program for first run

```
/TITLE
   Example 8.2. Data from Thomsen et al. (2004)
/SPECIFICATIONS
   DATA='c:\users\sony\desktop\eqs bog\eqs chap 8\thomsenelder.ess';
   VARIABLES=27; CASES=247;
   METHOD=ML; ANALYSIS=COVARIANCE; MATRIX=COVARIANCE;
/LABELS
   F1=rumination; F2=sadness; F3=sleep; F4= immune; F5=health care;
   V1=ecq1; V2=ecq2; V3=ecq3; V4=ecq4; V5=ecq5;
   V6=ecq6; V7=ecq7; V8=ecq8; V9=ecq9; V10=ecq10;
```

```
        V11=ecq11; V12=ecq12; V13=ecq13; V14=ecq14; V15=poms4d;
        V16=poms8d; V17=poms12d; V18=poms14d; V19=poms20d; V20=poms23d;
        V21=poms28d; V22=poms33d; V23=psqik; V24=leukocyt; V25=lymphocy;
        V26=consult; V27=telephon;
/EQUATIONS
        V1  =    1F1 + E1;
        V2  =    *F1 + E2;
        V3  =    *F1 + E3;
        V4  =    *F1 + E4;
        V5  =    *F1 + E5;
        V6  =    *F1 + E6;
        V7  =    *F1 + E7;
        V8  =    *F1 + E8;
        V9  =    *F1 + E9;
        V10 =    *F1 + E10;
        V11 =    *F1 + E11;
        V12 =    *F1 + E12;
        V13 =    *F1 + E13;
        V14 =    *F1 + E14;
        V15 =    1F2 + E15;
        V16 =    *F2 + E16;
        V17 =    *F2 + E17;
        V18 =    *F2 + E18;
        V19 =    *F2 + E19;
        V20 =    *F2 + E20;
        V21 =    *F2 + E21;
        V22 =    *F2 + E22;
        V23 =    1F3 + E23;
        V24 =    1F4 + E24;
        V25 =    *F4 + E25;
        V27 =    1F5 + E27;
/VARIANCES
        F1 to F5     = *;
        E1 TO E22    = *;
        E23          = 0;
        E24 TO E25   = *;
        E27          = 0;
/COVARIANCES
        F1 TO F5 = *;
        E7 TO E10 =*;
/PRINT
        FIT=ALL;
TABLE=COMPACT;
    /LMTEST
    PROCESS=SIMULTANEOUS;
    SET=PEE;
/END
```

Table 6 Example 2: output first run

```
    CHI-SQUARE =        731.570 BASED ON       285 DEGREES OF FREEDOM
    PROBABILITY VALUE FOR THE CHI-SQUARE STATISTIC IS       0.00000

MAXIMUM LIKELIHOOD SOLUTION (NORMAL DISTRIBUTION THEORY)

PARAMETER ESTIMATES (B) WITH STANDARD ERRORS AND TEST STATISTICS (Z)
STATISTICS SIGNIFICANT AT THE 5% LEVEL ARE MARKED WITH @.
```

(Continued)

Table 6 (Continued)

DEP.VAR.	PREDICTOR		B	BETA	S.E.	Z	R-SQUARED
V1 (ECQ1)							.572
	F1	(RUMINATI)	1.000	.756			
V2 (ECQ2)							.052
	F1	(RUMINATI)	.334*	.228	.099	3.361@	
V3 (ECQ3)							.513
	F1	(RUMINATI)	.820*	.716	.075	10.891@	
V4 (ECQ4)							.551
	F1	(RUMINATI)	.804*	.742	.071	11.307@	
V5 (ECQ5)							.096
	F1	(RUMINATI)	.405*	.311	.088	4.587@	
V6 (ECQ6)							.156
	F1	(RUMINATI)	.501*	.394	.086	5.853@	
V7 (ECQ7)							.236
	F1	(RUMINATI)	.364*	.486	.051	7.071@	
V8 (ECQ8)							.277
	F1	(RUMINATI)	.528*	.526	.069	7.684@	
V9 (ECQ9)							.540
	F1	(RUMINATI)	.874*	.735	.079	11.013@	
V10 (ECQ10)							.142
	F1	(RUMINATI)	.193*	.377	.035	5.439@	
V11 (ECQ11)							.289
	F1	(RUMINATI)	.609*	.538	.076	8.058@	
V12 (ECQ12)							.009
	F1	(RUMINATI)	.130*	.095	.093	1.392	
V13 (ECQ13)							.067
	F1	(RUMINATI)	.368*	.259	.096	3.816@	
V14 (ECQ14)							.000
	F1	(RUMINATI)	-.020*	-.016	.088	-.231	
V15 (POMS4D)							.663
	F2	(SADNESS)	1.000	.814			
V16 (POMS8D)							.623
	F2	(SADNESS)	.933*	.790	.068	13.700@	
V17 (POMS12D)							.576
	F2	(SADNESS)	.859*	.759	.066	13.015@	
V18 (POMS14D)							.333
	F2	(SADNESS)	.655*	.577	.070	9.293@	
V19 (POMS20D)							.623
	F2	(SADNESS)	.942*	.789	.069	13.691@	
V20 (POMS23D)							.406
	F2	(SADNESS)	.597*	.637	.057	10.447@	
V21 (POMS28D)							.321
	F2	(SADNESS)	.530*	.567	.058	9.096@	
V22 (POMS33D)							.325
	F2	(SADNESS)	.596*	.570	.065	9.169@	
V23 (PSQIK)							1.000
	F3	(SLEEP)	1.000	1.000			
V24 (LEUKOCYT)							.427
	F4	(IMMUNE)	1.000	.653			
V25 (LYMPHOCY)							.398
	F4	(IMMUNE)	.334*	.631	.105	3.175@	
V27 (TELEPHON)							1.000
	F5	(HEALTHCA)	1.000	1.000			

			COVA.	S.E.	Z	CORR.
F1,F2	(RUMINATI,SADNESS)		.213*	.041	5.151@	.426
F1,F3	(RUMINATI,	F3)	.158*	.044	3.625@	.260
F1,F4	(RUMINATI,	F4)	.283*	.102	2.783@	.283
F1,F5	(RUMINATI,	F5)	.209*	.065	3.219@	.229

```
F2,F3    (SADNESS ,    F3    )   .189*   .032    5.825@   .439
F2,F4    (SADNESS ,    F4    )  -.007*   .062    -.114   -.010
F2,F5    (SADNESS ,    F5    )   .159*   .045    3.526@   .247
F3,F4    (SLEEP   ,IMMUNE    )   .164*   .077    2.128@   .189
F3,F5    (SLEEP   ,HEALTHCA)    .170*   .051    3.308@   .216
F4,F5    (IMMUNE  ,HEALTHCA)    .082*   .109     .753    .063
E7,E8    (   ECQ7 ,  ECQ8   )   .029*   .027    1.068    .074
E7,E9    (   ECQ7 ,  ECQ9   )  -.122*   .028   -4.396@  -.329
E7,E10   (   ECQ7 , ECQ10   )   .094*   .016    5.832@   .429
E8,E9    (   ECQ8 ,  ECQ9   )   .124*   .038    3.261@   .256
E8,E10   (   ECQ8 , ECQ10   )   .046*   .020    2.359@   .162
E9,E10   (   ECQ9 , ECQ10   )  -.014*   .020    -.719   -.052
```

LAGRANGE MULTIPLIER TEST (FOR ADDING PARAMETERS)

ORDERED UNIVARIATE TEST STATISTICS:

```
                                           HANCOCK              STANDAR-
                                  CHI-      285 DF   PARAM.     DIZED    PREDICTED
NO   CODE     PARAMETER   SQUARE   PROB.    PROB.   CHANGE     CHANGE   RMSEA    CFI
--   ----     ---------   ------   -----    -----   ------     ------   -----    ---
 1    2  6    E13,E12     75.463   0.000    1.000    0.731      0.557   0.073   0.827
 2    2  6    E13,E5      56.155   0.000    1.000    0.579      0.484   0.075   0.818
 3    2  6    E5,E2       50.841   0.000    1.000    0.571      0.460   0.075   0.815
 4    2  6    E12,E5      35.308   0.000    1.000    0.453      0.382   0.077   0.808
 5    2  6    E22,E18     32.038   0.000    1.000    0.108      0.383   0.077   0.806
 6    2  6    E14,E12     26.027   0.000    1.000    0.400      0.325   0.078   0.803
 7    2  6    E14,E13     25.805   0.000    1.000    0.404      0.326   0.078   0.803
 8    2  6    E13,E2      23.332   0.000    1.000    0.427      0.311   0.078   0.802
 9    2  6    E21,E18     21.941   0.000    1.000    0.080      0.317   0.078   0.802
10    2  6    E12,E2      18.596   0.000    1.000    0.377      0.276   0.078   0.800
11    2  6    E14,E2      16.182   0.000    1.000    0.332      0.258   0.079   0.799
12    2  6    E21,E15     15.792   0.000    1.000   -0.058     -0.301   0.079   0.799
13    2  6    E7,E4       13.298   0.000    1.000    0.083      0.247   0.079   0.798
14    2  6    E18,E17     12.814   0.000    1.000   -0.062     -0.259   0.079   0.797
15    2  6    E16,E15     12.001   0.001    1.000    0.056      0.305   0.079   0.797
16    2  6    E23,E17     11.622   0.001    1.000   -0.067      0.000   0.079   0.797
17    2  6    E22,E21     11.149   0.001    1.000    0.053      0.226   0.079   0.797
18    2  6    E14,E5      11.117   0.001    1.000    0.240      0.214   0.079   0.797
19    2  6    E23,E21     10.309   0.001    1.000    0.062      0.000   0.079   0.796
20    2  6    E23,E19     10.262   0.001    1.000    0.064      0.000   0.079   0.796
21    2  6    E7,E5       10.137   0.001    1.000   -0.104     -0.183   0.079   0.796
 -    -  -        -          -       -        -        -          -       -       -
 -    -  -        -          -       -        -        -          -       -       -
 -    -  -        -          -       -        -        -          -       -       -
326   2  0    V27,F5       0.000   1.000    1.000    0.000      0.000   0.080   0.791
```

MULTIVARIATE LAGRANGE MULTIPLIER TEST BY SIMULTANEOUS PROCESS IN STAGE 1

PARAMETER SETS (SUBMATRICES) ACTIVE AT THIS STAGE ARE:

   PEE

```
        CUMULATIVE MULTIVARIATE STATISTICS        UNIVARIATE INCREMENT
        ----------------------------------        -----------------------------
                                                                  HANCOCK'S
                      CHI-                      CHI            SEQUENTIAL       PREDICTED
STEP   PARAMETER    SQUARE  D.F.   PROB.      SQUARE   PROB.    D.F.   PROB.   RMSEA    CFI
----   ---------    ------  ----   -----      ------   -----    ----   -----   -----    ---
  1    E13,E12      75.463    1    0.000      75.463   0.000    285    1.000   0.073   0.827
  2    E13,E5      132.223    2    0.000      56.761   0.000    284    1.000   0.067   0.853
  3    E5,E2       184.080    3    0.000      51.857   0.000    283    1.000   0.062   0.876
  4    E12,E5      221.392    4    0.000      37.312   0.000    282    1.000   0.058   0.893
  5    E22,E18     253.430    5    0.000      32.038   0.000    281    1.000   0.054   0.908
```

(Continued)

Table 6 (Continued)

6	E14,E12	279.355	6	0.000	25.926	0.000	280	1.000	0.050	0.919
7	E14,E13	305.276	7	0.000	25.920	0.000	279	1.000	0.047	0.931
8	E13,E2	330.662	8	0.000	25.386	0.000	278	1.000	0.043	0.942
9	E21,E18	355.934	9	0.000	25.272	0.000	277	1.000	0.038	0.954
10	E12,E2	376.296	10	0.000	20.362	0.000	276	1.000	0.034	0.963
11	E14,E2	392.916	11	0.000	16.620	0.000	275	1.000	0.031	0.970
12	E22,E21	409.050	12	0.000	16.134	0.000	274	1.000	0.027	0.977
13	E21,E19	423.669	13	0.000	14.619	0.000	273	1.000	0.023	0.983
14	E23,E21	438.877	14	0.000	15.208	0.000	272	1.000	0.018	0.990
15	E23,E19	452.692	15	0.000	13.815	0.000	271	1.000	0.012	0.996
16	E7,E4	464.912	16	0.000	12.220	0.000	270	1.000	99.999	1.000
17	E14,E5	476.892	17	0.000	11.980	0.001	269	1.000	99.999	1.000
18	E20,E9	486.917	18	0.000	10.025	0.002	268	1.000	99.999	1.000
19	E14,E6	495.198	19	0.000	8.281	0.004	267	1.000	99.999	1.000
20	E10,E5	502.991	20	0.000	7.793	0.005	266	1.000	99.999	1.000
21	E11,E4	510.668	21	0.000	7.677	0.006	265	1.000	99.999	1.000
22	E11,E1	520.487	22	0.000	9.819	0.002	264	1.000	99.999	1.000
23	E19,E12	527.605	23	0.000	7.118	0.008	263	1.000	99.999	1.000
24	E18,E17	534.563	24	0.000	6.959	0.008	262	1.000	99.999	1.000
25	E23,E17	541.251	25	0.000	6.688	0.010	261	1.000	99.999	1.000
26	E27,E15	548.202	26	0.000	6.951	0.008	260	1.000	99.999	1.000
27	E17,E11	554.650	27	0.000	6.448	0.011	259	1.000	99.999	1.000
28	E16,E15	560.829	28	0.000	6.179	0.013	258	1.000	99.999	1.000
29	E20,E15	569.934	29	0.000	9.105	0.003	257	1.000	99.999	1.000
30	E23,E4	575.947	30	0.000	6.012	0.014	256	1.000	99.999	1.000
31	E19,E9	581.642	31	0.000	5.696	0.017	255	1.000	99.999	1.000
32	E11,E10	586.690	32	0.000	5.048	0.025	254	1.000	99.999	1.000
33	E11,E5	591.605	33	0.000	4.915	0.027	253	1.000	99.999	1.000
34	E23,E5	596.564	34	0.000	4.959	0.026	252	1.000	99.999	1.000
35	E18,E5	601.457	35	0.000	4.892	0.027	251	1.000	99.999	1.000
36	E27,E8	606.166	36	0.000	4.710	0.030	250	1.000	99.999	1.000
37	E23,E8	612.168	37	0.000	6.001	0.014	249	1.000	99.999	1.000
38	E27,E24	616.159	38	0.000	3.991	0.046	248	1.000	99.999	1.000
39	E15,E10	620.133	39	0.000	3.975	0.046	247	1.000	99.999	1.000

Although all but two regression coefficients are significant (one-sided test, $\alpha = 0.05$), the fit could be better (CFI = 0.792, RMR = 0.089, SRMR = 0.080, RMSEA = 0.080 (0.073, 0.087)). A glance at the squared multiple correlations shows that some of the indicators have very small reliabilities – and what is more eye-catching, the five items with the lowest reliabilities (ecq2, ecq5, ecq12, ecq13 and ecq14) are exactly the five items that are worded in the opposite direction to the rest.

A look at the modification indices shows quite a few suggestions for letting items ecq2, ecq5, ecq12, ecq13 and ecq14 inter-correlate. This is no surprise, since the inter-correlations signal that these items have something in common that they do not share with the other items – and we know what it is: they are oppositely worded.

A preliminary component analysis of the ecq scale would have shown the scale to be two-dimensional, the two dimensions being made up of items worded positively and negatively respectively (and an item analysis on the complete scale would have eliminated the dimension with fewest items).

What then? We have three options:

1. To put in the suggested correlations.
2. To split the latent variable into two.
3. To skip the smaller of the two dimensions.

As the correlations will probably remain nearly constant and repeat themselves in every use of the ecq scale, and the last option is tantamount to throwing away gratis information, the choice is really between the first two options. However, as this is an illustrative example I decided on the first option, and I will leave it to you to explore the other two possibilities as an exercise.

A glance at the wording of the items poms14d and poms33d shows that introduction of the suggested correlation

$$E18, E22$$

is defendable.

The LM test suggests several correlations between items in the poms scale, but I am reluctant to include them until I have evidence that they are not a peculiarity of my sample but have been verified to show up in other uses of the scale too.

Figure 5 shows the rumination factor after these modifications.

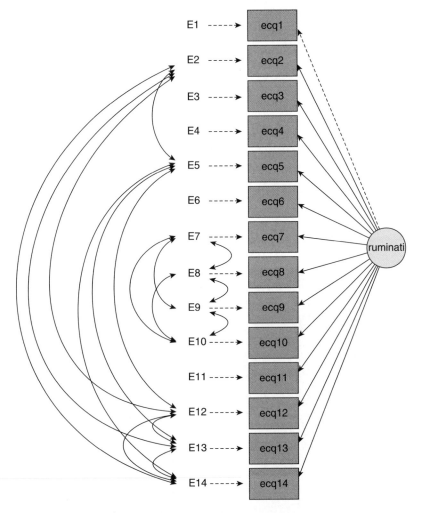

Figure 5 Example 2: rumination factor as modified for the second run

As is evident from Figure 5, a large model with many covariances can make the picture quite messy, and you can easily make mistakes when programming in 'Diagrammer'. In such situations 'Build EQS' is a good alternative.

The program is given in Table 7 and the output in Table 8.

Table 7 Example 2: program for second run

```
/TITLE
/TITLE
   Example 8.2. Data from Thomsen et al. (2004)
/SPECIFICATIONS
   DATA='c:\users\sony\desktop\eqs bog\eqs chap 8\thomsenelder.ess';
   VARIABLES=27; CASES=247;
   METHOD=ML; ANALYSIS=COVARIANCE; MATRIX=COVARIANCE;
/LABELS
   F1=rumination; F2=sadness; F3=sleep; F4= immune; F5=health care;
   V1=ecq1; V2=ecq2; V3=ecq3; V4=ecq4; V5=ecq5;
   V6=ecq6; V7=ecq7; V8=ecq8; V9=ecq9; V10=ecq10;
   V11=ecq11; V12=ecq12; V13=ecq13; V14=ecq14; V15=poms4d;
   V16=poms8d; V17=poms12d; V18=poms14d; V19=poms20d; V20=poms23d;
   V21=poms28d; V22=poms33d; V23=psqik; V24=leukocyt; V25=lymphocy;
   V26=consult; V27=telephon;
/EQUATIONS
   V1  =    1F1 + E1;
   V2  =    *F1 + E2;
   V3  =    *F1 + E3;
   V4  =    *F1 + E4;
   V5  =    *F1 + E5;
   V6  =    *F1 + E6;
   V7  =    *F1 + E7;
   V8  =    *F1 + E8;
   V9  =    *F1 + E9;
   V10 =    *F1 + E10;
   V11 =    *F1 + E11;
   V12 =    *F1 + E12;
   V13 =    *F1 + E13;
   V14 =    *F1 + E14;
   V15 =    1F2 + E15;
   V16 =    *F2 + E16;
   V17 =    *F2 + E17;
   V18 =    *F2 + E18;
   V19 =    *F2 + E19;
   V20 =    *F2 + E20;
   V21 =    *F2 + E21;
   V22 =    *F2 + E22;
   V23 =    1F3 + E23;
   V24 =    1F4 + E24;
   V25 =    *F4 + E25;
   V27 =    1F5 + E27;
/VARIANCES
   F1 to F5     = *;
   E1 TO E22    = *;
   E23          = 0;
   E24 TO E25   = *;
   E27          = 0;
```

```
/COVARIANCES
   F1 TO F5 = *;
   E7 TO E10 =*;
   E2,E5 = *;
   E2,E5 = *;
   E2,E12 = *;
   E2,E13 = *;
   E2,E14 = *;
   E5,E12 = *;
   E5,E13 = *;
   E5,E14 = *;
   E12,E13 = *;
   E12,E14 = *;
   E13,E14 = *;
   E18,E22 = *;
/PRINTE12,E13 = *;
   FIT=ALL;
   TABLE=COMPACT;
/LMTEST
   PROCESS=SIMULTANEOUS;
   SET=PEE;
/END
```

Table 8 Example 2: output second run

```
CHI-SQUARE =        433.303 BASED ON       274 DEGREES OF FREEDOM
PROBABILITY VALUE FOR THE CHI-SQUARE STATISTIC IS        0.00000


PARAMETER ESTIMATES (B) WITH STANDARD ERRORS AND TEST STATISTICS (Z)
STATISTICS SIGNIFICANT AT THE 5% LEVEL ARE MARKED WITH @.

                                                                R-
DEP.VAR.         PREDICTOR    B          BETA    S.E.    Z     SQUARED
-----------------------------------------------------------------------
V1  (  ECQ1  )                                                  .573
           F1   (RUMINATI) 1.000         .757
V2  (  ECQ2  )                                                  .036
           F1   (RUMINATI)  .276*        .189   .099   2.771@
V3  (  ECQ3  )                                                  .518
           F1   (RUMINATI)  .824*        .720   .075  10.969@
V4  (  ECQ4  )                                                  .565
           F1   (RUMINATI)  .814*        .752   .071  11.477@
V5  (  ECQ5  )                                                  .072
           F1   (RUMINATI)  .349*        .268   .088   3.953@
V6  (  ECQ6  )                                                  .163
           F1   (RUMINATI)  .512*        .404   .085   5.999@
V7  (  ECQ7  )                                                  .243
           F1   (RUMINATI)  .368*        .493   .051   7.174@
V8  (  ECQ8  )                                                  .275
           F1   (RUMINATI)  .526*        .524   .069   7.662@
V9  (  ECQ9  )                                                  .542
           F1   (RUMINATI)  .874*        .736   .079  11.033@
```

(Continued)

Table 8 (Continued)

```
V10  (ECQ10   )                                                .137
          F1   (RUMINATI)    .190*   .371   .035   5.345@
V11  (ECQ11   )                                                .280
          F1   (RUMINATI)    .599*   .529   .075   7.935@
V12  (ECQ12   )                                                .002
          F1   (RUMINATI)    .060*   .044   .093    .644
V13  (ECQ13   )                                                .047
          F1   (RUMINATI)    .308*   .217   .096   3.192@
V14  (ECQ14   )                                                .003
          F1   (RUMINATI)   -.068*  -.053   .088   -.779
V15  (POMS4D  )                                                .675
          F2   (SADNESS )   1.000    .822
V16  (POMS8D  )                                                .632
          F2   (SADNESS )    .932*   .795   .067  13.949@
V17  (POMS12D )                                                .585
          F2   (SADNESS )    .858*   .765   .065  13.250@
V18  (POMS14D )                                                .302
          F2   (SADNESS )    .618*   .550   .070   8.800@
V19  (POMS20D )                                                .623
          F2   (SADNESS )    .934*   .789   .068  13.814@
V20  (POMS23D )                                                .408
          F2   (SADNESS )    .593*   .639   .056  10.534@
V21  (POMS28D )                                                .306
          F2   (SADNESS )    .513*   .553   .058   8.873@
V22  (POMS33D )                                                .295
          F2   (SADNESS )    .563*   .543   .065   8.679@
V23  (PSQIK   )                                               1.000
          F3   (SLEEP   )   1.000   1.000
V24  (LEUKOCYT)                                                .431
          F4   (IMMUNE  )   1.000    .657
V25  (LYMPHOCY)                                                .394
          F4   (IMMUNE  )    .331*   .627   .105   3.156@
V27  (TELEPHON)                                               1.000
          F5   (HEALTHCA)   1.000   1.000


    COVARIANCES AMONG INDEPENDENT VARIABLES
    STATISTICS SIGNIFICANT AT THE 5% LEVEL ARE MARKED WITH @.


                                        COVA.    S.E.     Z      CORR.
    -----------------------------------------------------------------
    F1,F2    (RUMINATI,SADNESS  )       .213*   .042   5.125@    .423
    F1,F3    (RUMINATI,SLEEP    )       .151*   .044   3.474@    .248
    F1,F4    (RUMINATI,IMMUNE   )       .281*   .102   2.759@    .279
    F1,F5    (RUMINATI,HEALTHCA )       .211*   .065   3.253@    .231
    F2,F3    (SADNESS ,SLEEP    )       .190*   .033   5.800@    .436
    F2,F4    (SADNESS ,IMMUNE   )      -.008*   .063   -.129    -.011
    F2,F5    (SADNESS ,HEALTHCA )       .160*   .046   3.515@    .246
    F3,F4    (SLEEP   ,IMMUNE   )       .164*   .077   2.128@    .189
    F3,F5    (SLEEP   ,HEALTHCA )       .170*   .051   3.308@    .216
    F4,F5    (IMMUNE  ,HEALTHCA )       .081*   .110    .741     .062
    E2,E5    (  ECQ2  , ECQ5    )       .585*   .090   6.497@    .461
    E2,E12   (  ECQ2  ,ECQ12    )       .392*   .092   4.270@    .284
    E2,E13   (  ECQ2  ,ECQ13    )       .446*   .094   4.718@    .318
    E2,E14   (  ECQ2  ,ECQ14    )       .338*   .086   3.939@    .260
```

8.2 Analysis of the General Model

```
E5,E12   (    ECQ5  ,ECQ12 )   .467*   .083   5.635@    .388
E5,E13   (    ECQ5  ,ECQ13 )   .592*   .088   6.754@    .484
E5,E14   (    ECQ5  ,ECQ14 )   .247*   .074   3.324@    .218
E7,E8    (    ECQ7  , ECQ8 )   .028*   .027   1.016     .070
E7,E9    (    ECQ7  , ECQ9 )  -.126*   .028  -4.526@   -.340
E7,E10   (    ECQ7  ,ECQ10 )   .094*   .016   5.843@    .430
E8,E9    (    ECQ8  , ECQ9 )   .125*   .038   3.272@    .257
E8,E10   (    ECQ8  ,ECQ10 )   .048*   .020   2.421@    .167
E9,E10   (    ECQ9  ,ECQ10 )  -.012*   .020   -.623    -.045
E12,E13  (ECQ12     ,ECQ13 )   .743*   .098   7.617@    .558
E12,E14  (ECQ12     ,ECQ14 )   .401*   .083   4.849@    .325
E13,E14  (ECQ13     ,ECQ14 )   .409*   .084   4.858@    .327
E18,E22  (POMS14D ,POMS33D )   .108*   .021   5.110@    .369
```

The fit is excellent: CFI = 0.926, RMR = 0.042, SRMR = 0.053, RMSEA = 0.049 (0.040, 0.057). Observe that all regression coefficients except those of V12 and V14 are significant. I will delete these two items.

You may wonder why I did not delete these two variables after having seen the output from the first run.

The answer is a simple one. Even if the risk of deleting the two variables at an earlier stage was non-existent in this case, I *routinely* followed my habit of 'first you add variables and then delete variables' – and I recommend you follow the same rule.

It is now time to move on to the analysis of the hypothesized causal model.

Here, however, I must decide on how to handle the sleep quality factor. The 'one-indicator problem' is most often dealt with by fixing the error variance at 0.00. In most cases it is of course unrealistic to assume that measurement error is wholly absent, so I will deal with the problem in another way.

The average reliability of the (kept) items in the two ecq sub-scales is about 0.40 and the average reliability of the poms items is about 0.50. As the psqik1 question seems rather unproblematic, I will assume that the reliability of psqik1 is 0.50, and consequently fix the error variance of psqik1 at 50% of the total variance of psqik1 (cf. Chapter 2's Equation (3b)). I therefore substitute

$$E23=0.263$$

for

$$E23=0$$

If you use 'Diagrammer', double-click E23, and when the panel in Figure 6 pops up, fill it out as shown.

Of course this is a 'guesstimate', but it is more realistic than zero.

The model is shown in Figure 7, a program for the estimation of model parameters in Table 9 and the output in Table 10.

From Table 8 you can see that sadness and low sleeping quality go together, but it is obvious that this could be due to other causes than rumination. It is therefore no surprise that their correlation seems to be larger than that caused by their common 'cause' rumination.

Introducing a correlation between D2 and D3 takes care of this. I will leave it to the experts to consider a possible causal link between the two.

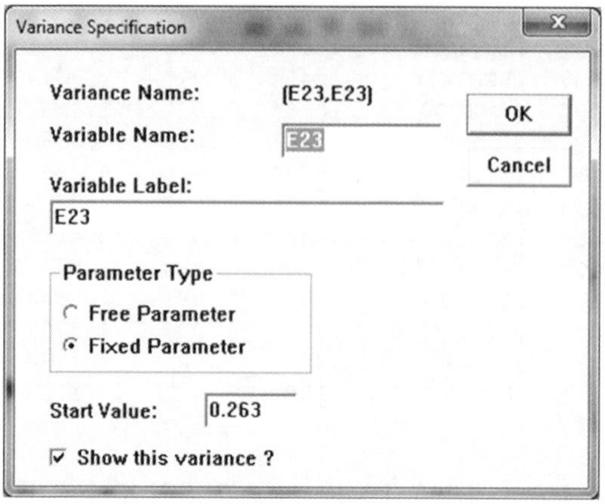

Figure 6 Example 2: setting the variance of E23

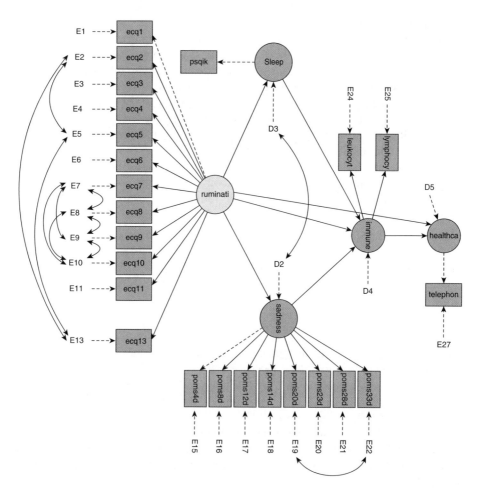

Figure 7 Example 2: the first 'causal' model

Table 9 Example 2: program for third run – first 'causal' model

```
/TITLE
    Example 8.2. Data from Thomsen et al. (2004)
/SPECIFICATIONS
    DATA='c:\users\sony\desktop\eqs bog\eqs chap 8\thomsenelder.ess';
    VARIABLES=27; CASES=247;
    METHOD=ML; ANALYSIS=COVARIANCE; MATRIX=COVARIANCE;
/LABELS
    F1=rumination; F2=sadness; F3=sleep; F4= immune; F5=health care;
    V1=ecq1; V2=ecq2; V3=ecq3; V4=ecq4; V5=ecq5;
    V6=ecq6; V7=ecq7; V8=ecq8; V9=ecq9; V10=ecq10;
    V11=ecq11; V12=ecq12; V13=ecq13; V14=ecq14; V15=poms4d;
    V16=poms8d; V17=poms12d; V18=poms14d; V19=poms20d; V20=poms23d;
    V21=poms28d; V22=poms33d; V23=psqik; V24=leukocyt; V25=lymphocy;
    V26=consult; V27=telephon;
/EQUATIONS
    V1  = 1F1 + E1;
    V2  = *F1 + E2;
    V3  = *F1 + E3;
    V4  = *F1 + E4;
    V5  = *F1 + E5;
    V6  = *F1 + E6;
    V7  = *F1 + E7;
    V8  = *F1 + E8;
    V9  = *F1 + E9;
    V10 = *F1 + E10;
    V11 = *F1 + E11;
    V13 = *F1 + E13;
    V15 = 1F2 + E15;
    V16 = *F2 + E16;
    V17 = *F2 + E17;
    V18 = *F2 + E18;
    V19 = *F2 + E19;
    V20 = *F2 + E20;
    V21 = *F2 + E21;
    V22 = *F2 + E22;
    V23 = 1F3 + E23;
    V24 = 1F4 + E24;
    V25 = *F4 + E25;
    V27 = 1F5 + E27;

    F2 = *F1+D2;
    F3 = *F1+D3;
    F4 = *F1 + *F2 + *F3 + D4;
    F5 = *F1 + *F4 + D5;
/VARIANCES
    F1 = *;
    E1 to E11 = *;
    E13 = *;
    E15 TO 22 = *;
    E23 = 0.263;
    E24 TO E25 = *;
    E27 =  0.00;
    D2 TO D5 = *;
```

(Continued)

Table 9 (Continued)

```
/COVARIANCES
    E7 TO E10 = *;
    E2,E5 = *;
    E2,E5 = *;
    E2,E13 = *;
    E5,E13 = *;
    E18,E22 = *;
    D2,D3 = *;
/PRINT
    FIT=ALL;
    TABLE=COMPACT;
/LMTEST
    PROCESS=SIMULTANEOUS;
    SET=PEE, PDD, BFF ;
/END
```

Table 10 Example 2: output from third run – first causal model

```
CHI-SQUARE =      398.821 BASED ON      236 DEGREES OF FREEDOM
PROBABILITY VALUE FOR THE CHI-SQUARE STATISTIC IS        0.00000

PARAMETER ESTIMATES (B) WITH STANDARD ERRORS AND TEST STATISTICS (Z)
   STATISTICS SIGNIFICANT AT THE 5% LEVEL ARE MARKED WITH @.

                                                                R-
   DEP.VAR.       PREDICTOR     B       BETA    S.E.    Z     SQUARED
   ----------------------------------------------------------------
   V1  ( ECQ1  )                                               .575
                 F1  (RUMINATI) 1.000   .758
   V2  ( ECQ2  )                                               .036
                 F1  (RUMINATI)  .275*  .189    .099   2.773@
   V3  ( ECQ3  )                                               .520
                 F1  (RUMINATI)  .824*  .721    .075  11.001@
   V4  ( ECQ4  )                                               .562
                 F1  (RUMINATI)  .810*  .749    .071  11.456@
   V5  ( ECQ5  )                                               .072
                 F1  (RUMINATI)  .349*  .268    .088   3.959@
   V6  ( ECQ6  )                                               .159
                 F1  (RUMINATI)  .505*  .399    .085   5.926@
   V7  ( ECQ7  )                                               .240
                 F1  (RUMINATI)  .366*  .490    .051   7.133@
   V8  ( ECQ8  )                                               .274
                 F1  (RUMINATI)  .524*  .523    .068   7.652@
   V9  ( ECQ9  )                                               .545
                 F1  (RUMINATI)  .875*  .738    .079  11.083@
   V10 (ECQ10  )                                               .135
                 F1  (RUMINATI)  .188*  .368    .035   5.303@
   V11 (ECQ11  )                                               .279
                 F1  (RUMINATI)  .597*  .529    .075   7.931@
   V13 (ECQ13  )                                               .048
                 F1  (RUMINATI)  .309*  .218    .096   3.211@
   V15 (POMS4D )                                               .671
                 F2  (SADNESS ) 1.000   .819
   V16 (POMS8D )                                               .634
                 F2  (SADNESS )  .936*  .796    .067  13.923@
   V17 (POMS12D)                                               .585
                 F2  (SADNESS )  .860*  .765    .065  13.202@
   V18 (POMS14D)                                               .302
                 F2  (SADNESS )  .619*  .549    .071   8.780@
```

8.2 Analysis of the General Model

```
V19 (POMS20D )                                            .624
        F2  (SADNESS )  .937*   .790   .068  13.775@
V20 (POMS23D )                                            .408
        F2  (SADNESS )  .595*   .639   .057  10.510@
V21 (POMS28D )                                            .308
        F2  (SADNESS )  .516*   .555   .058   8.901@
V22 (POMS33D )                                            .295
        F2  (SADNESS )  .564*   .543   .065   8.660@
V23 (PSQIK   )                                            .500
        F3  (SLEEP   ) 1.000    .707
V24 (LEUKOCYT)                                            .439
        F4  (IMMUNE  ) 1.000    .662
V25 (LYMPHOCY)                                            .387
        F4  (IMMUNE  )  .325*   .622   .104   3.134@
V27 (TELEPHON)                                           1.000
        F5  (HEALTHCA) 1.000   1.000
F2  (SADNESS )                                            .183
        F1  (RUMINATI)  .304*   .428   .052   5.828@
F3  (SLEEP   )                                            .132
        F1  (RUMINATI)  .222*   .363   .059   3.780@
F4  (IMMUNE  )                                            .192
        F2  (SADNESS ) -.768*  -.380   .318  -2.411@
        F3  (SLEEP   )  .936*   .397   .447   2.093@
        F1  (RUMINATI)  .424*   .295   .162   2.616@
F5  (HEALTHCA)                                            .058
        F4  (IMMUNE  )  .003*   .003   .077    .034
        F1  (RUMINATI)  .311*   .240   .094   3.317@


COVARIANCES AMONG INDEPENDENT VARIABLES
  STATISTICS SIGNIFICANT AT THE 5% LEVEL ARE MARKED WITH @.

COVA.   S.E.    Z       CORR.
-----------------------------------------------------------
COVARIANCES AMONG INDEPENDENT VARIABLES
  STATISTICS SIGNIFICANT AT THE 5% LEVEL ARE MARKED WITH @.


                              COVA.    S.E.       Z      CORR.
-----------------------------------------------------------
  E2,E5    ( ECQ2  , ECQ5  )  .585*    .090    6.497@    .461
  E2,E13   ( ECQ2  ,ECQ13  )  .445*    .094    4.716@    .318
  E5,E13   ( ECQ5  ,ECQ13  )  .592*    .088    6.751@    .483
  E7,E8    ( ECQ7  , ECQ8  )  .029*    .027    1.052     .073
  E7,E9    ( ECQ7  , ECQ9  ) -.125*    .028   -4.505@   -.339
  E7,E10   ( ECQ7  ,ECQ10  )  .095*    .016    5.869@    .432
  E8,E9    ( ECQ8  , ECQ9  )  .124*    .038    3.267@    .257
  E8,E10   ( ECQ8  ,ECQ10  )  .048*    .020    2.451@    .169
  E9,E10   ( ECQ9  ,ECQ10  ) -.012*    .020    -.594    -.043
  E18,E22  (POMS14D,POMS33D)  .108*    .021    5.113@    .369
  D2,D3    ( F2    , F3    )  .141*    .029    4.941@    .548



LAGRANGE MULTIPLIER TEST (FOR ADDING PARAMETERS)

ORDERED UNIVARIATE TEST STATISTICS:
                                       HANCOCK         STANDAR-
                          CHI-         276 DF  PARAM.  DIZED    PREDICTED
   NO  CODE  PARAMETER    SQUARE PROB. PROB.   CHANGE  CHANGE   RMSEA   CFI
   --  ----  ---------    ------ ----- -----   ------  -------  ----------
   1   2  6  E21,E18      15.037 0.000 1.000    0.062   0.239   0.051 0.929
   2   2  6  E21,E15      14.207 0.000 1.000   -0.056  -0.288   0.051 0.928
```

(Continued)

Table 10 (Continued)

3	2	6	E23,E17	12.144	0.000	1.000	-0.069	-0.310	0.051	0.927
4	2	6	E18,E17	11.382	0.001	1.000	-0.054	-0.223	0.051	0.927
5	2	6	E7,E4	11.181	0.001	1.000	0.076	0.229	0.051	0.927
6	2	6	E23,E19	10.540	0.001	1.000	0.066	0.295	0.051	0.926
7	2	6	E20,E9	10.529	0.001	1.000	-0.062	-0.214	0.051	0.926
8	2	6	E23,E21	9.423	0.002	1.000	0.061	0.256	0.052	0.926
9	2	6	E16,E15	9.414	0.002	1.000	0.050	0.280	0.052	0.926
10	2	22	F5,F3	9.346	0.002	1.000	0.595	1.067	0.052	0.926
11	2	6	E21,E19	9.241	0.002	1.000	0.045	0.225	0.052	0.926
12	2	6	E11,E4	8.677	0.003	1.000	-0.107	-0.220	0.052	0.926
13	2	6	E27,E15	8.585	0.003	1.000	0.093	0.000	0.052	0.925
14	2	6	E20,E15	8.280	0.004	1.000	0.041	0.227	0.052	0.925
15	2	6	E21,E13	8.106	0.004	1.000	-0.087	-0.161	0.052	0.925
16	2	6	E19,E15	7.845	0.005	1.000	-0.046	-0.253	0.052	0.925
17	2	6	E17,E11	7.742	0.005	1.000	0.069	0.196	0.052	0.925
18	2	6	E7,E5	7.711	0.005	1.000	-0.074	-0.128	0.052	0.925
19	2	6	E19,E9	7.148	0.008	1.000	0.055	0.186	0.052	0.925
20	2	6	E10,E5	6.687	0.010	1.000	0.050	0.119	0.052	0.925
21	2	6	E23,E4	6.655	0.010	1.000	-0.072	-0.232	0.052	0.925
22	2	22	F5,F2	6.648	0.010	1.000	0.357	0.548	0.052	0.925
23	2	6	E27,E8	6.358	0.012	1.000	-0.116	0.000	0.052	0.924
-	-	-	-	-	-	-	-	-	-	-
-	-	-	-	-	-	-	-	-	-	-
-	-	-	-	-	-	-	-	-	-	-
-	-	-	-	-	-	-	-	-	-	-
287	2	0	E23,E23	0.000	1.000	1.000	0.000	0.000	0.053	0.921

MULTIVARIATE LAGRANGE MULTIPLIER TEST BY SIMULTANEOUS PROCESS IN STAGE 1

PARAMETER SETS (SUBMATRICES) ACTIVE AT THIS STAGE ARE:
PEE PDD BFF

		CUMULATIVE MULTIVARIATE STATISTICS			UNIVARIATE INCREMENT					
STEP	PARAMETER	CHI-SQUARE	D.F.	PROB.	CHI-SQUARE	PROB.	HANCOCK'S SEQUENTIAL D.F.	PROB.	PREDICTED RMSEA	CFI
1	E21,E18	15.037	1	0.000	15.037	0.000	236	1.000	0.051	0.929
2	E22,E21	30.152	2	0.000	15.115	0.000	235	1.000	0.048	0.935
3	E21,E19	44.751	3	0.000	14.599	0.000	234	1.000	0.046	0.942
4	E23,E21	58.261	4	0.000	13.511	0.000	233	1.000	0.044	0.948
5	E23,E19	72.971	5	0.000	14.709	0.000	232	1.000	0.041	0.954
6	E7,E4	84.151	6	0.000	11.181	0.001	231	1.000	0.039	0.959
7	E20,E9	94.817	7	0.000	10.665	0.001	230	1.000	0.036	0.964
8	E18,E17	104.388	8	0.000	9.571	0.002	229	1.000	0.034	0.968
9	F5,F3	113.519	9	0.000	9.131	0.003	228	1.000	0.032	0.972
10	E21,E13	121.540	10	0.000	8.021	0.005	227	1.000	0.030	0.975

The LM test suggests two connections that are both (univariate) significant and – what is more important – make sense from a substantive point of view:

F5,F2 and F5,F3

However, although they are both (univariate) significant, their inclusion in the model adds little from a practical point of view. Also, if you choose to include one of them, the other will be insignificant. I therefore decide not to include any of them in the model in order to avoid over-fitting.

The fit is not too bad (CFI = 0.922, RMR = 0.043, SRMR = 0.057, RMSEA = 0.053 (0.044, 0.062)), but as mentioned several times, it takes more to accept a model: it must also be substantively meaningful.

In short, the model says that rumination raises the defense system of your body, both through a direct effect and by reducing sleep quality and causing depression. Also rumination has a direct effect on health care utilization, whereas the rise in the immune parameters does not seem to have an effect on health care utilization.

However, rumination could have a greater influence on the immune parameters than seen at first sight. For example, rumination has indirect effects on the immune parameters, both via sleep quality and via sadness, and, furthermore, we can measure that effect.

The effect of rumination on sleep quality is measured by the regression coefficient 0.222 and the effect of sleep quality on immunity is measured by the regression coefficient 0.936. So, from the rumination 'carried' to sleep quality (0.222), a share of 0.936, i.e. $0.222 \times 0.936 = 0.208$, is 'carried' through to immunity.

In the same way the indirect effect of rumination on immunity via sadness can be calculated as $0.304 \times (-0.768) = -0.233$. So the indirect effect of rumination on immunity is $0.208 - 0.233 = -0.025$, which, added to the direct effect (0.424), gives a total effect of 0.399.

If you add the order

$$EFFECT=YES$$

to the program in the /PRINT section, EQS will calculate total and indirect effects as given in Table 11, from which you can see that none of the relevant indirect effects are significant based on traditional criteria.

Table 11 Example 2: total, direct and indirect effects (extract)

```
DECOMPOSITION OF EFFECTS

    PARAMETER TOTAL EFFECTS

                                        STD.
DEP.VAR.         PREDICTOR      COEF    COEF    S.E.    Z
-----------------------------------------------------------
F2
          F1   -   F1           .304*   .428
          D2   -   F2          1.000    .904
F3   -   F3
          F1   -   F1           .222*   .363
          D3   -   F3          1.000    .932
F4   -   F4
          F2   -   F2          -.768*  -.380   .318   -2.411@
```

(Continued)

Table 11 (Continued)

```
     F3  -  F3     .936*    .397    .447    2.093@
     F1  -  F1     .398*    .277    .140    2.842@
     D2  -  F2    -.768    -.343    .318   -2.411@
     D3  -  F3     .936     .370    .447    2.093@
     D4  -  F4    1.000     .899
```

PARAMETER TOTAL EFFECTS (CONTINUED)

						STD.		
DEP.VAR.		PREDICTOR			COEF	COEF	S.E.	Z
F5	-	F5						
		F2	-	F2	-.002	-.001	.059	-.034
		F3	-	F3	.002	.001	.072	.034
		F4	-	F4	.003*	.003	.077	.034
		F1	-	F1	.312*	.241	.088	3.551@
		D2	-	F2	-.002	-.001	.059	-.034
		D3	-	F3	.002	.001	.072	.034
		D4	-	F4	.003	.003	.077	.034
		D5	-	F5	1.000	.970		

PARAMETER INDIRECT EFFECTS
STATISTICS SIGNIFICANT AT THE 5% LEVEL ARE MARKED WITH @.

						STD.		
DEP.VAR.		PREDICTOR			COEF	COEF	S.E.	Z
F4	-	F4						
		F1	-	F1	-.026*	-.018	.086	-.304
		D2	-	F2	-.768	-.343	.318	-2.411@
		D3	-	F3	.936	.370	.447	2.093@
F5	-	F5						
		F2	-	F2	-.002	-.001	.059	-.034
		F3	-	F3	.002	.001	.072	.034
		F1	-	F1	.001*	.001	.031	.034
		D2	-	F2	-.002	-.001	.059	-.034
		D3	-	F3	.002	.001	.072	.034
		D4	-	F4	.003	.003	.077	.034

I will leave it to the specialists to defend the direction of the arrows. However, if an amateur in the field is allowed to speculate, then is it not possible that depression – as measured by 'sadness' – influences rumination and not the other way round?

A last word of warning. Even if modifications to the model were guided by substantive thinking, I would feel safer if the same model could be shown to fit comparable data. If it is not possible to take another sample from the same population you could split your sample into two or more parts, and cross-validate between subsamples. But remember: you still have to assume that your original sample is representative of the population!

A shortcut in programming
Remember from your introduction to EQS programming (in Example 4.1) that a single paragraph called

/MODEL

could be substituted for the three paragraphs

/EQUATIONS

/VARIANCES

/COVARIANCES

This, of course, is most valuable if your model is large with many free and few fixed parameters. In Table 12a I repeat the three paragraphs of the program from Table 5, and in panel (b) you will see the one paragraph that can replace them.

Table 12 Example 2: use of the /MODEL paragraph

```
/EQUATIONS
    V1  = 1F1 + E1;
    V2  = *F1 + E2;
    V3  = *F1 + E3;
    V4  = *F1 + E4;
    V5  = *F1 + E5;
    V6  = *F1 + E6;
    V7  = *F1 + E7;
    V8  = *F1 + E8;
    V9  = *F1 + E9;
    V10 = *F1 + E10;
    V11 = *F1 + E11;
    V12 = *F1 + E12;
    V13 = *F1 + E13;
    V14 = *F1 + E14;
    V15 = 1F2 + E15;
    V16 = *F2 + E16;
    V17 = *F2 + E17;
    V18 = *F2 + E18;                                          (a)
    V19 = *F2 + E19;
    V20 = *F2 + E20;
    V21 = *F2 + E21;
    V22 = *F2 + E22;
    V23 = 1F3 + E23;
    V24 = 1F4 + E24;
    V25 = *F4 + E25;
    V27 = 1F5 + E27;
/VARIANCES
    F1 to F5     = *;
    E1 TO E22    = *;
    E23          = 0;
```

(Continued)

Table 12 (Continued)
```
    E24 TO E25 = *;
    E27        = 0;
/COVARIANCES
    F1 TO F5 = *;


/MODEL
(V1,V14)    ON F1;
(V15,V22)   ON F2;
(V23)       ON F3;
(V24,V25)   ON F4;
(V27)       ON F5;                                  (b)
E23         = 0;
E27         = 0;
COV F1-F5   = *;
```

Note that:

1. E and D variables are automatically added to the equations.
2. The first regression coefficient in each measurement model is automatically fixed at 1.00.
3. Variances are calculated automatically and only need to be stated in the /MODEL paragraph if they are fixed or a start value is required.

For the various options in the /MODEL paragraph consult the program manual (Bentler, 2006).

3 Longitudinal or Panel Models

Models where the measurements are taken at various points in time have at least two characteristics that differentiate them from models based on cross-sectional data:

1. The problem of direction as far as causal influences are concerned is less problematic because future events cannot affect the present.
2. Such models will often include correlations among error terms in measurement models across latent variables describing the same concept at different points in time (cf. Example 7.1).

Example 3 (continued from Example 6.2)
Examining the stability of alienation

Recall that the model I proposed in Figure 6.2 had a very bad fit. That model was a path model; it had only manifest variables. However, the structure of the model in Figure 6.2 is very similar to the model in Figure 7.2. In both cases the same variables are measured at two points in time. A reformulation of the model in Figure 6.2 incorporating latent variables as in the model in Figure 7.2 is shown in Figure 8.

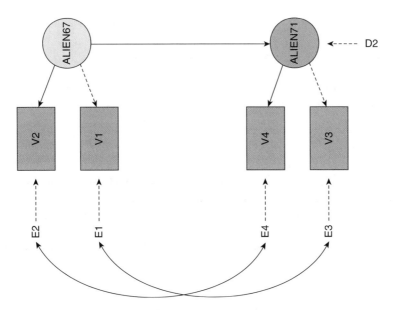

Figure 8 Example 3: model

A quick look will show that the model is not identified. It has 11 parameters to be estimated – three regression coefficients, two covariances and six variances – but we have only ten data points. Consequently the model must be simplified. If we assume that the two covariances are of the same magnitude, and that the same applies to the four E-variances, we have three degrees of freedom left over for testing.

The program is given in Table 13.

Table 13 Example 3: program

```
/TITLE
    Example 8.3. Data from Wheaton et al. 1977
/SPECIFICATIONS
    VARIABLES=4; CASES=932;
    METHOD=ML; ANALYSIS=COVARIANCE; MATRIX=COVARIANCE;
/LABELS
    V1=anomia67; V2=power67; V3=anomia71; V4=power71;
    F1=ALIEN67; F2=ALIEN71;
/EQUATIONS
    V1 =  F1 + E1;
    V2 = *F1 + E2;
    V3 =  F2 + E3;
    V4 = *F2 + E4;
    F2 = *F1 + D2;
/VARIANCES
    E1 TO E4 = *;
/COVARIANCES
    E3,E1 = *;
    E2,E4 = *;
```

(Continued)

Table 13 (Continued)

```
/CONSTRAINTS
   (E1,E1) = (E2,E2) = (E3,E3) =(E4,E4);
   (E3,E1) = (E4,E2);
/PRINT
   FIT=ALL;
   TABLE=COMPACT;
/MATRIX
   11.834
    6.947   9.364
    6.819   5.091  12.532
    4.783   5.028   7.495   9.986

/END
```

As usual the regression coefficients of the E terms, the coefficients of the D term and one regression coefficient for each of the two factors are fixed at one in order to obtain scales for these latent variables.

With these restrictions we get the output in Table 14, from which we can see that the model fits the data extremely well.

Panel models will be taken up in Chapter 11.

Table 14 Example 3: output

```
CHI-SQUARE = 1.436 BASED ON 3 DEGREES OF FREEDOM
   PROBABILITY VALUE FOR THE CHI-SQUARE STATISTIC IS .69705

   FIT INDICES (BASED ON MODIFIED INDEPENDENCE MODEL)
   -----------
   BENTLER-BONETT         NORMED FIT INDEX  =       .999
   BENTLER-BONETT NON-NORMED FIT INDEX  =    1.003
   COMPARATIVE FIT INDEX (CFI)          =    1.000
   BOLLEN'S            (IFI) FIT INDEX  =    1.001
   MCDONALD'S          (MFI) FIT INDEX  =    1.001
   JORESKOG-SORBOM'S  GFI  FIT INDEX    =     .999
   JORESKOG-SORBOM'S AGFI  FIT INDEX    =     .997
   ROOT MEAN-SQUARE RESIDUAL (RMR)      =     .076
   STANDARDIZED RMR                     =     .007
   ROOT MEAN-SQUARE ERROR OF APPROXIMATION (RMSEA) = .000
   90% CONFIDENCE INTERVAL OF RMSEA           (.000, .041)

PARAMETER ESTIMATES (B) WITH STANDARD ERRORS AND TEST STATISTICS (Z)
   STATISTICS SIGNIFICANT AT THE 5% LEVEL ARE MARKED WITH @.

                                                              R-
   DEP.VAR.            PREDICTOR      B      BETA   S.E.   Z   SQUARED
   ----------------------------------------------------------------
   V1   (ANOMIA67)  F1  (ALIEN67 )  1.000   .834   .695
   V2   (POWER67 )  F1  (ALIEN67 )   .845*  .787   .031  27.075@   .619
   V3   (ANOMIA71)  F2  (ALIEN71 )  1.000   .845   .713
   V4   (POWER71 )  F2  (ALIEN71 )   .839*  .798   .030  28.369@   .637
   F2   (ALIEN71 )  F1  (ALIEN67 )   .716*  .685   .038  18.834@   .469
```

				VARIANCE	S.E.	Z
FACTOR						
	F1	(ALIEN67)		8.201*	.545	15.056@
ERROR						
	E1	(ANOMIA67)		3.600*	.122	29.589@
	E2	(POWER67)		)3.600*	.122	29.589@
	E3	(ANOMIA71)		3.600*	.122	29.589@
	E4	(POWER71)		3.600*	.122	29.589@
DISTURBANCE						
	D2	(ALIEN71)		4.751*	.376	12.627@

		COVA.	S.E.	Z	CORR.
E1,E3	(ANOMIA67,ANOMIA71)	.906*	.122	7.449@	.252
E2,E4	(POWER67 ,POWER71)	.906*	.122	7.449@	.252

In this chapter you met the following concepts:

- the two-step rule
- the two- and four-step strategy
- direct, indirect and total effects

You have also been introduced to the EQS statements:

/MODEL   EFFECT=YES

Questions

1. State the consequences of measurement error in the dependent and independent variables in (traditional) regression analysis.

2. Comment on the various strategies for analyzing structural (causal) models.

3. Go through the various outputs in Example 2 and comment on the changes in the measurement part of the model.

4. Define direct, indirect and total effects, and explain how to calculate (by hand) the latter two.

5. Discuss the two-factor problem that could emerge from oppositely worded items. Discuss the pros and cons of various ways to take care of the problem.

6. Sometimes you are interested not only in the relations between latent variables, but also in their values (a problem taken up in Chapter 9). Imagine, for example, that you would like to compare the extent of alienation in 1967 and 1971 for the group of patients in Example 3. Then of course, you have to make sure that the measuring instrument functions in the same way for the two years. Can you say anything about this?

References

Bentler, P. M. (2006). *EQS 6 Structural equations program manual*. Encino, CA: Multivariate Software, Inc.

Buysse, D. J., Reynolds, C. F., Monk, T. H., Berman, S. R., & Kupfer, D. (1989). The Pittsburgh Sleep Quality Index: A new instrument for psychiatric practice and research. *Psychiatry Research, 28*(2), 305–306.

McNair, P. M., Lorr, M., & Dopplemann, L. F. (1981). *POMS manual* (2nd ed.). San Diego, CA: Educational and Industrial Testing Service.

Mulaik, S. A., & Millsap, R. E. (2000). Doing the four-step right. *Structural Equation Modeling, 7*, 36–73.

Roger, D., & Narajian, R. D. (1989). The construction and validation of a new scale for measuring emotion control. *Personality and Individual Differences, 10*, 845–853.

Shacham, S. (1983). A shortened version of the Profile of Moods Scale. *Journal of Personality Assessment, 47*, 305–306.

Thomsen, D. K., Mehlsen, Y. M., Hokland, M., Viidik, A., Olesen, F., Avlund, K. et al. (2004). Negative thoughts and health: Associations among rumination, immunity and health care utilization in a young and elderly sample. *Psychosomatic Medicine, 66*, 363–371.

PART 3
Advanced Models and Techniques

9

Mean Structures and Multi-group Analysis

> We have hitherto analyzed only *relations* among variables, but not been very interested in the *values* of the variables. In this chapter you will learn how to estimate means of latent variables and compare means across groups.
>
> As this necessitates estimation of intercepts in addition to regression coefficients, the chapter will introduce you to the analysis of *mean structures* by re-estimating the regression model from Example 4.1, but this time it will include the intercept.
>
> In order do so, the input covariance matrix must be supplemented by the means of the manifest variables.
>
> It is also time to look at how to estimate SEM in several groups at the same time and how to examine the degree to which models are equivalent across groups. You will learn how to judge the equivalence of a model across several samples through a systematic sequence of tests.
>
> Then you will move on to a larger model involving only manifest variables, although it has a complication: namely, two-way causation.

1 Identifying and Estimating Mean Structures

Until now we have only estimated covariance structures. We were only interested in *relations* between variables – be they manifest or latent – but not in the *values* of the variables.

As long as we are working only with manifest variables, hypotheses about means can be tested by traditional statistical techniques such as t-test, analysis of variance, multivariate analysis of variance, and the like, but these techniques cannot treat means of *latent* variables.

Now, let us look at the simple regression model

$$Y = \beta_0 + \beta_1 X + \varepsilon \qquad (1a)$$

Taking the expectation we get

$$\mu_Y = \beta_0 + \beta_1 \mu_X \qquad (1b)$$

It is this decomposition of the means of dependent variables that has given rise to the name *analysis of mean structures*. As is evident from (1b), this necessitates the estimation of regression intercepts and consequently the input sample covariance matrix has to be supplemented by the sample means.

As you will remember (from Chapter 4), the parameters of a covariance structure model are:

1. The regression coefficients.
2. The variances and the covariances of the exogenous variables.

In the analysis of covariance and mean structures these parameters must be supplemented by:

3. The means of the exogenous variables.
4. The intercepts of the endogenous variables.

The way a mean structure is formulated in EQS seems at first sight a bit complicated and confusing, but taking as our point of departure that (1a) and (1b) can be formulated as

$$Y = \beta_0 1 + \beta_1 X + \varepsilon \qquad (2a)$$

$$\mu_Y = \beta_0 1 + \beta_1 \mu_X \qquad (2b)$$

you will see that β_0 can be thought of as a coefficient of a 'variable' (in the following called Z) that is a constant taking on the value 1. Being a constant, Z has of course neither variance nor covariance to other variables. Let us now take a look at the model in Figure 1.

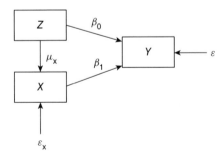

Figure 1 Estimating a simple regression function using EQS

When you regress X on Z the resulting regression function will leave out the slope parameter because Z is a constant. The only parameter in the regression function is then the intercept, which is of course the mean of X, μ_X.

As you can see from the figure, the direct effect of Z on Y is $\beta_0 1$ while the indirect effect is $\beta_1 \mu_X$. Consequently the total effect of Z on Y is $\beta_0 1 + \beta_1 \mu_X$. But according to (2b) this equals the mean of Y.

This all boils down to the following three rules:

1. The direct effect of a constant on an exogenous variable is the mean of that exogenous variable.
2. The direct effect of a constant on an endogenous variable is the intercept of that variable.
3. The total effect of a constant on an endogenous variable is the mean of that variable.

In one-group analysis, means and intercepts are in most cases of no interest. Nevertheless I will introduce mean structure analysis by estimating the intercept in the regression model from Example 4.1.

Example 1 (continued from Example 4.1)
Mapping European consumers' willingness to buy genetically modified food: estimating means and intercepts

By reformulating the model from Figure 4.2 (shown in Figure 2a) to include the intercept, we get the model shown in Figure 2b.

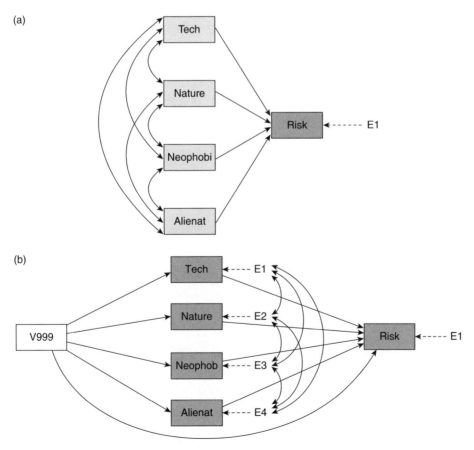

Figure 2 Example 1: a simple regression model without (a) and with (b) estimation of the intercept

Programs for the estimation of the two models are given in Table 1. Comparing the models in Figure 2 and the two programs you will note the following:

1. The 'variable' Z is called V999 in EQS in order to secure that no other variable has a higher number. Therefore Z will always come last in any list of variables in the output.
2. The former exogenous variables are now endogenous.
3. As they are no longer exogenous they do not have covariances that are parameters in the model. Therefore possible collinearity between them are now estimated as covariances between their E variables.
4. A new paragraph /MEANS has been added to the program.
5. In the /PRINT paragraph the command EFFECT=YES has been added.

Table 1 Example 1: programs

```
/TITLE
   Example 4.1.Data from Bredahl (2001)
/SPECIFICATIONS
   VARIABLES=5; CASES=481;
   METHOD=ML; ANALYSIS=COVARIANCE; MATRIX=COV;
/LABELS
   V1=RISK; V2=NATURE; V3=TECH; V4=NEOPHOB; V5=ALIENATI;
/EQUATIONS
   V1 =    *V2 + *V3 + *V4 + *V5 + E1;
/VARIANCES
   V2 = *;
   V3 = *;
   V4 = *;
   V5 = *;
   E1 = *;
/COVARIANCES
   V2,V3=*;
   V2,V4=*;
   V2,V5=*;
   V3,V4=*;
   V3,V5=*;
   V4,V5=*;
/MATRIX
   55.978
   18.673       36.468
  -10.343       -0.985      30.158
   16.471        1.610     -10.831      43.399
   11.252        6.845       0.364       2.288      12.220
/END


/TITLE
   Example 9.1.Data from Bredahl (2001)
/SPECIFICATIONS
   VARIABLES=5; CASES=481;
   METHOD=ML; ANALYSIS=COVARIANCE; MATRIX=COV;
/LABELS
   V1=RISK; V2=NATURE; V3=TECH; V4=NEOPHOB; V5=ALIENATI;
```

```
/EQUATIONS
    V1 = *V999 + *V2 + *V3 + *V4 + *V5 + E1;
    V2 = *V999 + E2;
    V3 = *V999 + E3;
    V4 = *V999 + E4;
    V5 = *V999 + E5;
/VARIANCES
    E2 TO E5 = *;
/COVARIANCES
    E2 TO E5 = *;
/MATRIX
    55.978
    18.673      36.468
   -10.343      -0.985     30.158
    16.471       1.610    -10.831    43.399
    11.252       6.845      0.364     2.288    12.220
/MEANS
    29.798      32.360     25.004    18.971    16.675
/PRINT
    EFFECT=YES;
    TABLE=COMPACT;
/END
```

Table 2 Example 1: Output

```
MAXIMUM LIKELIHOOD SOLUTION (NORMAL DISTRIBUTION THEORY)

PARAMETER ESTIMATES (B) WITH STANDARD ERRORS AND TEST STATISTICS (Z)
STATISTICS SIGNIFICANT AT THE 5% LEVEL ARE MARKED WITH @.

                                                                          R-
DEP.VAR.           PREDICTOR            B       BETA    S.E.      Z     SQUARED
-------------------------------------------------------------------------------
V1  ( RISK    ) V2  (NATURE  )        .368*    .297    .047    7.814@    .382
                V3  ( TECH   )       -.242*   -.178    .051   -4.714@
                V4  (NEOPHOB )        .270*    .238    .043    6.284@
                V5  (ALIENATI)        .672*    .314    .082    8.221@
                V999(  V999  )       7.636*    .000   2.357    3.239@          (4)
V2  (NATURE  ) V999(  V999  )       32.360*    .000    .276  117.401@    .000 (1)
V3  ( TECH   ) V999(  V999  )       25.004*    .000    .251   99.754@    .000
V4  (NEOPHOB ) V999(  V999  )       18.971*    .000    .301   63.092@    .000
V5  (ALIENATI) V999(  V999  )       16.675*    .000    .160  104.508@    .000


VARIANCES OF INDEPENDENT VARIABLES                                       (2)

                              VARIANCE    S.E.      Z
  -----------------------------------------------------
  ERROR
           E1  ( RISK    )    34.607*    2.234   15.492@
           E2  (NATURE   )    36.468*    2.354   15.492@
           E3  ( TECH    )    30.158*    1.947   15.492@
           E4  (NEOPHOB  )    43.399*    2.801   15.492@
           E5  (ALIENATI )    12.220*     .789   15.492@
```

(Continued)

Table 1 (Continued)

COVARIANCES AMONG INDEPENDENT VARIABLES (3)
STATISTICS SIGNIFICANT AT THE 5% LEVEL ARE MARKED WITH @.

```
                              COVA.     S.E.       Z       CORR.
-----------------------------------------------------------------
E2,E3  (NATURE  , TECH    )   -.985*   1.514    -.650      -.030
E2,E4  (NATURE  ,NEOPHOB  )   1.610*   1.817     .886       .040
E2,E5  (NATURE  ,ALIENATI)    6.845*   1.013    6.758@      .324
E3,E4  ( TECH   ,NEOPHOB  )  -10.831*  1.724   -6.284@     -.299
E3,E5  ( TECH   ,ALIENATI)     .364*    .876     .415       .019
E4,E5  (NEOPHOB ,ALIENATI)    2.288*   1.056    2.166@      .099
```

DECOMPOSITION OF EFFECTS

PARAMETER TOTAL EFFECTS
STATISTICS SIGNIFICANT AT THE 5% LEVEL ARE MARKED WITH @.

```
                                      STD.
DEP.VAR.   PREDICTOR      COEF        COEF    S.E.      Z
-----------------------------------------------------------------
V1  -  RISK
       V2   -NATURE        .368*      .297    .047    7.814@
       V3   - TECH        -.242*     -.178    .051   -4.714@
       V4   -NEOPHOB       .270*      .238    .043    6.284@
       V5   -ALIENATI      .672*      .314    .082    8.221@
       V999-  V999       29.798*      .000    .341   87.257@       (4)
       E1   - RISK        1.000       .786
       E2   -NATURE        .368       .297    .047    7.814@
       E3   - TECH        -.242      -.178    .051   -4.714@
       E4   -NEOPHOB       .270       .238    .043    6.284@
       E5   -ALIENATI      .672       .314    .082    8.221@
V2  -NATURE
       V999-  V999       32.360*      .000
       E2   -NATURE       1.000      1.000
V3  - TECH
       V999-  V999       25.004*      .000
       E3   - TECH        1.000      1.000
V4  -NEOPHOB
       V999-  V999       18.971*      .000
       E4   -NEOPHOB      1.000      1.000
V5  -ALIENATI
       V999-  V999       16.675*      .000
       E5   -ALIENATI     1.000      1.000
```

PARAMETER INDIRECT EFFECTS
STATISTICS SIGNIFICANT AT THE 5% LEVEL ARE MARKED WITH @.

```
                                      STD.
DEP.VAR.   PREDICTOR      COEF        COEF    S.E.      Z
-----------------------------------------------------------------
V1  -  RISK
       V999-  V999       22.162*      .000   2.351    9.425@       (4)
       E2   -NATURE        .368       .297    .047    7.814@
       E3   - TECH        -.242      -.178    .051   -4.714@
       E4   -NEOPHOB       .270       .238    .043    6.284@
       E5   -ALIENATI      .672       .314    .082    8.221@
```

The output in Table 2 deserves a few comments:

1. The coefficients showing the influence of V999 on the variables V2 to V5 are the means of the respective variables.
2. Since the variables E2 to E5 represent the variables V2 to V5, the variances of E2 to E5 are in reality the variances of V2 to V5.
3. In the same way the covariances between the E variables are in fact covariances between the V variables.
4. In the 'Decomposition of Effects' section of the output, we can calculate the mean of V1 (29.823) as the sum of the direct effect (the intercept from V999 to V5 (7.289)) and the indirect effect (22.533).

As you can see, the means in the output are exactly the same as in the input, so what is the point? Is it really necessary to *estimate* the means?

The answer is that if the model had been over-identified, the inputted means would not necessarily equal the estimated means, because the latter would then be freed from disturbing influences.

In Example 4.1 we had 15 'pieces of information' (5 variances and 10 covariances) on which to estimate 15 parameters (4 regression coefficients, 6 covariances and 5 variances), which left us with zero degrees of freedom. Now, we could add to our input information 5 means, but as the number of parameters to be estimated also grew by 5 (4 means and 1 intercept), we still have zero degrees of freedom and a just-identified model.

As you may have guessed from this example, degrees of freedom are rare goods in mean structure modeling. The problem is that the mean structure and the covariance structure must be identified *separately* – and it is obvious that identification of the mean structure is generally very problematic. In single-group models the mean structure is always just-identified unless at least one mean is fixed.

2 Comparing Covariance Structures Across Groups

You will often want to fit a model to more than one data set, e.g. for comparing two or more populations or for cross-validating within the same population.

Of course you can do separate analyses of the various samples, but there are several advantages in doing a simultaneous analysis in which the parameters in the various samples are estimated in one go.

You can test whether it is reasonable to assume that some or all parameters in the model are equal across samples, and estimation of parameters that (based on such tests) are considered equal can then be based on the combined data from all samples.

Often such analyses begin with a global test of equality of the covariance matrices for the various data sets. The argument is that if the same model describes the data equally well across groups, then the matrices are bound to be equal.

I cannot recommend the procedure. One problem is that the test does not build on a model of the data-generating process. With small or moderate sample sizes you run the risk that you will accept the null hypothesis of equal covariance matrices even if it is not possible to find a meaningful model that describes the data. Besides, the earlier mentioned problem of two-sided tests depending on sample size is itself a good reason for quitting this procedure altogether.

Testing a measuring instrument for cross-group equivalence

In order to compare research results across groups it is of course important to make sure that the measurements are comparable – that the measuring instrument works in the same way in the populations you want to compare (cf. the remarks in connection with Example 7.1 and Question 8.6).

Cross-group validity of a measuring instrument is usually checked by going through a series of tests, where the demands for the equivalence of the measuring instrument are increased step by step as we ask the following questions:

1. *Configural invariance*: Is the model structure the same across groups? That is, is the graphic picture of the measurement model the same across groups?
2. *Metric invariance*: Are the regression coefficients equal across groups? If so, the manifest variables are measured in the same scale units across groups.
3. *Scale invariance*: Are the item intercepts equal across groups? If so, the manifest variables are measured on common interval scales.
4. *Factor covariance invariance*: Are the factors interrelated in the same way across groups?
5. *Factor variance invariance*: Do the factors exhibit the same variation across groups?
6. *Error variance (and covariance) invariance*: Are the error variances (and covariances) equal across groups?

The last two questions secure equal reliabilities for the items and the complete measuring instrument across groups.

In Examples 2 and 3, you will need the input given in Table 3.

Table 3 Input for Examples 2 and 3

France 1994

n = 991	V10	V65	V23	V27	V45	V42
V10	3.5472					
V65	1.7071	4.0384				
V23	1.2193	1.1308	2.1313			
V27	0.1490	0.4255	0.5407	3.8371		
V45	0.1306	0.3621	0.1729	1.5280	4.5614	
V42	0.1176	0.0716	0.0708	1.1829	0.9593	4.7932
means	2.5005	2.9960	1.8729	3.0656	4.3582	4.2149

France 1998

n = 995	V10	V65	V23	V27	V45	V42
V10	2.7513					
V65	1.3850	3.4301				
V23	1.1782	1.1950	2.3008			
V27	0.4978	0.3907	0.6674	3.4849		
V45	0.3586	0.3484	0.3562	1.4290	3.9315	
V42	0.2071	0.2412	0.1996	1.0681	0.6606	3.8877
means	2.3658	3.0392	2.0050	3.1186	4.3779	4.5196

UK 1998

n = 1000	V10	V65	V23	V27	V45	V42
V10	3.3701					
V65	0.9896	3.7192				
V23	0.8806	1.1550	3.3682			
V27	0.2355	0.2035	0.3465	3.9896		
V45	0.1672	-0.0666	0.2016	1.5790	4.4350	
v42	-0.0615	-0.0290	0.1540	1.2053	0.7873	4.9876
means	2.8945	3.5201	2.4127	3.1595	3.5005	3.8717

Example 2
Does the FRL instrument work in the same way in the UK and in France?

The *Food-Related Lifestyle* (FRL) instrument is a 69-item battery, measuring 23 dimensions in five major domains (ways of shopping, cooking methods, quality aspects, consumption situations and buying motives). Since its invention (Brunsø & Grunert, 1995), it has been widely used in several European countries.

Let us test the intercultural validity of the FRL instrument across UK and French consumers in 1998 with data from Scholderer, Brunsø, Bredahl and Grunets (2004). In order to keep things simple and save space I will use only data from the two-factor dimension *consumption situations*, the items of which are listed in Table 4.

Table 4 Example 2: items used in the analysis

How are meals spread over the day? (snacks versus meals)

    (v10) I eat before I get hungry, which means that I am never hungry at meal time
    (v65) I eat whenever I feel the slightest bit hungry
    (v23) In our house, nibbling has taken over and replaced set eating hours

How important is eating-out? (social event)

    (v27) Going out for dinner is a regular part of our eating habits
    (v45) We often get together with friends to enjoy an easy-to-cook, casual dinner
    (v42) I do not consider it a luxury to go out with my family to have dinner in a restaurant

The model is shown in Figure 3, and a program for estimating the parameters in the two groups (without restrictions) is given in Table 5. You will observe that:

1. When doing multi-group analysis, the program is in fact a stack of programs, one for each group.
2. In the /SPECIFICATIONS paragraph you must state the number of groups, and also that the input data are the moment matrix, e.g. the covariances *and* the means (as in the previous example).
3. Special instructions such as /PRINT and /CONSTRAINTS are given only in the program for the last group.

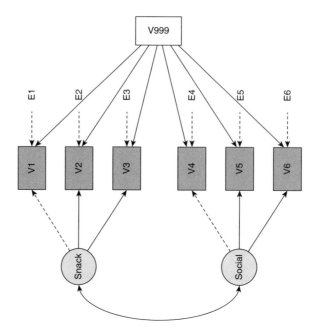

Figure 3 Example 2: model for UK and France 1998

Table 5 Example 2: program for test of configural invariance

```
/TITLE
Model built by EQS 6 for Windows in Group 1
/SPECIFICATIONS
   VARIABLES=6; CASES=1000; GROUPS=2;
   METHOD=ML; ANALYSIS=MOMENT; MATRIX=COVARIANCE;
/LABELS
   F1=snacks; F2=social;
/EQUATIONS
   V1 =    *V999 + 1F1 + E1;
   V2 =    *V999 + *F1 + E2;
   V3 =    *V999 + *F1 + E3;
   V4 =    *V999 + 1F2 + E4;
   V5 =    *V999 + *F2 + E5;
   V6 =    *V999 + *F2 + E6;
/VARIANCES
   F1 = *;
   F2 = *;
   E1 TO E6 = *;
/COVARIANCES
   F1,F2 = *;
/MATRIX
   3.3701
   0.9896   3.7192
   0.8806   1.1550   3.3682
   0.2355   0.2035   0.3465   3.9896
   0.1672  -0.0666   0.2016   1.5790   4.4350
  -0.0615  -0.0290   0.1540   1.2053   0.7873   4.9876
/MEANS
   2.8945   3.5201   2.4127   3.1595   3.5005   3.8717
/END
```

```
/TITLE
    Example 9.2. Data from Scholderer et al. (2004) F1998
/SPECIFICATIONS
    VARIABLES=6; CASES=995;
    METHOD=ML; ANALYSIS=MOMENT; MATRIX=COVARIANCE;
/LABELS
    F1=snacks; F2=social;
/EQUATIONS
    V1 =    *V999 + 1F1 + E1;
    V2 =    *V999 + *F1 + E2;
    V3 =    *V999 + *F1 + E3;
    V4 =    *V999 + 1F2 + E4;
    V5 =    *V999 + *F2 + E5;
    V6 =    *V999 + *F2 + E6;
/VARIANCES
    E1 TO E6 = *;
    F1 to F2 = *;
/COVARIANCES
    F1,F2 = *;
/MATRIX
    2.7513
    1.3850  3.4301
    1.1782  1.1950  2.3008
    0.4978  0.3907  0.6674  3.4849
    0.3586  0.3484  0.3562  1.4290  3.9315
    0.2071  0.2412  0.1996  1.0681  0.6606  3.8877
/MEANS
    2.3658  3.0392  2.0050  3.1186  4.3779  4.5196
/PRINT
    FIT=ALL;
    TABLE=COMPACT;
/END
```

When testing for metric invariance, you only have to put in the paragraph

```
               /CONSTRAINTS
               (1,V2,F1) = (2,V2,F1);
               (1,V3,F1) = (2,V3,F1);
               (1,V5,F2) = (2,V5,F2);
               (1,V6,F2) = (2,V6,F2);
```

The result of these two computer runs can be summarized as follows:

	Configural invariance	Metric invariance
χ^2 df and P	22.998 16 0.11	27.223 20 0.13
RMSEA	0.021 (0.000–0.039)	0.019 (0.000–0.035)
χ^2_{diff}, df and P		4.225 4 P = 0.376

No doubt each model would be accepted, if it were the only model, and furthermore the χ^2_{diff}-test does not show the second model to be significantly worse than the first, which – given the very large samples (about 2 × 1000) – is strong evidence in favor of the measuring instrument having *at least* metric invariance.

At our next step – testing for scale invariance – we add the following constraints:

$$(1,V1,V999) = (2,V1,V999);$$
$$(1,V2,V999) = (2,V2,V999);$$
$$(1,V3,V999) = (2,V3,V999);$$
$$(1,V4,V999) = (2,V4,V999);$$
$$(1,V5,V999) = (2,V5,V999);$$
$$(1,V6,V999) = (2,V6,V999);$$

and so you proceed, adding in turn the constraints

$$(1,F1,F2) = (2,F1,F2);$$

$$(1,F1,F1) = (2,F1,F1);$$
$$(1,F2,F2) = (2,F2,F2);$$

$$(1,E1,E1) = (2,E1,E1);$$
$$(1,E2,E2) = (2,E2,E2);$$
$$(1,E3,E3) = (2,E3,E3);$$
$$(1,E4,E4) = (2,E4,E4);$$
$$(1,E5,E5) = (2,E5,E5);$$
$$(1,E6,E6) = (2,E6,E6);$$

The results of this series of tests are given in Table 6.

Table 6 Example 2: marginal analysis

Type of invariance	χ^2 df and P			χ^2_{diff} and df		RMSEA	RMSEA increment
1. Configural	22.998	16	0.114			0.021	
2. Metric	27.223	20	0.129	4.225	4	0.019	– 0.002
3. Scale	249.272	26	0.000	222.049	4	0.093	0.074
4. Factor covariance	257.023	27	0.000	7.7516	1	0.092	– 0.001
5. Factor variance	260.864	29	0.000	3.841	2	0.090	– 0.002
6. Error variance	413.227	35	0.000	152.227	6	0.104	0.014

From Table 6 we can see that models 1 and 2 are accepted at any conventional significance level, while all other models are rejected. As mentioned above, this is a very good argument for the measurement model having *at least* metric invariance.

As mentioned several times, the χ^2_{diff}- test is of little value in such large samples. Therefore I will (like Scholderer et al.) fall back on RMSEA as my main measures of model fit.

In the RMSEA column we can see that the value of RMSEA (which for model 1 is 0.021) drops by 0.002 when we impose the restriction of metric invariance, whereas it increases by 0.074 when we also impose scale invariance. Adding restrictions on factor covariances and factor variances again reduces RMSEA, whereas adding the last restriction of equal error variances once more causes RMSEA to go up.

Our conclusion then is that the measuring instrument shows configural, metric, factor covariance and factor variance invariances, whereas scale invariance and error variance invariance are not supported by the data.

In this simple case you can short-circuit the process and do it all in one run. If you include all the constraints and add the paragraph

/LMTEST

the output will include the information given in Table 7.

Table 7 Example 2: LM test

```
LAGRANGE MULTIPLIER TEST (FOR RELEASING CONSTRAINTS)

CONSTRAINTS TO BE RELEASED ARE:

     CONSTRAINTS FROM GROUP   2

        CONSTR:    1    (1,V2,F1)-(2,V2,F1)=0;
        CONSTR:    2    (1,V3,F1)-(2,V3,F1)=0;
        CONSTR:    3    (1,V5,F2)-(2,V5,F2)=0;
        CONSTR:    4    (1,V6,F2)-(2,V6,F2)=0;
        CONSTR:    5    (1,V1,V999)-(2,V1,V999)=0;
        CONSTR:    6    (1,V2,V999)-(2,V2,V999)=0;
        CONSTR:    7    (1,V3,V999)-(2,V3,V999)=0;
        CONSTR:    8    (1,V4,V999)-(2,V4,V999)=0;
        CONSTR:    9    (1,V5,V999)-(2,V5,V999)=0;
        CONSTR:   10    (1,V6,V999)-(2,V6,V999)=0;
        CONSTR:   11    (1,F1,F2)-(2,F1,F2)=0;
        CONSTR:   12    (1,F1,F1)-(2,F1,F1)=0;
        CONSTR:   13    (1,F2,F2)-(2,F2,F2)=0;
        CONSTR:   14    (1,E1,E1)-(2,E1,E1)=0;
        CONSTR:   15    (1,E2,E2)-(2,E2,E2)=0;
        CONSTR:   16    (1,E3,E3)-(2,E3,E3)=0;
        CONSTR:   17    (1,E4,E4)-(2,E4,E4)=0;
        CONSTR:   18    (1,E5,E5)-(2,E5,E5)=0;
        CONSTR:   19    (1,E6,E6)-(2,E6,E6)=0;
```

	CUMULATIVE MULTIVARIATE STATISTICS				UNIVARIATE INCREMENT	
STEP PARAMETER	CHI-SQUARE	D.F.	PROBABILITY		CHI-SQUARE	PROBABILITY
1 CONSTR: 9	100.857	1	0.000		100.857	0.000
2 CONSTR: 16	176.749	2	0.000		75.893	0.000
3 CONSTR: 10	231.294	3	0.000		54.545	0.000

(Continued)

Table 7 (Continued)

4	CONSTR:	14	269.352	4	0.000	38.058	0.000
5	CONSTR:	5	287.053	5	0.000	17.702	0.000
6	CONSTR:	19	303.101	6	0.000	16.048	0.000
7	CONSTR:	6	318.329	7	0.000	15.228	0.000
8	CONSTR:	7	346.896	8	0.000	28.566	0.000
9	CONSTR:	11	354.044	9	0.000	7.149	0.008
10	CONSTR:	15	359.814	10	0.000	5.769	0.016
11	CONSTR:	17	364.368	11	0.000	4.554	0.033
12	CONSTR:	12	368.192	12	0.000	3.824	0.051
13	CONSTR:	18	371.049	13	0.000	2.857	0.091
14	CONSTR:	2	372.934	14	0.000	1.885	0.170
15	CONSTR:	1	375.961	15	0.000	3.027	0.082
16	CONSTR:	13	376.941	16	0.000	0.980	0.322
17	CONSTR:	8	377.164	17	0.000	0.223	0.637
18	CONSTR:	3	377.197	18	0.000	0.033	0.856
19	CONSTR:	4	377.199	19	0.000	0.002	0.962

In the last two columns you can see the increment in chi-square obtained by relaxing the various constraints, starting with the one that has the largest (positive) effect on chi-square.

As our interest concerns the constraints that are not significant, it seems obvious that our measuring instrument shows *at least* configural, metric and factor variance invariance, but bear in mind the excessive power of the tests with sample sizes of 2×1000.

Multi-group analysis of 'causal' models with latent variables

For the multi-group analysis of 'causal' models things become a little more complicated, because in addition to analyzing the measurement model you must also analyze the structural model.

As in all other cases, it is very important to make sure that the measurement model is valid before trying to analyze the structural model. So, I recommend using the two-step strategy mentioned in Chapter 8 and starting the analysis by going through the same sequence of steps as in Example 2.

Then you should continue with the structural model, first testing for the equivalence of the regression coefficients (and intercepts if this is relevant) and then the variances and covariances of the disturbances.

Usually error and disturbance variances (and covariances) are of least interest, so you can put error variances (and covariances) last in the sequence together with the disturbance variances.

Example 3
Are the good beautiful or the beautiful good?

It is generally agreed that a person's appearance affects other people's impressions of the person. A long line of evidence supports the view that physically attractive people are often attributed more positive qualities, and quite a few studies suggest that physically attractive people are more often seen as more intelligent than people that are less physically attractive (Byrne, London, & Reeves, 1968; Clifford & Walster, 1973; Landy

& Sigall, 1974; Sarty, 1975). However, there are also quite a few studies that point the other way: that persons with an attractive personality are perceived as more physically attractive (Gross & Crafton, 1977; Owens & Ford, 1978).

Felson and Bohrnstedt (1979) studied 209 girls and 207 boys from the sixth to the eighth grade (approximately 11–14 years of age) in order to find the direction of a (possible) causal effect between physical attractiveness and perceived academic ability – or if there perhaps exists a two-way causation. (Felson and Bohrnstedt in a single passage in their article write that the number of girls is 207 and the number of boys 209. However, the two figures are so close that, whichever is correct, it will not affect the conclusions.)

Felson and Bohrnstedt measured the following variables:

academic: Perceived academic ability, based on the item: Name who you think are the three smartest classmates.

attract: Perceived attractiveness, based on the item: Name the three girls (boys) in the classroom who you think are the most good-looking (excluding yourself).

GPA: Grade Point Average.

height: Deviation of height from the mean for a subject's grade and sex.

weight: Weight, adjusted for height.

rating: Ratings of physical attractiveness obtained by having children from another city rate photographs of subjects.

Their model is shown in Figure 4. I must admit, however, that I have cheated a bit: at present 'Diagrammer' does not allow reciprocal effects, so when programming you could instead use 'Build EQS'.

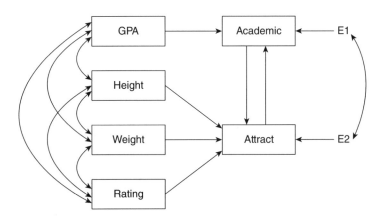

Figure 4 Example 3: Felson and Bohrnstedt's model

The reason why the model includes height and weight is that Felson and Bohrnstedt also wanted to test the following two hypotheses:

1. *Height* has a positive effect on *attract* for boys, but a negative or no effect for girls.
2. *Weight* has a negative effect on attract for both girls and boys.

Formulating the two regression equations as

$$\text{academic} = \text{attract} + \text{GPA} + E1$$
$$\text{attract} = \text{academic} + \text{height} + \text{weight} + \text{rating} + E2 \qquad (2)$$

it is evident that the model is identified because the two functions have no exogenous variables in common.

Note the two opposed arrows that depict the hypothesized effects between *academic* and *attract*. While the possible correlations among the exogenous variables only express traditional multicollinearity, the inclusion of a correlation between the error terms is more doubtful. The only reason Felson and Bohrnstedt give is that 'it is unrealistic in a simultaneous equation model to assume they are uncorrelated'. I would have preferred a substantive argument.

The data given in Table 8 can also be found on the book's website. Note that as the input consists of correlation coefficients and not covariances, the standard deviations have been added so that EQS can calculate the covariance matrix as a basis for estimating the model parameters. The means are also included in the data file but will not be used in this example.

When you try to estimate the models using the program in Table 9, you will get a lot of condition codes, and the program will not converge but recommend you choose better start values.

Table 8 Example 3: data input

```
Fels_fem
```

varname_	academic	attract	GPA	height	weight	rating
academic	1.00					
attract	0.50	1.00				
GPA	0.49	0.32	1.00			
height	0.10	-0.03	0.18	1.00		
weight	0.04	-0.16	-0.10	0.34	1.00	
rating	0.09	0.43	0.15	-0.16	-0.27	1.00
std dev	0.16	0.49	3.49	2.91	19.32	1.01
mean_	0.12	0.42	10.34	0.00	94.13	2.65

```
Fels_mal
```

varname_	academic	attract	GPA	height	weight	rating
academic	1.00					
attract	0.49	1.00				
GPA	0.58	0.30	1.00			
height	-0.02	0.04	-0.11	1.00		
weight	-0.11	-0.19	-0.16	0.51	1.00	
rating	0.11	0.28	0.13	0.06	-0.18	1.00
Std dev	0.16	0.49	4.04	3.41	24.32	0.97
mean_	0.10	0.44	8.63	0.00	101.91	2.59

It is better to try to locate the problem. In this case this is easily done. A quick look at Table 8 reveals that the standard deviations vary so much in size that they are bound to cause problems (cf. the comments in Section 4.6). I therefore multiplied the standard deviation and the mean for 'academic' by 10, and divided the standard deviation and mean for 'weight' by 100. The output can be seen in Table 10.

Table 9 Example 3: program, first run

```
/TITLE
Example 9.4. Data from Felson and Bohrnstedt (1979). Group 1: Girls.
/SPECIFICATIONS
DATA='C:\Users\Sony\Desktop\EQS bog\EQS Chap 9\Fels_fem_a.ESS';
VARIABLES=7; CASES=209; GROUPS=2;
METHOD=ML; ANALYSIS=COVARIANCE; MATRIX=CORR;
/LABELS
V1=academic; V2=attract; V3=GPA; V4=height;
V5=weight; V6=rating;
/EQUATIONS
V1 =    *V2 + *V3 + E1;
V2 =    *V1 + *V4 + *V5 + *V6 + E2;
/VARIANCES
V3 TO V6 = *;
E1 = *;
E2 = *;
/COVARIANCES
V3 TO V6 = *;
E1,E2 = *;
/END


/TITLE
Example 9.4. Data from Felson and Bohrnstedt (1979). Group 2: Boys.
/SPECIFICATIONS
DATA='C:\Users\Sony\Desktop\EQS bog\EQS Chap 9\Fels_mal_a.ESS';
VARIABLES=7; CASES=207; GROUPS=2;
METHOD=ML; ANALYSIS=COVARIANCE; MATRIX=CORR;
/LABELS
V1=academic;; V2=attract; V3=GPA; V4=height;
V5=weight; V6=rating;
/EQUATIONS
V1 =    *V2 + *V3 + E1;
V2 =    *V1 + *V4 + *V5 + *V6 + E2;
/VARIANCES
V3 TO V6 = *;
E1 = *;
E2 = *;
/COVARIANCES
V3 TO V6 = *;
E1,E2 = *;
/PRINT
FIT=ALL;
TABLE=COMPACT;
/END
```

In the output in Table 10 you will observe that 'R-squared' is not shown in connection with the regression functions as you have got used to, but instead there is a new statistic, the *Bentler-Raykov corrected R-squared*. The reason for this is that if you have reciprocal causation, the model could imply a correlation between the error/disturbance and one or more of the predictors. The Bentler–Raykov correction takes care of that.

As can be seen from the χ^2-test the fit is extremely good, and the various fit indices, which are not shown in order to save space, confirm this. As the fit is excellent it should be possible to simplify the model.

Table 10 Example 3: output for model A

```
MULTIPLE POPULATION ANALYSIS, INFORMATION IN GROUP   1

   PARAMETER ESTIMATES (B) WITH STANDARD ERRORS AND TEST STATISTICS (Z)
   STATISTICS SIGNIFICANT AT THE 5% LEVEL ARE MARKED WITH @.

                                                                    R-
DEP.VAR.           PREDICTOR      B      BETA    S.E.      Z      SQUARED
-------------------------------------------------------------------------
  V1  (ACADEMIC)
            V2  (ATTRACT )    -.036*   -.011   .517    -.069               (1)
            V3  (  GPA    )    .226*    .494   .036    6.241@
  V2  (ATTRACT )
            V1  (ACADEMIC)     .161*    .525   .035    4.601@              (1)
            V4  (HEIGHT  )     .000*    .003   .010     .050               (2)
            V5  (WEIGHT  )    -.020*   -.078   .015   -1.325               (3)
            V6  (RATING  )     .176*    .363   .027    6.448@

BENTLER-RAYKOV CORRECTED R-SQUARED COEFFICIENTS:
SQUARED CORRELATIONS BETWEEN DEPENDENT VARIABLES AND PREDICTORS

ACADEMIC=V1      .233
ATTRACT =V2      .404


   VARIANCES OF INDEPENDENT VARIABLES
   STATISTICS SIGNIFICANT AT THE 5% LEVEL ARE MARKED WITH @.

                             VARIANCE    S.E.       Z
-------------------------------------------------------
VARIABLE
            V3 (  GPA   )12.180*     1.194     10.198@
            V4 (HEIGHT  ) 8.468*      .830     10.198@
            V5 (WEIGHT  ) 3.733*      .366     10.198@
            V6 (RATING  ) 1.020*      .100     10.198@
ERROR
            E1 (ACADEMIC) 1.965*      .345      5.698@
            E2 (ATTRACT )  .143*      .014      9.981@


   COVARIANCES AMONG INDEPENDENT VARIABLES
   STATISTICS SIGNIFICANT AT THE 5% LEVEL ARE MARKED WITH @.

                                COVA.     S.E.       Z       CORR.
-------------------------------------------------------------------
    V3,V4    (  GPA   ,HEIGHT  )  1.828*    .716     2.555@    .180
    V3,V5    (  GPA   ,WEIGHT  )  -.674*    .470    -1.435    -.100
    V3,V6    (  GPA   ,RATING  )   .529*    .247     2.139@    .150
    V4,V5    (HEIGHT  ,WEIGHT  )  1.912*    .412     4.643@    .340
```

```
V4,V6    (HEIGHT  ,RATING  )   -.470*    .206   -2.279@    -.160
V5,V6    (WEIGHT  ,RATING  )   -.527*    .140   -3.759@    -.270
E1,E2    (ACADEMIC,ATTRACT )   -.037*    .105    -.355     -.070    (4)
```

MULTIPLE POPULATION ANALYSIS, INFORMATION IN GROUP 2

PARAMETER ESTIMATES (B) WITH STANDARD ERRORS AND TEST STATISTICS (Z)
STATISTICS SIGNIFICANT AT THE 5% LEVEL ARE MARKED WITH @.

```
                                                         R-
DEP.VAR.        PREDICTOR    B       BETA    S.E.    Z    SQUARED
------------------------------------------------------------------
V1  (ACADEMIC)
        V2   (ATTRACT )    .627*    .192    .585    1.071           (1)
        V3   ( GPA     )   .207*    .522    .030    6.927@
V2  (ATTRACT )
        V1   (ACADEMIC)    .139*    .453    .032    4.398@          (1)
        V4   (HEIGHT  )    .019*    .132    .010    1.967@          (2)
        V5   (WEIGHT  )   -.034*   -.171    .014   -2.484@          (3)
        V6   (RATING  )    .095*    .189    .030    3.150@
```

BENTLER-RAYKOV CORRECTED R-SQUARED COEFFICIENTS:
SQUARED CORRELATIONS BETWEEN DEPENDENT VARIABLES AND PREDICTORS

```
ACADEMIC=V1       .426
ATTRACT =V2       .313
```

VARIANCES OF INDEPENDENT VARIABLES
STATISTICS SIGNIFICANT AT THE 5% LEVEL ARE MARKED WITH @.

```
                         VARIANCE   S.E.      Z
-------------------------------------------------
VARIABLE
          V3  ( GPA    )16.322*    1.608   10.149@
          V4  (HEIGHT  )11.628*    1.146   10.149@
          V5  (WEIGHT  ) 5.915*     .583   10.149@
          V6  (RATING  )  .941*     .093   10.149@
ERROR
          E1  (ACADEMIC) 1.474*     .195    7.570@
          E2  (ATTRACT )  .165*     .016   10.149@
```

COVARIANCES AMONG INDEPENDENT VARIABLES
STATISTICS SIGNIFICANT AT THE 5% LEVEL ARE MARKED WITH @.

```
                              COVA.    S.E.     Z       CORR.
-----------------------------------------------------------------
V3,V4   ( GPA    ,HEIGHT  )  -1.515*   .966   -1.569    -.110
V3,V5   ( GPA    ,WEIGHT  )  -1.572*   .693   -2.268@   -.160
V3,V6   ( GPA    ,RATING  )    .509*   .275    1.850     .130
V4,V5   (HEIGHT  ,WEIGHT  )   4.229*   .649    6.521@    .510
V4,V6   (HEIGHT  ,RATING  )    .198*   .231     .860     .060
V5,V6   (WEIGHT  ,RATING  )   -.425*   .167   -2.543@   -.180
E1,E2   (ACADEMIC,ATTRACT )   -.103*   .115    -.898    -.209    (4)
```

```
CHI-SQUARE =         3.185 BASEDON         4 DEGREES OF FREEDOM
   PROBABILITY VALUE FOR THE CHI-SQUARE STATISTIC IS         .52743
```

The estimates of the coefficients seem partly to support Felson and Bohrnstedt's hypotheses (level of significance 0.05, one-sided test, region of rejection $Z > |1.65|$ – in the relevant direction!):

1. Perceived academic ability does not depend on attractiveness ($Z = -0.069$ for girls and 1.071 for boys), whereas the opposite effect seems to exist ($Z = 4.601$ and 4.398).
2. Height has nearly no effect on attractiveness for girls ($Z = 0.050$), but has a positive effect for boys ($Z = 1.967$).
3. Attractiveness does not depend on weight for girls ($Z = -1.321$), but does for boys ($Z = -2.484$).
4. E1 and E2 are not correlated ($Z = -0.355$ and -0.898, two-sided test).

Point 1 above answered the main research question, point 2 supports hypothesis 1 and point 3 partly supports hypothesis 2.

However, just as in traditional regression analysis, these are marginal tests, and you cannot use such tests to argue that several parameters should be removed at the same time.

We could of course exclude one parameter at a time, but due to collinearity this is perhaps not the most preferable procedure. Instead we can formulate a few reasonable models and compare them.

No doubt the effect from *attract* to *academic* and the correlations between the error terms should be excluded, while all correlations among exogenous variables should be maintained. These correlations are not given by the model but more or less by 'nature', and there would be no sense in restricting them to zero, even if they were not significant.

Having said that, there are still quite a few models that could all be substantively grounded and are also supported to a certain extent by the data.

Model B: One of Felson and Bohrnstedt's hypotheses was that height had a positive effect on *attract* for boys but a negative or no effect for girls. The data heavily support that hypothesis: not only is the effect for girls not significant by traditional standards, but in addition the regression coefficient is estimated as 0.000(!). Weight is also non-significant for girls but significant for boys, so it is tempting to remove this effect too. However, due to the rather strong correlation between weight and height, it is possible that weight would be significant if the effect of height is removed from the model.

So for model B, I exclude the effect from *attract* to *academic* and the correlation between the errors for both girls and boys, and in addition the effects of height for girls. Part of the output can be seen in Table 11.

Table 11 Example 3: partial output for model B

```
MULTIPLE POPULATION ANALYSIS, INFORMATION IN GROUP   1

STATISTICS SIGNIFICANT AT THE 5% LEVEL ARE MARKED WITH @.

                                                           R-
DEP.VAR.        PREDICTOR     B       BETA    S.E.    Z    SQUARED
-------------------------------------------------------------------
V1   (ACADEMIC)                                             .240
          V3  (  GPA  )      .225*    .490    .028   8.107@
```

```
V2    (ATTRACT )                                                      .405
         V1    (ACADEMIC)    .144*    .469    .016    8.742@
         V5    (WEIGHT  )   -.020*   -.078    .014   -1.402
         V6    (RATING  )    .178*    .367    .027    6.594@
```

MULTIPLE POPULATION ANALYSIS, INFORMATION IN GROUP   2

MAXIMUM LIKELIHOOD SOLUTION (NORMAL DISTRIBUTION THEORY)

PARAMETER ESTIMATES (B) WITH STANDARD ERRORS AND TEST STATISTICS (Z)
STATISTICS SIGNIFICANT AT THE 5% LEVEL ARE MARKED WITH @.

```
                                                                       R-
DEP.VAR.            PREDICTOR       B      BETA     S.E.     Z      SQUARED
---------------------------------------------------------------------------
V1    (ACADEMIC)                                                      .336
         V3    (  GPA   )    .230*    .580    .022   10.219@
         E1    (ACADEMIC)   1.000     .815
V2    (ATTRACT )                                                      .303
         V1    (ACADEMIC)    .138*    .455    .018    7.776@
         V4    (HEIGHT  )    .018*    .125    .010    1.821
         V5    (WEIGHT  )   -.034*   -.170    .014   -2.439@
         V6    (RATING  )    .097*    .194    .030    3.223@
         E2    (ATTRACT )   1.000     .835
```

In this case there is no need to do a χ^2_{diff}-test as you can be sure that this test will be insignificant. Also, the various fit indices (marginally) favor model B.

Model C: Although weight has the expected sign, and the coefficient is larger than in model A (as expected), it is still not significant. So for model C I will exclude weight for girls. The output is in Table 12.

Perhaps girls' attraction cannot easily be measured by 'hard measures' but depends more on 'soft' variables that are not very easy to describe in words? And perhaps it is not as much the weight in itself but how it is distributed that is of importance?

Model D: Even if *weight* is not significant for the girls but is significant for the boys, you could argue that the two regression coefficients are so close (−0.02 and −0.03) that for all practical purposes they could be considered equal. So model D is model B with an equality constraint on (V2V5).

Model E: As can be seen from Table 12, the effects (V1V3) and (V2V1) are not very different. So for model E, I will let the two effects be equal across the two groups, based on model C.

Model F: Model C with all regression coefficients equal across groups.

We can see from Table 13 that, *judged by themselves*, all six models are acceptable, and would have been accepted if only the same model were under consideration.

In such situations I have used RMSEA in earlier examples in this chapter as my main fit measure. Here, however, RMSEA is estimated as 0.000 for all six models. As a substitute I could fall back on the upper limit of the confidence interval for RMSEA, which shows that the choice must be between model C and model E – the last one being marginally favored. The various fit indices (not shown) also point to the two models, shown in Figure 5.

However, the differences in fit are very small and of limited interest for practical purposes. Also, whatever model you prefer, the main conclusions about the research questions (stated at the beginning of the example) would be the same.

Table 12 Example 3: partial output model C

```
MULTIPLE POPULATION ANALYSIS, INFORMATION IN GROUP  1

MAXIMUM LIKELIHOOD SOLUTION (NORMAL DISTRIBUTION THEORY)

PARAMETER ESTIMATES (B) WITH STANDARD ERRORS AND TEST STATISTICS (Z)
STATISTICS SIGNIFICANT AT THE 5% LEVEL ARE MARKED WITH @.

                                                           R-
DEP.VAR.         PREDICTOR      B       BETA    S.E.    Z     SQUARED
-----------------------------------------------------------------
V1   (ACADEMIC)                                                .240
          V3  (  GPA   )      .225*     .490    .028   8.107@
V2   (ATTRACT )                                                .396
          V1  (ACADEMIC)      .142*     .466    .017   8.630@
          V6  (RATING  )      .188*     .389    .026   7.206@


MULTIPLE POPULATION ANALYSIS, INFORMATION IN GROUP  2

MAXIMUM LIKELIHOOD SOLUTION (NORMAL DISTRIBUTION THEORY)

PARAMETER ESTIMATES (B) WITH STANDARD ERRORS AND TEST STATISTICS (Z)
STATISTICS SIGNIFICANT AT THE 5% LEVEL ARE MARKED WITH @.

                                                           R-
DEP.VAR.         PREDICTOR      B       BETA    S.E.    Z     SQUARED
-----------------------------------------------------------------
V1   (ACADEMIC)                                                .336
          V3  (  GPA   )      .230*     .580    .022  10.219@
V2   (ATTRACT )                                                .303
          V1  (ACADEMIC)      .138*     .455    .018   7.776@
          V4  (HEIGHT  )      .018*     .125    .010   1.821
          V5  (WEIGHT  )     -.034*    -.170    .014  -2.439@
          V6  (RATING  )      .097*     .194    .030   3.223@
```

Table 13 Example 3: fit measures for the various models

EQS (assuming Model A to be correct)

Model	chi	df	P	Chi diff	f dif	P diff	RMSEA upper
Model A	3.185	4	0.527				0.095
Model B	4.414	7	0.731	1.229	3	0.364	0.095
Model C	2.011	6	0.919	-1.174	2	1.000	0.032
Model D	4.884	8	0.770	1.699	4	0.791	0.056
Model E	2.055	8	0.979	-1.120	4	1.000	-
Model F	7.305	9	.605	4.120	5	0.903	0.067

As the model formulations B–F were partly data driven, the results of the analysis should be cross-validated on a new independent sample from the same population.

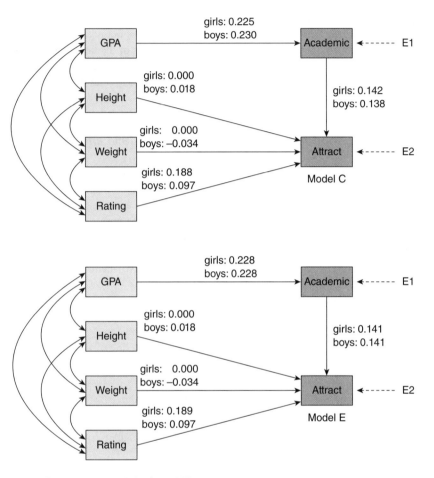

Figure 5 Example 3: models C and E

A brief remark on two-way causation

This is the first (and only) worked example of a cyclic model, and a few remarks are in order.

Recall from the last subsection of Chapter 6 that two conditions must be met to give a meaningful substantive interpretation of model parameters in a cyclic model:

1. As the regression coefficients in a loop are interpreted as the result of an infinite sum of loops, it is necessary that the sum is defined.
2. It is assumed that the whole process has come to an end.

If EQS succeeds in finding a solution you can be pretty sure that the first condition is fulfilled, but that is no guarantee that the second condition is fulfilled too.

Time series data are required to judge the second condition – and if such data were at hand you would probably specify a time series model.

3. Comparing Means of Latent Variables

We easily run out of degrees of freedom when trying to estimate mean structures in single-group studies and the same is the case in multi-group studies. If such a study is done in order to compare means of latent variables across groups, it is not possible to estimate the means in all groups in one go. However, if we fix the means of the latent variables in one group at zero, it is possible to estimate the means in the other groups, and these means will then express the *differences* in means between the various groups and the reference group.

Example 4
Comparing food-related lifestyle in France in 1994 and 1998

We will test the hypothesis that the two-factor means in the consumption situations dimension have not changed in France from 1994 to 1998.

In order to do so, we must make sure that the measures are comparable, i.e. that the measuring instrument functions in the same way at the two points in time. Otherwise, there is no sense in comparing the factor means (cf. Example 6.1).

So, we must demand that regression coefficients and regression intercepts are equal across groups – and of course also that the same general two-factor structure exists in both groups.

The model is shown in Figure 6 and the program in Table 14, which deserves a few comments.

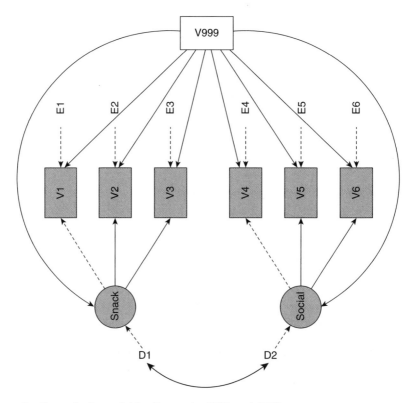

Figure 6 Example 4: model for France in 1994 and 1998

1. As the two factors are now dependent variables, they do not have variances and covariances. These are now carried by the two disturbances.
2. The corresponding regression coefficients and intercepts in the two models have been fixed to have the same values.
3. The means of 'Snacks' and 'Social' are fixed at zero in 'France 1994', but freely estimated in 'France 1998'.

Table 14 Example 4: program, first run

```
/TITLE
Example 9.3. Data from Scholderer et al. (2004) France 1994. Group 1
/SPECIFICATIONS
DATA='C:\Users\Sony\Desktop\EQS bog\EQS Chap 9\F94.ESS';
VARIABLES=6; CASES=991; GROUPS=2;
METHOD=ML; ANALYSIS=MOMENT; MATRIX=COVARIANCE;
/LABELS
V1=V1; V2=V2; V3=V3; V4=V4; V5=V5; V6=V6;
F1=snacks; F2=social;
/EQUATIONS
V1 =    *V999 + 1F1 + E1;
V2 =    *V999 + *F1 + E2;
V3 =    *V999 + *F1 + E3;
V4 =    *V999 + 1F2 + E4;
V5 =    *V999 + *F2 + E5;
V6 =    *V999 + *F2 + E6;
F1 =    0.0 V999 + D1;                                                       (3)
F2 =    0.0 V999 + D2;

/VARIANCES
  D1 = *;                                                                    (1)
  D2 = *;
  E1 TO E6 = *;
/COVARIANCES
D1,D2 = *;                                                                   (1)
/MATRIX
3.5472
1.7071   4.0384
1.2193   1.1308   2.1313
0.1490   0.4255   0.5407   3.8371
0.1306   0.3621   0.1729   1.5280   4.5614
0.1176   0.0716   0.0708   1.1829   0.9593   4.7932
/MEANS
2.5005   2.9960   1.8729   3.0656 4.3582   4.2149

/END


/TITLE
Example 9.3. Data from Scholderer et al. (2004) France 1998.Group 2
/SPECIFICATIONS
DATA='C:\Users\Sony\Desktop\EQS bog\EQS Chap 9\F98.ESS';
VARIABLES=6; CASES=991;
METHOD=ML; ANALYSIS=MOMENT; MATRIX=COVARIANCE;
/LABELS
V1=V1; V2=V2; V3=V3; V4=V4; V5=V5; V6=V6;
F1=snacks; F2=social;
```

(Continued)

Table 14 (Continued)

```
/EQUATIONS
V1 =      *V999 + 1F1 + E1;
V2 =      *V999 + *F1 + E2;
V3 =      *V999 + *F1 + E3;
V4 =      *V999 + 1F2 + E4;
V5 =      *V999 + *F2 + E5;
V6 =      *V999 + *F2 + E6;
F1 =      *V999 + D1;                                                    (3)
F2 =      *V999 + D2;
/VARIANCES
  D1 = *;                                                                (1)
  D2 = *;
  E1 TO E6 = *;
/COVARIANCES
  D1,D2 = *;                                                             (1)
/MATRIX
2.7513
1.3850    3.4301
0.4978    0.3907    0.6674    3.4849
0.3586    0.3484    0.3562    1.4290    3.9315
0.2071    0.2412    0.1996    1.0681    0.6606    3.8877

/MEANS
2.3658    3.0392    2.0050    3.1186    4.3779    4.5196
/PRINT
FIT=ALL;
TABLE=COMPACT;
/LMTEST
/CONSTRAINTS                                                             (2)
(1,V2,F1)    = (2,V2,F1);
(1,V3,F1)    = (2,V3,F1);
(1,V5,F2)    = (2,V5,F2);
(1,V6,F2)    = (2,V6,F2);
(1,V1,V999)  = (2,V1,V999);
(1,V2,V999)  = (2,V2,V999);
(1,V3,V999)  = (2,V3,V999);
(1,V4,V999)  = (2,V4,V999);
(1,V5,V999)  = (2,V5,V999);
(1,V6,V999)  = (2,V6,V999);
/END
```

The output is shown in Table 15

Table 15 Example 4: output, first run

```
    MULTIPLE POPULATION ANALYSIS, INFORMATION IN GROUP   1

    PARAMETER ESTIMATES (B) WITH STANDARD ERRORS AND TEST STATISTICS (Z)
    STATISTICS SIGNIFICANT AT THE 5% LEVEL ARE MARKED WITH @.

                                                              R-
    DEP.VAR.        PREDICTOR    B        BETA    S.E.    Z   SQUARED
    ---------------------------------------------------------------
    V1    ( V1   )                                            .443
              F1   (SNACKS ) 1.000       .665
              V999(   V999 ) 2.413*      .000    .053   45.445@
```

```
V2   ( V2     )                                            .382
         F1    (SNACKS  )   .994*    .618    .054   18.481@
         V999( V999    )  3.012*    .000    .055   54.493@
V3   ( V3     )                                            .451
         F1    (SNACKS  )   .801*    .672    .043   18.454@
         V999( V999    )  1.931*    .000    .043   45.184@
V4   ( V4     )                                            .588
         F2    (SOCIAL  )  1.000     .767
         V999( V999    )  3.045*    .000    .061   50.152@
V5   ( V5     )                                            .230
         F2    (SOCIAL  )   .680*    .480    .070    9.711@
         V999( V999    )  4.335*    .000    .055   79.174@
V6   ( V6     )                                            .128
         F2    (SOCIAL  )   .520*    .357    .056    9.210@
         V999( V999    )  4.357*    .000    .052   83.931@
F1   (SNACKS  )                                            .000
         D1    (SNACKS  )  1.000    1.000

F2   (SOCIAL  )                                            .000
         D2    (SOCIAL  )  1.000    1.000


    VARIANCES OF INDEPENDENT VARIABLES
    STATISTICS SIGNIFICANT AT THE 5% LEVEL ARE MARKED WITH @.


                              VARIANCE    S.E.     Z
    ---------------------------------------------------
    ERROR
              E1   ( V1   )1.945*    .130   14.966@
              E2   ( V2   )2.471*    .148   16.725@
              E3   ( V3   )1.205*    .082   14.718@
              E4   ( V4   )1.589*    .261    6.085@
              E5   ( V5   )3.503*    .199   17.609@
              E6   ( V6   )4.175*    .204   20.456@
    DISTURBANCE
              D1   (SNACKS )1.545*   .140   11.065@
              D2   (SOCIAL )2.264*   .282    8.020@


    COVARIANCES AMONG INDEPENDENT VARIABLES
    STATISTICS SIGNIFICANT AT THE 5% LEVEL ARE MARKED WITH @.


                              COVA.     S.E.     Z        CORR.
    ---------------------------------------------------------------
    D1,D2    (SNACKS ,SOCIAL  )   .400*    .091    4.401@   .214

MULTIPLE POPULATION ANALYSIS, INFORMATION IN GROUP  2

    PARAMETER ESTIMATES (B) WITH STANDARD ERRORS AND TEST STATISTICS (Z)
    STATISTICS SIGNIFICANT AT THE 5% LEVEL ARE MARKED WITH @.

                                                              R-
    DEP.VAR.         PREDICTOR    B       BETA    S.E.    Z   SQUARED
    -----------------------------------------------------------------
    V1   ( V1     )                                            .516
         F1    (SNACKS  )  1.000     .718
         V999( V999    )  2.413*    .000    .053   45.445@
```

(Continued)

Table 15 (Continued)

```
V2    ( V2     )                                                      .412
          F1    (SNACKS  )   .994*   .641   .054   18.481@
          V999( V999 )     3.012*   .000   .055   54.493@
V3    ( V3     )                                                      .413
          F1    (SNACKS  )   .801*   .643   .043   18.454@
          V999( V999 )     1.931*   .000   .043   45.184@
V4    ( V4     )                                                      .602
          F2    (SOCIAL  )  1.000    .776
          V999( V999 )     3.045*   .000   .061   50.152@
V5    ( V5     )                                                      .245
          F2    (SOCIAL  )   .680*   .495   .070    9.711@
          V999( V999 )     4.335*   .000   .055   79.174@
V6    ( V6     )                                                      .144
          F2    (SOCIAL  )   .520*   .379   .056    9.210@
          V999( V999 )     4.357*   .000   .052   83.931@
F1    (SNACKS )                                                       .000
          V999( V999 )      .014*   .000   .066    .210
F2    (SOCIAL )                                                       .000
          V999( V999 )      .092*   .000   .082   1.128
```

VARIANCES OF INDEPENDENT VARIABLES
STATISTICS SIGNIFICANT AT THE 5% LEVEL ARE MARKED WITH @.

```
                                VARIANCE   S.E.     Z
-----------------------------------------------------------
ERROR
         E1  ( V1   ) 1.355*    .102    13.219@
         E2  ( V2   ) 2.039*    .125    16.377@
         E3  ( V3   ) 1.315*    .081    16.328@
         E4  ( V4   ) 1.379*    .227     6.063@
         E5  ( V5   ) 2.972*    .170    17.455@
         E6  ( V6   ) 3.369*    .166    20.267@
DISTURBANCE
         D1  (SNACKS) 1.444*    .124    11.655@
         D2  (SOCIAL) 2.090*    .253     8.264@
```

MULTIPLE POPULATION ANALYSIS, INFORMATION IN GROUP 2

COVARIANCES AMONG INDEPENDENT VARIABLES
STATISTICS SIGNIFICANT AT THE 5% LEVEL ARE MARKED WITH @.

```
                               COVA.    S.E.    Z          CORR.
-----------------------------------------------------------------
   D1,D2   (SNACKS ,SOCIAL )   .553*    .084   6.559@        .318
```

With a χ^2 of 78.0011 with 24 degrees of freedom giving a *P*-value of 0.000, the model seems not to hold. However, such a conclusion is perhaps a little too hasty, because with a sample size of about 2 × 1000 the dependence of χ^2 on sample size becomes a problem.

Therefore I will (like Scholderer et al.) fall back on RMSEA as my main measure of model fit.

In this case RMSEA is 0.048 (0.036–0.059), and I will accept the model.

As the factor means in 1994 are fixed at zero, the 1998 means should estimate the *differences* between the 1994 and the 1998 factor means.

From the output we can see that none of the factor means are significantly different across the two measurements.

These, however, are marginal tests. In order to test the hypothesis that the two factor means *taken together* are equal, we must fix the 1994 factor means to be equal to the 1998 means, i.e. fix them both at zero.

I will not show the output from estimating this model (let us call it model B), but I can assure you that if it were the only model tested, it would be accepted based on the same measures as the model in Table 5 (model A).

You could also ask the question: 'If we accept model A as "true", is the fit of model B then significantly worse?'

You can test this with the χ^2-difference test:

	χ^2	f
Model B	79.271	26
Model A	78.011	24
Difference	1.260	2

This is not significant at any reasonable significance level, and we conclude that the two factor means *taken together* have not changed from 1994 to 1998.

What should I do if I want to compare the factor means in the UK and France?

You will remember that although the measuring instrument showed metric invariance across the UK and the French sample, it did not show scale invariance – the scale intercepts were different.

This situation is more the rule than the exception when the questionnaires used are in different languages. Intuitively it should be possible to 'regulate' the intercepts in order to place the measurements on a common scale. Scholderer, Grunert, and Brunsø (2005) show you how to do it.

In this chapter you met the following concepts:

- mean structure
- configural invariance
- metric invariance
- scale invariance
- factor covariance invariance
- factor variance invariance
- error variance invariance

You have also learned the following EQS statement:

/MEANS

Questions

1. List the various steps in testing a measuring instrument for cross-group equivalence. Comment on the rationale behind the procedure.

2. Referring to Example 7.1, compare the degree of democracy in the countries involved in 1960 and 1965.

3. Comment on the problems of cyclical models using examples from your own area of study or research.

References

Brunsø, K., & Grunert, K. G. (1995). Development and testing of a cross-cultural valid instrument: Food-related lifestyle. *Advances in Consumer Research, 22*, 475–480.

Byrne, D. O., London, O., & Reeves, K. (1968). The effects of physical attractiveness, sex and attitude similarity on interpersonal attraction. *Journal of Personality, 36*, 259–271.

Clifford, M. M., & Walster, E. (1973). The affect of physical attractiveness on teacher expectations. *Sociology of Education, 46*, 248–258.

Felson, R. B., & Bohrnstedt, G. W. (1979). Are the good beautiful or the beautiful good? *Social Psychology Quarterly, 42*, 386–392.

Gross, A. E., & Crafton, C. (1977). What is good is beautiful. *Sociometry, 40*, 85–90.

Landy, D., & Sigall, H. (1974). Beauty is talent: Task evaluation is a function of the performer's physical attractiveness. *Journal of Personality and Social Psychology, 29*, 229–304.

Owens, G., & Ford, J. G. (1978). Further considerations of the 'what is good is beautiful' finding. *Social Psychology, 41*, 73–75.

Sarty, M. (1975). *The 'pretty girl' as a sexual and reproductive stereotype*. Paper presented at the Western Psychology Association; summary from Department of Human Behavior, University of Southern California School of Medicine.

Scholderer, J., Brunsø, K., Bredahl, L., & Grunets, K. G. (2004). Cross-cultural validity of the food-related lifestyle instrument (FRL) within Western Europe. *Appetite, 42*, 197–211.

Scholderer, J., Grunert, K. G., & Brunsø, K. (2005). A procedure for eliminating additive bias from cross-cultural survey data. *Journal of Business Research, 58*(1), 72–78.

10

Incomplete and Non-normal Data

Missing data are more the rule than the exception in empirical research, and several solutions to the problem have been suggested. As will be argued in the opening paragraphs of this chapter, the most widespread ones are not wholly satisfactory.

Then you will learn about two more satisfying methods, the first of which is *full information maximum likelihood estimation* that makes it possible to estimate a model using all data at hand even if some data are missing. However, it turns out that even this technique is not without its drawbacks – the most serious being that you easily run out of degrees of freedom, because it is necessary to estimate means and intercepts.

Another possibility is to use *multiple imputation*, a technique that has grown in popularity during the last few years. Unfortunately this technique is not yet implemented in EQS, but you will learn how to do multiple imputation using SPSS.

Another common problem is the non-normality of data. No variable is strictly normal, and more often than not deviations from normality are so serious that they cannot be ignored. We take a look at the consequences of non-normality and the remedies most often used.

You will learn to use *bootstrapping*, which is an estimation procedure that makes no distributional demands at all.

Bootstrapping is some sort of Swiss army knife, capable of solving a lot of different problems in and outside of SEM, but as with all statistical methods it has its shortcomings.

Finally in the chapter you are introduced to the special procedures EQS uses to handle ordinal data.

1 Incomplete Data

It is very unlikely that you will undertake a large research project without meeting the problem mentioned in this heading. The most obvious consequence of incomplete data is that it could – depending on how you choose to handle the problem – reduce your sample. What is more serious is that it biases the estimation.

Of the many ways of coping with the missing data problem, the following seem to be the most popular:

1. *Listwise deletion* (LD for short): Delete all observations that have missing values on any variable.
2. *Pairwise deletion* (PD): Use LD for all pairs of variables.

3. *Mean imputation* (MI): Replace the missing value with the mean of the variable.
4. *Regression imputation* (RI): Estimate the value of the missing observation by regressing the variable on other variables.

It is obvious that the first method, which is the default in many computer programs (including SPSS and EQS), could easily reduce the sample size to an unacceptable level, and might also bias your estimates depending on the mechanism that produces the missing data.

If you use PD, the calculation of variances and covariances in the input matrix is based on all observations where the one or two variables involved are not missing. One problem with this procedure is that the various sample moments are based on different sample sizes. What sample size should then go into the calculation of test statistics and the like?

No doubt some rough rules of thumb could be put forward, but what is more serious is: if separate parts of the covariance matrix are based on different observations, you run the risk that the matrix will not be positive definite.

It is obvious that MI will reduce the sample variances and covariances, and as SEM is based on variances and covariances this too seems to be a bad solution to the problem.

RI also reduces estimates of variances and covariances, but to a lesser degree than MI.

None of these methods are very satisfying. Therefore in the following I will concentrate on the two methods mentioned above: *full information maximum likelihood* (FIML) and *multiple imputation* (MUI) – two methods that are much more preferable to the four listed above.

A few things are worth noting when working with incomplete data using FIML or MUI:

1. Calculations must be based on raw data – a matrix summary will not function.
2. You must estimate means and intercepts.

Full information maximum likelihood

FIML is the general name for ML based on individual observations in the raw data and not on a sample summary, whether this summary is supplied as input or calculated by the computer program as the basis for the estimation process.

In general the FIML procedure as implemented in EQS is the natural choice, because it allows ML estimation to be based on a data set with missing values and still make use of all available data without any form of imputation.

There is, however, one situation in which none of the above-mentioned methods including FIML will give consistent estimates. This is when the fact that a value is missing conveys information about its value. An example is when the probability that a respondent will not report his or her income is larger for higher incomes. In that case an empty cell in the data matrix indicates that the respondent may belong to the higher income classes. Even in this situation, however, FIML is less biased than any of the methods mentioned above.

Example 1
Analyzing incomplete data using FIML

I will use the Thomsen et al. (2004) data (from Example 8.2) to illustrate FIML estimation with incomplete data, estimating the first version of the measurement model after having deleted 20% of the measurements by simple random sampling. As usual, you can find the data ('missing 20') on the book's website.

The program, which is given in Table 1, is of course very similar to the one in Table 8.5. However, you will notice a few modifications.

In the /SPECIFICATIONS paragraph, you will meet

MATRIX=RAW

MISSING=ML

ANALYSIS=MOMENT

Until now the input to an analysis has been a covariance matrix or a correlation matrix supplemented with variances, and in the previous chapter these data were also supplemented with the variable means – in other words, our analyses were based on summary data.

You specify ML estimation with missing data (FIML) in the command MISSING=ML, and as you must estimate means and intercepts, you specify that the analysis should be based on the moment matrix (which in addition to the covariances also includes the means) and that the data are raw data. However, you do not input the sample means as in the previous chapter; EQS will estimate these based on the data.

Table 1 Example 1: program for ML estimation in case of missing values

```
/TITLE
    Example 8.2. Data from Thomsen et al. (2004) 20% missing data
/SPECIFICATIONS
    DATA='c:\users\sony\desktop\eqs bog\eqs chap 8\missing20.ess';
    VARIABLES=27; CASES=247; MISSING=ML;
    METHOD=ML; ANALYSIS=MOMENT; MATRIX=RAW;
/LABELS
    F1= rumination; F2=sadness; F3=sleep; F4=immune; F5=health care;
    V3=ecq1; V4=ecq2; V5=ecq3; V6=ecq4; V7=ecq5;
    V8=ecq6; V9=ecq7; V10=ecq8; V11=ecq9; V12=ecq10;
    V13=ecq11; V14=ecq12; V15=ecq13; V16=ecq14; V17=poms4d;
    V18=poms8d; V19=poms12d; V120=poms14d; V21=poms20d; V22=poms23d;
    V23=poms28d; V24=poms33d; V25=psqik; V26=leukocyt; V27=lymphocy;
    V28=consult; V29=telephon;

/EQUATIONS
    V3  = *V999 + 1F1 + E3;
    V4  = *V999 + *F1 + E4;
    V5  = *V999 + *F1 + E5;
    V6  = *V999 + *F1 + E6;
    V7  = *V999 + *F1 + E7;
    V8  = *V999 + *F1 + E8;
    V9  = *V999 + *F1 + E9;
    V10 = *V999 + *V999 + *F1 + E10;
    V11 = *V999 + *V999 + *V999 + *V999 + *F1 + E11;
    V12 = *V999 + *F1 + E12;
    V13 = *V999 + *F1 + E13;
```

(Continued)

Table 1 (Continued)

```
     V14 = *V999 + *F1 + E14;
     V15 = *V999 + *F1 + E15;
     V16 = *V999 + *F1 + E16;
     V17 = *V999 + 1F2 + E17;
     V18 = *V999 + *F2 + E18;
     V19 = *V999 + *F2 + E19;
     V20 = *V999 + *F2 + E20;
     V21 = *V999 + *F2 + E21;
     V22 = *V999 + *F2 + E22;
     V23 = *V999 + *F2 + E23;
     V24 = *V999 + *F2 + E24;
     V25 = *V999 + 1F3 + E25;
     V26 = *V999 + 1F4 + E26;
     V27 = *V999 + *F4 + E27;
     V29 = *V999 + 1F5 + E29;
/VARIANCES
     F1 TO F5 = *;
     E3 TO E24= *;
     E25 =  0.00;
     E26 TO E27 = *;
     E29 = 0;
/COVARIANCES
     F1 TO F5= *;
     E9 TO E12 = *;
/PRINT
     FIT=ALL;
     TABLE=COMPACT;
/LMTEST
     PROCESS=SIMULTANEOUS;
     SET=PEE;
/END
```

For obvious reasons only a very small part of the 36(!) pages of output is shown and discussed.

First in the output is a 'mapping' of the missing value patterns as given in Table 2. You will observe that only two observations do not have missing data, which is rather unrealistic. For data such as those used in this example, usually the number of missing values is concentrated in fewer observations – typically less than 20–25% of the total sample (my fault: remember, I and not the respondents chose the missing data mechanism). Consequently there are no less than 245 missing data patterns, the first of which has missing data for variables 2–6, 10–11, 14, 17 and 21–23. Next comes the following output, that is not shown in Table 2:

1. A sample covariance matrix based on pairwise deletion and a matrix showing the sample sizes for each pair of variables.
2. A description of the various variables like the one given in Table 4.4.
3. Estimates of the means and covariance matrix for the saturated model. This matrix is necessary for calculating residuals and the χ^2 statistic.
4. The estimated residual covariance/mean matrix.
5. The standardized residual matrix with listing of its largest entries.

Table 2 Example 1: output from analysis of incomplete data file (extract)

```
MAXIMUM LIKELIHOOD SOLUTION (NORMAL DISTRIBUTION THEORY)

   NUMBER OF CASES USED                  =  247
   NUMBER OF CASES WITH POSITIVE WEIGHT  =  247
   NUMBER OF CASES WITH MISSING DATA     =  247
   NUMBER OF MISSING PATTERNS IN THE DATA =  245

   IN THE SUMMARY OF MISSING PATTERNS, M REPRESENTS A MISSING VALUE

                                  VARIABLES
  PAT-     #       #      %               1                  2
  TERN  MISSING  CASES  CASES    1234567890123456789 0123456
  ----  -------  -----  -----
   1      11      1     0.40     M M M    MM M   M     MMMM
   2       8      1     0.40     M M M    M  M       M   M M
   3       8      1     0.40      M M     M  M       MM    MM
   4       4      1     0.40     M           M       MM
   5       5      1     0.40     M         M M       M  M
   6       5      1     0.40     M     M  MM         M
   7       2      2     0.81     M  M
   8       1      1     0.40     M
   9       2      1     0.40     M          M
  10       1      1     0.40                M
   -       -      -      -
   -       -      -      -
   -       -      -      -
  243      8      1     0.40     MM M    M          M MMM
  244     10      1     0.40     M MM MM M     M     MM M
  245      7      1     0.40     M     M M        MM  M M


   GOODNESS OF FIT SUMMARY FOR METHOD = ML

   INDEPENDENCE MODEL CHI-SQUARE          =    1871.991 ON   327 DEGREES OF FREEDOM

   INDEPENDENCE AIC =   1217.991    INDEPENDENCE CAIC =    -256.579
          MODEL AIC =     45.184           MODEL CAIC =   -1239.992

   -2LN(L) BASED ON THE UNSTRUCTURED MODEL =    10841.178
   -2LN(L) BASED ON THE   STRUCTURED MODEL =    11456.363

   LIKELIHOOD RATIO CHI-SQUARE =        615.184 BASED ON    285 DEGREES OF FREEDOM
   PROBABILITY VALUE FOR THE CHI-SQUARE STATISTIC IS         0.00000

   NEYMAN AND ANDERSON-DARLING TESTS ARE NOT COMPUTED
   BECAUSE ONLY 0 PATTERN HAS MORE THAN 4 CASES.

   GLS TEST OF HOMOGENEITY OF MEANS

   CHI-SQUARE =      5083.823 BASED ON   5065 DEGREES OF FREEDOM
   PROBABILITY VALUE FOR THE CHI-SQUARE STATISTIC IS         0.42332

   GLS TEST OF HOMOGENEITY OF COVARIANCE MATRICES

   CHI-SQUARE =       773.448 BASED ON    249 DEGREES OF FREEDOM
   PROBABILITY VALUE FOR THE CHI-SQUARE STATISTIC IS         0.00000
      NUMBER OF CASES USED FOR THE ABOVE STATISTIC IS             4
```

(Continued)

Table 2 (Continued)

```
GLS COMBINED TEST OF HOMOGENEITY OF MEANS/COVARIANCES

CHI-SQUARE =       5857.271 BASED ON     5314 DEGREES OF FREEDOM
PROBABILITY VALUE FOR THE CHI-SQUARE STATISTIC IS       0.00000

FIT INDICES (BASED ON COVARIANCE MATRIX ONLY, NOT THE MEANS)
-----------
BENTLER-BONETT      NORMED FIT INDEX  =   0.462
BENTLER-BONETT NON-NORMED FIT INDEX   =   0.463
COMPARATIVE FIT INDEX (CFI)           =   0.532
BOLLEN'S            (IFI) FIT INDEX   =   0.545
MCDONALD'S          (MFI) FIT INDEX   =   0.232
JORESKOG-SORBOM'S  GFI  FIT INDEX     =   0.761
JORESKOG-SORBOM'S AGFI  FIT INDEX     =   0.705
ROOT MEAN-SQUARE RESIDUAL (RMR)       =   0.091
STANDARDIZED RMR                      =   0.086
ROOT MEAN-SQUARE ERROR OF APPROXIMATION (RMSEA)    =   0.102
90% CONFIDENCE INTERVAL OF RMSEA (        0.095,       0.108)

FIT INDICES (BASED ON COVARIANCE MATRIX AND MEANS)
-----------
MCDONALD'S          (MFI) FIT INDEX   =   0.513
ROOT MEAN-SQUARE ERROR OF APPROXIMATION (RMSEA)    =   0.069
90% CONFIDENCE INTERVAL OF RMSEA (        0.061,       0.076)
```

The likelihood ratio chi-square value is calculated as the difference: 11456.363 − 10841.178. The test is not significant, but as is now our habit we rely more on fit measures because chi-square most often says more about the sample size than about the model being tested (refer to the section on statistical testing in Appendix A).

For the same reason the usefulness of the following three tests is limited.

They test if it is safe to assume that the various data patterns come from the same (homogeneous) population.

RMSEA is 0.069 (0.061, 0.076) – compare with 0.080 (0.073, 0.087) in the analysis based on the full data set. Most of the other fit measures are not very impressive, but remember that they do not take means and intercepts into consideration. Parameter estimates are given in Table 3 for comparison with Table 8.6.

Table 3 Example 1: Output from analysis of incomplete data file (extract)

```
MAXIMUM LIKELIHOOD SOLUTION (NORMAL DISTRIBUTION THEORY)

    PARAMETER ESTIMATES (B) WITH STANDARD ERRORS AND TEST STATISTICS (Z)
    STATISTICS SIGNIFICANT AT THE 5% LEVEL ARE MARKED WITH @.

                                                              R-
    DEP.VAR.        PREDICTOR    B       BETA    S.E.    Z    SQUARED
    -----------------------------------------------------------------
    V3  (   ECQ1  )                                           .528
            V999(    V999 )  1.542*   .000   .124   12.473@
            F1   (RUMINATI)  1.000    .727
    V4  (   ECQ2  )                                           .044
            V999(    V999 )  1.897*   .000   .148   12.831@
            F1   (RUMINATI)   .319*   .211   .119    2.675@
    V5  (   ECQ3  )                                           .559
            V999(    V999 )   .922*   .000   .086   10.673@
            F1   (RUMINATI)   .876*   .747   .084   10.473@
```

```
V6   ( ECQ4  )                                              .555
          V999( V999 )   .904*  .000  .088  10.216@
          F1   (RUMINATI)  .901*  .745  .089  10.145@
V7   ( ECQ5  )                                              .093
          V999( V999 ) 1.822*  .000  .138  13.170@
          F1   (RUMINATI)  .416*  .304  .105   3.948@
V8   ( ECQ6  )                                              .097
          V999( V999 ) 1.447*  .000  .121  11.998@
          F1   (RUMINATI)  .417*  .311  .106   3.921@
V9   ( ECQ7  )                                              .235
          V999( V999 )   .287*  .000  .046   6.203@
          F1   (RUMINATI)  .373*  .484  .058   6.456@
V10  ( ECQ8  )                                              .279
          V999( V999 )   .663*  .000  .073   9.039@
          F1   (RUMINATI)  .570*  .528  .081   7.056@
V11  ( ECQ9  )                                              .493
          V999( V999 ) 1.242*  .000  .105  11.862@
          F1   (RUMINATI)  .894*  .702  .092   9.698@
V12  (ECQ10  )                                              .102
          V999( V999 )   .146*  .000  .030   4.911@
          F1   (RUMINATI)  .164*  .319  .038   4.270@
V13  (ECQ11  )                                              .305
          V999( V999 ) 1.006*  .000  .091  11.011@
          F1   (RUMINATI)  .644*  .552  .087   7.420@
V14  (ECQ12  )                                              .010
          V999( V999 ) 2.002*  .000  .150  13.303@
          F1   (RUMINATI)  .142*  .102  .115   1.242
V15  (ECQ13  )                                              .056
          V999( V999 ) 1.637*  .000  .134  12.194@
          F1   (RUMINATI)  .351*  .236  .117   3.001@
V16  (ECQ14  )                                              .001
          V999( V999 ) 2.442*  .000  .174  14.065@
          F1   (RUMINATI)  .048*  .037  .116    .414
V17  (POMS4D )                                              .703
          V999( V999 )   .447*  .000  .058   7.768@
          F2   (SADNESS ) 1.000  .839
V18  (POMS8D )                                              .645
          V999( V999 )   .474*  .000  .056   8.417@
          F2   (SADNESS )  .899*  .803  .068  13.207@
V19  (POMS12D )                                             .512
          V999( V999 )   .345*  .000  .047   7.274@
          F2   (SADNESS )  .686*  .716  .063  10.967@
V20  (POMS14D )                                             .292
          V999( V999 )   .270*  .000  .051   5.322@
          F2   (SADNESS )  .589*  .540  .075   7.874@
V21  (POMS20D )                                             .593
          V999( V999 )   .314*  .000  .046   6.803@
          F2   (SADNESS )  .759*  .770  .060  12.624@
V22  (POMS23D )                                             .377
          V999( V999 )   .237*  .000  .040   5.873@
          F2   (SADNESS )  .536*  .614  .057   9.348@
V23  (POMS28D )                                             .324
          V999( V999 )   .165*  .000  .036   4.579@
          F2   (SADNESS )  .440*  .569  .054   8.175@
V24  (POMS33D )                                             .366
          V999( V999 )   .273*  .000  .046   5.885@
          F2   (SADNESS )  .598*  .605  .066   9.030@
```

(Continued)

Table 3 (Continued)

```
V25 (PSQIK    )                                                    1.000
         V999(    V999 )   .755*    .000   .071   10.701@
         F3   (SLEEP  ) 1.000     1.000
V26 (LEUKOCYT)                                                      .491
         V999(    V999 )  6.648*   .000   .442   15.030@
         F4   (IMMUNE ) 1.000      .701
V27 (LYMPHOCY)                                                      .438
         V999(    V999 )  1.773*   .000   .121   14.651@
         F4   (IMMUNE )   .335*    .662   .082    4.063@
V29 (TELEPHON)                                                     1.000
         V999(    V999 )   .922*   .000   .097    9.462@
         F5   (HEALTHCA) 1.000    1.000

COVARIANCES AMONG INDEPENDENT VARIABLES
STATISTICS SIGNIFICANT AT THE 5% LEVEL ARE MARKED WITH @.

                                   COVA.    S.E.      Z       CORR.
-----------------------------------------------------------------------
  F1,F2    (RUMINATI,SADNESS  )    .199*    .040    4.943@    .396
  F1,F3    (RUMINATI,SLEEP    )    .155*    .042    3.660@    .263
  F1,F4    (RUMINATI,IMMUNE   )    .247*    .091    2.718@    .249
  F1,F5    (RUMINATI,HEALTHCA )    .193*    .063    3.070@    .217
  F2,F3    (SADNESS ,SLEEP    )    .199*    .034    5.810@    .430
  F2,F4    (SADNESS ,IMMUNE   )   -.071*    .066   -1.075    -.091
  F2,F5    (SADNESS ,HEALTHCA )    .155*    .048    3.202@    .221
  F3,F4    (SLEEP   ,IMMUNE   )    .221*    .077    2.854@    .241
  F3,F5    (SLEEP   ,HEALTHCA )    .180*    .054    3.365@    .220
  F4,F5    (IMMUNE  ,HEALTHCA )    .026*    .110     .231     .019
  E9,E10   (   ECQ7 ,    ECQ8 )    .021*    .031     .685     .054
  E9,E11   (   ECQ7 ,    ECQ9 )   -.122*    .032   -3.792@   -.312
  E9,E12   (   ECQ7 ,ECQ10    )    .098*    .017    5.808@    .467
  E10,E11  (   ECQ8 ,    ECQ9 )    .138*    .048    2.905@    .261
  E10,E12  (   ECQ8 ,ECQ10    )    .039*    .022    1.771     .137
  E11,E12  (   ECQ9 ,ECQ10    )   -.017*    .022    -.779    -.062
```

Multiple imputation

You may have wondered why I chose the factor model and not the structural model from Figure 8.7 to demonstrate FIML estimation with missing data. The reason is simple: it is not possible to estimate the structural model if you have missing data, because the need for estimating means and intercepts eats up your degrees of freedom. This is not apparent from a calculation of variances, covariances, means and the number of parameters to be estimated. The crucial point is that the covariance structure and the means structure must be identified *separately*. In this case the covariance structure is over-identified while the means structure is under-identified – and the extra degrees of freedom in the covariance structure cannot save the identification of the means structure. This is a real limitation of this method if you have only a single sample.

As mentioned earlier, the alternatives offered by EQS (LD, PD and MI) are not very satisfying, so if you need to estimate the structural model and have missing values, EQS is of little help, and you have to turn to SPSS (or a similar program).

Fortunately SPSS has several options at your disposal. The 'Missing Values' module in SPSS is a rather large one that has its own manual of nearly 100 pages (SPSS, 2013) so I will barely scratch the surface.

The module is roughly divided into two sections that deal with:

1. A description and analysis of missing data patterns.
2. Imputation.

Although no imputation should be performed without a prior analysis of the patterns in the missing values, I will (for space reasons) leave it to you to explore the tools and go directly to imputation.

Remember that the problem with mean imputation and regression imputation is that they underestimate the variation in the data, because: (1) the spread in the data is reduced; and (2) the 'noise' in the regression estimation is not taken care of.

The solution to this problem is to use several regression imputations for estimating each of the missing values – the various imputations only differentiate themselves by the addition of a small amount of 'random noise'. In that way you end up with several imputed data sets.

Each of these is now analyzed as if they are a 'normal' complete data set, and – as a last step – the various model estimates are combined taking the above-mentioned 'regression noise' into consideration.

This is the principle in *multiple imputation*. It is by far the best imputation method and it is a good alternative to FIML.

So, MUI goes through the following three steps:

1. Create several complete data sets using RI.
2. Perform the desired analysis on each of the data sets.
3. Combine the various analyses into one.

All MUI methods build on predicting the missing values conditional on the non-missing variables – as does the simpler RI mentioned at the beginning of this chapter.

It is obvious that you must be very careful in choosing your regressors. As the purpose is to maintain the interrelations in the data, you choose regressor variables that correlate with the variables having missing values and regressors that covary with the reasons for the missing values. This means that you could run into difficulties if you use regressor variables that are not included in the model that is the basis of your later statistical analysis.

For comparison, I will demonstrate MUI using the same model and data as in Example 1.

Example 2
Analyzing incomplete data using MUI

Once again, open the .ess data set 'Missing 20' from the book's website, save it as an SPSS data file, and from the top menu choose 'Transform/Random Number Generators'. When the window in Figure 1 appears, be sure to check

'Set Active Generator'

'Set Starting Point'

'Fixed Value'

and set a starting point for generating 'random noise' in the imputation, so that you (if necessary) can replicate the analysis.

Next, choose 'Analyze/Multiple Imputation/Impute Missing Data Values' and the window in Figure 2 will appear. As is now routine, move the variables – all of them except 'id' and 'køn' (for the curious, this means 'sex' in Danish) – to the right panel. As you can see, the default number of imputations is 5, but change it to 10. Save the imputed data as 'Imputed.sav'. SPSS saves imputed data to one file and therefore puts in a variable 'Imputation'. The original data are saved in the same file as 'Imputation 0'.

As you can guess, clicking the various tabs in the window in Figure 2 gives you a rich palette of choices so that you can make a tailor-made imputation, based on a serious analysis of the pattern of missing values.

If you click the 'Method' tab in the window shown in Figure 2, the window in Figure 3 appears. To keep things simple I chose 'Automatic'.

As mentioned above, the imputed data sets are saved in a single file (see Figure 4). The reason is that most of the statistical procedures in SPSS can be carried out directly on this data file, because SPSS automatically splits the file using the variable 'Imputation' as the split variable.

However, EQS is not that clever, so you must split the file and then do the analysis as a multi-group analysis.

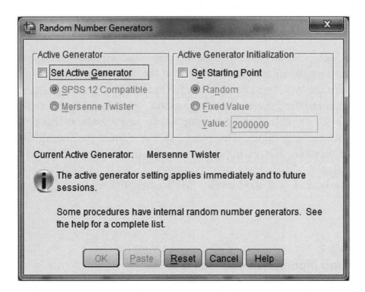

Figure 1 Example 2: choosing a starting point for random generation of 'noise'

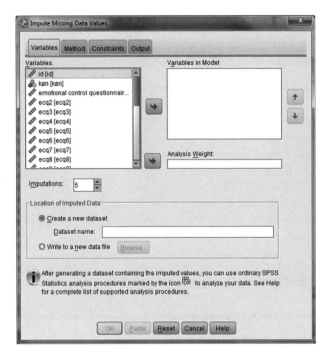

Figure 2 Example 2: choosing variables for multiple imputation

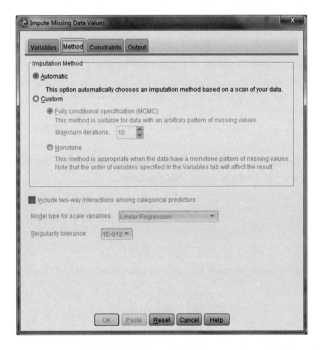

Figure 3 Example 2: choosing imputation method

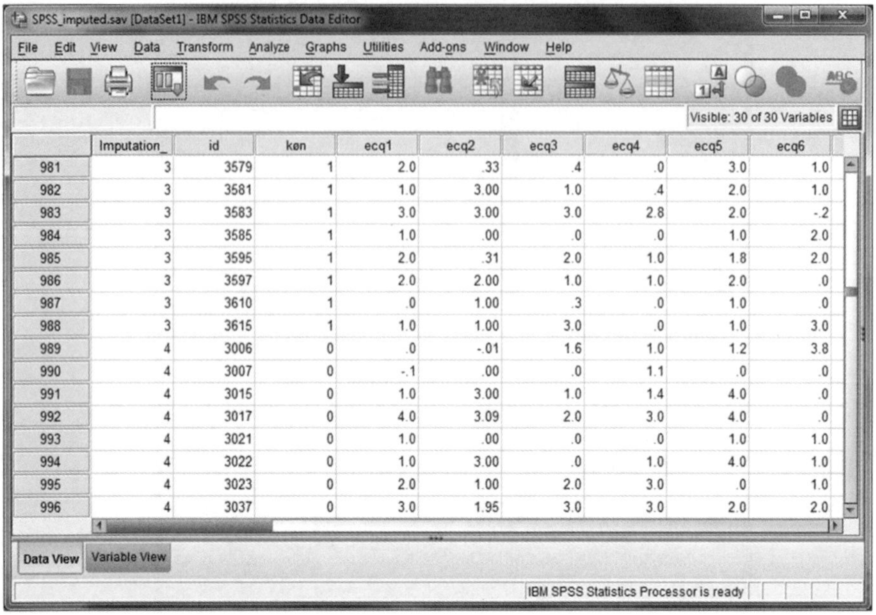

	Imputation_	id	køn	ecq1	ecq2	ecq3	ecq4	ecq5	ecq6
981	3	3579	1	2.0	.33	.4	.0	3.0	1.0
982	3	3581	1	1.0	3.00	1.0	.4	2.0	1.0
983	3	3583	1	3.0	3.00	3.0	2.8	2.0	-.2
984	3	3585	1	1.0	.00	.0	.0	1.0	2.0
985	3	3595	1	2.0	.31	2.0	1.0	1.8	2.0
986	3	3597	1	2.0	2.00	1.0	1.0	2.0	.0
987	3	3610	1	.0	1.00	.3	.0	1.0	.0
988	3	3615	1	1.0	1.00	3.0	.0	1.0	3.0
989	4	3006	0	.0	-.01	1.6	1.0	1.2	3.8
990	4	3007	0	-.1	.00	.0	1.1	.0	.0
991	4	3015	0	1.0	3.00	1.0	1.4	4.0	.0
992	4	3017	0	4.0	3.09	2.0	3.0	4.0	.0
993	4	3021	0	1.0	.00	.0	.0	1.0	1.0
994	4	3022	0	1.0	3.00	.0	1.0	4.0	1.0
995	4	3023	0	2.0	1.00	2.0	3.0	.0	1.0
996	4	3037	0	3.0	1.95	3.0	3.0	2.0	2.0

Figure 4 Example 2: saved imputed data sets

What now remains is to combine the 10 estimated models to form the final output. This must be done by hand.

If we let

$$m = \text{number of imputed data sets}$$

$$\hat{Q}^{(t)} = \text{parameter estimate based on sample } t$$

$$\sqrt{\hat{U}^{(t)}} = \text{estimated standard error based on sample } t$$

then the MUI estimate of a model parameter (e.g. a regression coefficients) is simply the mean of the m (= 10) estimates of that parameter:

$$\overline{Q} = m^{-1}\sum_{i=1}^{m}\hat{Q}^{(t)} \tag{1}$$

To obtain the standard errors is a bit more complicated.

The average within-imputation variance is computed using (1) above:

$$\overline{U} = m^{-1}\sum_{i=1}^{m}\hat{U}^{(t)} \tag{2}$$

You must, however, also compute the between-imputation variance:

$$B = (m-1)^{-1}\sum_{i=1}^{m}(Q^{(t)} - \overline{Q})^2 \tag{3}$$

Now, you combine (2) and (3) to obtain the total variance:

$$T = \overline{U} + (1 + m^{-1})B \tag{4}$$

and of course the standard error is then

$$SE = \sqrt{T} \tag{5}$$

and the Z-value is

$$Z = \frac{\overline{Q}}{\sqrt{T}} \tag{6}$$

This means lots of calculations by hand, but they can be easily done in a spreadsheet. The FIML and MUI estimates are given in Table 4 together with estimates based on the full data set. Estimates that are not statistically significant are in boldface ($\alpha = 0.05$, one-sided).

Table 4 Example 2: model estimates based on full data set, FIML and MUI

			Non-Missing	FIML	MUI
ECQ1	<---	RUMINATION	1.000	1.000	1.000
ECQ2	<---	RUMINATION	.334	.319	.342
ECQ3	<---	RUMINATION	.820	.876	.854
ECQ4	<---	RUMINATION	.804	..901	.879
ECQ5	<---	RUMINATION	.405	.416	.407
ECQ6	<---	RUMINATION	.501	.417	.399
ECQ7	<---	RUMINATION	.364	.373	.364
ECQ8	<---	RUMINATION	.528	.570	.582
ECQ9	<---	RUMINATION	.874	.891	.905
ECQ10	<---	RUMINATION	.193	.164	.155
ECQ11	<---	RUMINATION	.609	.644	.643
ECQ12	<---	RUMINATION	**.130**	**.142**	**.159**
ECQ13	<---	RUMINATION	.368	.351	.374
ECQ14	<---	RUMINATION	**-.020**	.048	.076
POMS4D	<---	SADNESS	1.000	1.000	.000
POMS8D	<---	SADNESS	.933	.899	.907
POMS12D	<---	SADNESS	.859	.686	.705
POMS14D	<---	SADNESS	.655	.589	.632
POMS20D	<---	Sadness	.942	.759	.764
POMS23D	<---	SADNESS	.597	.536	.505

(Continued)

Table 4 (Continued)

			Non-Missing	FIML	MUI
POMS28D	<---	SADNESS	.530	.440	.446
POMS33	<---	SADNESS	.596	.598	.627
PSIQ1	<---	SLEEP	1.000	1.000	1.000
LEUKOCYT	<---	IMMUNE	1.000	1.000	1.000
LYMPHOCY	<---	IMMUNE	.334	.335	.316
TELEPHONE	<---	HEALTHCA	1.000	1.000	1,000

			Non-missing	FIML	MUI
RUMINATION	<-->	SADNESS	.213	.199	0,205
RUMINATION	<-->	SLEEP	.158	.155	0,155
RUMINATION	<-->	IMMUNE	.283	.247	0,245
RUMINATION	<-->	HEALTHCA	.209	**.193**	0,190
SADNESS	<-->	SLEEP	.189	**.199**	0,202
SADNESS	<-->	IMMUNE	-.007	**.-071**	**-0,087**
SADNESS	<-->	HEALTHCA	.159	.155	0,157
SLEEP	<-->	IMMUNE	.164	.221	0,237
SLEEP	<-->	HEALTHCA	.170	.180	0,172
IMMUNE	<-->	HEALTHCA	**.082**	**.026**	**0,126**
ECQ7	<-->	ECQ8	.029	.021	0,026
ECQ7	<-->	ECQ9	-.122	-.122	-0,121
ECQ7	<-->	ECQ10	.094	.098	0,104
ECQ8	<-->	ECQ9	.124	.138	0,130
ECQ8	<-->	ECQ10	.046	.039	0,045
ECQ9	<-->	ECQ10	-.014	.017	-0,013

Missing data patterns

In this case the missing values were chosen by simple random sampling from all the measurements: the data were *missing completely at random* or *MCAR* (Rubin, 1976). This means that the probability that a value is missing is independent of one and every variable missing or not missing. Under this condition all the methods for dealing with missing data mentioned so far give consistent estimates, although of course only FIML and MUI are efficient in the statistical sense, because they use all available information in the data.

In all probability such a simple 'selection model' is very rare in practice. It is more realistic to assume that the probability that a measurement is missing is independent of its value *conditional* on the values of the non-missing variables. Even in this situation – called *missing at random* or *MAR* by Rubin – FIML estimation as implemented in EQS will give efficient and consistent estimates, while other methods will be inefficient and (in most cases) also lack consistency.

As mentioned earlier, FIML estimation will not be consistent if the MAR condition is not met, but FIML will still be less biased than other solutions to the missing data problem. This situation is called *non-ignorable* by Rubin.

2 Bootstrapping as an Aid to Deal with Non-normal Data

ML estimation is based on an assumption of multivariate normality of the manifest variables, and so are the large-sample properties of generalized least squares. If the data fail to meet this assumption, it could have serious consequences:

1. The program could run into convergence problems.
2. The asymptotic χ^2-values become excessively large.
3. The standard errors of parameter estimates are underestimated.

Even if you do not run into convergence problems, the last two problems could easily lead you astray in the interpretation of the output.

Now, there are several ways to cope with non-normality:

1. You can transform variables to (near-)normality.
2. If your distributions are non-normal but symmetric, perhaps one of the elliptical or heterogeneous kurtosis estimation methods (mentioned in Section 4.5) could be a solution.
3. You can use an estimation method that makes no distributional assumptions, such as LS or AGLS. However, as mentioned in Section 4.5, testing in LS is somewhat complicated when the variables are not multivariate normal, and AGLS makes large demands on the sample size.
4. Since the consequences generally lie more with test statistics than with parameter values, you can use GLS or ML, and then regulate the test statistics using so-called *robust statistics* (see e.g. Chou, Bentler, & Satorra, 1991). In many cases this may be the best way to solve the problem.
5. You can use bootstrapping – the topic of this section.

What then is bootstrapping?

Most statistical inference is based on the concept of a *sampling distribution* of a sample statistic, i.e. the distribution of a sample statistic taken across repeated samples of the same size from the same population. Now, we usually take only one sample, and consequently we do not have an actual empirical sampling distribution on which to base our inference. Instead we have to *derive* the sampling distribution from assumptions about the population from which the only sample was taken, e.g. an assumption of multivariate normality.

The idea behind bootstrapping is that you consider your sample to be your population. From this 'population' you take, say, 500 samples *with replacement*. From each sample you then calculate the required sample statistic. This gives you an empirical sampling distribution and an empirical standard error, and averaging the various sample statistics gives you an estimate of the parameter.

This in short is the principle of bootstrapping. It can be used to obtain empirical standard errors of whatever statistic you may want, including various fit indices, squared correlation coefficients, etc.

It is tempting also to use bootstrapping as a remedy for samples that are too small to give meaningful test results based on the asymptotic properties of ML or GLS. However, as the whole process is based on considering the original sample to represent the population from which it was taken, the sample should be large enough to guarantee stable estimates – and of course the sample selection should also be based on simple random sampling.

As you will probably have guessed, bootstrapping demands that the original data file is used as input – a covariance and mean summary of the data are not enough.

Example 3
Bootstrapping severely non-normal data

Once again we will return to the FRL scale (see Example 9.2). The quality domain of the FRL scale refers to health, price/quality relation, novelty seeking, preference for organic food, taste and freshness, and thus is a six-factor domain, each factor being measured by three items.

As you may expect everyone to prefer quality for money and good-tasting food, it is no surprise that the distribution of answers to the items measuring these two factors is concentrated at the upper end of the scales. As the skewness goes to the same side for all scales, skewness in itself is not necessarily a problem, but kurtosis could be due to the concentration of answers. The items used to measure these two dimensions are given in Table 5. As usual, you can find the data (france94quality.ess) on the book's website.

Table 5 Example 3: items used in the analysis

Price/quality relation	V64: I always try to get the best quality for the best price.
	V13: I compare prices between product variants in order to get the best value for money.
	V7: It is important for me to know that I get quality for all my money.
Taste	V5: I find taste in food products important.
	V21: When cooking, I first and foremost consider the taste
	V50: It is important to choose food products for their nutritional value rather than for their taste.

A quick look at the input data should be enough to convince you that the distributions are just as non-normal as you would have expected. If you estimate the model using ordinary ML, your output will include the statistics in Table 6, from which you can see that the multivariate kurtosis is indeed extremely high, and could very well motivate a bootstrapping.

Table 6 Example 3: partial output from an 'ordinary' ML analysis

```
CHI-SQUARE =            85.088 BASED ON        8 DEGREES OF FREEDOM
   PROBABILITY VALUE FOR THE CHI-SQUARE STATISTIC IS        0.00000



   MAXIMUM LIKELIHOOD SOLUTION (NORMAL DISTRIBUTION THEORY)

   PARAMETER ESTIMATES (B) WITH STANDARD ERRORS AND TEST STATISTICS (Z)
   STATISTICS SIGNIFICANT AT THE 5% LEVEL ARE MARKED WITH @.


                                                                   R-
   DEP.VAR.        PREDICTOR     B       BETA    S.E.     Z     SQUARED
   ------------------------------------------------------------------
   V1   (  64    )                                                .531
               F1   (QUALITY ) 1.000     .729
   V2   (  13   )                                                 .261
               F1   (QUALITY )  .939*    .511    .132    7.129@
   V3   (   7   )                                                 .091
               F1   (QUALITY )  .322*    .302    .053    6.046@
   V4   (   5   )                                                 .374
               F2   (TASTE   ) 1.000     .611
   V5   (  21   )                                                 .570
               F2   (TASTE   ) 1.481*    .755    .168    8.790@
   V6   (  V50  )                                                 .105
               F2   (TASTE   )  .853*    .324    .111    7.706@

   VARIANCES OF INDEPENDENT VARIABLES
   STATISTICS SIGNIFICANT AT THE 5% LEVEL ARE MARKED WITH @.


                             VARIANCE   S.E.      Z
   ---------------------------------------------------
   FACTOR
            F1   (QUALITY  )1.190*      .183    6.520@
            F2   (TASTE    ) .432*      .062    6.963@
   ERROR
            E1   (   64   )1.051*       .166    6.321@
            E2   (   13   )2.973*       .196   15.147@
            E3   (    7   )1.230*       .059   20.781@
            E4   (    5   ) .723*       .057   12.652@
            E5   (   21   ) .714*       .107    6.668@
            E6   (  V50   )2.682*       .128   20.960@

   COVARIANCES AMONG INDEPENDENT VARIABLES
   STATISTICS SIGNIFICANT AT THE 5% LEVEL ARE MARKED WITH @.



                                  COVA.   S.E.      Z      CORR.
   -----------------------------------------------------------------
     F1,F2    (QUALITY ,TASTE   )  .290*   .044   6.557@    .405
```

(Continued)

Table 6 (Continued)

SAMPLE STATISTICS BASED ON COMPLETE CASES

UNIVARIATE STATISTICS

```
VARIABLE                64          13          7           5          21
                        V1          V2          V3          V4         V5
  MEAN               5.7857      4.7425      6.1922      6.3712      5.9326
  SKEWNESS  (G1)    -1.3577     -0.5205     -1.8249     -2.1439     -1.4034
  KURTOSIS  (G2)     1.3526     -0.9432      3.7054      5.2541      1.9778
  STANDARD  DEV.     1.4970      2.0055      1.1635      1.0743      1.2885

VARIABLE                50
                        V6
  MEAN               4.7354
  SKEWNESS  (G1)    -0.4384
  KURTOSIS  (G2)    -0.5113
  STANDARD  DEV.     1.7310
```

MULTIVARIATE KURTOSIS

```
    MARDIA'S COEFFICIENT (G2,P) =     23.7688
    NORMALIZED ESTIMATE =             38.2416
```

A program for bootstrapping is given in Table 7 and part of the output in Table 8.

Table 7 Example 3: Program for 'naïve' bootstrapping

```
/TITLE
Naive bootstrapping
/SPECIFICATIONS
DATA='C:\Users\Sony\Desktop\EQS bog\EQS Chap 10\france94quality.ESS';
VARIABLES=6; CASES=994;
METHOD=ML; ANALYSIS=COVARIANCE; MATRIX=RAW;
/LABELS
F1= Quality; F2=Taste; V1=64; V2=13; V3=7; V4=5; V5=21;
V6=V50;
/EQUATIONS
V1 =   1F1 + E1;
V2 =   *F1 + E2;
V3 =   *F1 + E3;
V4 =   1F2 + E4;
V5 =   *F2 + E5;
V6 =   *F2 + E6;
/VARIANCES
  F1 = *;
  F2 = *;
  E1 = *;
  E2 = *;
  E3 = *;
  E4 = *;
  E5 = *;
  E6 = *;
/COVARIANCES
F1,F2 = *;
```

```
/PRINT
FIT=ALL;
TABLE=COMPACT;
/OUTPUT
PARAMETERS; STANDARD ERRORS;    !bootstrap model parameters and standard errors
DATA='EQSOUT.ETS';              !save information on each replication to the file
/SIMULATION
BOOTSTRAP=994;                  !size of bootstrap sample
REPLICATIONS=1000;              !number of replications
SEED=123456789.0;               !start of random generation
/END
```

Traditionally I have set the bootstrap sample to the same size as the original sample, although there is evidence that the bootstrapping process functions better if the bootstrap samples are smaller than the original one.

As you will have guessed, bootstrapping generates a lot of output, so only a small extract is given in Table 8.

Table 8 Example 3: partial output from bootstrapping

```
NUMBERED STATISTICS ARE
    1. TAIL PROBABILITY FOR MODEL CHI-SQUARE
    2. INDEPENDENCE MODEL CHI-SQUARE
    3. MODEL CHI-SQUARE
    4. JORESKOG-SORBOM'S  GFI  FIT INDEX
    5. JORESKOG-SORBOM'S AGFI  FIT INDEX
    6. BOLLEN'S           (IFI) FIT INDEX
    7. MCDONALD'S         (MFI) FIT INDEX
    8. BENTLER-BONETT     NORMED FIT INDEX
    9. BENTLER-BONETT NON-NORMED FIT INDEX
   10. COMPARATIVE FIT INDEX (CFI)
   11. ROOT MEAN-SQUARE RESIDUAL (RMR)
   12. STANDARDIZED RMR
   13. ROOT MEAN-SQUARE ERROR OF APPROXIMATION (RMSEA)
   14. CONFIDENCE INTERVAL FOR RMSEA (LOWER BOUND)
   15. CONFIDENCE INTERVAL FOR RMSEA (UPPER BOUND)
   16. CRONBACH'S ALPHA
   17. RELIABILITY COEFFICIENT RHO
   18. MINIMIZED MODEL FUNCTION VALUE
   19. INDEPENDENCE AIC
   20. INDEPENDENCE CAIC
   21. MODEL AIC
   22. MODEL CAIC

SUMMARY STATISTICS FOR ALL REPLICATIONS
----------------------------------------
```

STATISTIC	1	2	3	4	5
N	1000	1000	1000	1000	1000
COUNT > .05	0				
MEAN	0.0000	690.4059	94.3049	0.9702	0.9219
STANDARD DEV.	0.0000	74.3428	25.5664	0.0077	0.0203
SKEWNESS (G1)	21.4477	0.2776	0.5302	−0.4715	−0.4715
KURTOSIS (G2)	495.2252	0.0266	0.2642	0.1498	0.1498
LOWER 5%	0.0000	572.8400	56.9050	0.9563	0.8852
UPPER 5%	0.0000	813.0900	141.0300	0.9816	0.9516

STATISTIC	6	7	8	9	10
N	1000	1000	1000	1000	1000
MEAN	0.8734	0.9576	0.8632	0.7601	0.8721

(Continued)

Table 8 (Continued)

STANDARD DEV.	0.0350	0.0123	0.0347	0.0664	0.0354
SKEWNESS (G1)	-0.3808	-0.4923	-0.3776	-0.3813	-0.3813
KURTOSIS (G2)	0.1237	0.1931	0.1358	0.1270	0.1270
LOWER 5%	0.8149	0.9353	0.8053	0.6493	0.8130
UPPER 5%	0.9249	0.9757	0.9137	0.8577	0.9241
STATISTIC	11	12	13	14	15
N	1000	1000	1000	1000	1000
MEAN	0.1157	0.0631	0.1031	0.0845	0.1221
STANDARD DEV.	0.0202	0.0089	0.0154	0.0154	0.0152
SKEWNESS (G1)	0.9336	0.1339	0.1152	0.1117	0.1364
KURTOSIS (G2)	2.8884	-0.1217	-0.1189	-0.1217	-0.1372
LOWER 5%	0.0860	0.0486	0.0785	0.0598	0.0978
UPPER 5%	0.1506	0.0779	0.1294	0.1109	0.1482
STATISTIC	16	17	18	19	20
N	1000	1000	1000	1000	1000
MEAN	0.5396	0.6199	0.0950	660.4059	571.8803
STANDARD DEV.	0.0275	0.0231	0.0257	74.3427	74.3427
SKEWNESS (G1)	-0.1597	-0.2625	0.5302	0.2776	0.2776
KURTOSIS (G2)	-0.0111	0.4587	0.2642	0.0265	0.0266
LOWER 5%	0.4946	0.5824	0.0573	542.8400	454.3200
UPPER 5%	0.5829	0.6560	0.1420	783.0900	694.5700
STATISTIC	21	22			
N	1000	1000			
MEAN	78.3048	31.0909			
STANDARD DEV.	25.5664	25.5664			
SKEWNESS (G1)	0.5303	0.5303			
KURTOSIS (G2)	0.2642	0.2643			
LOWER 5%	40.9050	-6.3093			
UPPER 5%	125.0300	77.8150			

MULTIVARIATE KURTOSES

	(G2,P)	NORMALIZED
MEAN	23.1157	37.1907
STANDARD DEV.	2.2008	3.5408
SKEWNESS (G1)	-0.1822	-0.1822
KURTOSIS (G2)	-0.0174	-0.0173
LOWER 5%	19.4510	31.2950
UPPER 5%	26.4570	42.5660

PARAMETER ESTIMATES

PARAMETER	F1,F1	F2,F1	F2,F2	E1,E1	E2,E2
MEAN	1.2115	0.2958	0.4394	1.0269	2.9940
STANDARD DEV.	0.2968	0.0645	0.0857	0.2771	0.2158
SKEWNESS (G1)	0.1561	0.1407	0.1860	-0.2101	0.3410
KURTOSIS (G2)	0.7737	0.0977	0.0440	1.4805	1.1560
LOWER 5%	0.7920	0.1897	0.2998	0.5688	2.6488
UPPER 5%	1.7038	0.4015	0.5814	1.4154	3.3405

PARAMETER	E3,E3	E4,E4	E5,E5	E6,E6	V2,F1
MEAN	1.2123	0.7101	0.7159	2.6820	0.9352
STANDARD DEV.	0.0998	0.0896	0.1397	0.1233	0.1431
SKEWNESS (G1)	-0.2435	0.2235	-0.2918	0.0424	0.1375
KURTOSIS (G2)	0.5492	0.1054	0.4765	-0.0700	0.1883
LOWER 5%	1.0449	0.5648	0.4861	2.4767	0.7041
UPPER 5%	1.3699	0.8598	0.9294	2.8881	1.1763

```
PARAMETER         V3,F1      V5,F2     V6,F2
MEAN              0.3466     1.4851    0.8542
STANDARD DEV.     0.1436     0.2150    0.1427
SKEWNESS  (G1)    2.9270     0.7316    0.2442
KURTOSIS  (G2)   14.8964     0.8571    0.0900
LOWER    5%       0.1921     1.1761    0.6249
UPPER    5%       0.5464     1.8888    1.0957
```

Example 3
Partial output from bootstrapping

As you can see, all the fit measures are also bootstrapped, but I will concentrate on the model parameters. It seems that all the model parameters are in general agreement with the ones in Table 6 based on ordinary ML and so are the standard errors, although here the differences are a bit larger.

However, as the distributions of the variables are so far from normal, it could be dangerous to put too much confidence in Z-values and traditional confidence intervals based on the normal distribution. Let us instead construct Z-values based on the standard deviations in the distributions of the model parameters from Table 8. In Table 9 you can compare the bootstrap estimates with standard errors and Z-values with the corresponding results from ML estimation.

Table 9 Example 3: comparing ML estimates and bootstrap estimates

Parameter	ML			Bootstrapped estimates			
	estimate	s.e.	Z	Estimate	s.e=Std.	Z	90% c.i.
V2,F1	0.94	0.13	7.13	0.94	0.14	6.53	0.70 - 1,18
V3,F1	0.32	**0.05**	**6.05**	0.35	**0.14**	**2,41**	0.19 - 0.55
V5,F2	1.48	0.17	8.79	1.49	0.22	6.91	1.18 - 1.89
V6,F2	0.85	0.11	7.71	0.85	0.14	5.99	0.63 - 1.10
F1,F2	0.29	0.04	6.56	0.30	0.06	4.59	0.19 - 0.40

The standard errors based on standard deviations of the bootstrap estimates of the parameters are generally larger than those for the ordinary ML estimates – this is especially eye-catching for (V3,F1). Consequently, the Z-values based on bootstrapping are smaller than those for the ML estimates, although not so much smaller that any of the parameters become insignificant. Also, the parameter estimates are placed near the middle of the constructed confidence intervals.

What remains is a test of the model as a whole, i.e. a bootstrapped χ^2-test.

In fact, Bollen and Stine (1993) have invented an 'empirical χ^2-test' to be used in judging a model when using bootstrapping. The idea is as follows:

As the χ^2-test is a test of the (very unlikely!) hypothesis that your model is totally correct, the Bollen–Stine approach is to transform your input covariance matrix so that the model fits the (transformed) data exactly, but in other ways preserve its characteristics and then to do the bootstrapping on the transformed data. This is called 'model-based bootstrapping' by EQS.

To run a model-based bootstrap, you substitute the line

MBBOOTSTRAP=994

for

$$\text{BOOTSTRAP}=994$$

in the program in Table 7. As the output is similar to the one in Table 8, I only show the first section in Table 10, where (as you will guess) our main interest is in column 3.

Table 10 Example 3: model-based bootstrapping

STATISTIC	1	2	3	4	5
N	1000	1000	1000	1000	1000
COUNT > .05	835				
MEAN	0.3538	605.7522	10.5983	0.9965	0.9907
STANDARD DEV.	0.2852	70.2073	5.5489	0.0018	0.0048
SKEWNESS (G1)	0.5703	0.2875	1.3668	-1.3491	-1.3490
KURTOSIS (G2)	-0.8430	0.0222	3.5310	3.5230	3.5224
LOWER 5%	0.0077	496.9000	3.5517	0.9931	0.9820
UPPER 5%	0.8951	722.6800	20.7850	0.9988	0.9969

By comparing the ML χ^2 (85.09) with the B–S χ^2 (10.60) you will observe that the latter is much nearer to its expected value – which is the number of degrees of freedom (8). The upper 5% limit of the 90% confidence interval (3.55–20.79) is of course the critical one at a 0.05 level for the relevant χ^2-test. Since χ^2 in the original sample (85.09) exceeds that value, the test result is significant according to this traditional critical value. However, considering the large sample size this result is not very surprising, and using fit measures is a better basis for judging model fit.

You will have noticed that you can also bootstrap the various fit measures. You will, however, also have noticed that the chi-square resulting from the naïve bootstrapping (94.30) is not very useful. This goes for fit measures in general: if you need to bootstrap them, always use model-based bootstrapping.

Other Uses of Bootstrapping

Even if bootstrapping cannot cure all problems, it has other uses than for the analysis of non-normal data. You can, for example, use bootstrapping to compare the merits of different estimation methods and different models.

3 Analyzing Categorical Variables

In Section 4.5 I commented on the special problems involved if your data included ordinal (and thereby categorical) data. As you will remember, I generally favored analyzing such data as if they were continuous, if the following conditions could be met:

1. The variables can take on 'many' values.
2. The variables are 'nearly' normal, i.e. symmetric with kurtosis (see Appendix A) near zero.
3. A possible (limited) skewness falls on the same side for all variables.

I also mentioned that the first condition could generally be considered fulfilled if the scale had at least five values.

When the above conditions are not met you have to fall back on the special procedures for non-interval-scaled data. These procedures raise a lot of problems.

You will remember (from Section 4.5) that the special methods to analyze ordinal data assume that the ordinal measurements cover underlying continuous variables that fulfill the usual condition of being multivariate normally distributed, and the analysis is in a way based on this assumed underlying distribution. You, so to speak, introduce new latent variables in your model: your manifest *ordinal* variables are indicators of the underlying interval-scaled variables, and they again are indicators of the latent variables in your model.

As SEM is based on analyzing the covariance matrix of the measured variables, what we really would like to have is a way to estimate the covariance matrix of the underlying continuous variables based on the measured rank data.

Because an ordinal variable has neither measurement unit nor zero point, this is of course impossible. So we must look for a way to measure covariation that is in a way independent of measurement units. Such a measure is the correlation. So instead of using a covariance matrix as input, we must use a correlation matrix. But is it possible to uncover correlations in the underlying continuous variables? The answer is yes.

The problems that such a procedure raises are most easily seen if we turn the procedure round and start with a set of interval-scaled data and then group them as shown in Figure 5, which shows the covariation between height and weight as measured for 500 persons. Now assume that we classify the measured heights as follows:

heights < 160 cm are classified as '1'

160 cm ≤ heights < 180 cm are classified as '2'

height ≥ 180 cm are classified as '3'

In the same way weights are classified as follows:

weight < 60 kg are classified as '1'

60 kg ≤ weight < 90 kg are classified as '2'

weight ≥ 90 kg are classified as '3'

When we are analyzing ordinal data, we are in the opposite situation: we do not have the underlying continuous distributions, and our rank data are the only basis on which we can estimate the correlation in the underlying two-dimensional density function.

Although using ordinary correlations calculated on ranked data will generally underestimate the correlations of their continuous counterparts, the differences can be ignored if the above-mentioned three conditions are fulfilled. If they are not, special correlation measures must be calculated based on the ordinal variables 'on the surface'.

Such measures are the *polychoric* correlation coefficient if both variables are ordinal and the *polyserial* correlation coefficient if one variable is ordinal and the other is interval scaled.

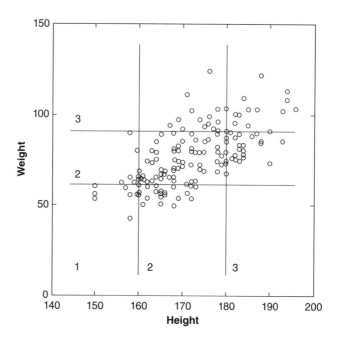

Figure 5 Categorizing interval-scaled data

In the present case the correlation between the interval-scaled variables is around 0.60, while the correlation between the ordinal variables is around 0.40, so ignoring the ordinality of the measurements is certainly not a good choice.

Figure 5 also points to a further problem.

If you want to analyze the covariation of two categorical variables using cross-tabulation, you know from your introductory course in statistics that this demands a certain minimum of observations per cell in a cross-tabulation. In SEM with several variables such a multidimensional cross-tabulation requires a very large sample indeed in order to avoid cells with no or few observations. Therefore the demands on sample size using these methods could easily grow to a size comparable with that of AGLS.

Analyzing ordinal data really puts EQS to work, so to be on the safe side, before starting the analysis, choose 'Build EQS/EQS Working Array' and add one or two zeros in order to increase the space that EQS has at its disposal.

Example 4 (continued from Example 8.1)
Estimating a measurement model analyzing ordinal data as ordinal

I will demonstrate the special procedure in EQS for handling categorical data by revising the program in Table 8.1 to take the categorical nature of the data into consideration. The necessary modifications to the /SPECIFICATIONS paragraph are shown in Table 11 together with the addition of a new paragraph /TECHNICAL and an addition to the /PRINT paragraph.

10.3 Analyzing Categorical Variables

Table 11 Example 2: analyzing the data as categorical

```
/TITLE
   Model built by EQS 6 for Windows
/SPECIFICATIONS
   DATA='C:\Users\Sony\Desktop\EQS bog\EQS Chap 10\bredahla.ess';
   VARIABLES=30; CASES=481;
   METHOD=LS,ROBUST; ANALYSIS=CORRELATION; MATRIX=RAW;              (1-4)
   CATEGORY=V1 TO V25;                                              (5)

/TECHNICAL                                                          (6)
IT=500

/PRINT
RETEST = CATSTART.EQS;                                              (7)
EIS;
FIT=ALL;
TABLE=COMPACT;
```

A few comments on the program in Table 11 are in order:

1. With categorical variables convergence problems are more common. Whereas ML and GLS estimation use standard start values for the iterations, LS uses start values based on the input data. So, using LS gives the iteration process a better start.
2. If you consider using categorical methods, it is obviously because you find it necessary not to ignore non-normality. Therefore ROBUST is required (see Section 4.5).
3. As mentioned above, categorical analyses are based on correlations and not covariances.
4. Categorical modeling always demands raw data.
5. The categorical variables are declared.
6. To be on the safe side, the number of iterations is set at its maximum (default is 30).
7. As a last measure against convergence problems, I ask for RETEST (see Section 4.6).

As you may have guessed, there is a great deal of output (about 50 pages!); only a small part of it will be discussed in the following.

Following citation of the input file are (see Table 12):

1. A description of the distribution of each categorical variable.
2. Information on the thresholds for the various discrete variables.
3. The polychoric correlation matrix between discrete variables.
4. The usual sample statistics you always get when the input is the raw data. We are warned that this information may not meaningful – and it is not, because the statistics presuppose interval-scaled variables.

Then comes the correlation matrix to be analyzed, but as this is the same as (3) because all variables are categorical, I will not show it.

As mentioned in Section 4.5, the problems associated with non-normal data are often more to do with the test statistics than with the parameter estimates.

Using robust estimation will add to the program output the so-called Satorra–Bentler chi-square (Satorra & Bentler, 1988, 1994) that regulates the normal chi-square for non-normality. Also, so-called 'robust standard errors' and 'robust Z-values' are added to the

Table 12 Example 4: analyzing data as categorical (ordinal) – output, first part

```
YOUR MODEL HAS SPECIFIED CATEGORICAL VARIABLES

    TOTAL NUMBER OF VARIABLES ARE        25
    NUMBER OF CONTINUOUS VARIABLES ARE    0
    NUMBER OF DISCRETE   VARIABLES ARE   25

    INFORMATION ON DISCRETE VARIABLES                                (1)

VARIABLE
NO.     NAME    CATEGORIES   CODE   FREQUENCY   PERCENT

 1      PR1         7          1        36       7.484
                               2        51      10.603
                               3        57      11.850
                               4       115      23.909
                               5        78      16.216
                               6        76      15.800
                               7        68      14.137

 2      PR2         7          1        41       8.524
                               2        50      10.395
                               3        64      13.306
                               4        73      15.177
                               5        76      15.800
                               6        95      19.751
                               7        82      17.048

 3      CR1         7          1        27       5.613
                               2        41       8.524
                               3        63      13.098
                               4       101      20.998
                               5        88      18.295
                               6        79      16.424
                               7        82      17.048


    RESULTS OF POLYCHORIC PARTITION                                  (2)

VARIABLE
NO.     NAME         AVERAGE THRESHOLDS

 1      PR1      -1.4349  -0.9103  -0.5253   0.0955   0.5249   1.0736
 2      PR2      -1.3675  -0.8801  -0.4616  -0.0652   0.3370   0.9504
 3      CR1      -1.5763  -1.0666  -0.6028  -0.0449   0.4263   0.9526


    POLYCHORIC CORRELATION MATRIX BETWEEN DISCRETE VARIABLES         (3)

                         PR1       PR2       CR1       CR2       CR4
                         V1        V2        V3        V4        V5
         PR1   V1       1.000
         PR2   V2       0.563     1.000
         CR1   V3       0.506     0.672     1.000
         CR2   V4       0.337     0.427     0.492     1.000
         CR4   V5       0.340     0.497     0.546     0.486     1.000
```

```
SAMPLE STATISTICS BASED ON COMPLETE CASES                                    (4)


*** NOTE *** CATEGORICAL VARIABLES LISTED ABOVE ARE INDICATORS OF LATENT
             CONTINUOUS VARIABLES.  THEIR UNIVARIATE AND JOINT STATISTICS
             MAY NOT BE MEANINGFUL.

UNIVARIATE STATISTICS
                              ---------------------

VARIABLE              PR1           PR2           CR1           CR2           CR4
                      V1            V2            V3            V4            V5
MEAN                  4.3472        4.4678        4.5530        4.7734        5.9751
SKEWNESS  (G1)       -0.1920       -0.3028       -0.2729       -0.3682       -1.5002
KURTOSIS  (G2)       -0.8782       -1.0553       -0.8235       -0.5731        1.6177
STANDARD DEV.         1.7801        1.8939        1.7470        1.6547        1.4316
```

tables of parameter estimates, and in the section of the output called 'goodness of fit summary for method robust' you will see some new fit measures. ROBUST can be used in connection with all the available estimation methods except AGLS.

In the section of the output called 'goodness of fit summary for method LS' you will find a chi-square of 1134.111 with 265 degrees of freedom, a CFI of 0.828, a standardized RMR of 0.075 and an RMSEA of 0.083 (0.078–0.088) (not shown). Below that you will find the fit measures shown in Table 13.

Table 13 Example 4: analyzing data as categorical – robust fit measures

```
ROBUST INDEPENDENCE MODEL CHI-SQUARE =       8176.502 ON     300 DEGREES OF FREEDOM

INDEPENDENCE AIC =      7576.502    INDEPENDENCE CAIC =     6023.741
        MODEL AIC =      511.638           MODEL CAIC =     -859.967

SATORRA-BENTLER SCALED CHI-SQUARE =     1041.6375 ON      265 DEGREES OF FREEDOM
PROBABILITY VALUE FOR THE CHI-SQUARE STATISTIC IS        0.00000

MEAN- AND VARIANCE-ADJUSTED CHI-SQUARE            =      310.392 ON    79 D.F.
PROBABILITY VALUE FOR THE CHI-SQUARE STATISTIC IS        0.00000

MEAN-SCALED AND SKEWNESS-ADJUSTED STATISTIC       =      117.959 ON    30 D.F.
PROBABILITY VALUE FOR THE CHI-SQUARE STATISTIC IS        0.00000

RESIDUAL-BASED TEST STATISTIC                     =     1435.277
PROBABILITY VALUE FOR THE CHI-SQUARE STATISTIC IS        0.00000

YUAN-BENTLER RESIDUAL-BASED TEST STATISTIC        =      359.143
PROBABILITY VALUE FOR THE CHI-SQUARE STATISTIC IS        0.00010

YUAN-BENTLER RESIDUAL-BASED F-STATISTIC     =           2.437
DEGREES OF FREEDOM  =                              265,    216
PROBABILITY VALUE FOR THE F-STATISTIC IS                0.00000

FIT INDICES
-----------
BENTLER-BONETT      NORMED FIT INDEX  =      0.837
BENTLER-BONETT NON-NORMED FIT INDEX   =      0.847
COMPARATIVE FIT INDEX (CFI)           =      0.865
BOLLEN'S          (IFI) FIT INDEX     =      0.865
MCDONALD'S        (MFI) FIT INDEX     =      0.330
ROOT MEAN-SQUARE ERROR OF APPROXIMATION (RMSEA)  =      0.092
90% CONFIDENCE INTERVAL OF RMSEA  (          0.087,         0.096)
```

You can compare the Satorra–Bentler scaled chi-square of 1041 with the unscaled value of 1134 and observe that the scaling has brought the expected value of the chi-square statistic a bit nearer its expected value under the null hypothesis, which is of course the degrees of freedom, 265.

Below the Satorra–Bentler scaled chi-square you will find the mean- and variance-adjusted chi-square and the mean-scaled and skewness-adjusted statistic (Satorra & Bentler, 1994), which are both further developments of the Satorra–Bentler chi-square.

Unfortunately the three chi-squares suffer from the same drawback: if you want to do a chi-square difference test in evaluating nested models, the difference is not distributed as chi-square.

If you need to do such a test, you should use one of the three residual test statistics, preferably one of the last two, because the first one could be ill-behaved in small samples.

However, the test is still significant, but considering the sample size this is not very surprising. The fit measures, however, could be better.

When going through the parameter estimates in Table 14, you should concentrate on the robust test statistics, which show that all parameters are significant (just as in Table 8.2 where the same data were analyzed as continuous) and the ranking of the influence of the exogenous factors on F5 is unaltered.

Table 14 Example 4: analyzing data as categorical – parameter estimates

```
LEAST SQUARES SOLUTION (NORMAL DISTRIBUTION THEORY)
    WITH ROBUST STATISTICS (LEE, POON, AND BENTLER OPTIMAL WEIGHT MATRIX)

    PARAMETER ESTIMATES (B) WITH STANDARD ERRORS AND TEST STATISTICS (Z)
    STATISTICS SIGNIFICANT AT THE 5% LEVEL ARE MARKED WITH @.

                                                          ROBUST
                                                                              R-
DEP.VAR.         PREDICTOR    B       BETA    S.E.    Z        S.E.    Z     SQUARED
---------------------------------------------------------------------------------
V1    ( PR1   )                                                              .316
              F5   ( F5 ) 1.000   .562
V2    ( PR2   )                                                              .542
              F5   ( F5 ) 1.310*  .736   .054   24.067@   .102   12.862@
V3    ( CR1   )                                                              .593
              F5   ( F5 ) 1.370*  .770   .059   23.050@   .109   12.601@
V4    ( CR2   )                                                              .395
              F5   ( F5 ) 1.118*  .629   .043   26.298@   .109   10.256@
V5    ( CR4   )                                                              .569
              F5   ( F5 ) 1.342*  .754   .057   23.543@   .121   11.071@
V6    ( CR5   )                                                              .618
              F5   ( F5 ) 1.398*  .786   .062   22.523@   .110   12.719@
V7    ( GA21  )                                                              .768
              F2   ( F2 ) 1.000   .876
V8    ( GA22  )                                                              .339
              F2   ( F2 )  .664*  .582   .038   17.522@   .066   10.111@
V9    ( GA23  )                                                              .293
              F2   ( F2 )  .618*  .541   .035   17.497@   .058   10.611@
V10   ( GA24  )                                                              .268
              F2   ( F2 )  .591*  .517   .034   17.464@   .061    9.686@
V11   ( GA25  )                                                              .157
              F2   ( F2 )  .452*  .396   .027   16.966@   .063    7.142@
V12   ( GA26  )                                                              .310
              F2   ( F2 )  .636*  .557   .036   17.511@   .062   10.184@
V13   ( GA31  )                                                              .451
              F1   ( F1 ) 1.000   .671
```

```
V14 ( GA32 )                                                              .530
         F1    ( F1 ) 1.085*   .728  .082  13.269@  .084  12.982@
V15 ( GA33 )                                                              .594
         F1    ( F1 ) 1.148*   .771  .090  12.714@  .087  13.191@
V16 ( GA34 )                                                              .466
         F1    ( F1 ) 1.017*   .683  .074  13.823@  .091  11.143@
V17 ( GA35 )                                                              .481
         F1    ( F1 ) 1.033*   .693  .075  13.698@  .078  13.214@
V18 ( GA41 )                                                              .298
         F3    ( F3 ) 1.000    .546
V19 ( GA42 )                                                              .462
         F3    ( F3 ) 1.245*   .680  .079  15.773@  .125   9.983@
V20 ( GA43 )                                                              .487
         F3    ( F3 ) 1.278*   .698  .082  15.560@  .149   8.600@
V21 ( GA44 )                                                              .538
         F3    ( F3 ) 1.343*   .734  .089  15.110@  .140   9.564@
V22 ( GA45 )                                                              .510
         F3    ( F3 ) 1.307*   .714  .085  15.362@  .141   9.253@
V23 ( GA52 )                                                              .613
         F4    ( F4 ) 1.000    .783
V24 ( GA53 )                                                              .593
         F4    ( F4 )  .984*   .770  .060  16.498@  .068  14.473@
V25 ( GA54 )                                                              .527
         F4    ( F4 )  .928*   .726  .056  16.459@  .081  11.448@
F5  ( F5   )                                                              .629
         F1    ( F1 ) -.181*  -.217  .019  -9.684@  .045  -4.074@
         F2    ( F2 )  .300*   .468  .035   8.510@  .045   6.682@
         F3    ( F3 )  .261*   .254  .025  10.656@  .057   4.608@
         F4    ( F4 )  .210*   .293  .036   5.761@  .043   4.864@

                                                          ROBUST
                               VARIANCE   S.E.     Z      S.E.     Z
---------------------------------------------------------------------
FACTOR
         F1   (    F1   )  .451*    .043   10.592@   .056    7.989@
         F2   (    F2   )  .768*    .071   10.797@   .062   12.407@
         F3   (    F3   )  .298*    .024   12.290@   .055    5.424@
         F4   (    F4   )  .613*    .058   10.632@   .058   10.594@
ERROR
         E1   (   PR1   )  .684*     ^
         E2   (   PR2   )  .458*     ^
         E3   (   CR1   )  .407*     ^
         E4   (   CR2   )  .605*     ^
         E5   (   CR4   )  .431*     ^
         E6   (   CR5   )  .382*     ^
         E7   (  GA21   )  .232*     ^
         E8   (  GA22   )  .661*     ^
         E9   (  GA23   )  .707*     ^
         E10  (  GA24   )  .732*     ^
         E11  (  GA25   )  .843*     ^
         E12  (  GA26   )  .690*     ^
         E13  (  GA31   )  .549*     ^
         E14  (  GA32   )  .470*     ^
         E15  (  GA33   )  .406*     ^
         E16  (  GA34   )  .534*     ^
         E17  (  GA35   )  .519*     ^
         E18  (  GA41   )  .702*     ^
         E19  (  GA42   )  .538*     ^
         E20  (  GA43   )  .513*     ^
         E21  (  GA44   )  .462*     ^
         E22  (  GA45   )  .490*     ^
```

(Continued)

Table 14 (Continued)

```
              E23  (    GA52   )  .387*     ^
              E24  (    GA53   )  .407*     ^
              E25  (    GA54   )  .473*     ^
DISTURBANCE
              D5   (    F5     )  .117*   .012    9.457@   .022    5.440@
```

COVARIANCES AMONG INDEPENDENT VARIABLES
STATISTICS SIGNIFICANT AT THE 5% LEVEL ARE MARKED WITH @.

```
                                                              ROBUST
                                    COVA.    S.E.     Z       S.E.     Z       CORR.
-----------------------------------------------------------------------------------
    F1,F2  (  F1  ,  F2  )   .038*   .006    5.960@   .035    1.083     .064
    F1,F3  (  F1  ,  F3  )  -.139*   .009  -14.828@   .027   -5.250@   -.380
    F1,F4  (  F1  ,  F4  )   .030*   .006    4.736@   .034     .879     .057
    F2,F3  (  F2  ,  F3  )   .021*   .005    3.998@   .027     .794     .045
    F2,F4  (  F2  ,  F4  )   .408*   .022   18.309@   .042    9.600@    .594
    F3,F4  (  F3  ,  F4  )   .053*   .006    8.699@   .027    1.947     .124
```

A final note!

After having read this chapter – and especially after having struggled with the exercises on the website – you will be well aware that a covariance or correlation summary of your data can hide lots of problems in the raw data, such as non-normality, non-linearities, outliers, etc. Give this some thought next time you read a journal article in which a covariance or correlation matrix is the only kind of data published.

In this chapter you met the following concepts:

- listwise and pairwise deletion
- mean imputation
- regression imputation
- multiple imputation
- FIML estimation
- function of log likelihood
- bootstrapping
- bollen–Stine χ^2-test

You have also learned the following EQS statement:

```
/SPECIFICATIONS              /SIMULATION
  MISSING=ML                   BOOTSTRAP=b
  ROBUST                       MBOOTSTRAP=B
  CATEGORY=Vx TO Vy            REPLICATION=r
                               SEED=x...y
                             /TECHNICAL
                               IT=x...
```

Questions

1. Judge the virtues and vices of various imputation methods.
2. State the characteristics of the three missing data concepts, namely 'missing completely at random', 'missing at random' and 'non-ignorable', and comment on the various methods for coping with the problem in each of the three situations.
3. Consider how bootstrapping could help solve problems that you might encounter, or have already encountered, in your own area of study or research.

References

Bollen, K. A., & Stine, R. A. (1993). Bootstrapping goodness-of-fit measures in structural equation modeling. In K. A. Bollen & J. S. Long (Eds.), *Testing structural equation models* (pp. 111–135). Newbury Park, CA: Sage.

Chou, C.-P., Bentler, P. M., & Satorra, A. (1991). Scaled test statistics and robust standard errors for non-normal data in covariance structure analysis: A Monte Carlo study. *British Journal of Mathematical and Statistical Psychology, 4*, 21–37.

Rubin, D. B. (1976). Inference and missing data. *Biometrika, 63*, 581–592.

Satorra, A., & Bentler, P. M. (1988). *Scaling corrections for chi square statistics in covariance structure analysis.* Paper presented at the American Statistical Association 1988 Proceedings of the Business and Economics Section, Alexandria, VA.

Satorra, A., & Bentler, P. M. (1994). Corrections to test statistics and standard errors in covariance structure analysis. In A. von Eye & C. C. Clogg (Eds.), *Latent variable analysis: Applications for developmental research* (pp. 399–419). Thousand Oaks, CA: Sage.

SPSS. (2013). IBM SPSS Missing Values 22.

Thomsen, D. K., Mehlsen, Y. M., Hokland, M., Viidik, A., Olesen, F., Avlund, K. et al. (2004). Negative thoughts and health: Associations among rumination, immunity and health care utilization in a young and elderly sample. *Psychosomatic Medicine, 66*, 363–371.

11

Latent Curve Models

> The last few decades have seen rapid growth in the amount of longitudinal data – both public (government) data and commercial data (e.g. panel data in marketing research) – and a growing interest in methods for the analysis of such data. SEM has much to offer in that context.
>
> The idea is that the repeated measurements are considered as manifestations of an underlying process that generates their so-called *trajectory* in much the same way as a latent variable generates the answers to items in a scale. This is the so-called *latent curve model*.
>
> You will learn the subject through a simple example. As is now (I hope) your habit, you start the analysis with the measurement model and then introduce the structural model.
>
> After this simple introduction to the subject, the last part of the chapter brings in more complicated matters: how to deal with metrics of time; how to interpret indirect effects; and how to expand the simple model in more elaborate directions.

1 What Is a Latent Curve Model?

Sometimes your research problem demands that you follow your 'respondents' (be they people, companies, geographic areas) over a shorter or longer period, taking measurements at various intervals in order to map the development through time.

Up to now you have met two examples where data were collected in two waves. In Examples 6.2 and 8.3 information on a group of patients was collected over an interval of four years to study the stability of alienation, and in Example 7.1 the degree of democracy in developing countries was measured in 1960 and again in 1965. But what if you want to follow these up, continuing to collect data in order to find answers to questions such as:

1. Is there a general trend in the data? Does a patient's feeling of alienation generally speaking increase, decrease or remain stable over time? Is democracy gaining or losing ground in developing countries or are things not changing?
2. Does every member (patient/country) of the group follow the same trend, or are there variations?
3. If the trend varies across group members, is it then possible to locate variables that could account for such variations?

A simple way to analyze such data is to use regression analysis (Appendix A), regressing the measure of interest on a time variable. To make things simple, I use a linear model:

$$y_{it} = \alpha_i + \beta_i \lambda_t + \varepsilon_{it}$$

where

y_{it} = the value of the variable of interest (1)

for 'respondent' i at time λ_t,

and ε_{it} is an error term fulfilling

the usual conditions

You can carry out a regression for each and every 'respondent' as well as for the group as a whole. However, this is perhaps not the most efficient way to analyze the data, e.g. in testing and comparing the various regression functions you have to do a lot of testing. In each test, you can control the risk α of making a type 1 error (i.e. the maximum probability of rejecting H_0, if H_0 is true; see Appendix A), but how large is α for the whole set of tests combined? Also, there is no way to judge the fit of the total model. These are not the only inconveniences in this choice of analysis strategy (Bollen & Curran, 2006).

So, let us look at a more effective way to analyze these sorts of data. As a start we could assume that the parameters α_i and β_i are stochastic variables:

$$y_{it} = \alpha_i + \beta_i \lambda_t + \varepsilon_{it}$$
$$\alpha_i = \mu_\alpha + \delta_{\alpha i}$$
$$\beta_i = \mu_\beta + \delta_{\beta i}$$

where

y_{it} = the value of the variable of interest (2)

for the respondent i at time λ_t

$\mu_\alpha = E(\alpha_i)$

$\mu_\beta = E(\beta_i)$

and ε_{it}, $\delta_{\alpha i}$ and $\delta_{\beta i}$ are error terms

fulfilling the usual conditions

In this way we take care of the possibility that the intercept and the slope may vary across respondents.

It is obvious that the model could also be interpreted as a confirmatory factor model as first proposed by Meredith and Tisak (1984, 1990) building on the work of Tucker (1958). Usually a factor model is used to model the connection between a series of questions in a questionnaire and some underlying construct that the questions are supposed to measure, e.g. a series of questions intended to measure depression or some other psychological variable of interest.

In this use of the factor analysis approach, we let a series of repeated measurements $y_1, y_2, \ldots, y_k$ on a variable take the place of the test questions in the above-mentioned example. These measurements are then regarded as indicators of the parameters in a model describing the trajectory generating the observations – for example, a curve describing the development in patients of feelings of alienation or the development of democracy in a selection of countries. Our model (2) can then be depicted as shown in Figure 1, where, in order to keep things simple, I assume that the measurements are taken three times at one-year intervals.

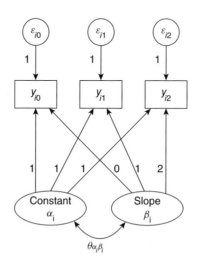

Figure 1 Linear latent curve model

As read from the model:

$$y_{i0} = \alpha_i + \varepsilon_{i0}$$
$$y_{i1} = \alpha_i + 1\beta_i + \varepsilon_{i1} \qquad (3)$$
$$y_{i2} = \alpha_i + 2\beta_i + \varepsilon_{i2}$$

cf. Equation (2).

What first catches the eye is that the regression coefficients that are usually at the center of interest in factor models are all fixed, and therefore not to be estimated. It is also apparent that the arrow from 'Slope' to y_{i0} is fixed at zero. I could just as well have excluded it from the drawing, but it has become common practice to include it.

In a way the scaling of time is somewhat arbitrary, but letting the first regression coefficient have the value 0 means that a_i represents the value of y_i at the time of the first measurement.

Since we are interested in the means of intercepts and slope, picturing the model in Figure 1 in 'EQS language' makes the picture a bit more complicated as can be seen from Figure 2. The constant V999 has been introduced and connected to the two factors, which makes the factors dependent variables. Since dependent variables do not have variances and covariances, information on the factors must be carried by their disturbances, so the covariance between the factors is now between their D variables.

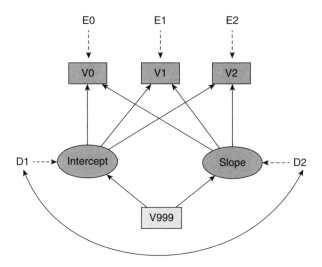

Figure 2 Linear latent curve model as depicted in EQS

2 The Two-Step Strategy in Latent Curve Modeling

In latent curve modeling (LCM) we follow a two-step strategy (introduced in Section 8.2). First we analyze the measurement model and then we bring in the causal model. But there is a difference.

If you compare the first step in Table 8.5 with the second step in Table 8.9, you will see that *all* variables in the second step ('the causal model') are also included in the first step ('the factor model').

This is not the case in LCM. Here the first step is to *describe* the trajectory without including any of the variables that are brought in during the second step to 'explain' the trajectory. So what we have in Figures 1 and 2 is the first step in any LCM.

Example 1
Does union negotiation raise wages?

Vella and Veerbek (1998), in a project on the influence of union membership on wages, interviewed 545 young men yearly over eight years. If we let 'lwage' be the logarithm of the wage, we will try to answer the first two questions mentioned above: (1) is there a trend in wages during the eight years; and (2) do all respondents follow the same trend or are there differences?

Now a trend could have many forms – it is not necessarily linear – so, as a first step, we will use SPSS to plot 'lwage' against 'year'. (Remember: it is always a good habit 'to draw before you calculate'!)

However, as is evident from Figure 3, the trend is as linear as you could ever require.

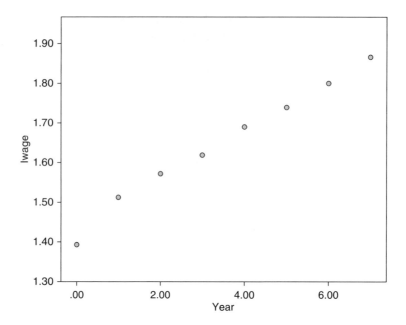

Figure 3 Example 1: linear trend at group level

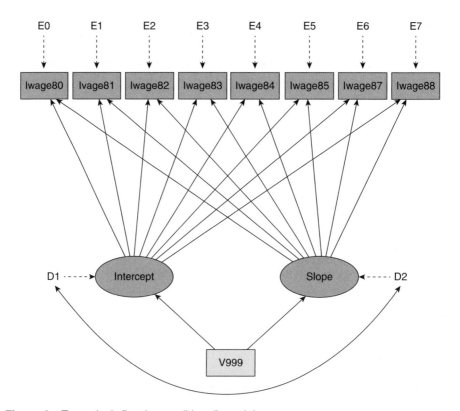

Figure 4 Example 2: first (unconditional) model

11.2 The Two-Step Strategy in Latent Curve Modeling

This also answers the first question raised above: there is a strong (linear) trend in wages at group level.

You should have no problems in formulating the model in Figure 4 and estimating it using the data 'wagepan' from the book's website. Before you look at the model estimates and the fit measures, it is a good idea to take a look at the sample statistics as given in Table 1.

It is obvious that there are problems with 'lwage84' whose kurtosis is extremely high (remember: kurtosis should preferably be smaller than 8–10). Consequently the normalized multivariate kurtosis coefficient is much larger than the suggested upper limit of 3–4.

Looking at the last line in the table, it is obvious that observation 41 is an outlier.

Table 1 Example 1: sample statistics from the first run (extract)

```
SAMPLE STATISTICS BASED ON COMPLETE CASES

                         UNIVARIATE STATISTICS

                         ---------------------


VARIABLE                 LWAGE80      LWAGE81      LWAGE82      LWAGE83      LWAGE84
                         V6           V12          V18          V24          V30
MEAN                     1.3935       1.5129       1.5717       1.6193       1.6903
SKEWNESS (G1)           -1.2328      -1.1622      -0.6908      -0.4056      -1.9834
KURTOSIS (G2)            3.2359       3.7696       3.3057       1.5347      18.6207
STANDARD DEV.            0.5575       0.5307       0.4974       0.4808       0.5242


VARIABLE                 LWAGE85      LWAGE86      LWAGE87      V999
                         V36          V42          V48          V999
MEAN                     1.7394       1.7997       1.8665       1.0000
SKEWNESS (G1)           -0.8767      -0.8902      -0.1434       0.0000
KURTOSIS (G2)            5.1196       3.7208       1.0168       0.0000
STANDARD DEV.            0.5225       0.5150       0.4669       0.0000


MULTIVARIATE KURTOSIS
                         ---------------------

    MARDIA'S COEFFICIENT (G2,P) =        172.9299
    NORMALIZED ESTIMATE =                159.5799


CASE NUMBERS WITH LARGEST CONTRIBUTION TO NORMALIZED MULTIVARIATE KURTOSIS:

    ------------------------------------------------------------------------

    CASE NUMBER      41              114            391          445          481

    ESTIMATE     36472.9198      4569.0505     4320.7030    3877.9628    3864.2667
```

Deleting observation 41 by inserting the line

$$DE=41;$$

in the /SPECIFICATIONS paragraph reduces the kurtosis of 'lwage84' from 18.62 to 1.26, quite a reduction! Unfortunately the normalized measure of multivariate kurtosis is only reduced from 159.58 to 110.13, so the distribution of the variables is still far from multivariate normal.

Now we have three options:

1. To continue deleting observations.
2. To choose another estimation method that could take care of excessive multivariate kurtosis, such as the elliptical and heterogeneous kurtosis methods mentioned in Section 4.5.
3. To continue using ML estimation but to regulate the test statistics to take care of the non-normality.

I will leave it to you to explore the first option, and since the second option is beyond the scope of this introductory text, I will choose the last one.

As in Example 10.4, I will therefore use robust estimation and substitute

$$METHOD=ML, ROBUST;$$

for

$$METHOD=ML;$$

in the program for the model in Figure 4. As demonstrated in Example 10.4, this will add to the program output both robust fit measures and robust test statistics for the parameters.

In the section of the output called 'goodness of fit summary for method ML' you will find a chi-square of 138 with 31 degrees of freedom, a CFI of 0.959, a standardized RMR of 0.083 and an RMSEA of 0.088 (0.071, 0.102) based on the covariance matrix alone, and an RMSEA of 0.080 (0.066, 0.093) based on both covariance matrix and means. Below that you will find the fit measures given in Table 2.

Table 2 Example 1: output from the second run (extract)

```
GOODNESS OF FIT SUMMARY FOR METHOD = ROBUST

  ROBUST INDEPENDENCE MODEL CHI-SQUARE =      1761.138 ON      28 DEGREES OF FREEDOM

    INDEPENDENCE AIC =    1705.138    INDEPENDENCE CAIC =    1556.767
          MODEL AIC =      54.975           MODEL CAIC =    -109.293

  SATORRA-BENTLER SCALED CHI-SQUARE =      116.9747 ON      31 DEGREES OF FREEDOM
  PROBABILITY VALUE FOR THE CHI-SQUARE STATISTIC IS      0.00000

  MEAN- AND VARIANCE-ADJUSTED CHI-SQUARE             =      77.542 ON     21 D.F.
  PROBABILITY VALUE FOR THE CHI-SQUARE STATISTIC IS      0.00000

  MEAN-SCALED AND SKEWNESS-ADJUSTED STATISTIC        =      46.474 ON     12 D.F.
  PROBABILITY VALUE FOR THE CHI-SQUARE STATISTIC IS      0.00001
```

```
RESIDUAL-BASED TEST STATISTIC                        =    99.102
PROBABILITY VALUE FOR THE CHI-SQUARE STATISTIC IS         0.00000

YUAN-BENTLER RESIDUAL-BASED TEST STATISTIC           =    83.783
PROBABILITY VALUE FOR THE CHI-SQUARE STATISTIC IS         0.00000

YUAN-BENTLER RESIDUAL-BASED F-STATISTIC              =     3.020
DEGREES OF FREEDOM  =                                   31,   513
PROBABILITY VALUE FOR THE F-STATISTIC IS                  0.00000

FIT INDICES (BASED ON COVARIANCE MATRIX ONLY, NOT THE MEANS)
-----------
BENTLER-BONETT      NORMED FIT INDEX  =      0.938
BENTLER-BONETT NON-NORMED FIT INDEX   =      0.946
COMPARATIVE FIT INDEX (CFI)           =      0.952
BOLLEN'S            (IFI) FIT INDEX   =      0.952
MCDONALD'S          (MFI) FIT INDEX   =      0.926
ROOT MEAN-SQUARE ERROR OF APPROXIMATION (RMSEA)   =   0.079
90% CONFIDENCE INTERVAL OF RMSEA   (     0.064,       0.094)

FIT INDICES (BASED ON COVARIANCE MATRIX AND MEANS)
-----------
MCDONALD'S          (MFI) FIT INDEX   =      0.924
ROOT MEAN-SQUARE ERROR OF APPROXIMATION (RMSEA)   =   0.071
90% CONFIDENCE INTERVAL OF RMSEA   (     0.058,       0.085)
```

You can compare the Satorra–Bentler scaled chi-square with a value of 116 with the unscaled value of 138 and observe that the scaling has brought the expected value of the chi-square statistic nearer its expected value under the null hypothesis, which is of course the degrees of freedom, 31.

However, the test is still significant, but considering the sample size this is not very surprising. Although the fit measures are generally OK, RMSEA indicates that there is room for improvement. Correlations between error terms are defendable (cf. Example 7.1).

Letting only neighboring error terms correlate has only a marginal effect on fit, while letting all error terms correlate will result in an under-identified model. As a compromise (and not to make the example too complicated) I will put in correlations between error terms that are at most three periods away. Part of the output is given in Table 3.

Table 3 Example 1: unconditional model, partial output from third run

```
MAXIMUM LIKELIHOOD SOLUTION (NORMAL DISTRIBUTION THEORY)

   VARIANCES OF INDEPENDENT VARIABLES
   STATISTICS SIGNIFICANT AT THE 5% LEVEL ARE MARKED WITH @.

                                                        ROBUST
                         VARIANCE   S.E.     Z         S.E.     Z
   -----------------------------------------------------------------

ERROR
          E6  (LWAGE80 )   .202*    .023    8.911@    .037    5.454@
          E12 (LWAGE81 )   .152*    .017    8.848@    .029    5.221@
          E18 (LWAGE82 )   .124*    .012    9.943@    .022    5.707@
```

(Continued)

Table 3 (Continued)

```
              E24  (LWAGE83 )   .111*    .011   10.361@   .017   6.388@
              E30  (LWAGE84 )   .098*    .010    9.857@   .015   6.476@
              E36  (LWAGE85 )   .123*    .013    9.358@   .028   4.343@
              E42  (LWAGE86 )   .104*    .016    6.357@   .027   3.818@
              E48  (LWAGE87 )   .045*    .019    2.381@   .021   2.113@

DISTURBANCE

              D1  (    F1   )   .125*    .020    6.225@   .021   5.944@
              D2  (    F2   )   .002*    .001    3.070@   .001   2.788@
```

COVARIANCES AMONG INDEPENDENT VARIABLES
STATISTICS SIGNIFICANT AT THE 5% LEVEL ARE MARKED WITH @.

```
                                                                 ROBUST
                              COVA.    S.E.     Z       S.E.     Z       CORR.
-------------------------------------------------------------------------------
E6,E12   (LWAGE80 ,LWAGE81 )  .017*    .017    1.038    .018    .948     .099
E6,E18   (LWAGE80 ,LWAGE82 )  .010*    .013     .764    .013    .728     .060
E6,E24   (LWAGE80 ,LWAGE83 )  .008*    .010     .800    .010    .801     .052
E12,E18  (LWAGE81 ,LWAGE82 )  .034*    .012    2.812@   .014   2.431@    .250
E12,E24  (LWAGE81 ,LWAGE83 )  .026*    .010    2.575@   .010   2.507@    .201
E12,E30  (LWAGE81 ,LWAGE84 )  .011*    .007    1.669    .007   1.510     .091
E18,E24  (LWAGE82 ,LWAGE83 )  .044*    .010    4.550@   .010   4.598@    .373
E18,E30  (LWAGE82 ,LWAGE84 )  .035*    .007    5.009@   .008   4.654@    .319
E18,E36  (LWAGE82 ,LWAGE85 )  .024*    .006    3.855@   .006   4.266@    .193
E24,E30  (LWAGE83 ,LWAGE84 )  .042*    .007    5.886@   .007   5.998@    .402
E24,E36  (LWAGE83 ,LWAGE85 )  .025*    .006    3.923@   .006   4.039@    .216
E24,E42  (LWAGE83 ,LWAGE86 )  .004*    .005     .734    .006    .696     .037
E30,E36  (LWAGE84 ,LWAGE85 )  .040*    .009    4.474@   .010   3.866@    .368
E30,E42  (LWAGE84 ,LWAGE86 )  .007*    .009     .774    .009    .778     .069
E30,E48  (LWAGE84 ,LWAGE87 )  .003*    .009     .322    .009    .304     .042
E36,E42  (LWAGE85 ,LWAGE86 )  .013*    .012    1.086    .012   1.080     .115
E36,E48  (LWAGE85 ,LWAGE87 )  .008*    .012     .673    .014    .585     .112
E42,E48  (LWAGE86 ,LWAGE87 )  .000*    .016     .011    .016    .011     .003
D1,D2    (   F1   ,    F2  ) -.004*    .003   -1.437    .003  -1.303    -.258
```

The fit is excellent: robust CFI = 0.992, RMSEA = 0.061 (0.032, 0.091) based on the covariance matrix alone, and RMSEA = 0.048 (0.024, 0.071) based on the covariance matrix and means.

The analysis answers the second question raised above. Since the variances are statistically significant for both 'Constant' and 'Slope', these two parameters vary across respondents.

So let us try to answer the third question and put in variables that could perhaps account for the individual differences in trajectories.

A conditional latent curve model

The model in Figure 4 is often called an *unconditional curve model*. It describes the trajectory *unconditional* on any variable that could have shaped it. If we put in independent variables that we think account for individual differences in trajectories, we obtain a so-called *conditional curve model*, which is the second step in our two-step strategy.

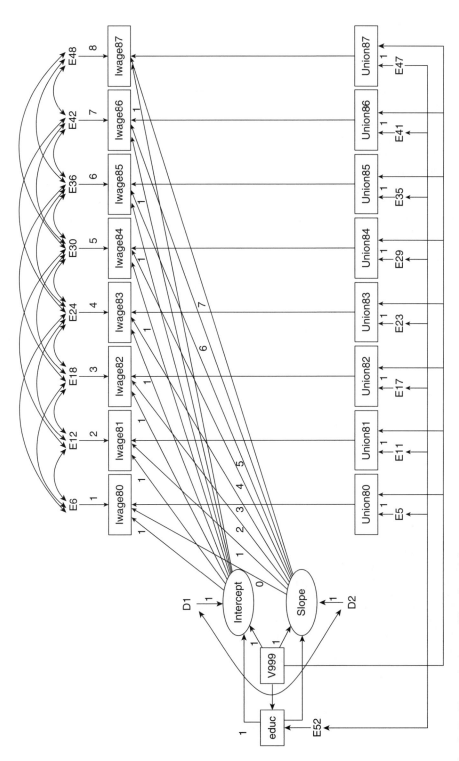

Figure 5 Example 1: conditional model

In their original article, Vella and Veerbek included 16 variables and a number of dummy variables to indicate industry and occupation. Since the purpose here is to illustrate a technique and not to solve a substantive research problem, I will include only two exogenous variables, 'years of schooling' and 'union membership', i.e. a dummy variable indicating whether the wage was negotiated with a union. See Figure 5.

Whereas 'years of schooling' is time independent, 'union' is time dependent.

You may wonder why I have not used 'Diagrammer' when drawing the figure; an explanation follows below.

The program is given in Table 4, but I had problems with the estimation. The process did not converge in 300 iterations. The problem could be that the choice of start values in EQS was not the best one, so I put in start values from the output from the final unconditional model, and for the means I took advantage of the statistics in the output from the first run. The same statistics are of course shown in the output from the second run in Table 6. These revisions are given in Table 5 and a partial output in Table 6. This time I had more luck: the program converged in six steps.

Table 4 Example 1: program for the conditional model (first run)

```
/TITLE
Example 11.1. conditional model, first run. Data from Vella and Veerbek
(1998)
/SPECIFICATIONS
DATA='c:\users\sony\desktop\EQS bog\EQS Chap 11a\wagepan2 41.ess';
VARIABLES=8; CASES=545;
METHOD=ML,ROBUST; ANALYSIS=MOMENT; MATRIX=RAW;
/LABELS
V5=union80;  V6=lwage80; V11=union81; V12=lwage81; V17=union82;
V18=lwage82; V23=union83; V24=lwage83; V29=union84; V30=lwage84;
V35=union85; V36=lwage85; V41=union86; V42=lwage86; V47=union87;
V48=lwage87; V52=educ;

/EQUATIONS
V6  = 1F1 + 0F2 + *V5  + E6;
V12 = 1F1 + 1F2 + *V11 + E12;
V18 = 1F1 + 2F2 + *V17 + E18;
V24 = 1F1 + 3F2 + *V23 + E24;
V30 = 1F1 + 4F2 + *V29 + E30;
V36 = 1F1 + 5F2 + *V35 + E36;
V42 = 1F1 + 6F2 + *V41 + E42;
V48 = 1F1 + 7F2 + *V47 + E48;
        V52 = *V999 + E52;
            V5  = *V999 + E5;
            V11 = *V999 + E11;
            V17 = *V999 + E17;
            V23 = *V999 + E23;
            V29 = *V999 + E29;
            V35 = *V999 + E35;
            V41 = *V999 + E41;
            V47 = *V999 + E47;
                F1 = *V999 + *V52 + D1;
                F2 = *V999 + *V52 + D2;

/VARIANCES
  E6  = *;
  E12 = *;
```

```
       E18 = *;
       E24 = *;
       E30 = *;
       E36 = *;
       E42 = *;
       E48 = *;
       E52 = *;
            E5  = *;
            E11 = *;
            E17 = *;
            E23 = *;
            E29 = *;
            E35 = *;
            E41 = *;
            E47 = *;
                 D1 = *;
                 D2 = *;

/COVARIANCES
       D2,D1 = *;
            E6,E12 = *;
            E6,E18 = *;
            E6,E24 = *;
                 E12,E18 = *;
                 E12,E24 = *;
                 E12,E30 = *;
                      E18,E24 = *;
                      E18,E30 = *;
                      E18,E36 = *;
                           E24,E30 = *;
                           E24,E36 = *;
                           E24,E42 = *;
                                E30,E36 = *;
                                E30,E42 = *;
                                E30,E48 = *;
                                     E36,E42 = *;
                                     E36,E48 = 0.008*;
                                          E42,E48 = 0.000*;
       E5,E11 = *;
       E5,E17 = *;
       E5,E23 = *;
       E5,E29 = *;
       E5,E35 = *;
       E5,E41 = *;
       E5,E47 = *;
       E5,E52 = *;
            E11,E17 = *;
            E11,E23 = *;
            E11,E29 = *;
            E11,E35 = *;
            E11,E41 = *;
            E11,E47 = *;
            E11,E52 = *;
                 E17,E23 = *;
                 E17,E29 = *;
                 E17,E35 = *;
                 E17,E41 = *;
```

(Continued)

Table 4 (Continued)

```
               E17,E47  =  *;
               E17,E52  =  *;
                      E23,E29  =  *;
                      E23,E35  =  *;
                      E23,E41  =  *;
                      E23,E47  =  *;
                      E23,E52  =  *;
                             E29,E35  =  *;
                             E29,E41  =  *;
                             E29,E47  =  *;
                             E29,E52  =  *;
                                    E35,E41  =  *;
                                    E35,E47  =  *;
                                    E35,E52  =  *;
                                           E41,E47  =  *;
                                           E41,E52  =  *;
                                                  E47,E52  =  *;

/PRINT
 FIT=ALL;
 EFFECT=YES;
 TABLE=COMPACT;
 RETEST='BLABLA.OUT;

/END
```

Table 5 Example 1: program for the conditional model (changes for the second run)

```
/TITLE
Example 11.1. conditional model, second run. Data from Vella and
Veerbek (1998)


V52 = 11.77*V999 + E52;
       V5  =  0.25*V999 + E5;
       V11 =  0.25*V999 + E11;
       V17 =  0.26*V999 + E17;
       V23 =  0.25*V999 + E23;
       V29 =  0.25*V999 + E29;
       V35 =  0.22*V999 + E35;
       V41 =  0.21*V999 + E41;
       V47 =  0.26*V999 + E47;
              F1 =  *V999 + *V52 + D1;
              F2 =  *V999 + *V52 + D2;

/VARIANCES
 E6  = 0.202*;
 E12 = 0.152*;
 E18 = 0.124*;
 E24 = 0.111*;
 E30 = 0.098*;
 E36 = 0.123*;
 E42 = 0.104*;
 E48 = 0.045*;
 E52 = *;
```

```
D1 = 0.125*;
D2 = 0.002*;

/COVARIANCES
D2,D1 = 0.004*;
    E6,E12 = 0.017*;
    E6,E18 = 0.010*;
    E6,E24 = 0.008*;
        E12,E18 = 0.034*;
        E12,E24 = 0.026*;
        E12,E30 = 0.0011*;
            E18,E24 = 0.044*;
            E18,E30 = 0.035*;
            E18,E36 = 0.024*;
                E24,E30 = 0.042*;
                E24,E36 = 0.025*;
                E24,E42 = 0.004*;
                    E30,E36 = 0.040*;
                    E30,E42 = 0.007*;
                    E30,E48 = 0.003*;
                        E36,E42 = 0.013*;
                        E36,E48 = 0.008*;
                            E42,E48 = 0.000*;
```

Table 6 Example 1: output for the second run of the conditional model

VARIABLE	UNION80	LWAGE80	UNION81	LWAGE81	UNION82
	V5	V6	V11	V12	V17
MEAN	0.2518	1.3932	0.2500	1.5149	0.2574
SKEWNESS (G1)	1.1434	-1.2304	1.1547	-1.1701	1.1101
KURTOSIS (G2)	-0.6926	3.2237	-0.6667	3.8478	-0.7678
STANDARD DEV.	0.4345	0.5580	0.4334	0.5291	0.4376
VARIABLE	LWAGE82	UNION83	LWAGE83	UNION84	LWAGE84
	V18	V23	V24	V29	V30
MEAN	1.5733	0.2463	1.6205	0.2518	1.7000
SKEWNESS (G1)	-0.6959	1.1775	-0.4100	1.1434	-0.2170
KURTOSIS (G2)	3.3563	-0.6135	1.5571	-0.6926	1.2557
STANDARD DEV.	0.4965	0.4313	0.4804	0.4345	0.4733
VARIABLE	UNION85	LWAGE85	UNION86	LWAGE86	UNION87
	V35	V36	V41	V42	V47
MEAN	0.2243	1.7402	0.2114	1.8005	0.2629
SKEWNESS (G1)	1.3222	-0.8809	1.4137	-0.8945	1.0774
KURTOSIS (G2)	-0.2519	5.1281	-0.0015	3.7287	-0.8392
STANDARD DEV.	0.4175	0.5227	0.4087	0.5152	0.4406
VARIABLE	LWAGE87	EDUC	V999		
	V48	V52	V999		
MEAN	1.8671	11.7647	1.0000		
SKEWNESS (G1)	-0.1466	-0.7488	0.0000		
KURTOSIS (G2)	1.0168	2.4434	0.0000		
STANDARD DEV.	0.4671	1.7484	0.0000		

```
                MULTIVARIATE KURTOSIS
                ---------------------

MARDIA'S COEFFICIENT (G2,P) =    177.6702
NORMALIZED ESTIMATE =             81.5207
```

(Continued)

Table 5 (Continued)

MAXIMUM LIKELIHOOD SOLUTION (NORMAL DISTRIBUTION THEORY)

    PARAMETER ESTIMATES (B) WITH STANDARD ERRORS AND TEST STATISTICS (Z)
    STATISTICS SIGNIFICANT AT THE 5% LEVEL ARE MARKED WITH @.

```
                                                      ROBUST         R-   DEP.
VAR.        PREDICTOR    B       BETA   S.E.   Z     S.E.    Z      SQUARED
-------------------------------------------------------------------------------
V5   (UNION80 )                                                       .000
          V999(   V999 )  .252*  .000   .019  13.507@  .019  13.507@
V6   (LWAGE80 )                                                       .374
          V5   (UNION80 ) .141*  .108   .044   3.206@  .041   3.417@
          F1   (   F1   ) 1.000  .603
V11  (UNION81 )                                                       .000
          V999(   V999 )  .250*  .000   .019  13.441@  .019  13.441@
          E11  (UNION81 ) 1.000 1.000
V12  (LWAGE81)                                                        .434
          V11  (UNION81 ) .154*  .129   .036   4.228@  .035   4.351@
          F1   (   F1   ) 1.000  .659
          F2   (   F2   ) 1.000  .091
V17  (UNION82 )                                                       .000
          V999(   V999 )  .257*  .000   .019  13.705@  .019  13.705@
V18  (LWAGE82 )                                                       .481
          V17  (UNION82 ) .114*  .103   .030   3.818@  .032   3.591@
          F1   (   F1   ) 1.000  .701
          F2   (   F2   ) 2.000  .193
V23  (UNION83 )                                                       .000
          V999(   V999 )  .246*  .000   .019  13.309@  .019  13.309@
V24  (LWAGE83 )                                                       .513
          V23  (UNION83 ) .077*  .070   .029   2.695@  .031   2.490@
          F1   (   F1   ) 1.000  .716
          F2   (   F2   ) 3.000  .296
V29  (UNION84 )                                                       .000
          V999(   V999 )  .252*  .000   .019  13.507@  .019  13.507@
          E29  (UNION84 ) 1.000 1.000
V30  (LWAGE84)                                                        .564
          V29  (UNION84 ) .101*  .093   .027   3.768@  .026   3.817@
          F1   (   F1   ) 1.000  .723
          F2   (   F2   ) 4.000  .399
V35  (UNION85 )                                                       .000
          V999(   V999 )  .224*  .000   .018  12.518@  .018  12.518@
V36  (LWAGE85 )                                                       .536
          V35  (UNION85 ) .094*  .077   .033   2.879@  .024   3.840@
          F1   (   F1   ) 1.000  .671
          F2   (   F2   ) 5.000  .463
V41  (UNION86 )                                                       .000
          V999(   V999 )  .211*  .000   .018  12.054@  .018  12.054@
V42  (LWAGE86 )                                                       .599
          V41  (UNION86 ) .043*  .035   .036   1.210   .032   1.358
          F1   (   F1   ) 1.000  .671
          F2   (   F2   ) 6.000  .555
V47  (UNION87 )                                                       .000
          V999(   V999 )  .263*  .000   .019  13.903@  .019  13.903@
V48  (LWAGE87 )                                                       .794
          V47  (UNION87 ) .029*  .027   .029   1.005   .033    .897
          F1   (   F1   ) 1.000  .724
          F2   (   F2   ) 7.000  .699
V52  (  EDUC  )                                                       .000
          V999(   V999 ) 11.765* .000   .075 156.799@  .075 156.799@
F1   (   F1   )                                                       .108
          V52  (  EDUC  ) .064*  .328   .011   5.987@  .011   6.041@
          V999(   V999 )  .640*  .000   .127   5.020@  .126   5.081@
```

```
F2   (   F2   )                                                                      .021
         V52  (   EDUC   )    .004*    .144    .002    2.218@    .002    2.439@
         V999 (   V999   )    .021*    .000    .021    1.013     .019    1.142
```

VARIANCES OF INDEPENDENT VARIABLES
STATISTICS SIGNIFICANT AT THE 5% LEVEL ARE MARKED WITH @.

```
                                                          ROBUST
                              VARIANCE    S.E.      Z      S.E.       Z
---------------------------------------------------------------------------
ERROR
         E5   (UNION80 )       .189*     .011    16.477@   .009    20.417@
         E6   (LWAGE80 )       .200*     .022     9.202@   .037     5.462@
         E11  (UNION81 )       .188*     .011    16.477@   .009    20.218@
         E12  (LWAGE81 )       .151*     .017     9.150@   .029     5.311@
         E17  (UNION82 )       .191*     .012    16.477@   .009    21.031@
         E18  (LWAGE82 )       .123*     .012    10.269@   .021     5.744@
         E23  (UNION83 )       .186*     .011    16.477@   .009    19.826@
         E24  (LWAGE83 )       .110*     .010    10.832@   .018     6.116@
         E29  (UNION84 )       .189*     .011    16.477@   .009    20.417@
         E30  (LWAGE84 )       .097*     .009    10.300@   .015     6.509@
         E35  (UNION85 )       .174*     .011    16.477@   .010    17.657@
         E36  (LWAGE85 )       .120*     .012     9.609@   .029     4.154@
         E41  (UNION86 )       .167*     .010    16.477@   .010    16.514@
         E42  (LWAGE86 )       .104*     .016     6.666@   .027     3.814@
         E47  (UNION87 )       .194*     .012    16.477@   .009    21.668@
         E48  (LWAGE87 )       .046*     .018     2.564@   .020     2.283@
         E52  (   EDUC  )    3.057*      .186    16.477@   .276    11.075@
DISTURBANCE
         D1   (   F1    )      .104*     .019     5.562@   .020     5.112@
         D2   (   F2    )      .002*     .001     3.053@   .001     2.774@
```

COVARIANCES AMONG INDEPENDENT VARIABLES
STATISTICS SIGNIFICANT AT THE 5% LEVEL ARE MARKED WITH @.

```
                                                                 ROBUST
                                    COVA.    S.E.      Z          S.E.      Z       CORR.
-----------------------------------------------------------------------------------------
   E5,E11   (UNION80 ,UNION81 )     .105*    .009    11.308@      .010    10.855@    .555
   E5,E17   (UNION80 ,UNION82 )     .082*    .009     9.267@      .010     8.669@    .433
   E5,E23   (UNION80 ,UNION83 )     .083*    .009     9.470@      .010     8.773@    .445
   E5,E29   (UNION80 ,UNION84 )     .075*    .009     8.563@      .009     7.908@    .395
   E5,E35   (UNION80 ,UNION85 )     .069*    .008     8.248@      .009     7.391@    .378
   E5,E41   (UNION80 ,UNION86 )     .055*    .008     6.931@      .009     6.133@    .312
   E5,E47   (UNION80 ,UNION87 )     .063*    .009     7.242@      .009     6.705@    .327
   E5,E52   (UNION80 ,  EDUC  )    -.022*    .033     -.664       .030     -.714    -.029
   E6,E12   (LWAGE80 ,LWAGE81 )     .017*    .016     1.046       .018      .931     .097
   E6,E18   (LWAGE80 ,LWAGE82 )     .011*    .012      .959       .013      .878     .073
   E6,E24   (LWAGE80 ,LWAGE83 )     .008*    .009      .874       .010      .805     .055
   E11,E17  (UNION81 ,UNION82 )     .103*    .009    11.132@      .010    10.724@    .544
   E11,E23  (UNION81 ,UNION83 )     .108*    .009    11.637@      .010    11.169@    .576
   E11,E29  (UNION81 ,UNION84 )     .097*    .009    10.684@      .010    10.125@    .516
   E11,E35  (UNION81 ,UNION85 )     .091*    .009    10.485@      .010     9.555@    .504
   E11,E41  (UNION81 ,UNION86 )     .087*    .008    10.275@      .009     9.181@    .491
   E11,E47  (UNION81 ,UNION87 )     .074*    .009     8.432@      .009     7.851@    .388
   E11,E52  (UNION81 ,  EDUC  )     .017*    .033      .510       .028      .599     .022
   E12,E18  (LWAGE81 ,LWAGE82 )     .034*    .012     2.881@      .014     2.416@    .247
   E12,E24  (LWAGE81 ,LWAGE83 )     .026*    .010     2.624@      .011     2.383@    .197
   E12,E30  (LWAGE81 ,LWAGE84 )     .009*    .007     1.437       .007     1.298     .078
   E17,E23  (UNION82 ,UNION83 )     .124*    .010    12.821@      .010    12.876@    .659
   E17,E29  (UNION82 ,UNION84 )     .119*    .010    12.381@      .010    12.362@    .627
   E17,E35  (UNION82 ,UNION85 )     .102*    .009    11.394@      .010    10.655@    .561
   E17,E41  (UNION82 ,UNION86 )     .091*    .009    10.567@      .010     9.573@    .509
```

(Continued)

Table 5 (Continued)

E17,E47	(UNION82 ,UNION87)	.081*	.009	9.063@	.010	8.557@	.422
E17,E52	(UNION82 , EDUC)	.005*	.033	.165	.026	.210	.007
E18,E24	(LWAGE82 ,LWAGE83)	.042*	.009	4.636@	.010	4.425@	.364
E18,E30	(LWAGE82 ,LWAGE84)	.034*	.007	5.063@	.008	4.585@	.315
E18,E36	(LWAGE82 ,LWAGE85)	.022*	.006	3.733@	.006	3.978@	.185
E23,E29	(UNION83 ,UNION84)	.131*	.010	13.367@	.010	13.566@	.700
E23,E35	(UNION83 ,UNION85)	.114*	.009	12.472@	.010	11.750@	.634
E23,E41	(UNION83 ,UNION86)	.101*	.009	11.559@	.010	10.463@	.571
E23,E47	(UNION83 ,UNION87)	.094*	.009	10.289@	.010	9.772@	.492
E23,E52	(UNION83 , EDUC)	-.006*	.032	-.198	.026	-.247	-.008
E24,E30	(LWAGE83 ,LWAGE84)	.041*	.007	6.010@	.007	5.963@	.397
E24,E36	(LWAGE83 ,LWAGE85)	.024*	.006	3.857@	.006	3.856@	.209
E24,E42	(LWAGE83 ,LWAGE86)	.003*	.005	.561	.006	.533	.028
E29,E35	(UNION84 ,UNION85)	.128*	.010	13.406@	.010	13.111@	.703
E29,E41	(UNION84 ,UNION86)	.114*	.009	12.609@	.010	11.780@	.643
E29,E47	(UNION84 ,UNION87)	.107*	.009	11.353@	.010	11.102@	.558
E29,E52	(UNION84 , EDUC)	-.031*	.033	-.946	.027	-1.130	-.041
E30,E36	(LWAGE84 ,LWAGE85)	.039*	.009	4.512@	.010	3.936@	.357
E30,E42	(LWAGE84 ,LWAGE86)	.006*	.008	.694	.008	.742	.059
E30,E48	(LWAGE84 ,LWAGE87)	.003*	.008	.428	.008	.423	.052
E35,E41	(UNION85 ,UNION86)	.122*	.009	13.549@	.010	12.350@	.715
E35,E47	(UNION85 ,UNION87)	.109*	.009	11.841@	.010	11.275@	.590
E35,E52	(UNION85 , EDUC)	.001*	.031	.042	.025	.051	.002
E36,E42	(LWAGE85 ,LWAGE86)	.012*	.011	1.027	.011	1.043	.105
E36,E48	(LWAGE85 ,LWAGE87)	.008*	.012	.674	.013	.589	.106
E41,E47	(UNION86 ,UNION87)	.108*	.009	12.005@	.010	11.256@	.601
E41,E52	(UNION86 , EDUC)	.017*	.031	.544	.024	.698	.023
E42,E48	(LWAGE86 ,LWAGE87)	.000*	.015	.012	.015	.012	.003
E47,E52	(UNION87 , EDUC)	-.014*	.033	-.410	.027	-.497	-.018
D1,D2	(F1 , F2)	-.004*	.003	-1.460	.003	-1.305	-.281

As my a priori expectation is that union-negotiated wages are higher, and that longer education has a positive effect on start wages as well as on the wage rises one can expect, one-sided tests are appropriate when testing regression coefficients.

From Table 6 we can see that union-negotiated wages have had a positive effect on the wage level during the period, but that this effect seems to have followed a negative trend from 1980 to 1987.

Longer education has a positive effect on the start wage as well as on the rate of increase in wage one can expect. However, the effect on rate of increase is much smaller than the effect on the start wage. Perhaps, as time goes by, other factors such as work experience play an increasing role.

The model fit is excellent (robust CFI = 0.991, RMSEA = 0.032 (0.020, 0.044) based on the covariance matrix alone, and RMSEA = 0.032 (0.019, 0.042) based on the covariance matrix and means). What most catches the eye is that none of the covariances involving 'educ' is significant, while most other covariances are highly significant.

It is tempting as a first step to exclude the insignificant covariances involving 'educ'. None of the correlations are numerically larger than 0.04.

However, this conflicts with one of my long-established rules: 'Never leave out correlations among exogenous variables'. So I decided to keep the insignificant covariances. Remember that correlations among exogenous variables are 'acts of nature' and, so to speak, outside your modeling.

An LM test would suggest putting in the covariances (V52, F1) and/or (V52, F2). A substantiated reason for this is that omitted variables that are incorporated in the disturbances and thus affect 'Constant' and 'Slope' also influence a respondent's schooling. There is a long list of such variables: parents' economic condition, and education and race, to mention just a few. I will, however, leave further modifications to you as an exercise.

Instead I will use the limited space at my disposal to discuss (in the next section) some general problems. But first a few words about 'Diagrammer' versus 'Build EQS' in the programming of latent curve models.

'Diagrammer' or 'Build EQS'?

It is apparent from Figure 6 that when modeling LCM in 'Diagrammer' the model easily becomes 'messy'. Remember: this model is a very simple one – I included only two explanatory variables. Think about what the model would look like if I included a few more explanatory variables – or if I included all 16 variables and the various dummies in Vella and Veerbek's original work!

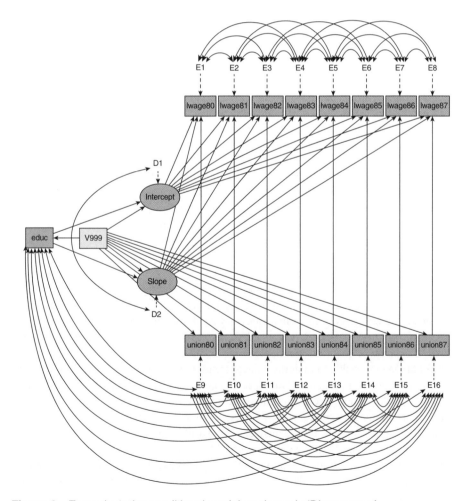

Figure 6 Example 1: the conditional model as drawn in 'Diagrammer'

This messiness has two consequences:

1. Drawing the covariances is time-consuming and you could very easily miss some of them.
2. If you need a graph of your model for publication, you will need a drawing program so that you can depict your model in a way similar to the one I have used in Figure 5.

In such situations 'Build EQS' is much to be preferred.

3 Some Special Problems and Extensions

In this section I will deal with two problems: (1) what to do if the trajectory is not linear and alternative coding of time; and (2) how to interpret the estimated parameters. Lastly in the chapter I will sketch a few extensions of the basic model.

Alternative codings of time

What will you do if an unconditional linear model does not seem to fit?

In other applications of SEM, the natural answer to this question is: 'let us free some fixed parameters'. You can 'unfix' all regression coefficients for the slope parameter except two. The most common thing is to fix the first at zero and the second at one. In this way you use the growth from the first to the second time period as your unit of measurement.

However, if you choose to 'unfix' regression coefficients it is perhaps a better idea to fix the last regression coefficient at one. If you do that, the regression coefficients are interpreted as the cumulative proportion of total (positive or negative) growth from the first measurement. Consequently, differences between regression coefficients reflect the proportion of total growth between the two measurements.

Freeing model parameters in order to improve the fit has one virtue: it maximizes fit with the lowest demands for observations.

It has, however, one serious drawback: making the coding of time dependent on the data is not very practical if you want to compare your results with other studies.

Instead you could try a quadratic trajectory as shown in Figure 7.

As you may have guessed, you need three waves to estimate a linear trend, four waves to estimate a quadratic trend, etc.

It is almost impossible to imagine a linear trend going on for ever – a digressive trend is much more likely in practice. However, the quadratic trend has a drawback in many situations: it will at some point in time reach its point of return and begin to decrease. What is needed in many situations is a digressive function with an upper asymptote. The exponential function could be the answer. This would, however, take us too far for an introductory text; instead, the reader is referred to du Toit and Cudeck (2001).

Sometimes you will find that the variable that defines the time dimension is not the best one, when you consider the purpose of your research. Then you have to redefine the time variable.

As an example, consider an analysis of development in children's reading ability, where you collect data in three waves (i.e. at three points in time). If in any wave there are children of different ages, it might perhaps be better to use age as a time metric.

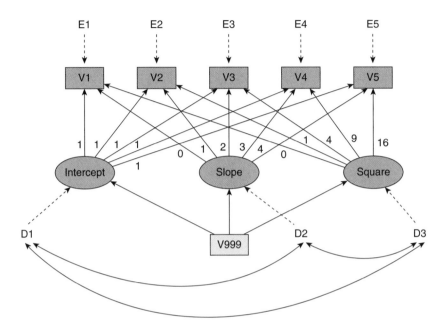

Figure 7 Quadratic trajectory

If children in the first wave are aged 6, 7 and 8 we have in fact three age cohorts. Following these three cohorts through three waves will result in a time variable having values 6, 7, 8, 9 and 10. However, we have only three observations on each child and consequently a lot of missing data: the first cohort will have missing values at 'times' 9 and 10, the second at 'times' 6 and 10, and the third at 'times' 6 and 7. It might perhaps also be a problem that the observations on children of the same age are not collected at the same time. For an extensive treatment of these problems see Bollen and Curran (2006).

Interpreting the model parameters

The regression coefficients linking the exogenous variables to the latent factors and to the growth variable ('lwage' in our example) are the parameters of main interest in the conditional model.

Until now we have looked only at the time-invariant variable's influence on the constant and the slope parameters in our trajectory, and in this case the influences were both highly significant. But does that mean that the time-invariant variable also has the same significant influence on our growth variable ('lwage') at all points in time? Not necessarily (Curran, Bauer, & Willoughby, 2004, 2006).

To keep things simple and in general terms, I have added in Figure 8 a time-invariant variable to the model in Figure 1, and at the same time introduced a few λ-terms to underpin that the following arguments are independent of the coding of time.

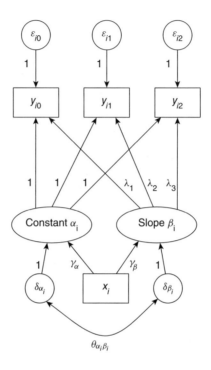

Figure 8 Conditional latent curve model based on the model in Figure 1

The following equations are just a repetition of (2) stating the *unconditional* model

$$y_{it} = \alpha_i + \beta_{1i} \lambda_t + \varepsilon_{it}$$
$$\alpha_i = \mu_\alpha + \delta_{\alpha i}$$
$$\beta_i = \mu_\beta + \delta_{\beta i} \tag{4}$$

with the same conditions. I now modify this model as follows to represent the conditional model in Figure 8:

$$y_{it} = \alpha_i + \beta_i \lambda_t + \varepsilon_{it} \tag{5a}$$
$$\alpha_i = \mu_\alpha + \gamma_\alpha x_i + \delta_{\alpha i} \tag{5b}$$
$$\beta_i = \mu_\beta + \gamma_\beta x_i + \delta_{\beta i} \tag{5c}$$

11.3 Some Special Problems and Extensions

By inserting (5b) and (5c) in (5a) we obtain

$$y_{it} = \mu_\alpha + \gamma_\alpha x_i + \delta_{\alpha_i} + (\mu_\beta + \gamma_\beta x_i + \delta_{\beta i})\lambda_t + \varepsilon_{it}$$
$$= (\mu_\alpha + \mu_\beta \lambda_t + \gamma_\alpha x_i + \gamma_\beta \lambda_t x_i) + (\delta_{\alpha_i} + \delta_{\beta_i}\lambda_t + \varepsilon_{it}) \quad (6)$$

Looking at the terms in the first parentheses in the second line, $\mu_\beta \lambda_t$ depicts the main effect of time on the repeated measure, $\gamma_\alpha x_i$ is the main effect of the time-invariant variable x_i and the last term $\gamma_\beta \lambda_t x_i$ is the interaction effect between the two. However, this interaction is also the indirect effect of x_i via the slope variable.

All of this boils down to the simple conclusion that the effect of the regressor x on the repeated measure depends on time λ_t and vice versa.

Often one of the two conditional effects on the repeated measurement (i.e. the effect of time conditional on a time-invariant regressor, or the effect of a time-invariant regressor conditional on time) is the main interest in a study, but most often an analysis stops short of that way of thinking.

Taking the expectation of (6), we get

$$\mu_{y_t} = \mu_\alpha + \mu_\beta \lambda_t + \gamma_\alpha x_i + \gamma_\beta \lambda_t x_i \quad (7a)$$

and after rearrangement

$$\mu_{yt} = (\mu_\alpha + \gamma_\alpha x_i) + (\mu_\beta + \gamma_\beta x_i)\lambda_t \quad (7b)$$

which clearly shows that, while the expected value of the repeated measurement is a linear function of time, this linear function depends on the value of the time-invariant variable x_i.

From the symmetry in (7a) you can get an analogous equation expressing μ_{yt} as a linear function of x_i, conditional on λ_t.

Example 1 (continued)

Let us take a look at the effect of time on 'lwage' conditional on years of education.

For this we need the means of F1 and F2. As you will remember from the comments to Figure 9.1, these are the total effects on the two factors from the constant V999. The line

EFFECT=YES

in the /PRINT paragraph includes total and indirect effects in the output. However, we are interested only in that part of the output given in Table 7.

We insert our estimates (from Table 7) $\hat{\mu}_\alpha = 1.393$, $\hat{\mu}_\beta = 0.067$, $\gamma_\alpha = 0.064$ and $\gamma_\beta = 0.004$ in (7b):

$$\mu_{yi/\lambda t} = (1.393 + 0.064 x_i) + (0.067 + 0.004 x_i)\lambda_t \quad (8)$$

Table 7 Example 1: estimating the means of intercept and slope

```
MAXIMUM LIKELIHOOD SOLUTION (NORMAL DISTRIBUTION THEORY)

  DECOMPOSITION OF EFFECTS

  PARAMETER TOTAL EFFECTS
  STATISTICS SIGNIFICANT AT THE 5% LEVEL ARE MARKED WITH @.

                                     STD.                    ROBUST
  DEP.VAR.    PREDICTOR     COEF     COEF     S.E.    Z      S.E.     Z
  ----------------------------------------------------------------------

  F1   -   F1
           V52   -   EDUC   .064*    .328    .011   5.987@   .011    6.041@
           V999- V999      1.393*    .000    .021  67.325@   .249    5.591@
           E52   -   EDUC   .064     .328    .011   5.987@   .011    6.041@
  F2   -   F2
           V52   -   EDUC   .004*    .144    .002   2.218@   .002    2.439@
           V999- V999       .067*    .000    .003  19.295@   .037    1.803
           E52   -   EDUC   .004     .144    .002   2.218@   .002    2.439@
```

Let us compare the trajectories for young men with 8 years of education and 18 years of education:

$$\mu_{yt/8} = (1.393 + 0.064 \times 8) + (0.067 + 0.004 \times 8)\lambda_t \qquad (9a)$$

$$\mu_{yt/18} = (1.393 + 0.064 \times 18) + (0.067 + 0.004 \times 18)\lambda_t \qquad (9b)$$

which gives

$$\mu_{yt/8} = 1.905 + 0.099\lambda_t \qquad (9c)$$

$$\mu_{yt/18} = 2.545 + 0.139\lambda_t \qquad (9d)$$

From this we can see that not only is the start wage higher for young men with 18 years of education, but while the yearly growth rate in wage is about 10% if you have 8 years of education, it is about 14% if you have 18 years of education.

That was a lot of calculating you had to do without much help from EQS, and in a serious analysis of this kind you also need to estimate variances and standard errors. Fortunately there is a calculator available at http://www.quantpsy.org/interact that will assist you (Preacher, Curran, & Bauer, 2006).

Some Extensions of the Latent Curve Model

In this chapter I have barely scratched the surface of the subject, and to give you some idea of the many possibilities that SEM offers in the analysis of panel-like data, I will sketch a couple of examples.

Example 2
Multivariate latent curve model: development of mathematical skills

Imagine we want to analyze the progress in math ability of a group of students measured once a year over four years. The model in Figure 9 is parallel to the one in Figure 4, with sex as the time-invariant variable and reading ability as the time-dependent variable.

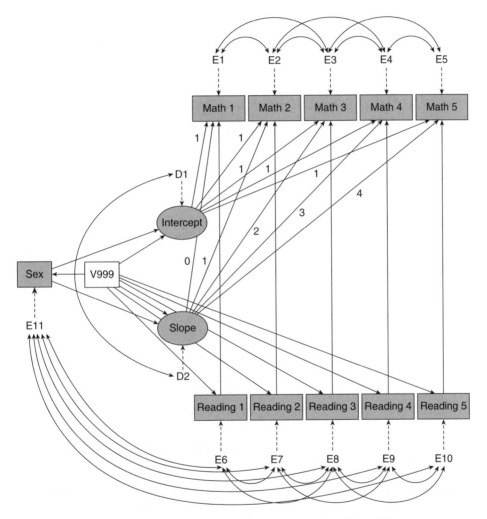

Figure 9 Example 2: math ability as a function of sex and reading ability

However, perhaps it would be a better foundation for the analysis to start by getting a feel for the trajectories of both math and reading ability as shown in Figure 10.

Introducing reading ability as a 'cause' of math ability can be done in several ways. You could substitute one-headed arrows between factors for one or more correlations between the disturbances in Figure 10, or – if you wish to keep year-by-year connections between math and reading abilities as in Figure 9 – you could analyze the data as a four-period cross-lagged panel design as in Figure 6.2. You could even combine the cross-lagged panel design with a linear curve model (Bollen & Curran, 2006: 210ff.).

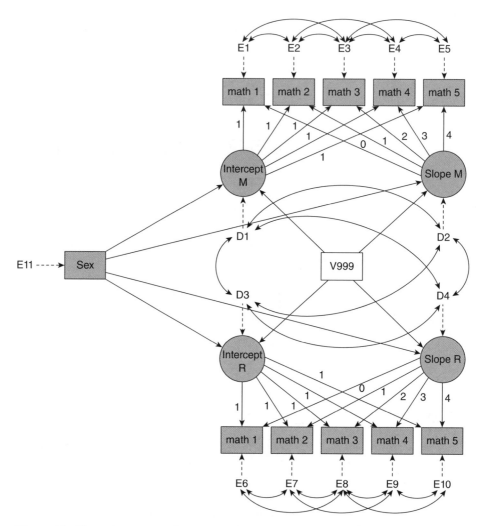

Figure 10 Example 2: unconditional model of trajectories of math and reading ability

Example 3
Multiple indicator model: democracy in developing countries

Imagine that you want to follow up the analysis of democracy in developing countries in Example 7.1 to find out whether democracy is gaining or losing ground over time. So you perform a third wave of data collection and construct the model in Figure 11.

You should compare this model with the one in Figure 7.2.

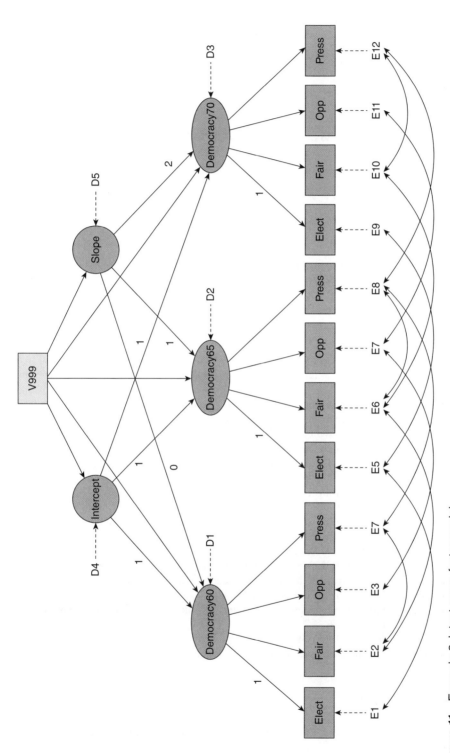

Figure 11 Example 3: latent curve factor model

In this chapter you met the following concepts:

- latent curve model
- trajectory
- unconditional and conditional LCM
- time-dependent and time-independent regressors

You have also learned the following EQS statements:

```
/SPECIFICATIONS

   DE=n;
```

Question

1. Compare LCM with other techniques for the analysis of longitudinal data. Discuss the virtues and vices of the various techniques using examples from your own field of study or research.

References

Bollen, K. A., & Curran, P. J. (2006). *Latent curve models: A structural equation perspective.* Hoboken, NJ: Wiley.

Curran, P.J., Bauer, D.J., & Willoughby, M.T. (2004). Testing and probing main effects and interactions in latent curve analysis. *Psychological Methods, 9,* 220–237.

Curran, P.J., Bauer, D.J., & Willoughby, M.T. (2006). Testing and probing interactions in hierarchical linear growth models. In C. S. B. S. M. Boker (Ed.), *Methodological Issues in Aging Research* (Vol. 1, pp. 99–129). Mahwah, NJ: Lawrence Erlbaum Associates.

du Toit, S. H., & Cudeck, R. (2001). The analysis of non-linear random coefficient regression models with LISREL using constraints. In R. Cudeck, S. du Toit, & D. Sörbom (Eds.), *Structural equation modeling: Present and future.* Lincolnwood, IL: Scientific Software.

Meredith, W., & Tisak, J. (1984). *On 'Tuckerizing' curves.* Paper presented at the Annual meeting of the Psychometric Society, Santa Barbara, CA.

Meredith, W., & Tisak, J. (1990). Latent curve analysis. *Psychometrika, 55*(1), 107–122.

Preacher, D. J., Curran, P. J., & Bauer, D. J. (2006). Computational tools for probing interactions in multiple linear regression, multilevel modeling, and latent curve analysis. *Journal of Educational and Behavioral Statistics, 31,* 437–448.

Tucker, L. R. (1958). Determination of parameters of a functional relation by factor analysis. *Psychometrika, 23,* 19–23.

Vella, F., & Veerbek, M. (1998). Whose wages do unions raise? A dynamic model of unionism and wage rate determinination for young men. *Journal of Applied Econometrics, 61,* 783–820.

Further Reading

Bollen, K. A., & Curran, P. J. (2006). *Latent curve models: A structural equation perspective.* Hoboken, NJ: Wiley.

Duncan, T. E., Duncan, S. C., & Strycker, L. A. (2006). *An introduction to latent variable growth curve modeling: Concepts, issues, and application* (2nd ed.). Mahwah, NJ: Lawrence Erlbaum Associates.

Appendices

A
Statistical Prerequisites

This appendix is intended as a statistical refresher, and can be read as an introduction to the book or consulted when necessary during reading of the main text.
The appendix contains the following sections:

1. Probability and Probability Distributions
2. Describing Your Data
3. Sample and Population (Including Estimation and Testing)
4. Correlation and Regression

1 Probability and Probability Distributions

If A_i for $i = 1, 2, 3, \ldots$ is a series of mutual exclusive and collective exhaustive *events*, having probabilities $P(A_i)$ of occurring, then X is called a *random variable*, if the value of X depends on A.

A *probability function* is a function $f(X)$ that assigns a probability to every possible value of X. If $f(X)$ is a probability function, then

$$\sum_i f(x_i) = 1.00 \tag{1}$$

if X is discrete, i.e. can only take on a countable number of values, and

$$\int_i f(x_i) = 1.00 \tag{2}$$

if X is continuous, i.e. can take on all values (possibly only in one or more intervals).
In this book, most often the event is that respondent i is included in a random sample from some population, and X_i is the value of some measurement taken on this respondent, e.g. his or her answer to a question in a questionnaire.

The normal distribution
The probability function you will most often meet in this book is the *normal distribution*. The normal distribution is a symmetrical, bell-shaped distribution, as can be seen from Figure 1. The normal distribution is continuous with probability function

$$f(x \mid \mu, \sigma^2) = (\sigma\sqrt{2\pi})^{-1} e^{-(x-\mu)^2/2\sigma^2} \tag{3}$$

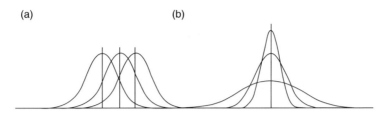

Figure 1 Normal distributions: (a) with the same σ but different μ; (b) with the same μ but different σ

The distribution has two *parameters* μ and σ^2 μ is the so-called *expected value* (the 'mean') of the distribution, and σ^2 is the *variance* (a measure of the 'spread'). I will have more to say on expected value and variance later on.

If for example you want to calculate the probability that a normally distributed random variable with μ =20 and σ^2 = 4 takes on values less than or equal to 25, you *standardize* the variable to have μ =0 and σ^2 = 1, by subtracting μ and dividing by σ:

$$P(X \leq 25 \setminus \mu = 20; \sigma^2 = 4) = P\left(\frac{X-\mu}{\sigma} \leq \frac{25-20}{2}\right) = P(Z \leq 2.5) = 0.994$$

The value 0.994 can be read from a table of the *standard normal distribution.*

The chi-square distribution

The chi-square distribution – usually denoted by χ^2 – is a continuous one-parameter distribution. Its parameter is usually denoted by ν (the Greek letter nu), which can take on all positive integer values. The distribution is right-skewed, the skewness declining with increasing values of ν. For ν → ∞ the chi-square distribution approaches a normal distribution. See Figure 2.

The main purpose of χ^2 is as a measure of a model's accordance with some data.

2 Describing Your Data

The most obvious way to describe your sample data is to depict the distribution in a histogram, but often you need only to summarize the characteristics of the distribution in a few figures.

The central tendency in a distribution of a variable X is most often summarized in the *mean* of the observations

$$\bar{X} = \frac{\sum_{i=1}^{n} X_i}{n} \qquad (4)$$

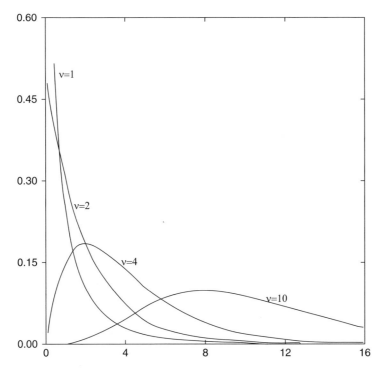

Figure 2 Chi-square distributions

where n is the sample size. Likewise the spread of the data is most often measured by the *variance*, the mean of the squared deviations around the mean

$$s^2 = \frac{\sum_{i=1}^{n}(X_i - \bar{X})^2}{n-1} \qquad (5)$$

In defining the variance as the *mean* of the squared deviations around the mean, you may wonder why I divided by $n - 1$ and not n in the expression (5). An explanation follows in Section 3.

Now, the variance is measured in other units than the data, which could be a little annoying, e.g. in dealing with people's heights measured in centimeters, the spread would be measured in square centimeters! To solve this problem we take the square root of the variance in order to obtain the *standard deviation*

$$s = \sqrt{s^2} = \sqrt{\frac{(X - \bar{X})^2}{n-1}} \qquad (6)$$

and thus return to the original measurement units.

The mean and variance (or standard deviation) say nothing (or little) about the shape of the distribution. We need a measure for describing the skewness. In EQS skewness is measured by

$$M_3 = \frac{\sum_{i=1}^{n}(X_i - \bar{X})^3}{ns^2} \tag{7}$$

If $M_3 = 0$, the distribution is symmetric, if $M_3 > 0$, it has a long upper tail, and if $M_3 < 0$, it has a long lower tail.

The last descriptor of univariate distributions is the *kurtosis*

$$M_4 = \frac{\sum_{i=1}^{n}(X_i - \bar{X})^4}{ns^4} \tag{8a}$$

Most often kurtosis is interpreted as a measure of 'peakiness' but in fact this descriptor is a bit more complicated (DeCarlo, 1997).

If you have a symmetric distribution – such as the normal in Figure 1 – you can think of it as consisting of three parts: the peak, the shoulders (in the normal case located around $\bar{X} - s$ and $\bar{X} + s$) and the tails.

For a normal distribution $M_4 = 3$. If $M_4 > 3$ the distribution is 'peakier' and has thicker tails than a normal distribution *with the same variance*. In other words, you can imagine that weight is pushed from the shoulders towards the peak and – in order to preserve variance – also towards the tails. If $M_4 < 3$, the weight is pushed from the peak and the tails towards the shoulders: the distribution gets flatter with thinner tails.

In EQS, Equation (8a) is normalized by subtracting 3, so that a normal distribution gets a kurtosis of zero:

$$M_4 = \frac{\sum_{i=1}^{n}(X_i - \bar{X})^4}{ns^4} - 3 \tag{8b}$$

3 Sample and Population

Usually your interest is not in the sample itself, but in making inferences about the population from which the sample was drawn. Then the sample statistics defined in (4)–(8) are considered *estimators* of the equivalent population parameters as shown in Table 1, where N is the size of the population.

For continuous variables integrals should be substituted for the summations. I have chosen to forgo the complications of distinguishing between finite and infinite populations – so in the following think about a finite population being large enough to consider it infinite!

Table 1 Sample statistics and population parameters

Sample	Population
$\bar{X} = \dfrac{\sum_{i=1}^{n} X_i}{n}$	$\mu = \dfrac{\sum_{j=1}^{N} X_j}{N}$
$s^2 = \dfrac{\sum_{i=1}^{n} (X_i - \bar{X})^2}{n-1}$	$\sigma^2 = \dfrac{\sum_{j=1}^{N} (X_j - \mu)^2}{N}$
$M_3 = \dfrac{\sum_{i=1}^{n} (X_i - \bar{X})^3}{ns^2}$	$\mu^3 = \dfrac{\sum_{j=1}^{N} (X_j - \mu)^3}{N\sigma^2}$
$M_4 = \dfrac{\sum_{i=1}^{n} (X_i - \bar{X})^4}{ns^4}$	$\mu_4 = \dfrac{\sum_{i=1}^{n} (X_j - \mu)^4}{N\sigma^4}$

Estimation and degrees of freedom

It seems reasonable to use

$$\hat{\sigma}^2 = \frac{\sum_{i=1}^{n}(X_i - \bar{X})^2}{n} \qquad (9)$$

as an estimator of σ^2. In fact it can be shown that $\bar{X}$ and $\hat{\sigma}^2$ are *maximum likelihood estimators* of the corresponding population parameters – that is, they give the values of the parameters that have the largest probability of producing the sample statistics.

However, it can be shown that (9) has a tendency to underestimate the population variance. This is no surprise, because ideally the unknown μ should be used in the numerator of (9), and the sample will of course cluster more around $\bar{X}$ than around μ. In order to correct for this, the denominator is reduced by one in (5). Of course this is no proof that reducing the denominator by one is the right thing to do, but it is!

Looking at the numerator, it consists of a sum of squares of n terms. However, these n terms are not independent. If you know the values of the first $n - 1$ terms, you also know the last term because of the restriction

$$\sum_{i=1}^{n}(X_i - \bar{X}) = 0 \qquad (10)$$

so you could say that, in a way, s^2 is the 'mean' of *independent* squared deviations around the sample mean.

s^2 is an *unbiased* estimator of σ^2. This means that if you take a 'large' number of samples from the population and calculate s^2 for every sample, then the average of s^2 across the samples – the expected value of the *sampling distribution* of s^2 – will equal σ^2.

The denominator $n - 1$ in (5) is called the *degrees of freedom*, and the general rule is that for each estimate based on sample information that is substituted for a parameter value, you lose one degree of freedom.

It is worth mentioning that as estimation in SEM is generally based on maximum likelihood estimation or other estimation methods with similar large-sample properties, all variances and covariances in the output are maximum likelihood estimates using n as the denominator, while the entries in the input covariance matrix are supposed to be unbiased estimates.

The standard deviation of a sampling distribution is called the *standard error* of that particular estimator. In the case of the sample mean, the standard error is

$$\sigma_{\bar{X}} = \frac{\sigma}{\sqrt{n}} \qquad (11a)$$

and is estimated as

$$s_{\bar{X}} = \frac{s}{\sqrt{n}} \qquad (11b)$$

If the sample is sufficiently large – or if the population from which it is drawn is normal – the sampling distribution of the mean is normal. This means that a 95% *confidence interval* for the mean can be constructed as

$$\mu \approx \bar{X} \pm 1.96s \qquad (12)$$

Meaning that there is a probability of 0.95 that the actual interval contains the (unknown) parameter μ.

Interval estimates for other parameters are constructed in similar ways.

Properties of estimators

The quality of estimators is judged on several criteria, of which the most important are as follows:

1. An estimator $\hat{\theta}$ is *unbiased* if $E(\hat{\theta}) = \theta$.
2. An estimator is $\hat{\theta}$ *efficient* if its sampling distribution has a small variance.
3. An estimator is *consistent* if it tends to be near the population parameter as the sample becomes larger. If an estimator is biased, consistency assures that the bias becomes smaller as the sample size increases.

4. An estimator is *sufficient* if it contains all information from the sample that bears on the unknown parameter. For example, $\bar{X}$ is a sufficient estimator of μ: once you have computed $\bar{X}$, no other sample statistic can add to the information about μ.

It can be shown that $\bar{X}$ is unbiased, consistent and sufficient. Further, $\bar{X}$ is the most efficient of all unbiased estimators of μ.

The central limit theorem

This theorem states that if X_i (i = 1, 2, 3,...,n) is a sequence of random observations from a population and $f(X_i)$ has a finite variance, then under fairly general conditions

$$\hat{\theta} = \sum_i \alpha_i X_i \qquad (13)$$

converges towards a normal distribution as $n \to \infty$.

This in fact means that most of the estimators you will meet in this book are asymptotically normally distributed.

Statistical testing

Often you will want to test a hypothesis about the population from which the sample is taken. The idea is that you make all calculations on the assumption that the hypothesis you want to support is false and if you then end up with an unlikely result, either a miracle has happened or your starting point, that your hypothesis is wrong, must be rejected. Usually the last interpretation is the more realistic of the two.

You go through the following steps:

1. Formulation of *null hypothesis* H_0 and *alternative hypothesis* H_1. H_1 is the hypothesis you want to support, and H_0 is the opposite hypothesis.
2. Determination of *significance level* α. α is the maximum probability for rejecting H_0 if H_0 is true; α is most often (arbitrarily) set at 0.05.
3. Choice of a *test statistic* (e.g. $\bar{X}$), the sampling distribution of which is known if H_0 is true.
4. Calculation of the value of the test statistic.
5. Calculation of the P-value, the probability of observing the actual value of the test statistic, or a value that casts even more doubt on H_0, assuming that H_0 is true.
6. Conclusion: if $P < \alpha$, reject H_0 (and accept H_1), otherwise accept H_0.

Example 1

Say you want to test the hypothesis that the mean length of a certain component in a large production batch is at least 25 cm, and you have drawn a simple random sample of 50 components from the batch.

Let us now go through the six steps above:

1. $H_0: \mu \leq 25$
   $H_1: \mu > 25$
2. α is (traditionally!) set at 0.05.
3. I choose to base my conclusion on the value of $\bar{X}$, which is normally distributed here with largest mean $\mu = 25$ and variance given by (11) if H_0 is true.
4. $\bar{X}$ is calculated at 26.5 cm with a standard error of 0.83.
5. $P(\bar{X} \geq 26.5 \mid \mu = 25) = P\left(Z \geq \dfrac{26.5 - 25}{0.83}\right) = P(Z \geq 1.81)$ where Z is standard normally distributed. This probability is read from a table of the standard normal distribution to be 0.035.
6. As the probability of getting a sample mean equal to or larger than the one observed is so small (smaller than α) if H_0 is true, we reject H_0, and conclude that (in all probability) $\mu > 25$.

One- and two-sided tests

The example above was a one-sided test. You will also meet two-sided alternative hypotheses such as

$$H_0: \mu = 25$$
$$H_1: \mu \neq 25$$

In this situation you will be interested in both positive and negative deviations.

The trouble with this formulation is that you know beforehand that H_0 is false. It is not very likely that $\mu = 25.000000000000\ldots$ and so on to infinity. If your sample is large enough you will reject H_0. So what is the rationale behind this sort of test?

You will meet this situation whenever you have a 'sharp' null hypothesis and a 'soft' alternative.

The chi-square test

I shall not go deeply into the actual calculations involved, but just point out that χ^2 is used to test the fit of a model to the data at hand. The model could have many forms, but whatever it is, the null and alternative hypotheses are

$$H_0: \text{the model fits the data exactly}$$
$$H_1: \text{the model does not fit the data}$$

Observe that when testing for model fit in SEM, the roles of the two hypotheses are interchanged. Now H_0 is the hypothesis you want the data to support, and as no model fits the data exactly, H_0 is false a priori with the consequences mentioned above.

4 Correlation and Regression

SEM is about mapping relations between variables, so traditional correlation and regression analysis is a natural primer for SEM.

You can calculate the means and the variances of two variables (call them X and Y), but you also need a measure of the interdependence of the two. To that end you can compute their covariance

$$s_{XY} = \frac{\sum_{i=1}^{n}(X_i - \bar{X})(Y_i - \bar{Y})}{n-1} \qquad (14)$$

which is an unbiased estimator of the population covariance

$$\sigma_{XY} = \frac{\sum_{i=1}^{N}(X_i - \mu_X)(Y_i - \mu)}{N} \qquad (15)$$

The covariance is a sort of 'mix' of the two variances (a variable's covariance with itself is its variance).

If $s_{xy} = 0$, the two variables are *linearly* independent; if $s_{xy} > 0$ the two variables are *positively correlated*, i.e. they covary *linearly* in the way that if one goes up, the other does too; and if $s_{xy} < 0$ they covary linearly in the opposite direction.

A problem with the covariance as a measure of correlation (linear interdependence) is that it has no upper or lower limit because its size depends on the units of measurement. So, how large numerically should a covariance be, before we accept that a (positive or negative) correlation is present?

If we standardize both variables

$$X_i^* = \frac{X_i - \bar{X}}{S_X} \text{ and } Y_i^* = \frac{Y_i - \bar{Y}}{S_Y} \qquad (16)$$

to have mean 0 and variance 1, and then calculate the covariance between the two

$$r = \frac{\sum(X_i^*)(Y_i^*)}{n-1} = \frac{\sum(X_i - \bar{X})(Y_i - \bar{Y})}{(n-1)s_X s_Y} = \frac{\sum(X_i - \bar{X})(Y_i - \bar{Y})}{\sqrt{\sum(X_i - \bar{X})^2 \sum(Y_i - \bar{Y})^2}} \qquad (17)$$

we obtain the so-called (*simple*) *correlation coefficient*, which is scale independent and bounded within the limits $-1 \leq r \leq 1$. Further, r^2 (*the coefficient of determination*) indicates the proportion of the variance that one variable has in common with the other.

Equation (17) is a biased estimate of the population parameter, which is defined as

$$\rho = \sum_{i=1}^{n} \left(\frac{X - \mu_X}{\sigma_X}\right)\left(\frac{Y - \mu_Y}{\sigma_Y}\right) \Big/ N \qquad (18)$$

Example 2
Estimating covariance and correlation coefficient

Bredahl (2001) used SEM in a cross-national study of factors influencing consumers' attitudes and buying intentions towards genetically modified food products (Example 4.1).

As an illustration I will use the first 20 observations on the variables 'tech' (attitude to genetic modification in food production) and 'risk' (perceived risk by using genetically modified food) from Example 4.1, as shown in Figure 3.

You can download the complete data set as an SPSS file from the book's website.

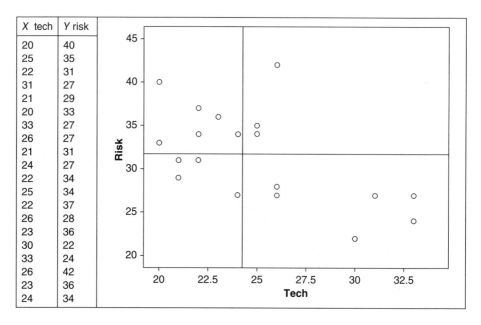

X tech	Y risk
20	40
25	35
22	31
31	27
21	29
20	33
33	27
26	27
21	31
24	27
22	34
25	34
22	37
26	28
23	36
30	22
33	24
26	42
23	36
24	34

Figure 3 Data for correlation and regression analysis

Means, variances, standard deviations and covariance are calculated as shown in Table 2.
In this case we have

$$r = \frac{-243.9000}{\sqrt{310.5500 \times 532.2000}} = -0.6000 \tag{19}$$

which gives $r^2 = 0.36$. The two variables have 36% of their variance in common.

Simple regression analysis

While the covariances and correlation coefficients are measures of covariation, and as such measures of what we could call a symmetric relationship, in (simple) regression analysis one variable (e.g. X) is called the *independent* variable or *predictor* or *regressor* and the other (Y) is called the *dependent* or *criterion* variable, and the purpose is to estimate the parameters in the model

$$Y_i = \beta_0 + \beta_1 X_i + \varepsilon_i \tag{20}$$

with the aim of predicting the value of Y from knowledge of the value of X.

Table 2 Calculation of sample statistics

	X = tech	Y = tech	$(X_i-\bar{X})^2$	$(Y_i-\bar{Y})^2$	$(X_i-\bar{X})(Y_i-\bar{Y})$
	20	40	23.5225	68.8900	−40.2550
	25	35	0.0225	10.8900	0.4950
	22	31	8.1225	0.4900	1.9950
	31	27	37.8225	22.0900	−28.9050
	21	29	14.8225	7.2900	10.3950
	20	33	23.5225	1.6900	−6.3050
	33	27	66.4225	22.0900	−38.3050
	26	27	1.3225	22.0900	−5.4050
	21	31	14.8225	0.4900	2.6950
	24	27	0.7225	22.0900	3.9950
	22	34	8.1225	5.2900	−6.5550
	25	34	0.0225	5.2900	0.3450
	22	37	8.1225	28.0900	−15.1050
	26	28	1.3225	13.6900	−4.2550
	23	36	3.4225	18.4900	−7.9550
	30	22	26.5225	94.0900	−49.9550
	33	24	66.4225	59.2900	−62.7550
	26	42	1.3225	106.0900	11.8450
	23	36	3.4225	18.4900	−7.9550
	24	34	0.7225	5.2900	−1.9550
Σ	497	634	310.5500	532.2000	−243.9000
Σ/20	24.85	31.70			
Σ/19			16.3447	28.0105	−12.8368
Σ/19			4.04	5.29	
	↑	↑	↑	↑	↑
	$\bar{X}$	$\bar{Y}$	S_X^2	S_Y^2	S_{XY}

It is assumed that:

1(a) the values of X are known and fixed a priori (e.g. through an experimental design); or

1(b) X is a stochastic variable that is uncorrelated with ε and whose distribution is independent of the regression coefficients.

In addition we assume that:

2. the error terms ε_i that depict the combined effects of all other factors having an effect on Y are uncorrelated and all have expected value 0 and the same variance.

Under these conditions the parameters of (20) can be estimated using least squares minimizing of the variance of ε_i.

If the error terms can be assumed to be normally distributed, you can calculate confidence intervals for the population parameters and test various hypotheses about them.

If the variables are standardized before the analysis, the regression coefficients are usually called *beta coefficients*.

Example 3
Simple regression analysis using SPSS

You use the same data set as in the previous example. After opening the data set in SPSS, choose 'Analyze/Regression/Linear' as shown in Figure 4a, and the window in Figure 4b will appear. Select the variable *risk*, and by clicking the top little arrow, move the variable from the left panel to the box marked 'Dependent'. Then select the variable *tech* and move it to the box marked 'Independent' by clicking the appropriate little arrow. When you click 'OK', the output in Table 3 will be shown.

(a)

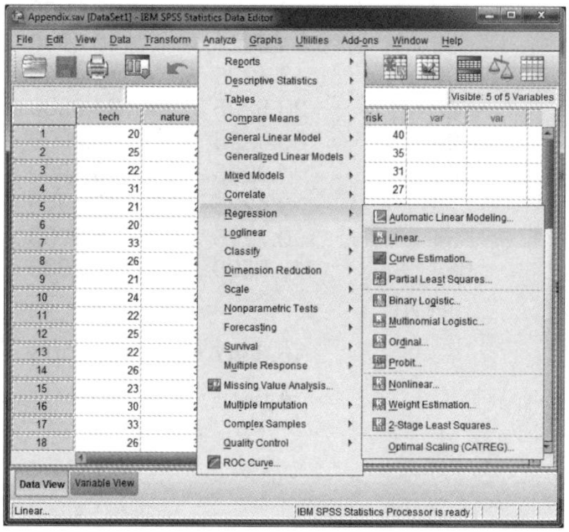

(b)

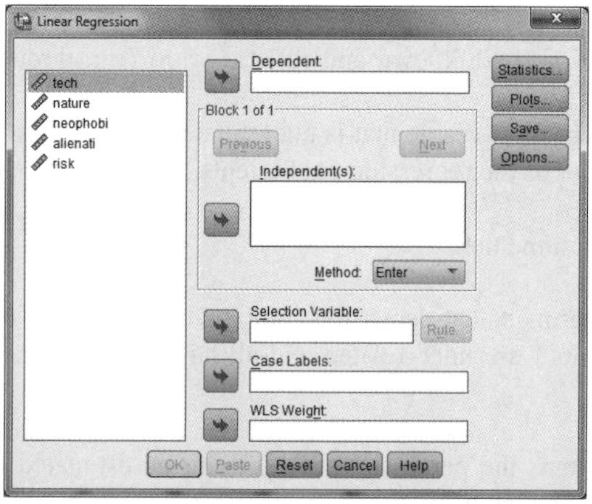

Figure 4 Example 3: the first steps in regression analysis in SPSS

In the first table, note that (in connection with regression analysis) SPSS calculates the correlation coefficient as positive, although we know from (18) that, in this case, it is negative! This is because SPSS uses the same algorithm as in the calculation of the multiple correlation coefficient – see next section. I will postpone commenting on the output in the second table to the next section on multiple regression.

In the third table you will find estimates of the parameters making up the line shown in Figure 5. The equation for the estimated regression line is

$$\hat{Y} = 51.217 - 0.785X \tag{21}$$

and the standard deviation of the error term is estimated at 4.350. It is found in the first table, where it is called *Std. Error of the Estimate*.

Table 3 Example 3: output from SPSS

Model Summary

Model	R	R Square	Adjusted R Square	Std. Error of the Estimate
1	.600(a)	.360	.324	4.350

a Predictors: (Constant), tech

ANOVA (b)

Model		Sum of Squares	df	Mean Square	F	Sig.
1	Regression	191.554	1	191.554	10.122	.005(a)
	Residual	340.646	18	18.925		
	Total	532.200	19			

a Predictors: (Constant), tech
b Dependent Variable: risk

Coefficients (a)

Model		Unstandardized Coefficients		Standardized Coefficients		
		B	Std. Error	Beta	t	Sig.
1	(Constant)	51.217	6.211		8.246	.000
	tech	-.785	.247	-.600	-3.181	.005

a Dependent Variable: risk

Next to the estimates 51.217 and −.785 are the standard errors of the two estimates. If ε_i (for $i = 1, 2, \ldots, n$) follow the same normal distribution with mean 0, then $t = b_j / std(b_j)$ has a *t*-distribution with $n - 2$ degrees of freedom (because we have estimated two parameters in the regression line, β_0 and β_1; the degrees of freedom are a parameter in the t-distribution). The t-distribution resembles the normal distribution, but has fatter tails. However, the more degrees of freedom, the more the t-distribution approaches the normal distribution.

Even if ε_i is not normally distributed, the sampling distributions of β_0 and β_1 are asymptotically normally distributed – by the central limit theorem – which makes testing possible if the sample is sufficiently large.

Next to the standardized coefficients (Beta), we find the t-values for the two (unstandardized) regression coefficients, and in the last column are the *significance probabilities* or *P*-values of a test of $H_0 : \beta_j = 0$ against $H_0 : \beta_j \neq 0$. As is evident, this null hypothesis is rejected for both coefficients at any reasonable level of significance.

Multiple regression

Introducing another predictor, using

$$Y_i = \beta_0 + \beta_1 X_{1i} + \beta_2 X_{2i} + \varepsilon_i \tag{22}$$

does not make any principal difference but adds to the calculations and opens up problems associated with *collinearity*. Co-linearity is the correlation among regressors. If the regressors covary, it is easy to see that it could be difficult to measure their individual effects on the criterion variable – and consequently the standard errors of the regression coefficients are increased.

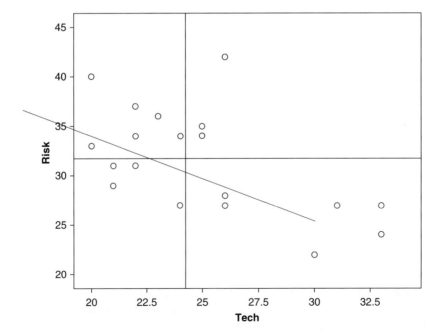

Figure 5 Example 3: regression line

The correlation coefficient between the actual Y-values and the values $\hat{Y}_i$ predicted by the estimated regression function is called the *multiple correlation coefficient*, usually designated R. The square of R is called the *multiple coefficient of determination*, and as you will have guessed it shows how large a proportion of its variance Y shares with the regressors taken as a whole, or as is usually expressed: how large a proportion of the variation in Y that is 'explained' by variation in the regressors.

R^2 is upward biased – especially if the number of regressors is large compared with the number of observations. The *adjusted* R^2, defined as

$$R^2_{adjusted} = 1 - (1 - R^2)\frac{df}{n-k} \tag{23}$$

where df is the degrees of freedom and k the number of regressors, adjusts R^2 downwards in order to compensate for this.

Perhaps you might expect the sum of the simple correlation coefficients squared to equal R^2, i.e.

$$R^2 = r^2_{X_1Y} + r^2_{X_2Y} \tag{24}$$

but this is only true in the absence of collinearity.

Example 4
Multiple regression analysis using SPSS

If in addition to 'tech' we use 'alienation' (alienation to the marketplace) from the same data set as the regressor, we get the output given in Table 4.

Table 4 Example 4: output from multiple regression analysis

Model Summary

Model	R	R Square	Adjusted R Square	Std. Error of the Estimate
1	.818(a)	.669	.630	3.219

a Predictors: (Constant), alienati, tech

ANOVA (b)

Model		Sum of Squares	df	Mean Square	F	Sig.
1	Regression	356.002	2	178.001	17.174	.000(a)
	Residual	176.198	17	10.365		
	Total	532.200	19			

a Predictors: (Constant), alienati, tech
b Dependent Variable: risk

(Continued)

Table 4 (Continued)

Coefficients(a)

Model		Unstandardized Coefficients		Standardized Coefficients	t	Sig.
		B	Std. Error	Beta		
1	(Constant)	23.856	8.265		2.886	.010
	tech	-.344	.214	-.263	-1.609	.126
	alienati	1.041	.261	.650	3.983	.001

a Dependent Variable: risk

In the first table you will find the multiple correlation coefficient R, the (multiple) coefficient of determination R^2, the adjusted R^2 and the standard error of estimate, i.e. the standard deviation of ε.

The sum of squares in the second table is defined as follows:

Regression sum of squares: $$\sum_i (\hat{Y}_i - \bar{Y})^2 \qquad (25a)$$

Residual sum of squares: $$\sum_i (Y_i - \hat{Y})^2 \qquad (25b)$$

Total sum of squares: $$\sum_i (Y_i - \bar{Y})^2 \qquad (25c)$$

The regression sum of squares is that part of the sum of squares for Y that is 'explained' by the regression function, while the residual sum of squares is the 'unexplained' sum of squares measuring the deviations of the observations from the regression line – or in the case of multiple regression, the regression plane.

As you may have guessed (and as you can easily verify)

$$R^2 = \frac{\sum_i (\hat{Y}_i - \bar{Y})^2}{\sum_i (Y_i - \bar{Y})^2} \qquad (26)$$

The F-test is a traditional analysis of variance F-test of the hypothesis

$$H_0 : \beta_j = 0 \text{ for all values of } j \text{ or } H_0 : R^2 = 0 \qquad (27)$$

and is then a test of the regression function taken as a whole.

As can be seen from the second table, the regression function is highly significant, and from the third table it appears that only alienation is significant. But remember: these are two-sided tests. The one-sided P-value for 'tech' is 0.063, so if you have formulated a one-sided hypotheses *before* observing the data, 'tech' is nearly significant at the traditional significance level of 0.05.

References

Bredahl, L. (2001). Determinants of consumer attitudes and purchase intentions with regard to genetically modified foods – results of a cross-national survey. *Journal of Consumer Policy, 24*, 23–61.

DeCarlo, L. T. (1997). On the meaning and use of kurtosis. *Psychological Methods, 2*(3), 292–307.

Further Reading

Kutner, M., Nachtsheim, C., & Neter, J. (2004). *Applied linear regression models* (rev. edn). New York: McGraw-Hill.

B
Glossary

acyclic model Consider the graphical picture of a model with variables (manifest or latent) connected by one- and two-headed arrows. If it is not possible by following one-headed arrows to return to the variable where you started, the model is *acyclic*, otherwise it is *cyclic*

binary variable A variable that can have only one of two values, e.g. the variable 'sex'

Bollen–Stine χ^2-test When using bootstrapping with non-normal data, the 'traditional' χ^2-test will be misleading, and instead you use the Bollen–Stine χ^2-test, which is based on an 'empirical' χ^2-distribution calculated across the bootstrapped samples

bootstrapping A resampling method where you construct a sampling distribution of a *statistic* by drawing a large number of simple random samples with replacement from your original sample (which serves as a 'population'), all samples having the same size as your original one

causal relation Although the word *cause* is used in everyday language without causing misunderstandings, the concept of causality is rather dim and a more stringent definition can only be given within a scientific *model*. A causal relation can be seen as a 'force' from one event or concept – the 'cause' – to another event or concept – the 'effect'. Since we cannot observe this 'force', the definition is an *operational definition* that allows listing of the criteria that a relationship must fulfill in order to be called 'causal'. Most often three criteria are used: (1) a co-occurrence or covariation; (2) a time difference between the two, the cause coming before the effect; and (3) the grounded exclusion of other possible explanations of the fulfilling of the other two conditions than that of a 'causal relation' (whatever that means!)

coefficient of determination This is the same as the correlation coefficient squared, R^2. It can be interpreted as the fraction of variance in the dependent variable that is 'explained' by an equation

component loading The correlation or covariance between a variable and a *principal component*. Factor loading is defined analogously

component score The value of a principal component. Factor score is defined analogously

component score coefficient	The coefficient of a variable when a *component score* is expressed as a linear function of the variables involved. Factor score coefficient is defined analogously
conceptual definition	As you would find in a math book or in an encyclopedia, new concepts are defined with reference to concepts defined earlier or (in the case of an encyclopedia) to concepts that are assumed to be better known. An *operational definition* defines a concept through the method used to measure it: 'temperature' is what you measure using *this* thermometer, 'intelligence' is what you measure using *this* test
conditional latent curve modelling	Latent curve modeling (LCM) that includes variables that are supposed to influence the trajectory of the LCM
confirmatory analysis	Verification (confirmation) of a model (theory) formulated a priori, e.g. before you look at the present data. If the analysis is not confirmatory it is *exploratory*, i.e. you explore your data in order to find some meaning in them and perhaps be able to formulate a model without having very precise ideas in mind. The distinction is, however, not as absolute in practice as in theory
confirmatory factor model	A factor model with parameter restrictions
constraint	See *parameter constraint*
construct	Same as *latent variable*
convergent and discriminant validity	Criteria for judging the validity of a measuring instrument
correlation matrix	A *matrix* whose element in the i, j position is the correlation between the ith and jth variable
covariance matrix	A *matrix* whose element in the i, j position is the covariance between the ith and jth variable
Cronbach's α	A commonly used measure of reliability for *summated scales*
cyclic model	Consider the graphical picture of a model with variables (manifest or latent) connected with one- and two-headed arrows. If it is possible by following one-headed arrows to return to the variable where you started, the model is *cyclic*, otherwise it is *acyclic*
data matrix	A *matrix* whose element in the i, j position is the ith respondent's (or whatever the analytical unit may be) value on the jth variable
default	The method the computer program would choose if not instructed otherwise, e.g. maximum likelihood is the default estimation method in EQS
degrees of freedom	In general, the degrees of freedom (df) of an estimate of a parameter are equal to the number of independent 'pieces of information' that go into the estimate minus the number of parameters used as intermediate steps in the estimation of the

	parameter itself (e.g. in estimating a variance, *df* is the sample size minus one, since the sample mean is the only intermediate step). In the case of SEM, the *df* is (in most cases) the number of non-redundant entries in the sample covariance matrix ('pieces of information') minus the number of parameters to be estimated
direct effect	See *total effect*
disturbance	The combined effects of all omitted variables on a dependent variable in a structural model. Usually called δ. However, EQS uses that designation (called 'D' in programs and output) only if the dependent variable in that equation is latent
eigenvalue	Every symmetric $p \times p$ matrix – and that includes covariance and correlation matrices – has associated with it p *eigenvalues* (some of which could be identical). If the eigenvalues are all positive, the matrix is said to be *positive definite* (if they are all negative, it is *negative definite*). If they are non-negative, the matrix is *positive semi-definite*. As the eigenvalues can be interpreted as the variances of the *principal components* of the matrix, covariance and correlation matrices must necessarily be (at least) positive semi-definite. However, some calculations used in the estimation process are not defined for positive semi-definite covariance matrices, so you have a problem if your sample covariance matrix is not positive definite
elbow plot	A graphic depiction of the variances of the *principal components* or factors in decreasing order. Also called *scree plot*
elliptical least squares, elliptical general least squares, elliptical reweighted least squares	Estimation methods available in EQS, but not covered in this book
endogenous variable	A variable whose value is determined by other variables in the model
equivalent models	It is always possible to construct at least two different models that are equally good in 'explaining' the data. Such models are called equivalent
error	See *measurement error*
estimation method	The method by which the parameters in a model are estimated. In EQS the following estimation methods are available: (1) ML or maximum likelihood (2) LS or least squares (not treated) (3) GLS or generalized LS (4) ELS or elliptical LS (not treated) (5) EGLS or elliptical GLS (not treated) (6) ERLS or elliptical reweighted LS (not treated)

	(7) HKGLS or heterogeneous kurtosis GLS (not treated) (8) HKRLS or heterogeneous kurtosis RLS (not treated) (9) AGLS or arbitrary distribution GLS
estimator	A sample statistic that is used to estimate a parameter
exogenous variable	A variable whose value is only determined by variables not included in the model
exploratory factor model	A factor model without parameter restrictions
FIML	Short for 'full-information maximum likelihood' estimation. ML estimation based on raw data and not on a data summary. An estimation method used to estimate a model in the case of missing data
fit measure	A fit measure (or fit index) is a measure of a model's agreement with the data. It is, however, worth noting that a good fit does not guarantee that the model is in agreement with the 'real world', i.e. that it is 'correct' (see also *equivalent models*). Fit measures are classified as 'absolute', 'relative', 'non-central chi-square based', 'information theoretic'
fixed parameter	See *parameter constraint*
free parameter	See *parameter constraint*
generalized least squares	One of the estimation methods available in EQS
GLS	Short for 'generalized least squares', one of the estimation methods available in EQS
goodness of fit	The degree to which a model is in agreement with the empirical data. It is, however, worth noting that a good fit does not guarantee that the model is in agreement with the 'real world', i.e. that it is 'correct'. See also *fit measure* and *equivalent models*
heterogeneous kurtosis generalized least squares, heterogeneous kurtosis reweighted least squares	Estimation methods available in EQS, but not covered in this book
identification	The process of finding out whether there are enough data to estimate a model
implied covariance matrix	Every model formulation implies a certain pattern in the covariances between the various variables in the model. This pattern is summed up in the implied covariance matrix. If the model is in good agreement with the data, the difference between the sample covariance matrix on which the estimation is based and the implied covariance matrix should be small. This difference is called the *residual covariance matrix*

imputation	Replacing missing values in your data with other data. In mean imputation you replace missing values with the mean of the variable in question; in regression imputation you regress the variable with missing values on other variables in the data set and use the regression function to estimate the missing value; in multiple imputation you make several imputations, each resulting in a separate data set, and then you estimate your model for every data set. Finally the various models are combined to be your final model
independence model	A model with zero correlation between all manifest variables
indicator	A manifest variable that is used as a measuring instrument for a latent variable
indirect effect	See *total effect*
information-theoretic fit measure	See *fit measure*
interval scale, interval-scaled variable	A scale with a zero point and a unit of measurement, but both are arbitrary, i.e. chosen and agreed upon. Examples are temperature scales (Celsius and Fahrenheit). Standard methods in SEM require (at least) interval-scaled data. See also *nominal* and *ordinal scale*
item analysis	The process of selecting the best items for a (summated or non-summated) measuring instrument. It can be done using 'reliability analysis' (for summated scales) or exploratory factor analysis in SPSS or confirmatory factor analysis in EQS
iterative	All estimation methods in EQS are iterative, i.e. they start with some values for the parameters to be estimated and then gradually improve the fit step by step until a satisfactory fit is obtained
just-identified	A *model* is just-identified if it has zero *degrees of freedom*
Kaiser criterion	A criterion used to decide how many *principal components* or factors to keep for further analysis
latent curve model	A model describing and perhaps also 'explaining' the change-over time in some variable of interest
latent growth model	Same as *latent curve model*
latent variable	A variable for which no generally agreed measuring instrument exists. Examples are intelligence, preference and satisfaction (cf. *manifest variable*)
LCM	Short for 'latent curve modeling'
least squares	One of the estimation methods available in EQS
listwise deletion	Deletion of any observation with missing values on any variable that goes into the analysis, i.e. using only complete cases

manifest variable	A variable that is measurable, i.e. there is a well-defined and usually generally agreed way of measuring it. Examples of such variables are temperature, length, number of cigarettes sold
matrix	A rectangular arrangement of numbers in rows and columns. An example is the data matrix where X_{ji} is the value of variable j on observation i. In this book the observation is most often a person, and the variable an answer to a question in a questionnaire
maximum likelihood estimation	One of the estimation methods available in EQS
mean imputation	See *imputation*
mean structure	In SEM you most often analyze covariance structures, i.e. you analyze the covariances and try to 'explain' them. In doing so, EQS fixes all means and intercepts at zero. Sometimes you are also interested in estimating means and intercepts, and want to 'explain' them too. So, your covariance structure must be supplemented with a mean structure, and the sample means must be added to the sample covariances in the input
measurement error	The error of a measuring instrument. The error involved in using an indicator for a latent variable. Traditionally called ε but in EQS called 'E'. However, EQS uses E in all models where the dependent variable in an equation is manifest – whether it is in a measurement model or in a structural model
measurement model	A model that describes the connection between a latent variable and its (manifest) indicators
ML estimation	Short for 'maximum likelihood' estimation, one of the estimation methods available in EQS
model	A simplified 'picture' of the phenomenon you want to study. The 'picture' could be an informal 'mental' one, a graphic model, a set of mathematical equations or whatever you find most practical to get an overview of a complicated world. Scientific work is characterized by the use of formal models
multiple imputation	See *imputation*
nested model	A model is nested under another model if it can be obtained by placing restrictions on the latter model
Nominal scale	A scale used only to classify respondents as belonging to a certain group. An example is coding sex as male=0 and female=1
non-central chi-square distribution	A generalization of the 'normal' chi-square distribution. In connection with SEM the non-central chi-square distribution can be considered as the distribution that the test statistic will follow if the null hypothesis is wrong
non-cyclic models	See *cyclic model*

non-recursive	Roughly the same as cyclic. See *cyclic model*
non-summated scale	The use of the separate items as measures for a construct without summing them
operational definition	See *conceptual definition*
order condition	A necessary condition for the identification of cyclic models
ordinal scale, ordinal variable	A scale that indicates a rank (e.g. measuring preference by ranking)
over-identified	A *model* is over-identified if its *degrees of freedom* are positive
P-value	In statistical testing, the probability of observing the actual value of a statistic or one that casts even more doubt on the null hypothesis, assuming it is true
pairwise deletion	*Listwise deletion* on any pair of variables
parallel measurements	Two measurements are called parallel if (1) they have the same 'connection' with the concept they are supposed to measure and (2) their measurement errors are equal
parameter	A measure that describes a population or a model
parameter constraint	A constraint placed on the estimated values of a parameter. A parameter is unconstrained or *free* if it is to be estimated from the data with no restrictions on the estimated values. In EQS a parameter can be restricted to have a certain value, two or more parameters can be restricted to have the same (estimated) value, two or more parameters can be restricted to satisfy a linear restriction, a parameter can be restricted to have an upper and/or lower bound or the parameter can be missing, i.e. it can be fixed at zero
parceling	Grouping indicators and using summaries of the groups (parcels) as manifest variables
parsimony	In connection with SEM, the word means 'simple' or 'uncomplicated'. We usually look for simple models with as few parameters as possible
path model	A model with no latent variables
pilot sample	A smaller sample taken prior to the main sample, e.g. in order to test a questionnaire
positive definite matrix	See *eigenvalue*
positive semi-definite matrix	See *eigenvalue*
principal components	Principal components are linear functions of the data. The first principal component is the linear function with the largest variance, the second principal component is the linear component with the second largest variance under the condition that it is uncorrelated with the first, etc. There are as many (non-correlated) principal components as there are variables in your data set.

	However, some of them could be identical. The variances of the principal components are the *eigenvalues* of the *covariance* or *correlation matrix*
principal components analysis	A method for summarizing data in fewer variables (the first few *principal components*) with minimum loss of information or for determining the number of dimensions in a data set
rank condition	A sufficient condition for the identification of cyclic models
ratio scale, ratio-scaled variable	An interval scale with a fixed zero point (e.g. scales measuring weight and length). See also *interval scale*
recursive model	Roughly the same as non-cyclic. See *cyclic model*
recursive rule	A recursive model is always identified
regression imputation	See *imputation*
relative fit measure	See *fit measure*
reliability	A measuring instrument has (large) reliability if it has a small amount of measurement error
reliability coefficient	A measure of reliability having values in the interval 0.00 to 1.00; the higher, the better
residual covariance matrix	See *implied covariance matrix*
rotation	A transformation of component axes or factor axes to obtain a simpler factor structure that is easier to interpret
sampling distribution	The probability distribution of a *statistic* across an infinite number of samples of the same size as the one at hand and from the same population
saturated model	A model with the maximum number of parameters and therefore exact fit to the data
scree plot	See *elbow plot*
SEM	Short for 'structural equation modelling'
SSCP matrix	Short for 'sum of squares and cross-products matrix'
standard deviation	A measure of the spread in the distribution of a statistical variable or in a data set
standard error	The *standard deviation* in the *sampling distribution* for a *parameter*
standardized coefficient	Also called beta coefficient. A regression coefficient based on standardized variables.
standardized variable	A variable with a mean of 0.00 and a variance of 1.00
start value	The initial parameter value used in *iterative* estimation methods

statistic	A measure that describes a sample. Sometimes a statistic is used as an *estimator* for the corresponding *parameter*
structural model	A model describing the (suggested) 'causal' connections among the variables, as opposed to the measurement model that describes the connection between *latent variables* and their (*manifest*) indicators. If a model includes latent variables the structural model describes 'causal' relations between latent variables. If the model only includes manifest variables the whole model is structural
summated scale	A summated scale is obtained by adding scores obtained by answering a series of questions. One of the most popular is the Likert scale: the respondents are asked to indicate their agreement with each of a series of statements by checking a scale from, for example, 1 (strongly disagree) to 5 (strongly agree) and the scores are then added to make up the scale
***t*-rule**	A necessary (but not sufficient) condition for identification: the number of data points should be at least as large as the number of parameters to be estimated
theory	See *model*
three-indicator rule	A sufficient condition for identification of a confirmatory factor model
total effect	The effect of one variable on another variable. It is the sum of the *direct effect* and the *indirect effect*, i.e. the effects that are mediated by one or more other variables
trajectory	The path that a moving object follows through space as a function of time. The object might be a projectile or a satellite. In SEM a trajectory is used in connection with a *latent curve model* as a description of the change over time in some variable of interest
two-indicator rule	A sufficient condition for identification of a confirmatory factor model
two-step rule	As a first step, you consider the model to be a confirmatory factor model (you substitute two-headed arrows for all one-headed arrows between latent variables), and you confirm that such a model would be identified. As a second step you look at the structural part of the model. Imagine that all the latent variables were manifest, and confirm that such a model would be identified. If these two conditions are met, the original model is identified.
two-step strategy	When your model includes latent variables and 'causal' relations, it is preferable to analyze the model in two steps. First the model is analyzed as if it was a measurement model (a confirmatory factor model) and then the total model is analyzed. One reason for this is that if your measurement model does not have a satisfactory fit, it is pointless analyzing the structural part of the model. A four-step strategy has also been proposed, starting with an exploratory factor model

unconditional latent curve modeling	LCM that describes the trajectory of a latent curve model, but does not include variables that are supposed to influence the trajectory
under-identified, not identified	A *model* is under-identified if its *degrees of freedom* are negative
unique variance	An expression of validity
validity	A measuring instrument has (large) validity if it measures exactly the concept it is supposed to measure and nothing else
zero B-rule	A sufficient condition for identification. If a path model has no variable with both incoming and outgoing arrows, it is always identified
zero model	A model where all parameters have the value 0
χ^2-distribution	The distribution of the χ^2-statistic used to test the model fit
χ^2-difference test	A test for the difference in fit between two *nested models*

C
EQS Statements

(Defaults appear in boldface.)

Paragraph/statement	Abbreviation and examples	Meaning	First mentioned in connection with Example
/TITLE		Title of the analysis/model	4.1
/SPECIFICATIONS			4.1
CASES	CA = 500	Number of cases	4.1
VARIABLES	VA = 8	Number of variables	4.1
MATRIX	MA =	Specifies the form of input data	4.1
	MA = **COV**	Covariance matrix	
	= RAW	Raw data	
	= COR	Correlation matrix	
	= MOM	means and covariances	
METHOD	ME =	Estimation method to be used	4.1
	ME = **ML**	Maximum likelihood	
	= LS	Least squares	
	= GLS	Generalized LS	
	= ELS	Elliptical LS	
	= EGLS	Elliptical GLS	
	= ERLS	Elliptical reweighted GLS	
	= HKGLS	Heterogeneous kurtosis GLS	
	= HKRLS	Heterogeneous kurtosis RLS	
	= AGLS	Arbitrary distribution GLS	
	= XX,ROBUST	Robust statistics on method XX	

Appendix C

Paragraph/statement	Abbreviation and examples	Meaning	First mentioned in connection with Example
DATA_FILE	DA = XXX.XXX	Name of external file where input data reside	7.2
ANALYSIS	AN =	Type of matrix on which the calculations should be based	4.1
	AN = **COV**	Covariance matrix	
	= COR	Correlation matrix	
	= MOM	Means and covariance matrix	
GROUPS	GR = m	Number of input samples	9.2
MISSING	MI =	Specifies how to handle missing data	10.1
	MI = **COMPLETE**	Discard cases with missing values	
	= ML	ML using all cases	
	= PAIR	Pairwise present computations	
CATEGORY	CAT = Vx,Vy,Vz	List of categorical variables	10.4
/LABELS	Vx = XXX e.g. (V1 = ANOMIA67)	Labels manifest and latent variables	4.1
/EQUATIONS	e.g. V5=*V1+*V2+ *V3+*V4+E5 F5=*F1+*F4+D5	Specifies the model '*' signals that the coefficient is to be estimated from data	4.1
/VARIANCES	e.g. V1=* V2=*	List of variances that are parameters in the model	4.1
/COVARIANCES	V1,V2=* V1,V3=*	List of covariances that are parameters in the model	4.1
/MATRIX		To be followed by the input matrix in the program in cases where the data do not reside in an external file	4.1

(Continued)

(Continued)

Paragraph/statement	Abbreviation and examples	Meaning	First mentioned in connection with Example
/STANDARDDEVIATIONS		To be followed by the input standard deviations in the program	4.1
/MEANS		To be followed by the input means in the program	9.1
/MODEL		A paragraph that can be substituted for the three paragraphs /EQUATIONS /VARIANCES /COVARIANCES	8.2
/RELIABILITY	SCALE Vx TO Vy	Models a one-factor model with indicators Vx to Vy and calculates reliability coefficients alpha and rho	7.3
/PRINT		If you demand more output than the default, you list your requests here	6.2
FIT	FI = ALL	Prints full range of fit measures Default: only chi-square, AIC, CAIC, NFI, NNFI and CFI are printed	6.2
TABLE	TA = **EQUATION**	Equations are printed as equations	6.2
	= COMPACT	Equations are printed in compact forms	6.2
	= MATRIX	Equations are printed in matrix form	6.2
RELIABILITY	RELIABILITY = YES	Prints the full range of reliability coefficients	7.2
EFFECT	EF = YES	Effect decomposition into direct, indirect and total effects	8.2
/CONSTRAINTS	e.g. (V2,F1) = (V6,F2)	Place constraints on parameters	7.1

Paragraph/statement	Abbreviation and examples	Meaning	First mentioned in connection with Example
/LM TEST		LM test used to test the effect of making fixed parameters freely estimated	
PROCESS =	e.g. PR = SEP = SIM = SEQ	Specify the sequence in which the tests are being performed: separate, simultaneous or sequential	7.2
SET =	e.g. SET = PEE, GVF	Restricts the type and number of parameters to be tested	7.2

Author Index

Aaker, D.A. 18, 25, 124, 147
Abbott, M. 7, 26
Akaike, H. 131, 147
Alwin, D.F. 125, 147
Armstrong, J. Scott 54, 70
Arbuckle, J. L. 14, 25
Avlund, K. 216, 279

Bagozzi, R.P. 14, 20, 25, 147, 184
Bandalos, D.L. 33, 46
Bass, F.M. 16, 19, 25, 75, 141, 144,
Bauer, D. J. 299, 302, 306
Bearden, W. O. 70
Beck, A.T. 12, 25,
Bentler, P.M. 14, 26, 90, 91, 99, 105, 125, 128, 132, 147, 168, 184, 212, 216, 263, 273, 279, 184,
Berman, S. R. 191, 216
Bisp, S. 37, 46
Blalock, H. M. 14, 26,
Bohrnstedt, G.W. **232**, 248
Bollen K. A. 36, 46, 79, 90, 91, 105, 150, 181, 269, 279, 281, 299, 304, 306
Bonnett, D.G. 132, 147
Bozdogan, H. 131, 147
Bredahl, L. 37, 46, 74, 106, 227, 248, 317, 325
Brown, W. S. 144, 147
Browne, M.W. 79, 91, 106, 125, 147
Brunsø, K. 227, **247**, 248
Buysse, D. J. 191, 216
Byrne, D.O. **232**, 248

Campbell, D.T. 44, 46
Cha, J. 134, 147
Child, D. 70
Childers, T.L. 10, 26, 162, 184
Chin, W.W. 134, 147, 183, 184
Chou, C.-P. 263, 279
Clifford, M. M. **232**, 248
Crafton, C. **233**, 248
Cronbach, L. 36, 46,
Cudeck, R. 298, 306
Curran, P. J. 281, 299, 302, 304, 306

Davis, J. A. 145, 147
Day, D.A. 18, 25, 124, 147

DeCarlo, L.T. 312, 325
de Gruijter, N. M. 46
DeVellis, R.F. 46
Dominick, B.A. 17, 26
Dopplemann, L. F. 191, 216
Duncan, O. D. 14, 26
Duncan, S. C. 308
Duncan, T. E. 308
Dunteman, G. H. 70
Durkheim, E. 5, 26
du Toit, S. H. 298, 306

Erbaugh, J. 12, 25

Felson, R.B. **233**, 248
Finney, S.J. 33, 46
Fiske D.W. 44, 46
Ford, J. G. **233**, 248
Fornell, C. 134, 147, 183, 184

Goldberger, A. S. 14, 26
Grant, B. 95, 106,
Gross, A. E. **233**, 248
Gruber, C. 95, 106
Grunert, K. G. 37, 46, **227, 247, 248**
Guttman, L. 41, 46

Hancock, G. R. 106,
Harman, H. 52, 70
Haws, K. L. 70
Heckler, S. 10, 26, 162, 184
Henseler, J. 134, 147, 183, 184
Herschberger, S.I. 104, 106
Hokland, M. 216, 279,
Houston, M. J. 10, 26, 162, 184
Hume, D. 15, 16, 26

Jackson, D. N. 69, 70
Johnson, R.A. 69, 70
Joireman, J. 7, 26
Jöreskog, K.G. 14, 125, 147,

Kim, J.-O. 68, 70
Kline, R. B. 183, 184
Kupfer, D. J. 191, 216

Landy, D. **232**, 248
Lavidge, J. C. 5, 26
Lawley, D.N. 68, 70
Lee, S. 104, 106,
Lind, J. C. 133, 147
London, O. **232**, 248
Lorr, M. 191, 216

Marcoulides, G.A. 106
Mardia, K.V. 100, 106
Maxwell, A. E. 68, 70
McArdle, J. J. 14, 26
McDonald, R. P. 14, 26
McDonald, R. 67, 70
McNair, P. M. 191, 216
Mehlsen, Y. M. 216, 279
Mendelson, M. 12, 25
Meredith, W. 281, 306
Millsap, R.E. 190, 216
Monk, C. F. 191, 216
Morrison, D.F. 52, 70
Mueller, C.W. 68, 70
Mueller, R.O. 106
Mulaik, S.A. 75, 68, 70, 190, 216
Mullahy, J. 6, 26
Muthén, B. 125, 147

Narajian, R. D. 191, 216
Netemeyer, R. G. 70,
Nielsen, N.A. 37, 46
Norušis, M.J. 54, 70

Olesen, F. 216
Owens, G. 238, 248

Paivio, A. 172, 184
Preacher, D.J. 302, 306

Raykov, T. 178, 181, 184
Reeves, K. **232**, 248
Reynolds, C.F. 191, 216
Roger, D. 191, 216
Rubin, D.B. 262, 279

Sarty, M. **233**, 248
Satorra, A. 263, 273, 276,
Scholderer, J. 227, **232**, **246, 247, 248**
Schumacker, R.A. 106
Shacham, S. 191, 216
Shapiro, A. 180, 184
Sigall, H. **233**, 248
Simon, H.A. 17, 26,
Spearman, C. 13, 26
SPSS 257, 279
Steiger, J. H. 133, 147
Steiner, G. A. 5, 26
Stine, R.A. 269, 279
Strycker, L. A. 306
Summers, G. F. 125, 147
Sörbom, D. 125, 147
Sørensen, E. 37, 46, 163, 184

Thomsen, D.K. 191, 216, 250, 279
Thurstone, L.L. 13, 26, 67, 70
Thurstone, T. 13, 26
Tisak, J., 281, 306
Tucker, L. R. 281, 306

van der Kamp, L. J. Th. 46,
Veerbek, M. 283, 306
Velicer, W. F. 69, 70
Vella, F. 283, 306
Viidik, A. 216
Vinzi, V. E. 134, 147, 183, 184

Walster, E. 238, 248
Wang, H. 134, 147, 183, 184
Ward, C. H. 12, 25
Wheaton, B. 125, 147
Wichern, D.W. 73, 74
Wilkinson, L. 95, 106
Willoughby, M. T. 299, 306
Wold, H. 134, 147, 183, 184
Wright, S. 13, 26

Yi, Y. 20, 25

Subject Index

acyclic graphs, 19
acyclic models, 20
Adjusted Goodness of Fit Index (AGFI), 132
'alternative forms' measure, 31, 41
analysis of variance, 3, 19, 219, 324
analysis of covariance structures, 24
Arbitrary distribution generalized least squares (AGLS), 90, 91–92, 94, 263, 272, 275
automatitation of test procedures, 103

behavioral science research, nature of, 3, 9
Bentler-Raykov corrected R-squared **236**
Beta coefficients, 320, 322, 334
bias and bias correction, 190, 250
Bollen-Stine boot-strapped chi-square, 269–70
bootstrapping, 263–70
  model-based, 269–70
build EQS 112–115
  or 'Diagrammer' 297–98

categorical variables, analysis of, 92, 270–78
  see discrete data, analysis of
causal models
  multi-group analysis of, 232
  in non-experimental research, 14–21
  types of, 17–21
causation
  depiction of, 11, 74–75
  establishment of, 14–17
  two-way (reciprocal), 19, 141–46, **232–38**, 241
central limit theorem, 32, 33, 315
centroid, distance from, 96
chi-square (χ^2) distribution, 79, 310–11
  non-central, 130, 131, 133–34
chi-square (χ^2) test, 79, 103–04, 316
  empirical, 269
chi-square difference test, 157, 166, 229, 229–31
classical test theory, 2746, 30, 183
closed systems, 1517
coefficient of determination, 39, 88, 130, 181, 189–90, 317, 323
collinearity, 74, 95, **238**, 322, 323
column vectors, 22
common factors, 66, 68, 69

common variance, 42, 59, 68
communalities, 42, 59, 68
compact output, 136–37
comparative fit index (CFI), 132, 134
component scores and component loadings, 51, 54, 59, 151
component score coefficients, 51, 59, 60
component variance, 53, 59
concepts
  clarification of, 173
  definition of, 33–34
  measurement of, 8–10, 27–50
conceptual definition, 33–34
concurrent validity, 43
conditional latent curve model, 288–97, 299–302
confidence intervals, 314, 319
  bootstrapped, 269–70
configural invariance, 226, 228–29
confirmatory factor models, 14884, 187, 190
  and item selection, 162–75
congeneric measurements, 30, 36, 59, 177
'connections' between concepts, 5–6, 10, 12
consistency of measuring instruments, 41
consistency of an estimator, 79, 90, 250, 262–63, 314–15
constraints, 76–77, 149,156–57, 175–76, 227, 231–32
  and LM-test, 175–76, 231–32
construct validity, 43–44
content validity, 43
convergence problems, 93, 263, 273
convergent correlation, 45
convergent validity, 44
correlation,
  convergent, 45
correlation coefficient, 28, 31, 35, 95, 181, 317, 321, 323–24,
  polycloric, 271–278
  polyserial, 271
correlation matrices, 23, 36, 44, 52, 68, 83–84, 94, 107–112, 193,
  for categorical variables, 271–78
covariance, 7, 317–18
covariance-based SEM, 134, 183

Subject Index

covariance matrices, 22–25, 68, 75–76, 79, 150, 151, 220, 314
    empirical (see also sample and implied), 79
    not positive definite, 94–95
    residual; see residual matrices
    sample and implied, 79, 24–25
    test for equality of, 225
co-variation, 15
criterion validity, 43
Cronbach's alpha (α), 35–41, 59, 66, 162
    In EQS, 128, 177–79
cross-group equivalence (of a measuring instrument), 226–232
cross-validation, 225
cyclic graphs, 19
cyclic models, 141–46, **232–41**
    identification in, 141–144

data-entering and data-import, 97–98, 107, 112
data matrix, 21
definitions, 23, 33–34
degrees of freedom, 22, 75, 79, 225, 313–14, 322
dependent variables, 7-8, 80, 318
determinant, 86–87, 95
Diagrammer, 4, 115–22, 137–40, 159–62, 203, **233**
    or 'Build EQS', 200, 297–98
discrete variables, analysis of,
    see categorical variables, analysis of,
    se categorical variables
discriminant validity, 44–45
disturbance, 6, 17, 80, 120, 183, 232, **236**, **243**, 304,

econometrics, 14
eigenvalue, 59, 68, 94
elbow plot, 52–53, 59, 62–63
elliptical least squares (ELS), 90, 91
elliptical generalized least squares (EGLS), 90, 91
elliptical reweighted least squares (ERLS), 90, 91
endogenous variable, 8, 76, 80, 143–44, 220–22
EQS,
    data-entering and data-import, 97–98, 107–112
    examination of output, 92–101
    model and notation, 79–80
    programming in, 80-90, 112–122
equivalence of measuring instruments, 226–**232**
equivalent models, 104–05
error, 9, 11, 76–77, 80, 148–49, 150
error messages, 92–102
error variances, 42, 59, 76,
error variance/covariance invariance, 226–32
estimators, properties of, 314-15
exogenous variables, 8, 76, 80, 143-44, 220-22
expected values, 17, 133, 310
experimental data/experiments, 14–15, 20
exploratory factor analysis, 66–69, 148–49, 162, 190
extreme attitudes, 34

F-test, 324
factor analysis, 13–14, 47–70
    compared with component analysis, 69
factor indeterminacy problem 67
factor means
    comparing **242–47**
factor variance/covariance invariance, 226–32
fatigue factor, 41
first principal component, 49
fit indices, 130–34
    absolute, 131, 132–33
    based on non-central χ^2-distribution, 130, 133–34
    information theoretic, 130, 131
    relative, 130, 131–32
fixed/fixing parameters, 76–77, 102, 150, 113, 203, **242**, **247**,
formative indicators, 181–83
full-information maximum likelihood (FIML) estimation, 250–56
full-information methods of parameter estimation, 90

general model, 190–212
generalized least squares (GLS) estimation, 91, 95
Goodness of Fit Index (GFI), 132,
graphic interface in EQS
    see Diagrammer

Hancock P-values, 169
Heterogeneous kurtosis generalized least squares (HKGLS), 91
Heterogeneous kurtosis reweighted least squares (HKRLS), 91
historical data, 15–16

identification, 75–79
    of acyclic models, 123–24
    of confirmatory factor models, 150
    of cyclic models, 141–44
    of the general model, 186–87
    of mean structures, 225
independence model, 131–32, 134
imputation of missing data, 250
    multiple, 256–262
incomplete data, 249–63
Incremental Fit Index (IFI), 132
independent variables, 7–8, 80, 318
indirect effects, 209–10, 220, 225
    in latent curve models, 301–02
interactions in latent curve models, 301–02,
intercepts, 7, 83, 220–21, 225, 226, 281, 302
item analysis, 36–41, 47, 56–66, 162
iteration process, 128–130
iterative estimation methods, 68, 79, 91

just-identified models, 75, 76, 77, 104, 190, 225

Kaiser criterion, 53
kurtosis, 91, 92, 99–101, 263, 264–66, 285–86, 312

Lagrange multiplier (LM) test, 166–70, 175–76, 199, 208, 231–32, 296
lambda (λ) coefficients, 11
latent curve models, 280–306
  coding of time in, 298–99
  conditional 288–97, 300–302
  unconditional, 288, 300,
  indirect effects and interactions in, 301–02
latent curve as factor model, 281
latent variables, 9–10
  benefits of, 12–13
least squares estimation, 17, 24, 90–91
  see also: Arbitrary distribution generalized least squares (ADGLS), elliptical least squares (ELS), elliptical generalized least squares (EGLS), elliptical reweighted least squares (ERLS), partial least squares, two-stage least squares,, weighed least squares
likelihood function, 68–69, 79
Likert scale, 8, 61
limited-information methods of parameter estimation, 90, 144
LISREL (Linear Structural Relations), 14, 131, 132,
listwise deletion of data, 249–50,
loading on a component or factor, 51, 53–54, 59,
longitudinal (panel) models, 212–15, 280–306

Mahalanobis' squared distance (D^2), 96–97, 101
manifest variables, 9–12, 14, 20, 28, 32, 45, 66, 76, 79, 80, 83, 123–147
matrices and matrix algebra, 21–25
maximum likelihood (ML) estimation, 68, 79, 83, 101, 250, 263, 313
  Asymptotic qualities of, 79, 101
McDonald's fit index (MFI), 133
mean 310, 312
mean imputation (MI) of missing values, 250, 257
mean structure 219–**32**,
  identification of, 225
  in multi-group studies, 225–**32** **242–47**
  comparing means of latent variables **242–47**
measurement error, 9, 12–13, 80, 190, 203
measurement model, 10–11, 13, 27, 29, 33, 68, 69, 77, 80, 148–184, 185–190, 212, 226–**232**, 272–278, 283,
metric invariance, 226, 229–30, 231, **247**
missing at random (MAR), 262–63
missing completely at random (MCAR), 262
missing data, 249–263
missing data patterns, 252–53, 262–63
multicollinearity, 7
multidimensionality, 33, 6066,
multi-group analysis, 219–248
  of causal models, **232–41**
  comparing means of latent variables **242–47**

multiple imputation (MUI), 256–62
multivariate kurtosis, 91, 100–101, 264, 285–86
multiple regression, 7, 74–75, 81–90, 185, 322–24
multitrait-multimethod (MTMM) technique, 44–45
multivariate normality, 79, 91, 96, 101, 263

negations in summated scales, 35
negative variance, 94
nested and non-nested models, 134, 157, 166, 276,
noise, 7, 17, 19, 41, 47, 53, 66, 80, 141, 180, 257, 258
non-experimental data, analysis of, 14–21
normal distribution, 32, 79, 91, 92, 97–101, 309–10, 312, 315
  deviations from, 91–92, 95–101, 263–70
normed fit index (NFI), 132
non-normed fit index (NNFI), 132
null hypothesis, 87, 103–04, 133, 225, 315, 316, 322,

oblique rotation, 54–55, 66, 151
observation space, 22
observational data, 15
one-indicator problem, 203
one-sided tests,101, 104, 156, 296, 304, 316, 324
one-step strategy, 190
operational definition, 15, 33–34
optimal scales, 47–51
order condition, 143–44
ordinal scaled data, 92, 270–78
outliers, 95–101
overidentified models, 75, 78, 124, 143, 190, 225, 264

P-value, 121, 127, 134, 156, 169, 315, 324
pairwise deletion (PD), 94, 249–50, 252
panel data, 125–30, 212–15, 280–306
parallel measurements, 30, 35, 41,
parallel tests for judging reliability, 30
parameters, *free, fixed* and *constrained*, 76–77
parceling, 33
parsimony, 102, 131, 156,
partial least squares, 134, 183
path analysis, 13–14, 123–47
pilot sample, 41
polychoric correlation coefficient, 271, 273–74
polyserial correlation coefficient, 271
positive definite and positive semi–definite matrices, 93, 94–95, 250,
predictive validity, 43
principal component, definition of, 51–52
principal components analysis, 51–66
  compared with factor analysis, 66–69
  as item analysis, 56–66, 162
probability and probability distributions, 309–10

rank condition, 143, 144
rank data, 271
   see ordinal scaled data
random sampling, 264
randomization, 31, 192
   scale items, 192
Raykov's rho (ρ), 178
reciprocal (or two-way) causation, 19, 141–146, **232–38, 241**
   see also cyclic graphs and cyclic models
recursive rule, 123–24
reflexive indicators, 181–83
regression analysis, 3, 7, 10, 17, 19, 20–21, 23–25,74–75, 81–90. 96, 281, 316–24
regression imputation of missing values, 250, 257
regression sum of squares, 324
regression coefficients, 10, 20, 76, 84, 87–88, 123–24, 150, 166, 181, 189–90, 220, 225, 226, 282, 298, 319–20, 322
relative fit measures, 131–32
reliability, 27–32, 35–41, 176–80, 183, 198
   true, 41
reliability analysis, 36
   see also item analysis
   in EQS, 177–180
reliability coefficient, 28, 176–80
reliability of summated scales, 35–41, 177–180
reproducibility of results, 27
residual matrices, 24–25, 86–87, 90, 91, 127–29, 130, 133, 180,
residual sum of squares, 324
restrictions, 92, 157, 159
   see also constraints
Reticular Action Model (RAM), 14
'reverse' use of statistical tests, 103, 127
revision of models, 102, 159
robust statistics, 92, 263, 273, 286–88
root mean square of approximation (RMSEA), 121, 133–34, 231, **239, 246,**
root mean square residual (RMR), 133
rotation (of components and factors), 13, 53–55, 62, 66, 68, 149, 151
row vector, 22

Sample or population?, 159
sample size, 92, 101–102, 103–104, 225, 231, **246,** 250, 272,
sampling distribution, 48, 134, 263, 314, 315,
   empirical, 263
Satorra-Bentler scaled chi-square, 273, 276
saturated model, 131, 252
scale invariance, 226, 230–31, **247**
scales
   finding the dimensionality of, 61–66
   optimal, 47–51
   summated and non-summated, 32–36
scree plot,
   see elbow plot

significant and non-significant factors, 66
skewness, 92, 99, 264, 276, 312
social science research, nature of, 3, 9, 12,
Spearman-Brown formula, 31, 35, 41
specific factor 42, 66–67, 68
specific variance, 42, 59, 177
split-half measurements, 31–32, 35, 41
standard deviation, 23, 78, 84, 99, 112, **235,** 269, 311, 314
standard error, 87, 190, 263, 314,
   bootstrapped, 269
   empirical, 263
   in multiple imputation, 260–61
standardized parameter values 88, 181
standardized residual covariances, 127
standardized variables, 23, 52, 96, 317
start values for parameter estimation, 68, 78, 93, 273
statistical inference, 103, 263, 312–325,
stochastic independence, 17
structural equation modeling (SEM)
   covariance-based, 134, 183
   definition of, 13
   estimation methods for, 90–92
   exploratory use of, 102–03
   history of, 13–14
   problems with, 103–05
   steps in, 73–74
   use in experimental research 20
structural equation models
   describing, 11, 79–80
   errors in, 11, 13
structural models with missing data, 265
subscripts on parameters, 11, 80
sum of cross products, 22
sum of squares, 22, 313, 324
sum of squares and cross products (SSCP) matrix, 22
summated scales, 8–9,12, 32–41
   construction of, 8–10, 36–44, 55–66
   reliability of, 35–41, 176–180

t-distribution, 322
t-rule, 76, 153
tau (τ) equivalence, 30, 36, 41, 59, 177, 178
test-retest reliability, 30–31, 41
theory, 4–6
three-indicator rule, 150, 153
time, codings of, 298–99
time-dependent and time-independent regressors, 290
time sequence, 15, 21, 144–45
total effect, 209–10, 220–21,
trajectory, 282, 283, 288, 298–99
trend, 280, 283
   see also trajectory
true variance, 28
two-indicator rule, 150

two-sided tests, 104, 225, 316
two-stage least squares estimation, 144
two-step rule, 186–87, 190
two-step strategy, 190
   in latent curve models, 283
two-way causation, 19, 141–46, **232–38**, **241**
   see also reciprocal causation

unconditional latent curve model, 288, 290, 298, 300, 304, 312
underidentification, 75, 143, 256
   empirical, 78
unidimensional scales, 33, 34, 55–66, 162
unique validity variance, 181

validity of measuring instruments, 180–81, 183
variable space, 22
variance, 311
   see also: analysis of variance, common variance, communalities, component variance, negative variance
   as a measure of amount of information, 47–51
Varimax rotation, 54, 151
Vectors, 22

Wald (W) test, 166,
weighted least squares, 91

zero-B rule, 123, 125